The Glacier Park Reader

NATIONAL PARK READERS

Lance Newman and David Stanley, series editors

The Glacier Park Reader

Edited by
David Stanley

THE UNIVERSITY OF UTAH PRESS
Salt Lake City

THE GLACIER NATIONAL PARK CONSERVANCY
Columbia Falls

A COPUBLICATION WITH THE
Glacier National Park Conservancy.

The Defiance House Man colophon is a registered trademark
of The University of Utah Press. It is based on a four-foot-tall
Ancient Puebloan pictograph (late PIII) near Glen Canyon, Utah.

LIBRARY OF CONGRESS CATALOGING-IN-PUBLICATION DATA
Names: Stanley, David, 1942- editor.
Title: The Glacier Park reader / edited by David Stanley.
Description: Salt Lake City : University of Utah Press, [2017] | Series: National park
    readers | "Glacier is a place of paradox, at once serene and violent, breathtakingly
    beautiful and somber, even sometimes almost ominous. Vibrant life thrives within the
    apparent calm of the scenery, and people from all walks of life come to the park and
    interact with each other, encountering the wilderness, learning its ways, and telling
    stories about their experiences. In this collection, I have put together a variety of those
    stories written between 1889 and 2016, along with Native American oral narratives
    of gods, animals, and men that date back much further. My intention has been to
    portray the park in all its diversity, richness, and beauty. I hope this collection does it
    justice."—Last paragraph of introduction. | Includes bibliographical references. |
Identifiers: LCCN 2017031819 (print) | LCCN 2017033268 (ebook) | ISBN
    9781607815891 () | ISBN 9781607815884 (pbk.)
Subjects: LCSH: Glacier National Park (Mont.)—History. | Tales—Montana—Glacier
    National Park. | Indians of North America—Montana—Glacier National Park—
    Folklore. | Mountaineers—Montana—Glacier National Park—Folklore. | Animals—
    Montana—Glacier National Park.
Classification: LCC F737.G5 (ebook) | LCC F737.G5 G45 2017 (print) | DDC
    978.6/52—dc23
LC record available at https://lccn.loc.gov/2017031819

Frontispiece: *Running Eagle Falls* by Kathryn Stats, 30" x 24", oil on linen panel.
Used by permission of the artist. All rights reserved.

Printed and bound in the United States of America.

For my daughter Kate

CONTENTS

VI. ANIMALS

VII. MODERN TIMES

Illustrations follow page 187

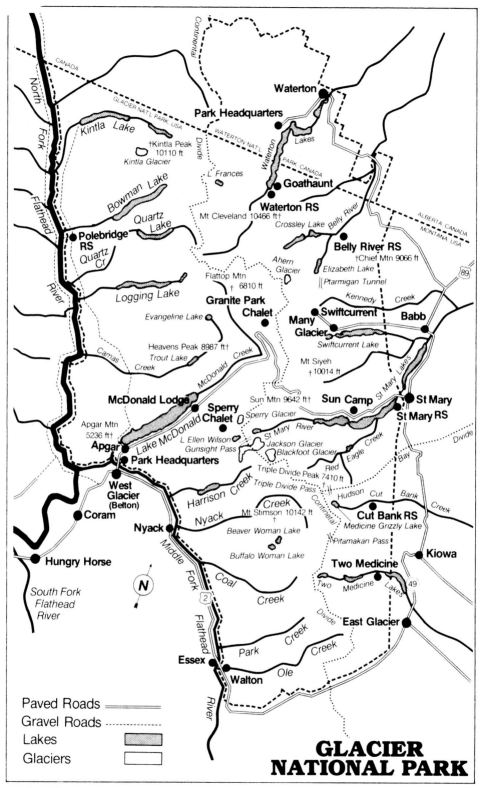

GLACIER
NATIONAL PARK

INTRODUCTION

David Stanley

Glacier National Park was established in 1910 largely in recognition of its spectacular geology: glaciated U-shaped valleys, paternoster lakes (so named because they resemble rosary beads on a cord), cup-shaped basins called cirques containing tarns (tiny lakes), and hanging valleys from which fall shimmering waterfalls hundreds of feet high. The jagged peaks, sculpted by masses of moving ice over millennia, include sharply pointed horns, thin vertical walls called arêtes, and incised notches and passes. About sixty living glaciers up to a square mile in size were a major attraction for visitors in the early days of the park; they are now rapidly disappearing.

Glacier remains a place of astounding beauty where a roadside stop, a brief walk along a trail, a hike, a backpacking trip, or a mountain scramble reveals landscapes stunning in form, colors, and contrasts. In any of Glacier's valleys, one might stand amid a mosaic of wildflowers—red-orange Indian paintbrush, scarlet monkey flower, creamy-white beargrass, brilliant yellow glacier lilies, and the deep blues of lupine, penstemon, gentian, and larkspur. Beyond the meadow may be a turquoise-blue lake or a clear-flowing stream, its bed glowing with the red, green, and buff stones that form the park's sedimentary rock layers. In the background, near-vertical mountain walls frame evergreen forests, and in the far distance, bare rock cliffs shelter glaciers and permanent snowfields, all outlined against what Montanans like to call "the Big Sky." These panoramas, to me, are what make Glacier so timeless, so serene.

Glacier is also one of the continent's most important sanctuaries for wildlife, from the valley-floor forests to the highest alpine meadows, cliffs, and summits. Two dozen kinds of fish swim in the lakes and streams, and hundreds of kinds of birds live in or pass through Glacier, from tiny hummingbirds to golden and bald eagles. Within the park roam virtually all of the large mammals of North America: moose, elk, whitetail and mule deer; bobcat, lynx, and cougar; ermine, mink, otter, pine marten, fisher, badger, and wolverine; mountain goat and bighorn sheep; fox, coyote, and gray wolf; black bear and grizzly. Even a few bison and pronghorn live on the eastern prairies of Glacier's Canadian partner, Waterton Lakes National Park.

Vital to the carnivores are the ubiquitous vegetarians, from chipmunks, red squirrels, jackrabbits, and snowshoe hares to hoary and yellow-bellied marmots, four species of ground squirrel, and the increasingly rare pika. There are also pack rats, beavers, porcupines, skunks, flying squirrels—animals of unusual appearance and fascinating behavior. Taken together, Glacier and Waterton National Parks are a crossroads where a variety of ecological zones come together, thus accounting for the tremendous variety of plant and animal life and some of the greatest biological diversity of all North American parks.

I first encountered this wonderland at the age of eighteen, when I was lucky enough to get a summer job doing trail maintenance, the first of six summers at the most physically challenging job I ever had. I had never lived in the West before, and I was unprepared for the wealth of life behind scenery that, after all, was choked with snow and frozen solid six months of the year. My first June in the park I found surprisingly chilly—drizzly days with clouds wreathing the peaks and mud, mosquitoes, and blisters on my feet.

Early in July, two other guys and I were sent into the Red Eagle Valley followed by a packer on a horse with a string of mules and enough food for ten days. We lodged in a mouse hotel called a snowshoe cabin where old-time rangers had sheltered while on winter patrol for poachers. As the rookie in the group, I got the upper bunk up against the logs, which the mice used as freeways during the night. It took awhile to get used to the scrabbling of little claws just above my head.

On that first trip into the valley we were trudging along, following veteran foreman Bud Clark, one of the most respected (and laconic) trail men who ever worked in the park. He stopped suddenly at the edge of a meadow and drawled, "Might want to hold up a minute." At the far end of the meadow a dark patch moved—deer or moose, I thought, until it turned sideways, and we saw the unmistakable shoulder hump of a grizzly. Bud led us on a good long bypass through the woods.

Within a couple of weeks, we'd seen two more grizzlies just outside the cabin, headed peacefully up the valley. Clearing the trail to the old Curly Bear fire lookout, we spotted a cougar flashing into the woods. A few weeks later, reconnoitering the abandoned trail to Red Eagle Pass, we surprised a couple of dozen heavily antlered bull elk chewing their cuds in an alpine meadow. Our foreman picked up a group of ptarmigan chicks huddled in the alpine moss and cupped them in his hands. The scenery began to be inhabited for me, and I began to absorb stories about the park—and to tell them myself.

The park's ample wilderness and wildlife can temporarily mask, for new visitors, the long and complex human history of the region. The area that became the park has for millennia been an arena for interactions—sometimes friendly and cooperative, sometimes hostile—among a variety of peoples. Native Americans have explored these mountains for thousands of years (the often-repeated assertion that Indians were afraid of the mountains and rarely entered them is patently untrue). Although Euro-American historians and Natives alike still debate the origins of the tribal groups in the area, by the time the first European trappers and fur traders arrived in the late eighteenth century, the Niitsitapi people (the Blackfeet or Blackfoot) dominated the east side of the mountains and plains from northern Alberta to southern Montana. The southernmost group, the Pikuni, lived and hunted primarily in what is now north-central Montana. West of the mountains lived the Ktunaxa (Kootenai), Upper Kalispel (Upper Pend d'Oreille), and Salish (Flathead). The western groups, especially the Ktunaxa, crossed the park's passes several times a year to hunt bison on the plains. Blackfeet war parties bent on obtaining horses crossed the mountains in the other direction. Raids, skirmishes, ambushes, and full-scale battles sometimes occurred.

The arrival of French and British Canadians from the north and U.S. explorers from the east created more interaction and more conflict. Some of the first written descriptions of the native peoples of the area came from the remarkable David Thompson, who surveyed the region at the end of the eighteenth century, made contact with tribal groups, kept an extensive journal, and drew maps with astonishing accuracy. A few years later, in 1806, Meriwether Lewis, homeward bound near the end of the Lewis and Clark Expedition, led three other men in following the Marias River to within twenty miles of the current park boundary. On Two Medicine River, a tussle erupted with a group of eight Blackfeet warriors. One, perhaps two, warriors died in the fight—the only violent conflict with Natives in the three-plus years of the expedition.

As trade in beaver pelts and bison hides expanded, a flood of trappers, traders, and missionaries (notably Father Pierre-Jean De Smet, a Belgian) came into the region. The traders brought with them household goods, tools, trinkets, and—increasingly—firearms and whiskey, usually adulterated. Several arrivals became what were disparagingly termed "squaw men," marrying Native women and settling down as adopted members of the tribal group. Some set up trading posts, some trapped, some hunted and raided along with their hosts. Despite the reputation of the Blackfeet as one of the most hostile and warlike tribes of the West, a number of these men—Hugh Monroe and James Willard Schultz, for example—lived for many years among the Blackfeet and prospered. Schultz, in fact, became a writer of some note and was the first Easterner to publicize the mountain country of northwest Montana and its inhabitants. Among his works are *Running Eagle*, the saga of Hugh Monroe, and *Medicine Grizzly*, a book about Pitamakan, the legendary woman warrior of the Blackfeet.

Schultz's articles in *Forest and Stream* magazine attracted the attention of the magazine's editor, George Bird Grinnell, one of the greatest conservationists of the nineteenth and twentieth centuries. In 1885, Grinnell made his first trip to the east side of what eventually became Glacier National Park, hunting with Schultz and local Blackfeet guide William Jackson; they explored the St. Mary and Swiftcurrent Valleys, naming lakes, mountains, and glaciers along the way.

In the mid-1890s, rumors of mineral wealth in the region began to spread. Soon there were short-lived booms in gold, silver, copper (including an unsuccessful mine in the center of the current park developed by Mrs. Nat "Libby" Collins, the "Cattle Queen of Montana"), and petroleum. The pressure exerted by greedy miners and Congress's indifference to the treaty rights of the Blackfeet led to the federal government's 1896 purchase of the east side of the mountains from the tribe for $1.5 million, or about $3 an acre. Almost immediately, miners poured into the east-side valleys, intent on quick riches. Traders and merchants wanting to buy cheap and sell high arrived. Trees were felled for mine timbers, shacks, and firewood. The boomtown of Altyn in the Swiftcurrent Valley sprang up and then almost immediately died away when the lack of mineral wealth became evident.

Grinnell, who had helped to broker the sale of the tribal lands to the federal government, then began publishing descriptive essays about the region, including "The Crown of the Continent" (1901) in the *Century Magazine*, an article that began nine years of political maneuvering to turn the area—at the time, a forest reserve—into a national park. Three years earlier, in 1898, California conservationist John Muir had visited Lake McDonald and called it, in an article in *The Atlantic*, "the greatest care-killing scenery on the continent."

The area also continued to be a place of occasional conflict and controversy. Blackfeet and local settlers continued to hunt in the mountains while newly appointed forest rangers tried to stop them. Residents of the Flathead Valley and homesteaders on the west side of the mountains generally opposed the creation of a national park, fearing they would lose economic and recreational resources. Yet other locals had already begun building the first basic cabins and hotels on the west side of Lake McDonald, even importing a steamboat (on a wagon!) to cater to a trickle of tourists arriving on the Great Northern Railway, which had finally completed (in 1893) its main line from St. Paul, Minnesota, to Seattle across Marias Pass on the southern boundary of the reserve.

On May 11, 1910, President William Howard Taft signed the enabling legislation that established Glacier as the nation's ninth national park. At that point, one or two thousand Blackfeet lived on their reservation bordering the east side of the park. A few scattered rangers patrolled 1,500 square miles. A dozen or so families lived around Lake McDonald, and a few homesteaders were settled along the North Fork of the Flathead River. Occasional hunters and tourists visited, especially on the west side, where geologists Raphael Pumpelly and Lyman Sperry had first explored some of the few active glaciers in the contiguous United States. Once the park was established, the Great Northern Railway, led by its president Louis Hill, began a major investment in tourist facilities—hotels, backcountry chalets, "tepee camps," roads, and trails—to lure passenger traffic to the railroad.

Very quickly, curious travelers arrived to experience this new park, following on the heels of Schultz, Grinnell, and Walter McClintock, who had come to the east side to report on the customs of the Blackfeet. About the same time, a number of intrepid, adventurous writers—many of them women—visited the west side of the soon-to-be-established park, including the witty Carrie Adele Strahorn, who found tourist facilities in the early 1890s decidedly inadequate. She was followed by Helen Fitzgerald Sanders, who also visited and wrote about the Flathead Indian Reservation southwest of the park. In the first decade after the park's establishment, visitors included historian Agnes C. Laut and Mary Roberts Rinehart, an immensely popular American author who completed a three-week, three-hundred-mile horseback trip through Glacier in 1915, then returned in 1916 with her husband and three sons for a hair-raising wooden boat excursion down the North and Middle Forks of the Flathead River.

A few years later, Vachel Lindsay, author of "The Congo" and other popular poems, along with his friend Stephen Graham, arrived to explore the backcountry of the park. The great painter and sculptor of the Old West, Charles M. Russell, was already spending summers at a cabin on Lake McDonald, and other artists—including Winhold Reiss, John Fery, Maynard Dixon, and Kathryn Leighton—were recruited and funded by the Great Northern Railway to paint the park's landscapes and the Blackfeet people, part of a massive publicity effort by the railroad to attract tourists.

My own experience forty years later reflects the remarkable diversity of residents and visitors. Within a few days of my arrival, I became aware that the green-uniformed rangers with the Smokey Bear hats were either "permanents," who lived and worked at the park year-round, or "seasonals," men and women hired for the summer. The park's wide array of tourist facilities—hotels, motels, cafes, gift shops, camp stores—employed hundreds of summer employees, most of them in those days college students from the Midwest. Some local residents, both Native Americans and Anglos, worked seasonally for the park on road and trail crews or found temporary work serving the tourists who came from every state and dozens of foreign countries. The park also supported fire lookouts, campground caretakers, maintenance workers, horse wranglers for tourist trips, and packers, the men who led strings of mules into the backcountry to supply those of us who worked there. These last were a colorful crew, dressed in classic cowboy garb and sporting a vocabulary that was new to me—terms for horse and mule gear like "alfogies" and "manties," accompanied by some rip-roaring cussing, usually at the mules.

Parks seem to attract interesting characters—eccentrics, tricksters, storytellers, loners, and curmudgeons. I soon began hearing stories about Norman Clyde, the California mountaineer who—legend has it—climbed forty-two peaks in forty-three days in 1921, many of them first ascents and most of them solo (not recommended). And there was Joe Cosley, the ex-ranger who became a trapper and an outlaw; John George "Kootenai" Brown, the mountain man who was appointed the first superintendent of Waterton; Albert "Death-on-the-Trail" Reynolds, the lonely ranger at the U.S. end of Waterton Lake; and homesteader Josephine Doody, the moonshiner of the Middle Fork, who supported herself nicely during Prohibition with the help of railroad crews making her deliveries.

Even the well-known writer Thomas Wolfe, author of *Look Homeward, Angel*, came to the park in 1938 and recorded his impressions in *A Western Journal* (published posthumously in 1951). In his characteristically unbridled prose, he described traveling the newly completed Going-to-the-Sun Road:

> the stupendous hackled peaks now—the sheer basaltic walls of glaciation, the steep scoopings down below, the dense vertices of glacial valley slopes and forest—and climbing climbing to the Logan Pass so down

again terrifically, and the glacial wall beside the enormous hackled granite peaks before, the green steep glaciation of the forest, the pouring cascades, and the streams below—and down and down the miraculous
road into the forest, and by rushing waters, and down and down to the
McDonald Lake.

The park's rocks are neither basalt nor granite, but never mind.

With so many disparate groups of people interacting with each other, stories were bound to emerge. Tourists in search of information on trails, campsites, glaciers, and animal life heard stories from park workers and passed them
on to each other. As a laborer on the trail crew, I absorbed accounts of rescues
of injured hikers, vivid descriptions of bear maulings, and cautionary tales
of drownings, falls, and other accidents, along with tall tales about giant fish
(some of them fur-bearing) and other unusual animals such as snow snakes
and rhinoceros-sized grizzly bears.

The underlying theme of these stories was the total unpredictability of
the park. A thunderstorm could come up over the Continental Divide with
no warning, catching hikers on exposed ridges or mountaintops, drenching
and frightening them at the same time. An unattended campfire, a carelessly
dropped cigarette, or a sudden lighting strike could ignite a full-fledged forest
fire in a matter of minutes. A spring downpour could melt the snowpack and
wipe out trails, roads, and bridges in a few hours. A benign-looking snowfield could turn out to be glare ice, sending the unwary hiker on a long and
painful slide into the rocks below. Rockfalls, avalanches, yawning crevasses
in the glaciers, sudden whiteout snowstorms, crumbling trail edges, unstable
log crossings over streams, slippery cliffs by waterfalls and creeks—all threatened the careless, the inexperienced, and the unprepared with major injury
or sudden death.

And then there were bears. Glacier's animal symbol, designed and sponsored by the Great Northern Railway soon after the park was created, is the
mountain goat, a relatively benign and slightly goofy-looking bearded creature
that can scale vertical cliffs with remarkable agility. But it was bears—mainly
grizzlies—that became the focus of most Glacier tales, stories that emphasized
their strength, speed, and intelligence. It was said that a mother bear with cubs
would attack without provocation, that certain bad-tempered and aggressive
"boars" (males) would stalk and attack hikers and campers out of sheer cussed-
ness, that any bear could turn rogue, intimidating unwary hikers and campers

and stealing their food. If you ran into a grizzly, said some, you should climb a tree. Others said to lie down, curl up in a fetal position, and hope the bear leaves you alone. Still others said you could talk calmly to the bear while backing away (all of these strategies have worked, sometimes). However, everyone agreed, "Don't run. A bear can run as fast as a horse."

The fact is that ten people were killed by bears in the park between 1967 and 2015, usually while hiking or camping, though during that time frame far more people have died of heart attacks, car accidents, falls from mountains, and drownings. Still, the presence of bears creates a certain alertness in visitors—it's their bearish unpredictability and the thought, as former fire lookout Doug Peacock has said, that humans are not at the top of the food chain in grizzly country.

Fascination with grizzlies—and apprehension about them—has led to dozens of legends and lots of writing from people like Andy Russell, Edward Abbey, Doug Peacock, Don Burgess, and Christine Byl. Entire books of bear stories have been collected and published, enough to keep the reader occupied for years (these are best read *after* visiting the park, by the way). And, not surprisingly, lots of folklore has emerged on how to avoid bear confrontations, from little bells on hikers' shoelaces to air horns. Current wisdom, by the way, says, "Make lots of noise and carry bear spray."

Glacier is a place of paradox—at once serene and violent, breathtakingly beautiful and somber, even sometimes almost ominous. Vibrant life thrives within the apparent calm of the scenery, and people from all walks of life come to the park and interact with each other, encountering the wilderness, learning its ways, and telling stories about their experiences. In this collection, I have put together a variety of those stories written between 1889 and 2016, along with Native American oral narratives of gods, animals, and men that date back much further. My intention has been to portray the park in all its diversity, richness, and beauty. I hope this collection does it justice.

PART I

NATIVE PEOPLE

The Glacier Park area has been familiar territory for Native Americans for a very long time. Rich archeological sites at lakes like Middle and Lower Waterton and Lower St. Mary's show thousands of years of usage, and the *piskun* or buffalo jumps—sites where Indian people worked together to stampede bison over steep cliffs to obtain meat, hides, and other parts—are numerous in the region. The east side of the mountains, the rolling plains from the North Saskatchewan River to the Yellowstone, was the home of the Niitsitapi (the Blackfoot Confederacy), who regularly traversed the plains to hunt bison and harvest other resources. They also used these valleys extensively for edible and medicinal plants, minerals for paint, forest timber for firewood and lodgepoles, and wild game for meat and fur. In addition, they occasionally crossed the mountains to raid the northwestern plateau nations for horses. At the same time, the people of the northwestern plateaus—especially the Ktunaxa (Kootenai), the Kalispel, the Salish (Flatheads), and the Nez Perce—made frequent excursions through the mountains to "go for buffalo"—to hunt bison on the prairies, dry the meat, then pack it back to their home villages. Skirmishes and even full-scale battles were common as the tribes competed for food, territory, and power.

The arrival of Euro-American explorers, traders, trappers, prospectors, and soldiers spelled an end to the free movement of Native Americans as their lands were coerced from them and their resources were sequestered or destroyed. Many died from introduced epidemics and attacks by settlers and military forces. They were increasingly confined to reservations, which in turn became smaller and smaller through nominal purchase, treaties and other agreements, forced cessions, allotments, and unauthorized white encroachment.

As soon as Glacier National Park was established in 1910—half of it obtained through forced cession by the Blackfeet—the Great Northern Railway and park superintendents sought to involve the Blackfeet people in advertising the wonders of the park. Indian people in "native costume" met trains at East Glacier, sold souvenirs (including hat racks made from the horns of the millions of bison slaughtered in the 1870s), performed "native dances," showed visitors the tepees where some of them lived in the summer, and had their photos taken for small tips. The Blackfeet became known, in advertising, as the "Glacier Park Indians." This gloss of publicity tended to obscure the fact that Native Americans had suffered greatly after the bison were wiped out: their reservations were diminished, food rations were cut, and disease, starvation, and alcohol took a terrible toll. Yet the people, and their cultural traditions, survived.

Jack Gladstone (b. 1958) is a contemporary Native American performing artist of Blackfeet heritage. A musician, singer, and songwriter, Gladstone gives lectures and presentations and composes songs that focus on the complex history of the Blackfoot Confederacy and their interactions with the Glacier Park region. Gladstone's Native America Speaks lecture series, presented every summer at various locations throughout the park, was established in 1985 and is the longest continuously running indigenous speaker series in national park history.

His song "Legends of Glacier" (2002) represents the deep and continuing meaning that his people find in the mountain country, which the Blackfeet people call "the Backbone of the World." The song is available on Gladstone's album, *Tappin' the Earth's Backbone* (2002), as well as on his compilation disc, *Buckskin PoetSongs* (2005). He explains, "This was written to accent the point that the land we now call Glacier National Park has a story to tell. In learning stories from our indigenous peoples, we discover a relationship whose roots extend back many thousands of years."

Grandmother's stories ignited the spark
Now warming the heart of a man
Fantastic odysseys, requested dreams,
Were part of our first human clans
Elders have summoned the auras of old

Remembered and treasured through time
Don't be surprised. This land comes alive
And Legends of Glacier survive.

Gray Wolf and Beaver Chief caretake the land
The heart is the Sun's beating drum.
Owl eyes and eagle wings perfect the view
Where spirit and matter are one.

Permit your wings to transcend the things
Consuming and cluttering life
You're one on one with Creator Sun
And Legends of Glacier survive.

Ahh—Listen deep to the voice
That calls from our home long ago
We're on the knife edge of time
We feel, but never quite know.

The youngest of all of her children are us.
The ones still learning respect
The soul awakens, the heart is revived
And Legends of Glacier survive.
Keep Legends of Glacier alive.
Legends...

MY INTRODUCTION TO THE BLACKFEET

Walter McClintock

1910

Yale-educated Walter McClintock (1870–1949) first saw northwestern Montana in 1896, where he soon came to know William Jackson, veteran Piegan scout and guide for James Willard Schultz and George Bird Grinnell. McClintock spent much of the next two decades with the Blackfeet people, observing their ceremonies and taking photographs. Later, he published (with the Southwest Museum in Los Angeles) a series of studies of Blackfeet culture, including monographs on medicine bundles, tipis, dance, warrior societies, and ceremonies. His books on the Blackfeet—*The Old North Trail* (1910) and *Old Indian Trails* (1923)—are major studies of the Blackfeet way of life during the early reservation period. *The Old North Trail; Or, Life, Legends and Religion of the Blackfeet Indians* explores ceremonies and spiritual practices in addition to describing the Old North Trail, which ran parallel to the east slope of the Rocky Mountains from Canada to Mexico and had been used by Native Americans for thousands of years. This excerpt from pages 6–27 of that work describes McClintock's first journey across the ranges that would later become Glacier National Park. The route in question was from the Middle Fork of the Flathead River, up Nyack Creek, and over Cut Bank Pass—the pass most commonly used by Native Americans.

I first visited the country of the Blackfeet as a member of a Government expedition under Gifford Pinchot, Chief of the Forest Service of the United States, which had been sent into the north-west by the National Forest Commission, to report upon the advisability of forming certain national forest reserves.

Siksikakoan (Blackfoot-Man), also known as William Jackson, was a noted Indian scout, who had served in the Indian campaigns under Generals Miles and Custer....Siksikakoan continued his scouting service until the close of the Indian wars on the northern plains, when he returned to his tribe on the Blackfeet Reservation. He erected a cabin on Cutbank [usually spelled "Cut Bank"] River, at the foot of the Rocky Mountains. He gradually built up a well-equipped ranch, and owned large herds of cattle and horses. He lived there till the winter of 1899, when he died, as the final result of injuries received during his life of adventure and hardship as a scout.

When the forestry work was completed and my Government associates had departed, Siksikakoan and I were camped together in the forest country of the Flathead Indians, on the western slope of the Rocky Mountains. One evening, by our camp-fire, I agreed to his proposal that we should return to the Blackfeet Reservation on the eastern side of the range; "for there," said he, "I have many horses and cattle. The mountains are not far distant, where the hunting is good, and the lakes and streams are full of fish. We shall be in the midst of my people, and I will introduce you to the leading chiefs of the Blackfeet."

It was at the beginning of summer, when we started on our journey across the Rocky Mountains, toward the country of the Blackfeet. Our outfit was carried on the backs of pack horses. The trail was difficult and overgrown and frequently blocked by windfalls. Siksikakoan led the way with his axe, while I followed driving the pack horses. On the western slope of the Rockies the forests are very dense, because of the mild climate and abundant rainfall. The trees grow to a large size and the undergrowth is luxuriant. We rode through glades, where the rank masses of weeds and grasses were shoulder high, and passed chains of beautiful lakes, hidden in the gloomy recesses of the forest, where huge tamaracks, firs and spruces grew to the water's edge, and extended high up on the sides of the mountains. This was the haunt of deer, wapiti [elk] and moose, many of their tracks being visible in the soft ground along the lake shores.

We surprised a large bear sunning himself in the trail, but he quietly and quickly disappeared into the forest. The trail led through a broad valley and along the bank of a swift mountain stream, climbing continually upwards towards the Continental Divide. When we reached a high altitude, the trees became gnarled and stunted, and we were frequently enveloped in heavy clouds. Here were many tracks of big-horn, and we saw a band of Rocky Mountain goats high up on the mountain side. Hoary marmots, or whistlers greeted us from the cliff with their shrill calls, but they were so timid that they quickly disappeared on our approach. We entered a huge basin, surrounded by towering peaks—a superb and vast amphitheatre about four miles wide from side to side. At the bottom was a sparkling lake, with wooded shores, surmounted by a circular mountain wall with a sheer height of 3,000 feet. It was fed by many streams, which had their sources in the glaciers and fell over precipitous cliffs with a constant roar, reverberating like thunder from the surrounding walls of rock.

The Indians have given to the main range of the Rocky Mountains the appropriate name "Backbone-of-the-World." Standing on the summit of the Cutbank Pass (7,861 feet), we were surrounded by dazzling glaciers and stupendous mountains mantled with snow. The intense brightness of the snow-fields was relieved by the dark green covering of forests, which lined the valleys far below. Four miles to the north lay the Triple Divide—the Crown of the Continent, where the water-shed divides between the Pacific Ocean, Hudson Bay, and the Gulf of Mexico. Directly south was the sharply-pointed Flinch's peak [now Flinsch Peak], which lifted its towering mass like a cathedral spire 5,000 feet above the valley. It is impossible from the illustration to realise the sheer precipitousness of this peak.

On the west were Mt. James [Mt. Stimson] (10,155 feet), Mt. Pinchot (9,332 feet), and Ram Mountain, so called because [it was] frequented by many Rocky Mountain rams. To the north-west was Mt. Blackfoot (9,591), and the magnificent Blackfoot Glacier, a vast expanse of ice and snow. Beyond rose the summit of Mt. Jackson (10,023), and under its shoulder the Harrison Glacier, with its wonderful ice cascades. Turning farther to the north, we could see a multitude of peaks. Among them were Mt. Siyeh (or Mad Wolf, 10,004); Little Chief (9,542); Going-to-the-Sun (9,594); Four Bears; Almost-a-Dog (8,911); Mt. Grinnell (8,838), and the Grinnell Glacier; Mt. Red Eagle, and the Red Eagle Glacier, which is the source of Red Eagle Creek. The Grinnell Glacier is fenced on the west by a remarkable serrated ridge of the Continental Divide known as "The Garden Wall."

In close proximity are the Gun-sight Pass (its contour resembling a gun-sight), and the Sperry Glacier; the Sexton Glacier, with its half mile of ice front, and the Swift Current Pass. Words fail to describe the magnificence of the glaciers and waterfalls, and the majesty and impressive beauty of the numerous high peaks and stupendous mountain ranges. Although this country is practically unknown, the difficult trails being frequented only by hunters, trappers, and Indians, its scenic wonders are probably unsurpassed by any within the United States. The region should be reserved by the Government as a National Park and Game Preserve.

From the summit of the Pass, Siksikakoan pointed out the course of our trail eastward, following the Cutbank River through a long, winding valley, with high, snow-covered mountain ranges on either side. Beyond stretched the tawny plains—the country of the Blackfeet, resembling a distant ocean in its level expanse, and extending eastward many hundreds of miles into the dim and hazy horizon. We descended from the summit of Cutbank Pass between two small glacier lakes. In their dark and still waters, the surrounding crags and mountain walls were clearly reflected and many miniature icebergs were floating, having fallen from the fronts of the overhanging glaciers.

The travelling on the eastern side of the Rockies was much easier and in marked contrast with our difficult ascent of the western side. We now followed a trail worn deep into the ground by generations of Blackfeet and other Indian tribes, when they crossed and recrossed the Rocky Mountains on their war and hunting expeditions. We entered a forest at the head of the canyon, where the snow clung heavily to the balsams and pines. As we descended, the snow disappeared and the air became balmy.

The climate east of the mountains is more severe, because subject to extreme changes of temperature. Hailstorms are frequent, and snowstorms often occur in midsummer. In winter there are terrible blizzards, during which the thermometer drops to 50° below zero (Fahrenheit).

We camped after sunset in a beautiful, natural park of luxuriant bunch-grass, fragrant with wild flowers and surrounded by forests of spruce and pine.

Early next morning—our last day in the mountains—we again took up the trail through the canyon of the Cutbank River. As the sun's rays entered the canyon, the massive walls of rock, towering overhead, became a brilliant red, while the high peaks glistened with colours as varied as the rainbow's. In crossing the summit of a high rocky ridge, we had an extended view of the forest-covered valley below, and the course of the river winding through open glades and grassy meadows, until it passed through the entrance of the canyon. Beyond were the foothills, or high, grass-covered ridges, lying in front of the canyon entrance, like a mighty barrier. Here the luxuriant vegetation of the mountains abruptly ended and the dry grass of the prairies began.

After riding through the foothills, we crossed an old trail, running north and south, now overgrown with grass. Siksikakoan explained that it was the Old North Trail. It is no longer used by the Indians, its course having been broken in many places by the fences and towns of the white man's advancing civilisation. Yet the old horse trail and travois tracks were still plainly visible, having been worn deep by many generations of travelling Indians.

We rode out over the treeless plains until, from the crest of a ridge, about twenty miles from the main range of the Rockies, we looked down upon a scene, which I will never forget because of its novel and exceeding beauty. In a luxuriant tract of meadow, and on the shore of a lake, lay the tribal camp of the Blackfeet, pitched in the form of an enormous circle. The undulating ridges which surrounded it were brilliant with blue lupines and velvet-leaf sun-flowers. Great herds of horses were contentedly feeding on the rich bunch grass. Smoke from the evening fires was rising from the lodges. A faint breeze, laden with a pleasant fragrance from the meadows, brought distinctly the sounds of an Indian camp, the shouts of men and women, the crying of children, the barking of many dogs and the slow, measured beating of Indian tom-toms in dances and ceremonial gatherings.

After entering the Blackfeet camp, I accompanied Siksikakoan while he visited the lodges of the different chiefs. As we sat smoking a friendly pipe together, he explained to them that I had come from the Great Father (President of the United States), for the purpose of protecting the forests of their country, that they might be preserved for future generations. In this way I first met Chief Mad Wolf (Siyeh), their greatest orator, the high priest of their Sun-dance and the owner of the Beaver Medicine Bundle (an important ceremonial). This was the beginning of a mutual bond of sympathy and attachment, unusual between an Indian and a white man, which developed gradually into a strong and lasting friendship.

On my first night in the Blackfeet camp, I chose to sleep outside the camp circle in a meadow, not far from Mad Wolf's lodge, because the weather was clear and warm and I had no fear of being molested by the Indians. I was within hearing of any ceremonials that would take place in Mad Wolf's lodge and nothing of moment could occur in the encampment without my knowledge.

I placed my blanket-bed on the prairie-grass, and, instead of the lodge covering for a roof, I had the magnificent canopy of the night-sky, spangled with an innumerable multitude of stars. On account of the clearness of the atmosphere over the plains, these sparkling orbs of light shone with a rare brilliance and splendour, and appeared lower down in the horizon than I had ever seen elsewhere. Lying on my back and gazing up into the wonderful beauty of the heavens gave me an overwhelming sense of the infinity of God's universe and my own littleness by comparison.

I was not, however, to be entirely free from disturbance. While lying upon my blankets, my attention was attracted by two wandering Indian boys, who had been startled by the weird and ghostly appearance of my bed. They were standing at a short distance conversing together in awed whispers. When I gave a sudden jump and rattled the white canvas covering, they took to their heels, believing that I was a ghost. During the night, I was again aroused by the hot breath of a large animal upon my face. Being awakened from a deep slumber, I imagined that it was a grizzly bear standing over me. Jumping from my blankets with a yell, I found that it was an Indian horse, which had been standing quietly, with lowered head, over my bed. My outfit had aroused his curiosity, but my actions were so precipitate and my appearance, clad in white, so startling, that he quickly stampeded with frightened snorts.

At first I was at a loss to know how to secure suitable board and lodging in the Blackfoot camp. Their diet of dried meat and meat stews was to me neither appetising nor sufficiently nourishing. The difficult problem was, however, solved for me in a very satisfactory way by my friend Big Eyes. I had gained the good will of himself and wife through the interest I had taken in their children. To show their appreciation, his wife, Ips-e-nik-ki, who was skilled in the making of lodges, presented me with an Indian tipi, decorated with pictographs of interesting events in her husband's life. With the acquisition of a tipi, I had my own home in the camp, but it was necessary to do my own cooking and to care for my own horses and outfit, for the Blackfeet have no servants, and I had not taken a wife.

I soon discovered that my diet of bacon, cereals, and dried fruits was no more pleasing to the Blackfeet than theirs was to me. After Spotted Eagle, the medicine man, had dined with me, he said that he had never been able to understand how people could live on the food eaten by white men. He told me of a journey he had once taken with some officers of the United States Army, "with whom he could stay no longer than a week, because of the strange food they ate."

When the Sun festival was finished and the Indians separated, I accompanied Siksikakoan to live on his Blackfoot ranch, not far from Mad Wolf's home on Cutbank River. I found him to be a man of fine mind and practical common sense, resourceful and fearless in emergencies and thoroughly equipped in all that goes to make an ideal guide and companion in the wilds. Under him I learned woodcraft, the handling of the broncho, the mysteries of the "diamond hitch" and the location of the old Indian trails leading across the plains and through the mountains. He was a natural orator and had standing and influence in the councils of his tribe. He spoke English fluently as well as the Blackfoot and Sioux tongues, and was thoroughly familiar with the ancient customs and traditions of his people. It was under his influence that I became deeply interested in the Blackfeet, and through his friendship that I was gradually brought into an intimate association with their leaders.

During my first summer among the Blackfeet, I rode over the reservation, visiting them in their camps and in their homes. Many interesting subjects crowded themselves upon my mind and enlisted my energies. I carried a medicine case containing simple remedies with which I was sometimes able to relieve the sick and help the injured. I endeavoured in every way to aid their advancement towards the white man's civilisation, helping in the cultivation of the ground, herding horses and cattle, and cutting timber in the mountains for building their cabins, fences, and corrals. When the sun was hot in midsummer, I helped them to make hay in the luxuriant meadows of the river bottoms. Although that kind of work was hard, it never seemed to dull my mind to the wonderful and ever-changing beauty of prairie, river, and distant mountains. In the clear days of autumn, when the bite of frost was in the air, I joined their hunting expeditions across the broad plains and into the Rocky Mountains.

I now look back with the deepest pleasure upon the freedom of that life, the delight of living and of working in that exhilarating mountain atmosphere. Those who spend sleepless nights, because of the absorbing and nerve-racking occupations of modern civilisation, may well envy my nights of refreshing sleep, while wrapped in my blankets beside some swiftly flowing mountain stream, or on the plains under the open sky. The life of the Indian, so close to the heart of nature, the companionship with inspiring mountains, sunlit plains, lakes and rivers, the ceaseless, but ever beautiful succession of lights and colourings, while day waned into night and night gave place to day, and the wonderful colour transformations, which came and went with the changing seasons, all these fascinated and held me with an irresistible grip.

It required, however, a long period of cordial relations to overcome the natural prejudice of the Indians against a white man, but I gradually gained their confidence, which I was careful never to abuse. I lived with them, not merely for pleasure and adventure, but chiefly for the purpose of gaining as full a knowledge as possible of their characteristics and customs, their traditions and religion. I realised that I had an unusual opportunity of studying a remarkable race of people, who properly belonged to the Stone Age, whose religion and social organisation had come down from a distant past, free from contact with any other religion or culture. The younger generation were indifferent to their ancient customs and religion and it seemed that this primitive and most interesting people must soon lose their identity and disappear for ever.

2

MY-STU-BUN, CROWFEATHER ARROW'S REVENGE

Percy Bullchild
1985

Many early explorers, travelers, and historians of the Glacier Park region have claimed that Native Americans did not venture into the mountains, either because they preferred other country or because they feared evil spirits or ghosts. Neither of these ideas is true; Native American groups visited the mountains frequently to obtain game, medicinal herbs, mineral colors for paints, and lodgepoles for their tepees. Many young men embarked on vision quests in the mountains as well, and the mountains often play an important role in Native American myths and legends.

The Blackfeet people, largely a plains people who relied on the buffalo, or bison, for much of their sustenance, nevertheless made frequent forays into the mountains. They knew the best passes, which they used for horse raids against the Salish (Flatheads), Kalispels, and Ktunaxa (Kootenais) of the western slopes. They knew, too, the valleys and canyons, where they frequently wintered in groves of cottonwood trees, particularly along the Two Medicine and Cut Bank Rivers, which eventually join to form the Marias River.

Percy Bullchild was a full-blood Blackfeet who spent virtually all of his life on the reservation. Toward the end of his life, he began collecting and writing down narratives of Blackfeet life, relying especially on his memories of legends told by his paternal grandmother, Catches Last, who passed away in 1927. In addition, Bullchild collected myths and legends from dozens of other elderly Blackfeet. His collection was published in 1985 as *The Sun Came Down: The History of the World as My Blackfeet Elders Told It* (reprinted by University of Nebraska Press in 2005). It is regarded as one of the finest collections of traditional narratives from any of the western tribal groups. The narrative that follows centers on the figure of Napi or Oldman, the creative force among the Blackfeet people who created the world. But Napi is also a trickster, capable of pranks, mischief, disruption, and human emotions. In this narrative, he is disguised as My-stu-bun, Crow-feather Arrow, and he is angry because the people rejected his gift of plumes and feathers but accepted those of Bellyfat, a great man within the tribe. This was in a time long ago, before the Blackfeet acquired horses.

My-stu-bun came mysteriously. No one knew where he had come from, just himself knew who he really was. He knew he had transformed himself into another being. Crowfeather Arrow was really Oldman, Napi. He was put here on Mother Earth to teach the children of Creator Sun and Mother Earth how to live like them, a sinless life. But he had made a few mistakes with the people already, so now he was trying to break away from Creator Sun's rulings. He was tempted to live like his subjects, the people of Mother Earth, and at the same time to retain the power that was entrusted to him by Creator Sun. He was also stealing that power entrusted to him by Creator Sun to gain himself a wife. But wrong never holds up no matter what, and no matter how much power is entrusted to you, that power never works when you are using it for the wrong purpose.

My-stu-bun, Crowfeather Arrow, was very embarrassed over what he had done, cheating to get a wife for himself. At the same time he was mad at all of the people, they were all against him for what he had done, or so he thought.

My-stu-bun was going to show them a lesson they must learn, not to make fun of anyone. He was going to have revenge and make them suffer for what they had done to him, belittling him, making fun of him, harassing him. This wasn't all that true, but that's what Crowfeather Arrow had in his mind, that all were against him and making fun of him for what he had tried to do.

Crowfeather Arrow bided his time, waiting for the best time to get revenge on the people. It had to be something to affect all of the people, the children of Mother Earth and Creator Sun.

…his chance for revenge came at last. The people were getting very hungry. The buffalo was on the move and it was hard for them to keep up with the herds of buffalo. Being on foot wasn't easy, their leg power was the only thing that got them places.

Crowfeather Arrow, seeing the people moving here and there about every other day looking for the buffalo, got an idea to get that revenge he wanted. He must hide the buffalo so the people wouldn't find them at all.

Using that supernatural power entrusted to him by Creator Sun, he rounded up all of the buffalo and hid them all in a mountain canyon. This particular canyon was at the head of the present-day Cut Bank Creek and Cut Bank

Canyon, to the south of Saint Mary Lake. The people were camped just east of there in the hills, still looking for the buffalo.

All of the men of the camp and other camps all over were out in mass to find the herds of buffalo. The deer and the antelope, the elk, moose, and other game, even the fowls that were food to the people were just too hard to get—they were so much faster than the buffalo and so much harder to kill. It was easier to kill a lot of buffalo. They were stampeded over high steep places in herds. Many are killed in the fall, and those that might be still alive are trampled to death by others falling on them. There, enough meat was gotten for even a big camp of people to last them for quite a while.

Even the dried meat that was stored away was eaten up, [and] some of the older people were beginning to get weak from the lack of fresh meat as every one of the Plains people depend on the meat as the main source of energy and vitamins.

All of the people seemed to be starving from the lack of fresh meat—except Crowfeather Arrow. For some reason he still had lot of energy, even some to spare. This, Bellyfat had observed of him. Bellyfat was now watching Crowfeather Arrow very close, from the time Crowfeather Arrow got up out of bed until he retired for the night.

Bellyfat was up way before daylight and was hiding up on a little knoll that was thick with quaking aspens. From this clump of quaking aspens where he hid, he had a good observation of almost everything surrounding the place.

Just at daylight, it was no problem for Bellyfat to see from his hiding place all those that got out of their tipis and went for their usual morning strolls. He kept his eyes on Crowfeather Arrow's tipi. Crowfeather Arrow also got up before the other people got up, and right away went sneaking out of camp right to a thick clump of quaking aspens not far from where Bellyfat was hiding. Bellyfat seen him disappear into the quaking aspens. A little while after, a beautiful white crow came up out of the thickets. Bellyfat wasn't a type to be fooled easily, he knew right away what it was all about. He kept his eyes on this white crow, he knew that it was no other than Crowfeather Arrow.

Crowfeather Arrow was on his way to eat. He knew where the herds of buffalos were, where he hid them. Crowfeather Arrow was getting his fill each day and letting the rest go hungry. He was very wise, but not as wise as Bellyfat. For some reason he had a feeling someone was watching him this one morning. Flying up out of the thick quaking aspens, he watched very close down on ground. He circled around and around, that feeling of someone watching his every movement. He went into bigger circles and was quite high in the air, he was trying very hard to see who was watching him. Bellyfat was too well hidden to be seen, especially from the air. He just kept his eyes on Crowfeather Arrow, the white crow that was flying.

After he made very sure no one was watching, he flew to the north. He was trying to fool whoever might be watching him, he thought whoever was doing the watching might come out and follow him to the north.

Bellyfat was just too smart for that. He didn't move, he just kept his eyes glued on the white crow flying north.

Crowfeather Arrow, the flying crow, was tricky this morning. As he flew, his eyes were looking back and all over to see if someone was watching where he flew to....

Crowfeather Arrow, the white crow, finally sure of himself, turned and came flying back towards the camps. It took time to get back to where the camps were, but reaching them, he didn't come down. He went on flying to the south now. His worries were all for nothing, it was just his imagination that he thought someone was watching him. He flew on towards Cut Bank Canyon, and there he circled for awhile to make very sure again no one was watching him.

Before the crow came back, while it was still flying out of sight far, far to the north, Bellyfat made a dash for the clump of quaking aspens that Crowfeather Arrow had disappeared into. Sure enough, there in the center of this thicket, laid in a heap, was Crowfeather Arrow's clothing—his breechclout, his leggings, his buckskin shirt, everything he owned. Being very sure of this, Bellyfat ran back to his hiding place not too far away, and hid again.

Bellyfat just made it back to his hiding place when the crow came flying back from that north side, zigzagging towards the camps, just trying to make sure no one seen him. Coming closer to the camps, the crow went way down low, just above the treetops where hardly anyone would notice him.

The crow flew to the clump of quaking aspens to the west of them, and went right down into the thicket where his clothing laid. It wasn't long after this that Crowfeather Arrow came walking out of the thickets and hurried down to his tipi.

Crowfeather Arrow's hunger got the best of him again. He must go and fill his greedy stomach up. He got up very early again, just getting daylight, and to the thickets again he went. But there was always one that got up before him, and that was Bellyfat. Bellyfat…finally seen the crow take a roundabout course towards the south.…Bellyfat jumped from his hiding place and ran with all his might southward to Cut Bank Canyon, where the crow had disappeared again.

Bellyfat, coming into the canyon, followed the creek up as far as he dared to go. He hid himself very near a small park, an opening in the timber where the creek ran through. Over this area, the crow had to fly over. Right near the creek's edge, Bellyfat transformed himself into a dead beaver lying on its back.

Bellyfat didn't have too long to wait. As he laid there in the form of a dead beaver, with his eyes open to observe everything around him, he seen the crow as it came flying out of the thickets quite a ways to the west.…

Crowfeather Arrow…was keeping his eyes open for anything that looked suspicious. Coming over the small park, the opening in the timber where the creek ran through, his gazing eyes seen a dead beaver laying there. A beaver was a tender morsel for a crow, a treat that couldn't be passed up.…

The crow lit a little ways from the dead beaver.…All at once he jumped towards the head of the beaver and he pecked at the slightly open eye of this dead beaver, which the beaver didn't expect. The dead beaver winced at this eye-pecking.…

As the crow flew out of sight, Bellyfat transformed himself back into his real self and slowly walked back toward the camps, his eye hurting quite a bit from that good peck the crow had done to him. He knew he had to try harder to catch that Crowfeather Arrow so he could find out about all of the buffalo.

It was several days before Crowfeather Arrow attempted to go and get something to eat, this time getting up extra early. Bellyfat didn't waste any time this morning, he left the area before Crowfeather Arrow transformed into a white crow.…Bellyfat didn't get to the head of Cut Bank Creek any too soon. He just made it there and hid, where there came that white crow flying proudly, coming over the north ridge of Cut Bank Creek.…

The crow flew on up the canyon and disappeared somewhere along those several canyons that come into Cut Bank Canyon. It was a long time when he reappeared in Bellyfat's view, coming out from one of the several canyons. Just as the crow reappeared,…Bellyfat transformed himself into a deer. Crowfeather Arrow just loved deer meat when it was fresh, like a person does.

Coming down fast to where the dead deer laid, [Crowfeather Arrow] almost lit on him, when it dawned on him that this may be a trick too. So he skipped the deer and lit on the ground not too far from it. The crow would hop on the dead deer every once in a while, it would peck at the most tender places of the animal, places where he knew it would hurt if he were alive….

After several more peckings, the crow got careless. This sweet flesh of the fresh deer meat was just too tasty. He didn't jump off the deer carcass any more, he was just pecking away, trying to tear more meat off to eat.

Under the crow and in the form of a dead deer laid Bellyfat. He was almost jumping up from the pain that the crow was causing to his body. But he thought about the people all near starving, so he tried his best not to give up so easily….All at once the crow made its wrong move, hopping to the middle of the deer's front legs. That was it. The deer made a fast grab for the crow as he transformed quickly back into his rightful origin, Bellyfat, a human. It was a lucky grab, he caught the crow by its legs and held it.

Getting back to the camps near Saint Mary's Lake, Bellyfat got himself a piece of rawhide rope while he held on to the crow with the other hand. With this raw-hide rope Bellyfat tied the crow's legs together very tight so the rope wouldn't slip off. He then ran the rope over one of the tipi poles at the very top inside of this tipi, right where the smoke vent was, where all of the smoke went when the fire was a-going. The crow hung down from the tipi poles, head down.

[Bellyfat] went out of his tipi and on out to the open, away from the camp. There he picked an armful of sage…, a pile of sage and a pile of wood. Belly-fat took both piles inside of his tipi. He make a fire, and as the fire started to burn good, Bellyfat piled the sage on top of the dry wood. Right away it started a thick smoke, and right away the crow began to plead with Bellyfat to put the fire out so it wouldn't smoke anymore.

Bellyfat went in after he knew the smoke had cleared from the inside, and what he seen made him laugh and laugh. From above, the crow was hanging down head first. He was burnt black and his eyes were just red….

Crowfeather Arrow, the now black crow, wanted freedom. He didn't want to spend much more time up there, he must tell the truth. The black crow told Bellyfat where to go and how to get there. "Up there in that canyon," which is the present-day Cut Bank Canyon.

Bellyfat didn't waste any time. The people were very hungry, very near starvation. If it weren't for the roots and edible leaves, they would have already starved. Right to the canyon he went, found the place where he was told to go, and sure enough, up one of the blind canyons with a lot of fresh green grass and fresh water were the thousands of buffalo. Bellyfat made his way around to the back of them. He spooked them to the entrance of this long large canyon of Cut Bank Creek. Running back to this entrance, Bellyfat stood there with his bow and arrows and killed many of the buffalo as they came running out.

Bellyfat butchered all the buffalo he had killed, dressed them all out, and hung them up on the limbs all over the place. Some he piled up where it was cool, then back to the camps he went with the good news and what he could carry of the entrails of the buffalo. Seeing the tasty entrails in his arms, the people lost no time to get a-going to where he had hung all of the fresh meat.

As for him, he went back to his tipi and told the now black crow to promise never to try to starve his people again.... The crow readily promised never to do that again, so Bellyfat untied him and let him down off of the poles. As he let him loose to fly away, Bellyfat hollered after him, "All of the crows to come, after this, shall all be black like you are now, to remember never to try to starve the people again."

As the crow flew away, he was readily agreeing to what Bellyfat was talking about—"*aw, aw, aw, aw.*" In our Piegan language, *aw* or *ah* means yes, agreeing to. To this day, you can hear the crow still agreeing to that promise as they say "*aw, aw, aw,*" and they are still black.

3

THE LAST GREAT BATTLE OF EAGLE HEAD

As told by Eagle Head to his grandson George Comes at Night
1978

Chief Mountain is a monolith, an outrider of the Lewis Overthrust, part of an immense mass of rock that was pressed eastward by tectonic activity many millions of years ago. Depending on the angle of view, Chief can be seen as a rectangular block or a towering pillar rising from the plains, exactly on the border of the Blackfeet Reservation and Glacier National Park. For centuries, Chief has been a landmark, visible for a hundred miles or more, and it was noted as "the King" or "the Chief" by early trappers and traders even before the exploratory visit of Meriwether Lewis and his three men in 1806. Because of Chief's prominence and isolation, many young Natives have sought it as a site for their vision quests, and many legends have accrued around the mountain. In the 1890s, for example, Henry Stimson (later secretary of war under Franklin D. Roosevelt) and a companion climbed Chief via the nearly vertical east face, finding on top the weathered remains of a buffalo skull, which had been used as a pillow by a young man seeking a vision many years before. Other Anglo-American writers—including James Willard Schultz, Harold McClintock, and George Bird Grinnell—have taken note of this tradition.

In the late 1970s, George Comes at Night, a citizen of the Blackfeet Nation, began collecting and writing down traditional narratives of his people. One of these was a story told by his grandfather, Eagle Head, about his climb of Chief Mountain and his experiences there during his journey to become a member of one of the many honorary warrior societies. After his vision quest, Eagle Head participated in many raids and battles against the Gros Ventres, the Cut Throats (Sioux), and other traditional enemies, and he met success in all.

Eagle Head's story remains the only published narrative about a vision quest on Chief related by a Native American. It first appeared in *Roaming Days: Warrior Stories*, edited by Jane Bailey and published by the Blackfeet Heritage Program in Browning, Montana, in 1978.

The time had come for Eagle Head to embark on a career as a medicine man and a warrior. In order to achieve this he had to fast to get a sleep vision, to obtain a sacred helper. He wanted to be a real man, a warrior, to be a member of the Doves or Raven Carriers or All Friends Society. Eagle Head decided to have his fasting place be on top of Chief Mountain.

He said to his mother, "I want to take my fast. As of now I am unable to take part in dances, war parties and the happy feast gatherings of the Doves or Raven Carriers."

His mother told him, "My dear son, if you should succeed in your fast for a secret helper, how proud I would be to see you returning with a war party, waving enemy scalps, singing the victory song, riding and driving enemy horses before you." His sister wanted him to join the Siezers, who wore the best clothes, were the best singers and were good dancers. But his mother wanted him to join the Raven Carriers, who were always successful in their undertakings. He asked his mother which medicine man or sun priest he should get to pray for his safety in his lone vision sleep on Chief Mountain. His mother, Mink Woman, told him to get Black Otter, owner of the sacred thunder pipe bundle.

So Eagle Head went out, brought his horses in, and roped one top buffalo horse, a real fast brown horse. He led it to Black Otter's lodge, gave him the horse and said, "Haiya, oh, powerful, Sun-favored thunder pipe man. I am to undergo a lone fast. Help me. Pray for me."

Black Otter asked him, "Where are you going to make your fast?"

Eagle Head told him, "On top of Chief Mountain."

Black Otter said, "It is a holy mountain. You will not fail in your sleep on it, to obtain a sacred helper."

Eagle Head helped his mother and sister build a sweat lodge for Black Otter. The two men crawled in, threw their blankets out and sat naked. They had an old lodge skin over it. In its center, a small pit was dug. Nearby, the women folks had a fire going and were heating the rocks. Black Otter had his sacred pipe, a wooden bowl with water and a buffalo tail. When the rocks got red hot, the women pushed them in and Eagle Head rolled them into the pit with his stick. The old man dipped his buffalo tail into the bowl by him and sprinkled water over the rocks; steam began to fill the lodge. He prayed to the Above Ones, to the Sun, the Night Light (moon) and to his own sacred helper to aid Eagle Head in his coming raids and undertakings. Then he sang some of his thunder pipe songs. Eagle Head also prayed to the Above Ones, for success in his undertakings, and for long life and happiness for his family and tribe. The steam sweat over, they reached out for their clothes and blankets, wrapped on their blankets and went to the creek to bathe and dress.

Eagle Head woke up about daybreak the following morning, thinking of the ordeal ahead, which he was to undergo alone. The camp was along the St. Mary's River, east of lower St. Mary's Lake. About noon he brought in his horses, caught one for his mother, Mink Woman, and one for his sister, Fine Woman. The three of them rode off to Chief Mountain with Black Otter. On the west side a ridge goes gradually up the mountain. Right near the top it is steep. They tied their horses there and the woman folks climbed up, bringing two buffalo robes and a blanket for him to use; one robe to lie on, the other robe and blanket to cover up with. He had his gun for safe guard. Near sun down Black Otter prayed again to his secret helper, to the Sun and to the Night Light to protect Eagle Head in his sleep. Then he and the women left.

If a person fasting doesn't have a vision on the fourth night, he is done for. Some animal is afraid of him, afraid to be his sacred helper. He must leave the place and try again at a later date and in another place.

On the third night of his sleep, he saw a Cougar, a long-tailed one, come out of the timber and stop to look at him. He said to the Cougar, "You are powerful, always successful in your wanderings and kills. Help me. I am poor." But the Cougar went back into the timber.

As the fourth night came on, he prayed hard to the Above Ones before his sleep. In his sleep vision the Cougar came out of the timber again and said to him, "You want me to be your sacred helper, but you must do certain sacrifices to the Above Ones. Then I will help you along."

The morning after that fourth night, the party of three came after him. Eagle Head was weak from thirst and hunger. His mother brought him water so he took a little drink, not enough to hurt or upset himself. Half way down to camp he took another drink. Before they left the top of Chief Mountain, Black Otter asked him if he'd had any luck. Eagle Head told him of the vision, of a certain land animal who was to be his secret helper. They were all glad. When they arrived at camp he ate a light meal and later on, ate some more. The next day he rested and stayed in camp.

The second day Eagle Head and Wolf Tail, his friend, caught their saddle horses and rode up to [East] Flat Top Mountain. They tied their horses at the bottom slope and climbed the steep side. Half way up they jumped seven big horn sheep, killed two, gutted them and dragged them down to their horses. They quartered them up, rode home to camp and had big horn steaks for their evening meal.

4

THE JEALOUS WOMEN

James Willard Schultz

1916

James Willard Schultz (1859–1947) came from a prosperous family in Boonville, New York, but as a young man he was determined to "go West," which he did at age eighteen. Arriving at Fort Benton, Montana, by steamboat, he found work with James Kipp, the famous Native American trader of the region. Eventually, Schultz married a young Blackfeet woman, Nät-ah'-ki, and was adopted into the Pikuni tribe as Apikuni (sometimes spelled "Appekunny"); several features in the Swiftcurrent Valley of Glacier Park are named for him.

After visiting the St. Mary Lakes for the first time in 1883, Schultz began exploring and hunting in the area, eventually settling nearby with his wife. In 1885, he began sending articles about his experiences with the Pikuni, and with the mountains that became the eastern half of Glacier, to George Bird Grinnell, editor of *Forest and Stream*, one of the leading outdoor magazines of the time. Grinnell published them as a series that eventually became Schultz's first book, *My Life as an Indian: The Story of a Red Woman and a White Man in the Lodges of the Blackfeet* (1907). Schultz went on to write thirty-seven books (plus five published posthumously), many of which were somewhat fictionalized accounts of his life with the Pikuni people and were avidly read by young people. Of especial note are *With the Indians in the Rockies* (1912) and *Blackfeet Tales of Glacier National Park* (1916). The best study of Schultz's life is Warren L. Hanna's *The Life and Times of James Willard Schultz* (1986).

Schultz spent much time and effort trying to have "white man's names" removed from the peaks, lakes, and streams of Glacier Park, to be replaced by historically authentic—or, in some cases, what Schultz thought were appropriate—names from the Pikuni people of the east side of the park and the Ktunaxa (Kootenai) people on the west. He was largely unsuccessful in this effort.

Schultz often represented himself as a conscientious observer and student of Native American culture, as illustrated in this chapter from *Blackfeet Tales of Glacier National Park* (pages 226–32). Schultz uses as the basis for the book a visit he made to the reservation and the park in the summer of 1915, when he and his Pikuni friends explored many of the valleys on the east side of the park where

Native people had formerly gone to hunt, gather plants, and hold ceremonies. In this chapter, Schultz records a Ktunaxa legend about what was then called McDermott Lake (now Swiftcurrent Lake) in the Swiftcurrent Valley. It should be noted that polygamy was common among the Native people of the area, in part because of the appalling rate of casualties to young men from war, hunting, and accidents.

IKS-I'-KWO-YI-A-TUK-TAI (SWIFT CURRENT RIVER)
SEPTEMBER 1

We moved up here the other day and made camp beside one of the most lovely lakes in all this Rocky Mountain country. In my time we called it Beaver Woman's Lake. It is now McDermott [currently Swiftcurrent] Lake. And what a name that is for one of Nature's gems! There are names for other lakes and peaks here just as bad as that, but we shall have nothing to say about them here. Only by an act of Congress can we get what we want done, and we have faith that within a reasonable time all these mountains and lakes and streams will bear the names of the great chiefs, medicine men, and warriors who traversed them before the white man came.

Some of us—all excepting our two old men and the women—have been riding over the different trails here, viewing the glaciers and other places of interest, especially Iceberg Lake, where we saw a mass of ice as large as a house part from the glacier, splash down into the deep lake, and disappear, and after a time come up from the depths to the surface and create another commotion of the waters. It was a grand sight!

Tail-Feathers-Coming-over-the-Hill says that the lake with the unpronounceable white man's name—McDermott—should be called Jealous Women's Lake; that away back in the days of his youth, when the Kootenai Indians occasionally came to camp and hunt with the Blackfeet, he had a youthful friend of the mountain tribe who told him the following story:

THE JEALOUS WOMEN

"In those days a young Kootenai, good of heart, a great hunter, and very brave, married twin sisters so alike that except for one thing they could not be told apart: one was a slow, the other a very fast, talker.

"In time the fast talker, named Marmot, became jealous of her sister, Camas, complaining all the time that she had to do the most of the lodge work, and that she was sure Camas said bad things about her to their man. Camas denied all this. 'I have never tried to place myself first with our man,' she said. 'We are twins; I love you dearly; our man's heart is so big that it holds us both in equal love. Now, be sensible! Cast out your bad thoughts for they are all wrong.'

"But Marmot persisted in believing that she was neglected; that her sister had all their man's affection; and she finally went to him with her complaint. He laughed. 'I love you just as much as I do your sister,' he said. 'Now, just think back and show me when and in what way I have shown that she is first with me!'

"Marmot sat down and thought. She thought a long time; remained silent. The man was very patient with her; he waited for her answer, but it did not come. At last he said: 'Well, you have thought a long time. Have you found one thing in which I gave her preference?'

"'No, I haven't, but all the same I believe that you love her best,' Marmot answered; and got up and went about her work.

"The man shook his head, made no answer to that, and took up his weapons and went hunting down the river. At the time he was camped right here at this lake.

"The man had not gone far, moving slowly, carefully, through the timber and brush along the river, when he heard ahead a great splashing in the water, and, going closer, found that it was caused by two otters playing. They would chase each other in the water, then climb the bank and go as swift as arrows from a bow down a slide that they had made, and again chase and tumble each other over in the water. The man crept closer to the slide, an arrow in his bow, another in his hand, and, watching his chance, shot one of the players. He tried to get the other, but it dived and was gone before he could fit the other arrow to his bow: 'It is too bad that I didn't get the other. I would have liked a skin of these medicine skins for each of my women,' he said to himself.

"He took the otter home and handed it to Camas. 'That is yours,' he said. 'There were two of them. To-morrow, Marmot, I will get the other for you, and then you will each have a strong medicine skin.'

"Marmot said nothing, but looked cross.

"The man went hunting the next day but he could not find the other otter. He searched the river for many days and could not find one.

"And as the days passed, Marmot became more and more angry, and finally said to her sister: 'I have proof now that our man loves you best. He gave you the otter; he does not even try to get one for me. He hunts other animals every day, bighorn, goats, animals that live nowhere near the haunts of the otter.'

"'Now, don't be foolish!' Camas answered. 'You know as well as I do that he has tried and tried to get the other otter for you. But at the same time he has to get meat for us: that is why he hunts the mountain animals.'

"'Camas, the two of us can no longer live in this lodge,' cried Marmot. 'You are a bad woman! I hate you! I will fight you any way you say to see which of us shall be our man's one wife!'

"Then it was that, for the first time, Camas became angry: 'We have no weapons to fight with,' she answered, 'but I propose this: We will swim this lake across and back and across and back until one of us becomes tired and drowns! Now, crazy woman, what do you say to that?'

"'Come on! Come on!' Marmot cried, and ran to the shore and tore off her clothes. So did Camas, and the two rushed into the water and began their swim of hate. They crossed the lake; turned and came back; crossed again and started back, Camas well in the lead. She reached the shore in front of the lodge, dragged herself out on the shore, and turned. Her sister had gone down. There was not even a ripple on the still water. Marmot was drowned. Hardly knowing what she did, she put on her clothes and went into the lodge and cried and cried. The man came home. She was still crying. He asked her where Marmot was, and she cried all the harder, but at last told him all. Then the man cried. Together the two mourned for a long time, and searched the lake for the body of the lost one, and could not find it. So they moved away from the unhappy place and returned to the camp of their people, but it was a long time, a very long time, before they ceased mourning, and never again would they go anywhere near the lake.

"Yes, this is the Lake of the Jealous Women!"

5

MOUNTAIN SHEEP BOY

Peter Beaverhead

ca. 1959

In 1959–60, anthropologist Leslie B. Davis conducted research among the Upper Pend d'Oreille (Kalispel) people of the region west of Glacier National Park. Most of the narratives that Davis collected were from Peter Beaverhead (b. 1899), who also authored a book, *Mary Quequesash's Love Story: A Pend d'Oreille Indian Tale.* Though the narrative below is not specifically connected with the Glacier Park region, it is representative of many of the traditional tales concerning the transformation of humans to animals and vice versa. Many are set in the high mountains of the region. This story also shows the encroaching influence of European narrative traditions, such as the reliance on exact time and the implicit warning against pride. The narrative was first published in Davis's *Remnant Forms of Folk Narrative among the Upper Pend d'Oreille Indians* (pages 28–30).

Long ago, a man and his family lived high in mountain sheep country. Every day the man hunted mountain sheep and his wife gathered wild roots. Their son played around in the rocks. After several weeks there the man had to hunt and hunt to find any game. The sheep weren't coming down the nearby trail they had always followed from place to place. His wife was finding fewer and fewer roots. They were eating less and less and they were becoming very hungry. One evening their son stopped playing earlier than usual. He came back to the tipi, sat before his parents, and asked, "Why is it that you can kill no sheep and can get no roots? I'm getting very hungry." His father told him that the sheep were still there. He saw fresh sign each morning, but he was never waiting for them at the right time. His mother told the same thing about the roots. The boy said, "I know the time when the sheep pass and I know the time when the roots come up. The sheep pass at exactly midnight, but not before or after. That's when the roots grow, but toward morning they work themselves back underground. Only the sick ones stay above ground." He went on, "My father, tonight you will be waiting just before midnight along the sheep trail. You will soon see a large herd of sheep coming. You will kill only one. Bring it back without letting it touch the ground. Bring it through the rear of the tipi. If

I'm asleep wake me." Then he turned to his mother and said, "Mother, tonight at exactly midnight you will go to where you dig roots. Build a fire and you will see many roots there. Now I am going to bed."

So then the boy's parents waited as they had been told. At midnight they went out. The boy's mother built a fire and was surprised to see the ground covered with roots. She began digging them up. The boy's father waited until he heard the sound of horns hitting stone. He saw many sheep coming up the trail out of their hiding place. He picked a fat one, killed it, and carried it on his back, not letting it touch the ground anywhere. When he got home his wife had already raised the back side of the tipi for him. He woke his son. The boy got up and directed his father to cut the sheep open down the middle. Then he was to remove all the tripe and was told to cut out all the fat along the backbone. He was to separate out the meat there from the backbone fat and give it to his son to eat. Then he told his parents to go ahead and eat their fill.

The next evening he told his father, "Tonight you will kill the baby sheep for me. When you skin it leave the ears, hooves, tail and everything on the hide. After that you may kill any sheep you want. Just give me the fat next to the backbone." The boy had met a stranger who had told him when to find the sheep and roots, and to bring to him a young sheep's hide with everything on it.

The boy's father killed a baby sheep. After carefully skinning it he gave the hide to his son. Time went on. Soon they had much dried meat and roots. One day Father asked his son, "Why don't you let your mother eat some of that backfat you've been eating. Don't you think she might like to eat some, too?"

The boy listened quietly. Then he reached behind him and covered himself with the sheepskin. He made sure that his head, arms, and legs were covered and then he began to cry. His father tried to comfort him, but he tired and his wife tried to comfort her son. The parents went to sleep and left their son there crying. Later the man got up and looked at his son. His son looked very much like a young sheep. Father called to his wife, "Look. Look at our son. I think he has become a sheep. Jump up. Let's try to catch him. Watch the door and I'll go behind him." Then the boy jumped up and ran around inside the tipi, his parents trying to hold him. But he escaped out the back of the tipi. They lost him in the woods. They waited week after week for him to return and his father hunted for him each day. Soon they had no more dried meat or roots and they became very hungry. They decided to go down the mountain to the village of their people. There they told what had happened in the mountains.

The next spring they returned to their mountain camp. The father looked for his son without success. One night as he sat waiting for the sheep to pass he saw a big, fat sheep leading the herd. The sheep walked up to him in his hiding place and said, "Now look at me, look at me closely. I'm your son. I'm full-grown now. I have my own father and mother in the herd behind me. The one that is following me is my brother, the next is my older brother, and the one after him is my uncle."

Then the sheep-boy told his father of his other relations on down through the herd. He told his father to shoot the last sheep because he wasn't any relation. The boy's father and mother intended to stay on the mountain until they starved to death. Each night Father was to shoot the last sheep. Then they had plenty of dried meat and roots again.

One night his son came to him on the trail and said, "My father, I would like to see my mother just as I am once more. Bring her with you tomorrow night so I may speak with her." They waited the next night. The lead sheep stopped and said, "Hello, Mother. I am your son although I don't look like him. This will be the last time I speak with you. But I and my herd will pass through here each year when you camp here. You, my father, always shoot the last sheep. From now on I will not speak with you. I have my own home now and I am happy. You should never worry about me. I will be fine. When you see the herd coming you will always know I am the leader. Goodbye, my father, and you, my mother."

Then his father shot the last sheep. Soon they had enough meat to last them all winter and they returned to their people. The next year they went back to their hunting place. After a time they had plenty of meat and roots. But one night Father decided to shoot a big, fat sheep that wasn't last in line. He shot one in the middle of the herd, and another one, and another one. He began gathering those he had killed but he couldn't find any of them. In his excitement he hadn't seen them coming to life and running away.

So he went back to his wife and told her that he hadn't seen any sheep. But as they already had plenty of meat they started home. Toward the middle of the next summer they packed and headed for their hunting place. They set up their tipi and he went out to look at the game trail, expecting to see it covered with sign. But the trail was overgrown with brush and there were no tracks anywhere. He sat there all night but no game went by. His wife told him she hadn't found any roots either. Father knew then that his son controlled the game and the roots. He knew, too, that he had broken the law when he shot the wrong sheep the year before. They talked it over and decided to stay there anyway until they died. So they lived on until they died without ever seeing their son again. That is all.

PART II

EXPLORERS

Beginning, perhaps, with explorer and trader David Thompson at the end of the eighteenth century, Anglo-American men explored the edges of what later became Glacier National Park. Following Meriwether Lewis's exploratory probe in 1806, which brought him and his three men within twenty miles of the current park boundary, fur trappers and traders looked for beaver, hide hunters sought bison, and prospectors staked hopeful claims for gold and silver, then copper, then petroleum. Boundary commissions surveyed and marked the 49th parallel, the Canada-U.S. borderline, and a few military expeditions—notably, those led by A. W. Tinkham in 1853 and Lts. Charles A. Woodruff and John T. Van Orsdale in 1873—investigated the region and crossed the mountains. Yet the lowest and most accessible pass over the mountains remained something of a mystery—largely unused, even by Natives, and suspected but not found by railroad surveyors. That was the case until a bitterly cold night in December 1889, when surveyor James F. Stevens climbed to the top of what is now called Marias Pass (the Marias River had been named by Meriwether Lewis in honor of one of his cousins, Maria, but the word is now pronounced "muh-RYE-us") and determined that it would be ideal for the new transcontinental railroad, the Great Northern.

The railroad's tracks reached the pass in the autumn of 1891, and by 1893 trains were connecting St. Paul, Minnesota, with Seattle. Once the park was established in 1910, the railroad, under the leadership of its president, Lewis W. Hill—son of the railroad's founder, James J. Hill—built trails, roads, hotels,

chalets, and tent camps to accommodate the expected throngs of summer visitors. Part of Hill's publicity campaign to encourage passenger traffic involved
hiring well-known artists such as Winold Reiss and John Fery to paint the
park's landscapes and the Blackfeet Indians. In 1917, the railroad sponsored the
artist Maynard Dixon (1875–1946), who spent the summer exploring the park's
mountains and lakes and the Blackfeet Indian Reservation. Now regarded as
one of the foremost artists of the American West, Dixon was also a poet whose
collected poems, *Rim-Rock and Sage*, were finally assembled and published in
1977, more than thirty years after his death. Included is this poem, "Camp in
the Rockies," from his summer in Glacier:

> Cold September moonlight in the mountains:
> The silent pale-gleaming tent below the dark and steep-edged peaks,—
> The dutch-oven, black in the red-fading coals,—
> The dish towels hanging rigid with cold in the frosty air,—
> The faint smell of bacon and aromatic smoke of spruce,…
> Sleepers warm in the tent,
> And small sharp stars, wintry, remote in the north.
> —*Montana, 1917.*

6

FROM *MY REMINISCENCES*

Raphael Pumpelly
1918

One of the nation's best-known geologists and explorers, Raphael Pumpelly (1837–1923) built a worldwide reputation for his exploratory trips to Asia in the 1870s, including China, Mongolia, and the Gobi Desert. In 1882–83, he was hired by railroad magnate Henry Villard of the Northern Pacific Railroad to survey the Northwest for possible extensions of the railroad as well as for agricultural, mineral, and forest potential. With William R. Logan (later to be named the first superintendent of Glacier) as his guide, Pumpelly attempted to cross the mountains from east to west via Cut Bank Pass (its current spelling), but deep snowdrifts blocked their way. The following year, Pumpelly and Logan, along with Lt. John Van Orsdale (who had led a party over Cut Bank Pass in the 1870s), made their way up the Middle Fork of the Flathead River and Nyack Creek, where Pumpelly located the glacier now named for him. This was the first active, living glacier discovered and named in the park. The Northern Transcontinental Railroad Survey had to be suspended when the Northern Pacific experienced financial failure; many years later, in his eighties, Pumpelly recorded his adventurous life in *My Reminiscences* (1918). This segment describes the two surveys.

It was my intention to find an abandoned Indian trail up the Cutbank River, and cross the mountains to the Flathead plains. Wishing to explore some rough country, I sent all the party, except Logan, my head packer, by an easy trail to wait for me at the crossing of the Cutbank River. When I reached the crossing there was no trace of the party, and I supposed they would be found camped further up the valley. In vain we rode till within a mile of the gorge where the river leaves the mountains. Suddenly we saw a smoke signal rise from a hill near the gorge—a thin column broken into three successive puffs; then an answering signal from a distant hill. There was no doubt that Indians were there, and Logan said they were probably Crees from Canada. We were only about twenty-five miles from the border. The Crees were a hostile tribe, and we had only one pistol with us, for our arms were with the [baggage] train.

We thought it best to go back to the [Blackfeet] agency, and from there follow the tracks of our train. It was already twilight. Lighted only by the stars, we
rode all night, crossing deep valleys and their streams with doubtful bottoms.
Woe to the rider where these rivers have bottomed in a certain black shale, for
the black mass is worse than quicksand. In the chill of an icy wind we rested
a half-hour.

In the morning we looked down on the agency, wondering whether the
"madness" of the Indians might not have led to a tragedy. We had been gone
twenty-six hours, and had traveled in all about ninety miles, leading the horses
for the last ten.

After having rested our mounts and eaten, I hired a wagon, and tying our
horses to the back, and telling the driver to follow the tracks of the pack-train,
we slept all day on the bottom boards. The party was found several miles too
far downstream.

When we reached the mouth of the gorge the next afternoon, I sent Logan
and a man ahead to find the trail. I was soon startled by three reports of a gun
echoing among the cliffs. Remembering the Indian signals of the day before,
I seized a carbine, and galloped up the gorge. Suddenly my horse snorted,
as a struggling grizzly bear rolling down hill fell dead before me. Then came
another shot, and soon a cinnamon bear followed. Logan had said that he was
so afraid of grizzlies that nothing could make him tackle one. I did not care for
the [bear] steak we cooked, but the artist caught some big trout.

The Cutbank descends through a wonderful gorge between limestone cliffs
2,000 feet high. Its upper and steep part was buried deep in hardened snow.
Below the pass was an amphitheater—or *cirque*—its walls thickly covered with
ice that extended nearly down to a deep blue lake, near which we camped amid
heavy rain and high wind. At night the horses were so uncomfortable that they
stood half-way in our tents. The next day, in brilliant sunshine, we cut our way
upward in the ice to the top of the amphitheater wall. We were on the pass, on
a narrow ridge between the *cirque* whose wall we had climbed and the walls of
two amphitheaters on the other side of the Continental Divide. A great thickness of snow covered valleys and crests. We had come too early in the season
and we were clearly not prepared to surmount the difficulties of the wild and
unknown region that we looked over. I find in my notes that we next ascended
the headwaters of the Two-Medicine River, to try the pass of that name, but
found the way blocked by great landslides and ice. The way up the river lay
along a beautiful lake between mountains that rose 3,000 to 5,000 feet above

it, while beyond it, from between two *cirques*, a narrow cliff-bound peak towered 3,000 feet above the valley. I find that this is named Pumpelly Pillar on the recent Government map of Glacier National Park.

We left the Flathead River to cross the great range of the Rocky Mountains [in the summer of 1883]. Our route lay up the valley of the middle fork, and what is now called Nyack creek on the Government map of Glacier National Park by Mathes. This map, by the way, is a model of topographic work. I think it took us two weeks of hard work to make our way to the continental divide. For much of the way the Nyack flowed between walls that rose 2,000 to 3,000 feet on either side. These were clothed with a superb forest of pines and larches. Reconnoitering in advance, we slowly picked our way 1,000 to 1,500 feet above the swollen creek. Once something happened that might have wrecked the expedition. The pack train was led by the usual bell-mare. The mule that came next was stopped by catching its pack against a tree, and did not dare to move. The next mule, bound to follow the mare, and trying to pass, hit its pack against the other one's, and went rolling and bouncing down the steep incline. One after another six more did the same. Five lodged on their backs 800 feet below, and one fell clear down, and was carried off by the river. The men descended to save at least the packs. Not one of the five mules was hurt! They had kept their legs folded under their bellies in rebounding, and they had always landed on their packs.

On one of them were the boxes of food tempting the packers to eat before the work to be done. Suddenly two more mules bounded over the men's heads, and landed, feet up, below. They, too, were unharmed. I would not have told this adventure were it not that Sargent and, I think, Dana are living witnesses.

I had noticed an opalescent hue in the stream, and that, as we came above a tributary, the color became milky. This meant the probable existence of a glacier at the source, though none was known in the United States Rockies. With one of the party I ascended a mountain which I suppose to be the one now called Stimson. Standing here, within the arc of a great curve of the divide, we looked out on a long series of sharply cut peaks rising from deeply snow-covered ranges. And to the north, descending from the very crest, there was a clearly defined glacier that seemed to end at the top of a high cliff. Through our field-glasses we could see that a block of ice, perhaps a quarter of a mile square, was missing at one side of the face.

Farther up the stream Logan and I ascended a valley coming from the direction where I had seen the glacier. In a little over a mile we entered an amphitheater about two miles wide. Two thousand feet above, at the top of the *cirque*, the almost vertical wall of rock continued upward to form the terminal face of the glacier—itself a cliff of perhaps 500 feet of ice.

The missing block of ice was now accounted for. It had plunged down the 2,500 foot wall, and its acquired impetus had carried it several hundred feet up the opposite slope of the *cirque*, plowing a broad swath through a dense forest of large Douglas firs, whose trunks and branches, still holding their bark, lay in every position, like gigantic jack-straws. The fact that everywhere else the forest of trees of the same size was intact seemed to indicate a recent advance of the glacier, after a period of rest at least as long as the age of the trees.

Since my visit a large number of glaciers have been found farther north along the divide. What I saw was merely the lowest point of a glacier whose edge extends about two miles around the top of the *cirque*. From this ten superb waterfalls plunge down the precipitous wall of the *cirque* to unite 3,000 feet below.

A few years ago Professor L. B. Sperry came to ask the location of a glacier which people in Montana said I had found, and they had named after me. Later he sent me a photograph on which appears evidence that it breaks off regularly in great square blocks, as in my time.

Professor Sargent, who was making a reconnaissance with reference to forests, said that it was a remarkable fact that some of the plants and trees here, nearly 6,000 feet above the sea, belonged to vegetation of the much warmer Puget Sound botanical province. He accounted for this, if I remember rightly, by the possibility of frequent influence of the Chinook winds from the warm current on the west coast.

The presence of glaciers from here northward is probably due to moisture brought by the same wind. They are remnants of greater ones of the ice period, when they filled the amphitheaters and flowed down the valleys. They end now at the top of the *cirque* walls 6,500 to 7,000 feet above the sea, excepting the Agassiz glacier whose lowest point is at about 5,800 feet.

Our way to the pass lay about 1,000 feet below the crest around the upper part of an amphitheater. I had looked down upon it the year before. It was now wholly bare of snow. The surface was covered with loose limestone shale that, on the steep declivity, made very difficult the footing of the animals. We had one accident, losing a horse carrying Sargent's voluminous collections and all of our guns. A slip of his hind feet carried him over, striking the ground only three times as he fell about 1,500 feet.

On July 10, 1882, I had found this *cirque* filled to the top with snow, the eastern approach to the pass ice-bound and the valley of the Cutbank deeply buried under snow. Now (August 4, 1883) *cirque*, pass, and valley were wholly free from snow and ice. It is well to remember these dates if you ever think of visiting Glacier National Park, for among these limestone mountains—from lofty crests and in *cirques*—you will see the grandest scenery in the United States; and the best time to see it is when, from high lying snow-fields, waterfalls are plunging 2,000 feet down almost vertical steeps.

7

FROM *SPORT AMONG THE ROCKIES*

The Record of a Fishing and Hunting Trip
in North-Western Montana

Charles Spencer Francis
1889

Following the trail established by the articles of James Willard Schultz and George Bird Grinnell, four young men from Troy, New York, set off on a hunting and fishing trip to northwest Montana in August 1888. One of the party was Charles Spencer Francis (1853–1911), son of the editor of the *Troy Daily Times*. Referring to himself as "the Scribe"—his companions were called "the Sport," "the Artist," and "the Commodore," and the party "the Four Trojans"—Francis composed twenty-five letters later published in sequence in the newspaper. The following year, he arranged to have the letters published in a leather-bound edition of only fifteen copies, with forty-nine bound-in photographs (in 2012, one of these volumes was offered for sale by a New York rare book dealer for $55,000). The party arrived by train at Great Falls, Montana, where they were met by their guides: Joe Kipp (a mixed-blood trader) and Schultz, plus another guide named Bill, a cook named Charlie, and a wrangler, along with horses, mules, two heavy prairie schooners (canvas-topped wagons), and a mountain of supplies. Proceeding by way of the agency on the Blackfeet Indian Reservation, they explored the Cut Bank and St. Mary Valleys, hunting and fishing as they went. They shot, by their account, at least half a dozen bighorns, two grizzlies, and an elk, and they dined primarily on the bighorns, game birds, and trout. The area was obviously a paradise of game in the days before the Great Northern Railway crossed Marias Pass, and this account gives a fine picture of one of the first tourist parties to explore the east side of the mountains. The following excerpts are from Francis's Tenth and Eleventh Letters, written after they had entered the Cut Bank Valley.

THE VILLAINOUS MOSQUITO

But sleep we could not. The hearty supper and the strong coffee undoubtedly had a good deal to do with our restlessness, but the mosquitoes would probably not have allowed us to sleep under other and more favorable conditions. Our camp was pitched in a low place close by the water and in high grass, and was entirely surrounded by brush, which kept off the wind and allowed the indefatigable mosquito to vigorously and successfully prosecute his wicked designs upon us. Never before in our lives did we have such a fight with the infernal insect. He sang and he bit, he bit and he sang, and even completely enveloping our heads with our blankets and leaving only a little breathing hole did not protect us from the diabolical music and the fiendish assaults of the pests. Some of our Trojan sportsmen tried the experiment of using forcible language, but it proved unavailing, and there we lay kicking and thrashing and throwing our arms about us until daylight.

Next morning we proceeded as far as Willow creek, where, while our dinner was being prepared, the Sport did a little fly-fishing. Almost with tears in his eyes he mournfully told us on his return of an immense trout, at least two feet long, that had carried away his leader and flies with the greatest ease imaginable. While we enjoyed the smaller trout he did catch for our dinner, we all sympathized with him in the loss of his marvelous fish—and we believed his yarn!

After dinner we covered fifteen miles more in Cut Bank, where we camped for the night. This short ride afforded all members of the party great sport with shotguns. Each Trojan sportsman bagged his share of game, which consisted of prairie chickens, blue grouse, and mallard and teal ducks. Arriving at Cut Bank just before dark, the Sport and the Scribe hurriedly put together a fly-rod and in a few minutes caught trout enough for supper. So our bill of fare that evening included numerous kinds of game, and was in reality a game supper all of our home friends would have thoroughly enjoyed.

FROM ELEVENTH LETTER

On the morning of the seventh day…the weather was simply perfect, and as we contemplated going up the valley of Cut Bank for the purpose of reaching better hunting grounds, everybody was astir at an early hour. Charlie's cheery salutation of "Roll your bones, boys, for breakfast," produced a commotion in camp shortly after daybreak. We were told it was impossible to go farther with wagons, for only a short distance from camp began a long pine forest which continued unbroken for eight or ten miles, through which no wagon-road had even been cut. Besides, gulches and "jump offs" made "schooner" travel out of the question. A very fair, plainly-defined trail, traveled solely by Kootenay Indians and a few mining prospectors, led up through the valley and over the summit of the Rockies by Cut Bank pass. By trail of course we mean a pathway over which a horse can travel, but, as we had occasion to find out from actual experience, there was not much room to spare on either side of the animal between the trees.

The herder "rounded up" the horses, and our two pack mules, Patrick Henry and Jenny Lind, were pressed into service for the first time. And what loads we put on those poor mules' backs! When Patrick Henry was ready to start very little could be seen of the statesman's namesake except his ears and tail. In arranging the loads on the pack-saddles of the mules and extra horses, we were shown the mysteries of the "diamond hitch," so familiar and dear to the heart of the Rocky mountain train-driver. It was, indeed, mysterious to us how the knots were made and the ropes used, but eventually Joe and his assistants reported everything ready and we prepared to mount. Notwithstanding grunts of disapproval on the part of mules and horses, the ropes had been drawn so tightly and so securely fastened it was impossible for anything on the packs to either drop off or be brushed off.

A MAGNIFICENT VIEW

Starting westward and following the trail upward to a considerable height before we reached the pine forests a most beautiful scene presented itself to our vision. In front of us, ten or fifteen miles away, could be seen the lofty peaks of the high, upper ranges of the Rockies. On the left and only a few miles distant, a magnificent mountain proudly raised its head fully 4,000 feet above us. Its upper face on the side toward us presented a sheer fall of at least 2,000 feet, and the edge of the timber growth below was everywhere as plainly defined as though a straight line had been drawn right across the mountain.

FOLLOWING THE TRAIL

At several points the trail led us to ticklish places, and a misstep on the part of the horses we were riding would undoubtedly have resulted in our tumbling down a distance of 500 or 600 feet to the bottom of the cañon, and confirmed the truth of the assertion made by timid friends at home that we were "a lot of foolish fellows to undertake such a crazy trip to a locality so far out of the world." As we proceeded farther and farther up the trail the valley grew narrower and narrower. It was evident, judging from the appearance of the trail, that few persons had passed over it this season. Now and then the indistinct print of a moccasined foot and the impression made by the shoeless cayeuse [cayuse] pony indicated that Indians had crossed the trail a few weeks before us. Several times Patrick Henry and Jenny Lind were compelled to succumb in mire-holes caused by little rivulets from springs above forming "sinks" on the trail, and had to be, literally speaking, lifted out of their predicaments. We rode directly behind Jenny, and very often the side of the little mule's pack would strike a sapling three or four inches thick, which one would naturally think must cause the animal to stop. But not so. Jenny Lind was an old mountaineer. She had been there before and knew all about it. She kept right on, ploughing her way ahead, until the sapling, passing under the load, would fly back and resume its former position.

DAMAGING TO SHINS

As previously stated, the trail was narrow, and at best there was little room to spare between the trunks of trees and our legs as we sat astride our beasts. Collisions between the two were inevitable: they could not be avoided. The lower branches of the pine trees were just low enough to strike our horsemen, and between looking out for "low bridge" and unsuccessfully trying to save our shins from injury we were kept busy enough. The Artist, true to his profession, had an eye for the beautiful, and, as a matter of course, the sublime scenery on all sides commanded his enthusiastic admiration. Alas, our companion was so wrapped up in the magnificent panorama presented to his vision that he became oblivious of everything else: he didn't keep in mind the fact that he was riding over a seldom used Rocky mountain trail: he forgot the obstacles Nature had thrown in our pathway.

WE HAVE A SCARE

Suddenly, as we were slowly picking our way along the rough and uneven trail, we heard a most blood-curdling shriek followed by appeals for speedy help from the Artist, who was heading the van by several hundred yards. Thoughts rushed upon us of his having met a grizzly bear; or more likely, that, his horse having fallen, our friend was hanging by his arms over a lofty precipice! Consternation seized us. Poor boy—the life of our party: always light-hearted: never complaining—what had happened to him? We hurried forward to our companion's aid, and, turning an abrupt corner, beheld a sight which so convulsed us with laughter that we could with difficulty remain in our saddles.

BRUSHED OFF HIS HORSE

There before us was our even-tempered Artist dangling in the air, his arms and shoulders stretched over the branch of a tree, while his feet were still "mixed up" in the stirrups, and he was at least a foot from the saddle. His horse "Carribou" had evidently taken in the situation and stopped at the first shriek of his rider. What a situation! What an unartistic plight! Literally speaking our friend had been brushed off his horse into a tree by a limb extending across the trail, and the operation was executed so quickly that before he had time to recover from his surprise he found himself suspended in mid-air. After the spectacle had been enjoyed by us all for several minutes, sympathetic hands extricated the Trojan from his dilemma, and he was restored to his former position on old Carribou's back. But after that, during the day, the Artist invariably kept one eye on the trail while the other absorbed the beauties of the landscape. None of the Trojans escaped shin "barking:" all were compelled to suffer more or less of it, and it is believed to-day examination would reveal on the legs of every sportsman in that party scars received by too close an acquaintance with the pines along the Cut Bank trail.

8

THE CROWN OF THE CONTINENT

George Bird Grinnell
1901

George Bird Grinnell (1849–1938) was born to a prosperous family in New York City; in fact, when he was a boy, his family lived on the former estate of the great naturalist, John James Audubon, overlooking the Hudson River. Grinnell studied zoology at Yale University and soon after graduation accompanied, as a naturalist, George Armstrong Custer on a military expedition into the Black Hills of South Dakota. With help from his father, Grinnell eventually became the editor and publisher of *Forest and Stream*, perhaps the leading outdoor journal of the time. Grinnell became intrigued with northwestern Montana after receiving—and publishing—articles by James Willard Schultz about hunting, fishing, exploring, and interacting with the Blackfeet Indians on the east side of the mountains. Grinnell eventually visited Schultz three times between 1885 and 1891, exploring the St. Mary and Swiftcurrent Valleys, climbing on the glacier that was soon named for him, and hunting mountain goats, bighorns, and deer.

By the time of his last visit, Grinnell had become convinced that the region should be protected as a national park, and he used the columns of *Forest and Stream* and his influential contacts in Congress to press for that designation. This article, condensed here, was originally written in 1891 for *The Century Magazine*, but was—for never-explained reasons—not published until 1901, when Grinnell used it as part of his campaign for the national park. He had behind-the-scenes aid and encouragement from Louis Hill, soon to be president of the Great Northern Railway, who envisioned summer passenger traffic enhancing his revenues. After at least three failed attempts, the bill was passed by Congress and signed into law by President Taft on May 11, 1910.

Grinnell went on to a long and distinguished career as a naturalist, writer, editor, and anthropologist. He published many books and articles on Native American tribes of the West, including *Blackfoot Lodge Tales*—using mostly oral texts collected by Schultz—and *Blackfeet Indian Stories*. The "Crown of the Continent" phrase, by the way, is Grinnell's; he used it to refer to the fact that within Glacier there is a point, Triple Divide Peak at the head of the Cut Bank Valley, from which waters flow to Hudson Bay, the Gulf of Mexico, and the Pacific Ocean. The phrase, as in "Crown of the Continent Ecosystem," is often used today to refer to the nearly unbroken wilderness of northwestern Montana and western Alberta.

Far away in northwestern Montana, hidden from view by clustering mountain-peaks, lies an unmapped corner—the Crown of the Continent. The water from the crusted snowdrift which caps the peaks of a lofty mountain there trickles into tiny rills, which hurry along north, south, east, and west, and growing to rivers, at last pour their currents into three seas. From this mountain-peak the Pacific and the Arctic oceans and the Gulf of Mexico receive each its tribute.

Here is a land of striking scenery. From some bold headland that rises abruptly from the plain, one looks eastward over naked yellow prairie. Near at hand, the ground is undulating, rising and falling like the swell of a troubled sea, but smooth and quiet in the far distance. Away to the east rise from the level land the three sharp pinnacles of the Sweet Grass Hills. On a clear day the dark column of smoke from the coal-mines of Lethbridge is seen seventy miles to the northeast. Here and there the yellow of the plain is broken by winding green watercourses, along which grow fringes of cottonwoods and willows, and at intervals little prairie lakes gleam like silver in the sun.

If one turns his back upon the prairie and looks west and south, the view is barred by a confused series of unknown mountains. Here are cañons deeper and narrower than those of the Yellowstone, mountains higher than those of the Yosemite. Some are rounded and some square-topped, some are slender pinnacles, and others knife-edged and with jagged crests, each one a true sierra. Many are patched with snow, and the highest wear their white covering from year's end to year's end. Along their verdureless slopes slow-moving ice rivers still plow their deliberate way, relics of mightier glaciers, the stiffened streams of which in a past age fashioned the majestic scenery of to-day. These old glaciers dug out for themselves channels between the mountains, and, when the ice melted, left deep cañons, the walls of which sometimes rise vertically from three to four thousand feet above the course of the stream flowing through the valley; or, again, they stand farther back, and are faced by long steep slopes of rock fragments fallen from the heights above. Often this talus is bare, or it may be covered with a dense growth of sturdy pines up to the limit— here less than eight thousand feet—where trees will no longer grow.

This is the Blackfeet land, and for the Indians it is historic ground. A century ago it was owned by the Snakes [probably Shoshones] and the Crows. In those old times, we are told, there was no war. Members of one tribe visited the camps of others, and after friendly meetings parted in peace. But already the white man had come, and had introduced among the Indians the temptation to war, as well as the means for carrying it on. Horses brought up from the south reached the Snakes, Flatheads, and Crows, and at length became known to the Blackfeet....About this time, too, the French traders from Montreal had supplied them with guns, powder, and ball. They had learned how to use these new weapons, and so had gained confidence in themselves. Their descendants of to-day have said to me: "Then first we learned to take courage, and to venture out of the timber on to the prairie, and to make journeys to war."

In their raids for horses the Blackfeet pressed farther and farther southward, driving their enemies before them, at first beyond the St. Mary's River and then beyond the Yellowstone. The Crows retreated southward and the Snakes southwest over the mountains; yet because of the great abundance of the buffalo on the plains, hunting and war-parties of their enemies were constantly invading the territory which the Blackfeet had conquered, and so the Chief Mountain country was always a debatable ground where Blackfeet, Crows, Snakes, Gros Ventres, Crees, Assinaboins, Flatheads, Kootenais, and Stonies came to hunt, trap, and—when they met—to fight. All the prominent landmarks have their legends, stories of religion or of mythic heroes or of adventurers of later times. The Blackfeet remained the possessors of the territory, and though bit by bit their lands have been taken from them by the whites, they still retain the country of the Chief Mountain [St. Mary] Lakes.

It was once a great game country. Over the far-stretching prairie roamed countless thousands of buffalo, and their advancing hosts creeping up along the mountain-sides covered the foot-hills and surged up the narrow valleys, as the swelling tide overflows the reefs and fills up the estuaries on some rocky shore. Far and near the prairie was black with them, and then again, in obedience to some mysterious impulse, the mighty herds receded and left it bare. In those days deer and elk without number fed in the river-bottoms. Antelope dotted the plain. Moose, elk, and mountain bison had their homes in the thick timber, and wore deep trails through it from park to park, and down to the water, and again up to the high naked buttes, where they liked to lie in the sun. Still higher, along the faces of rock slides and cliffs, are the hard-trodden paths worn by the mountain-sheep and the white goats, which dwell above the timber-line, and only now and then pass through the forest.

The game is almost all gone now from mountain and plain. Buffalo and bison are extinct everywhere, but in the dense forest a few moose, elk, and deer still exist, and, as of old, bears prowl through the timber, tearing to pieces the rotten logs for worms, or turning over great stones to find the ants and beetles on which they prey. On the high lands game is more abundant. The cliffs are still climbed by the nimble sheep and the sure-footed white goats, and there is no reason why the hunter should starve. During the migrations there are swans, geese, and ducks in great numbers; five species of grouse are found on the mountains; the streams and lakes swarm with trout and whitefish; and in early autumn the hillsides are covered with huckleberries.

The region is one of great precipitation. The warm west winds, which bring their freight of vapor from the distant Pacific, are chilled when they strike the cold high peaks of the main range, and their moisture is condensed, and much of it falls as rain or snow. Looking from the summit of Mount Allen, at an elevation of about eleven [actually nine] thousand feet, I have seen half a dozen tall peaks which lay west of my station, all apparently smoking like so many factory chimneys. A fresh wind was blowing, and not a cloud was to be seen in all the blue arch, yet from each of these cold pinnacles of rock a long streamer of heavy mist swung off to the southeast, hanging level in the air as the smoke of a passing steamer hangs over the sea, hiding the view; and in the shadow of each streamer of cloud more or less rain and snow was falling. It is this precipitation that maintains the glaciers which still lie on the north sides of all the higher mountains of this region.

My earlier visits were hunting-trips, and my time was spent climbing the mountains near the lakes for game, or fishing in the wind-swept waters; but I soon learned that the region was unexplored, and when from the summits of peaks about the lakes I looked back into the range and saw others yet unnamed, I felt a great desire to learn something more of this unknown country. Since that time I have been to the head of unexplored tributaries of Cut Bank, up the valley of Red Eagle Creek, to the head of the Upper St. Mary's River, as well as to the head of all the branches of Swift Current and a long way up Kennedy's Creek.

No words can describe the grandeur and majesty of these mountains, and even photographs seem hopelessly to dwarf and belittle the most impressive peaks. The fact that it is altogether unknown, the beauty of its scenery, its varied and unusual fauna, and the opportunities it offers for hunting and fishing and for mountain climbing, give the region a wonderful attraction for the lover of nature.

Beyond the head of the lower lakes wagons cannot go, and the traveler who wishes to reach the heads of any of the streams must leave his wagon and start into the mountain with a pack-train. This means that all his possessions— his food, his bedding, and his camp furniture—must be lashed on the backs of horses or mules, and so carried through the dense forests and up the steep mountain-sides. This is a pleasant mode of traveling, though it is slow and entails much more labor than traveling in a wagon. It has, however, the great advantage that it makes one independent. With a pack-train the explorer can go almost where he pleases. Neither dense brush, close-standing timber, nor steep hills furrowed by deep ravines can stop him; wherever a man can ride, a packhorse can follow.

Wherever it is possible, those who travel through unexplored mountains make use of old game-trails, for in its migration from place to place the game selects the easiest paths, and these wild animals have been the real road-makers in Western exploration. Mountain men have an old saying: "The deer made the first trails; the elk followed the deer, the buffalo the elk, and the Indians the buffalo; after the Indians came the trapper; then an army officer came along and discovered a pass."

In these rough mountains the most practicable routes for horses are in the stream valleys or just above them; but at best progress is slow. In a bad country accidents and delays occur continually. Animals become wedged in between trees, fall down while crossing swift-running streams, lose their footing on steep mountain-sides, and roll far down the hill. Many of these mishaps involve the repacking of the animal, and when to this is added the fact that the train is winding about to avoid obstacles, now climbing hills and again descending into valleys, it will easily be seen that, however long the day's march may be in hours, it seldom covers many miles.

On the September day in 1891 when our party of five men set out to try to reach the head of the St. Mary's River above the lakes, we were late in getting away from camp. This is always to be expected on the first day's march. Pack-saddles and "riggings" are to be fitted to the horses, provisions, cooking-utensils, and blankets to be sorted out and made up into packs; and this, with the loading of the animals, takes a great deal of time. After a day or two, when each packer knows just where every article belongs, the work is much more quickly done. At length the last rope is made fast, and the leader of the train rides off up the trail. The pack-horses fall in behind him, and the other riders, after giving a last look over the abandoned camp-ground to see that nothing has been left behind, take their places in the line, distributing themselves along it, so that each man has in front of him one or two animals which are his special charge. He must keep them from lagging and must watch their loads.

The trail follows up the west shore of the [Upper St. Marys] lake, for two miles passing through dense growths of aspens, and then into a long, wide prairie which is crossed here and there by the wooded courses of little streams. To the right, or west, and little more than a mile distant, tower the cliffs of Single Shot Mountain; while across the lake, hills wooded with dense pine forests rise toward Milk River Ridge and the point of Divide Mountain. About seven miles above the end of the upper lake is the true gate of the mountains. Here two long points, from Red Eagle Mountain on one side and from Goat Mountain on the other, jut out into the lake and almost meet, forming the Lower Narrows. The northern face of the ledge from Goat Mountain is vertical and can be climbed at only one point, and there by a very steep trail. Most people prefer to ascend this on foot, leading their horses, and a little excitement is usually given to the scramble by the rocks which, loosened by the horses' hoofs, come bounding down the slope. Occasionally it happens that a pack-horse loses its footing and rolls down, hoofs over load. This is worse for those below than a fifty-pound rock, because less easily avoided.

After climbing the point of rocks, the trail winds through the green timber near the foot of Goat Mountain, and then passes out on to the steep slide-rock, which in many places extends from the lake shore, in a slope broken only by cliffs, up to the walls of rock forming the mountain's crest. Ever ascending, the trail climbs this slide-rock, following an ancient path trodden into the rock by the game, and at length passes along a narrow ledge with precipices above and below. A little alder-grown trickle of water crosses here, and this was where our party met with its first accident.

For a few yards below the crossing, the sharply sloping mountain-side is overgrown with alders, and then breaks off in a cliff one hundred feet high. The trail is twelve or fifteen inches wide, but appears narrower, for the summer's growth of weeds, grass, and alder sprouts extends out over it. The man who was in advance was on foot, leading a pack-horse. After him came another loaded animal, and this was closely followed by two horsemen. When these were within a few yards of the brook crossing they heard a yell of dismay from the man in front, and then a shout: "The black mare has rolled down the hill!" Slipping off their horses and leaving them standing in the trail, they ran forward, and reached the scene of disaster just in time to see the second pack-horse spring upon a large flat rock which lay in the way, and as its four unshod feet came down on the smooth stone, it slipped, lost its footing, and rolled slowly off the trail. It had not fairly got started before the men had it by the head and had stopped its descent, holding it by the loosened hackamore. The animal made one or two struggles to regain its footing, but the brush, the slope, and its load made it impossible for it to rise, and it lay there while the three men held it. Meanwhile the black mare by a lucky chance had regained her feet before reaching the precipice, and was now making her way up the slope toward the trail.

To get the pack off the fallen beast was the first thing to be done. A man climbed down the rocks behind the horse, so as to be out of the way of its feet if it should flounder, and cut the lacing which attaches the hook to the lash cinch, thus freeing the load, which was then readily pulled aside, and with a little effort and help the horse stood on its feet and was led up to the trail, and then on to a grassy bench where there was a little level ground. The other horses were then carefully led past the dangerous point, and as it was now late in the afternoon, and the work of repairing damages would occupy an hour or two, we camped here, and after stretching ropes across the trail so that the horses could not go back, turned them loose to forage on the ledges. While supper was being cooked, a large white goat came out to the edge of the cliff three hundred yards above us, and made a leisurely inspection of the camp.

Two days later we had made some progress up the untraveled valley of the Upper St. Mary's and had camped on the edge of a narrow grassy park in the valley of the south branch of the river. This is much the larger of the two streams, and its milky water shows the presence of glaciers at its head, while the north fork is clear.

On the left of the camp towered the vertical cliffs of Citadel Mountain; the high wooded shoulder running down from Mount Reynolds was to the right, and before us, up the valley, stood the peak of Fusillade and the rounded mass of Mount Jackson.

The following day's march was very laborious. For the first few miles no obstacles more formidable than fallen timber, dense alders, and mire were met with; but after we had passed the point of Citadel and turned south, progress became very difficult and slow. Many years ago an avalanche had swept down the valley and overthrown its great trees, which now lay piled up on the ground like giant jackstraws, barring the way, and it was necessary to climb a shoulder which runs down between the valley and Citadel Mountain. The ascent of this was steep, and the ground was thickly overgrown with tough brushwood, standing shoulder-high, among which lay the rotting trunks of great trees fallen years before. The combination was very discouraging, and it was not long before the horses became so tired that they refused to face the brush, and I had to dismount and lead my animal, breaking a trail as I went. To add to our discomfort, rain began to fall about midday, and in a very short time all hands were thoroughly soaked. After an all-day struggle with brush, fallen timber, and hills, we found ourselves at night in a little grassy meadow lying between two old moraines, almost at timber-line and only a few hundred yards from the foot of the great glacier which runs down from the mountain to the south. Here we made our camp, and a few stunted spruces gave us half a dozen lodge-poles. Though wet and weary, the men, as they worked to make camp that night, carried about with them a feeling of contentment born of dif-ficulties overcome and an object attained, and one of them referred to the lit-tle party as the "get there" brigade.

The camp stood on the east side of the valley. To the south and southeast were the moraines and ice-fingers stretching down from the great Blackfoot Glacier, and behind these the sloping mass of ice rises toward the mountain's crown. East were the vertical walls of Citadel Mountain; to the west stood Mount Jackson, and to the north was Fusillade. The Blackfoot Glacier is by far the most imposing that I have seen in the Rocky Mountains south of the Cana-dian boundary. From our camp in this valley we could see only a small part of its lower end, but I have looked on this mountain from two different points of view, at a distance of a dozen miles, and have seen that the glacier covers the whole northern side of the mountain. The mass of the ice lies behind (south of) Citadel Mountain and west of the great crest of rock from the eastern side of which flow waters running into Red Eagle Creek. At the foot of this main ice is a lofty cliff, and over this pour great milky streams, the volume of which seems at least one half of the water which flows into the St. Mary's Lake.

Mount Jackson, one of the highest mountains to be seen, is a rounded mass, in part ice-covered, as is also the high ridge by which it joins the shoulder of the Blackfoot Mountain. North of Jackson is a deep valley which separates it from Fusillade Mountain. At the head of this valley is a little lake [Gunsight Lake], and beyond the lake a low saddle, over which a trail across the range could easily be made. On the west side of this pass is another little lake, from which a stream runs southwestward toward the Pacific Ocean. The wall of rock separating these two lakes is not more than one hundred yards in thickness, and to tunnel it would afford a passage for a railway with but slight grade.

We spent nearly two weeks in this wonderful spot, climbing the mountains and hunting goats and sheep and ptarmigan. Goats were abundant and tame, but the member of the party who had the nearest view of them was one who had never before been in the Rocky Mountains. He was laboriously working his way up some vertical cliffs, and, needing both hands to climb with, had strapped his rifle on his back. As he raised himself up over a rock he met face to face, and not forty feet away, a large goat coming toward him. The two saw each other at the same moment, and at first astonishment held each motionless. In a moment the goat recovered himself and started back up the mountain, and by the time the hunter had freed his gun, the game had disappeared behind some rocks and was not seen again.

A goat-hunting incident gave Fusillade Mountain its name. We had moved our camp to the little lake below that peak, and one morning two of the men climbed high up on its side in pursuit of a dozen or twenty goats which made it their feeding-ground. The day had passed, and we had heard no shot, and from the camp could see the goats still feeding undisturbed. Just about sunset, as we were eating supper, the report of a gun was heard far above us. Glasses were leveled, and as shot after shot rang out and echoed along the mountainside, we saw puffs of blue smoke rising from a point far below the goats. These at first did not seem to be interested in the shooting. Very likely they had never before heard a gun. But at length, when the balls began to strike near them, they jumped about a little, and at last, looking like so many flies crawling up a wall, all slowly clambered up the mountain and passed out of sight over the top. When all had disappeared, the hunters, who had been shooting at long range and had not expected to hit anything, rose from their places of concealment and started down toward the camp. They had come but a short distance when over the top of the mountain all the goats appeared again and crawled deliberately down the seemingly vertical wall back to their feeding-ground.

Two miles from where St. Mary's River leaves the lower lake, it is joined from the west by a large stream known as Swift Current. The valley of this river is narrow where it joins that of the St. Mary's but above this it becomes wider. The mountains which inclose it on each hand, at first lower and round-topped, gradually become bolder and higher, and at last are continuous walls two thousand feet in height, broken at intervals by "basins," each one narrow at its mouth, but often wide within, from which pour torrents fed by melting snows, or by springs high up in the rocks. Swift Current valley is straight, and as one rides along toward its head he can see the long, narrow mountain which separates its two branches, and the great mass of ice which supplies water for the southernmost of the two. Up this valley for perhaps fifteen miles, passing through the groves of aspens and the grassy parks which lie on the north of the stream, runs a well-worn Indian trail. On the south side, the heavily timbered mountains, still the home of a few moose, stand close to the river. At intervals along the stream are little lakes, and the fifth of these [now called Swiftcurrent Lake], counting from its mouth, receives the two main branches into which Swift Current is here divided. Just below this lake are the falls of Swift Current, two broken cataracts or steep cascades, one of fifty and the other of seventy-five feet, beautiful waterfalls, but insignificant in comparison with their surroundings.

The first day's journey up the stream usually carries one to a large grassy park below the falls, where Indian hunting-parties make their permanent camps. Once these mountains abounded in sheep and goats, and everywhere about this park may be seen the sites of old Indian camps, with rotting lodge-poles, old fireplaces, and piles of bone and hair, showing where game has been cut up and hides dressed. Above this park the trail forks, the right-hand branch following up the north arm of the river toward Mount Wilbur, and the other, which is blind and not easy to find or to follow, crossing a shoulder of Mount Allen and keeping on the south side of the south branch of the river to its head. On this arm of the stream are two glacial lakes, each a mile long, the westernmost of the two lying at the foot of the great precipice, beneath a large glacier.

When the old camp-ground is reached, the pack-animals are quickly caught and relieved of their loads, unsaddled and turned loose. Meantime one of the men has taken the ax, and stepping off among the pine timber, is felling straight, slender poles. Before long, other men go to him, and bring the lodge-poles to the camp, where they are smoothed and three of them tied together at the proper height, to make a frame for our dwelling. These having been raised and their butts spread so as to form a tripod, other poles are set up against the forks, and the top of the lodge is tied to the last pole. When this is in position, the canvas is spread over the frame. Then the front of the lodge is pinned together, the outside poles fixed in the ears, the border of the lodge pinned to the ground, and we have a comfortable house which is warm, water-tight, and windproof. The fire is built on the ground in the middle of the lodge; the beds are spread about the walls. Outside saddles and ropes are neatly piled up, and we are at home for a night or for a month. The evening meal is eaten about dark, and the hours before bedtime are spent about the fire. The camp is roused at dawn, and while breakfast is being cooked, some one goes out, finds the horses, and drives them close to the camp. After breakfast, while some make up the packs and tear down the lodge, others catch and saddle the animals, which are soon packed, and before long the train is strung out over the trail on the day's march.

On my first visit to Swift Current Glacier [later named after Grinnell himself] I approached it by climbing up the face of the precipice at its foot. The climb was long and hard, and though we started about three o'clock in the morning, it was long after dark that night when we returned to the camp. Most of the time after we reached the ice was devoted to examining it, though we stopped long enough during the ascent to kill a great bighorn, the tracks of which we found in the new snow on the edge of the glacier. Following these footprints, which led in the direction we were going, on rounding a point of rocks we saw the sheep standing in a snow-drift on the mountain-side far above us. A quick shot was made, and with one bound he disappeared from view; but on climbing up to where he had stood, we saw from the blood and footprints in the snow that he was hard hit and could not go far. He had turned down the mountain, and one of the men followed him down the cliffs and over the snow-banks till he found him dead at the foot of a precipice. The other two men went on higher, and spent some hours upon the glacier, which was then, in November, covered with new snow.

On another occasion, some years later, I found this glacier melting rapidly in early September. It was everywhere extensively crevassed and pierced by deep wells, into which the brooks which seamed the surface of the ice poured with loud roarings. Indeed, the rush of many waters here was fairly appalling. The tinkle of the streams above, the echoing fall of the plunging torrents, and the hiss of the confined water rushing along beneath the ice, made up a volume of sound so great that ordinary conversation could not be heard. It was here and at this time that I carelessly put myself in a position of serious danger. Though unprepared for ice work, I was anxious to climb an arm of the glacier which led directly to the mountain's crest, and not realizing the steepness of the ascent, I set out. Before I had gone half a mile over the ice, I wished myself back on the rocks again, for the incline was constantly increasing. I knew that if I lost my footing and began to slide down the sloping ice I should not stop until I had fallen into one of the bottomless pits or crevasses of the main glacier; and a man who has fallen into one of these would have but a very short time in which to think over his past life. To attempt to retrace my steps would be greatly to increase the danger of making a fatal slip. There was no course except to keep on climbing. I made my way to the border of the finger of ice which was embraced by the two shoulders of the mountain; but next to the rock it had melted away, and I looked down into a deep trench there, which ran back far under the ice, and from the blackness below came up the roar of the torrent and the rumble of great rocks crashing against the stream-bed as they were hurried along by the water. Keeping near the edge of the ice, I slowly and carefully climbed higher and higher, and at length reached a place where a point of solid rock jutted out to within six feet of the edge of the ice. Here I sprang across the chasm and landed safely on the mountain-side.

About the heads of Swift Current there is abundant opportunity for a mountaineer to stretch his legs. The north branch takes its rise in two streams, one heading in an odd double glacial lake at the foot of Mount Wilbur, and the other among lower mountains to the northeast. At the foot of Wilbur, and lying against the vertical cliffs which rise without a break thousands of feet above it, is a little glacier less than half a mile square, which is constantly pushing out into the lake [Iceberg Lake]. The waters carried by the eddying winds against this ice undermine it, and as this goes on, sections of the glacier fall off into the water, so that the little lake is dotted with a multitude of tiny icebergs, which, driven hither and thither by the wind, glitter in the sunlight until at last they melt, the supply being kept up by other fallen masses of glacier. So here in the Rocky Mountains we have a little iceberg factory. The basin or little valley from which this stream flows is narrow and hemmed in on three sides by marvelous rock walls. Apparently vertical, this barrier rises for thousands of feet, terminating in a serrated ridge, over which it would seem that nothing but a bird could pass. Although seemingly vertical, these precipices can at some points be scaled by an active man, and from their summits one looks down into the narrow valley of Belly River, walled in by high gray and glacier-bearing mountains.

Our work in the mountains is not all pleasure. Often we have a "spell of weather" which forbids climbing or hunting. A blizzard sweeps over the range, and deep snows and bitter cold confine us to the lodge, and we await the advent of a favoring chinook to melt the snow. At such times short excursions are made with the shot-gun for ducks or grouse, or we wade through the drifts over the lower lands and try to find the lynxes and coyotes the tracks of which are seen in the snow, or even the bears, which have not yet entered on their long winter sleep. Much of the time, however, is spent in the lodge, where, after the few books in the camp have been exhausted, we are driven to entertain one another with stories.

Men who have seen much of the wild life of the old frontier have usually a good store of interesting reminiscences, if they can be induced to talk. As a rule, however, they are rather silent; but days of confinement often lead to the discovery among the company of some man who has an unexpected fund of good stories. Many of these will treat of personal adventure or of curious observations on the habits of birds and mammals. If Indians are in the party, they will sometimes tell stories of their own—tribal traditions of the beginnings of things, of the time when their gods lived upon the earth and mingled with the people, of the magic doings of powerful medicine-men, besides many tales of the prowess of ancient warriors of their tribe. Often these weather-bound story-tellings will bring out enough interesting material to fill a volume. The tales are sometimes related with great power and even beauty. Little time is wasted in a word-painting; it is the action which the story-tellers deal with. Terse, epigrammatic phrases and the expressive gestures of the sign-language with which they supplement their spoken words lend a wonderful force to their narrations.

A special interest attaches to the traditional stories of the Indians, of which each tribe has its own, handed down from generation to generation by word of mouth. Such a story is the Blackfoot account of how the people first received arms. "Old Man," it must be explained, is the Blackfoot Creator and chief god.

The old men say that Old Man, soon after he was born, made the people. Instead of giving them long fingers, he made their hands like those of the bear, and they dug roots and ate berries for food.

In those days the buffalo used to eat people. It was a long time before Old Man found this out, but one day he came along and saw them feasting on a woman they had just killed. Then Old Man felt very badly; he sat down on a rock and cried, and tore out his hair, and tried to think what he could do to save the people. "Hai-yah!" he cried, "I have not made these people right. They cannot defend themselves." He sat a long time thinking what to do, and at last he knew; so he went to where there were some people, and split their hands, making long fingers instead of short claws. Then he made some bows, arrows, and knives, and taught the people how to use them. He made their right arms the strongest, so that they could bend the bow with great force.

"Now, people," he said, "you will survive; now you can defend yourselves. Kill plenty of buffalo next time they come. The meat is good to eat, and the robes will make you warm clothing."

By and by the buffalo came again, and the people did as the Old Man had told them. The first arrow struck a buffalo in the side.

"Oh, my brothers," he cried, "a great fly bites me!" and he fell down and died.

The people killed many more buffalo, and at last those still alive saw that the people were shooting them. "You people, you people," they cried out, "do not kill any more of us! We will never eat any of you again."

Then Old Man, who was sitting on a rock looking on, said to them: "Hold on! We will gamble to see which shall be eaten." He called all the animals to help the people, and they all came. First the elk played against the buffalo and lost. The different animals in turn gambled against the buffalo and lost. On the third day, all had played except the mouse. His turn was now come. He took the bones [for the stick game] in his little paws, and all the people and animals shouted: "Take courage, little mouse! Take courage, little mouse!" The mouse took courage, and made his paws go so fast that the buffalo could not tell which one held the bone with the black mark. They guessed the wrong one and lost. Then every one shouted, they were so glad. The people strung their bows and killed many fat cows, enough to give all the animals a feast.

Afterward Old Man gave the buffalo skulls to the mice. Even to this day you will see that they make their home in them. This is how Old Man paid them for saving his people.

9

FROM *OUR NATIONAL PARKS*

John Muir
1902

One of the great conservationists in American history, John Muir (1838–1914) explored the Sierra Nevada on foot, advocated for wilderness preservation, visited wild areas from California to Alaska, and founded the Sierra Club. His writings inspired generations of Americans with his eloquent descriptions of the "range of light" (the Sierras), the cathedral groves of sequoias, the falls of Yosemite, even the dipper, the little bird of the rushing streams called "water ouzel." In 1898, Muir traveled around the West, observing the "forest reservations" (national forests) of that time. Many of those reservations, including part of the Flathead Reserve, became national parks such as Glacier. Muir's articles in *Harper's Weekly* and *The Atlantic*, and his later book, *Our National Parks* (first published 1902, reprinted in revised form in 1916), brought the issue of wilderness preservation to the consciousness of American readers. This brief excerpt is from the book's 1902 edition (pages 17–19).

Wander here [in the Bitterroot Valley, south of Missoula] a whole summer if you can. Thousands of God's wild blessings will search you and soak you as if you were a sponge, and the big days will go by uncounted. If you are business-tangled, and so burdened with duty that only weeks can be got out of the heavy-laden year, then go to the Flathead Reserve; for it is easily and quickly reached by the Great Northern Railroad. Get off the track at Belton Station [West Glacier], and in a few minutes you will find yourself in the midst of what you are sure to say is the best care-killing scenery on the continent—beautiful lakes derived straight from glaciers, lofty mountains steeped in lovely nemophila-blue skies and clad with forests and glaciers, mossy, ferny waterfalls in their hollows, nameless and numberless, and meadowy gardens abounding in the best of everything. When you are calm enough for discriminating observation, you will find the king of the larches, one of the best of the Western giants, beautiful, picturesque, and regal in port, easily the grandest of all the larches in the world. It grows to a height of one hundred and fifty to two hundred feet, with a diameter at the ground of five to eight feet, throwing out its branches into the light as no other tree does. To those who before have seen only the European larch or the Lyall species of the eastern Rocky Mountains, or the little tamarack or hackmatack of the Eastern States and Canada, this Western king must be a revelation.

Associated with this grand tree in the making of the Flathead forests is the large and beautiful mountain pine, or Western white pine (*Pinus monticola*), the invincible *contorta* or lodge-pole pine, and spruce and cedar. The forest floor is covered with the richest beds of *Linnea borealis* I ever saw, thick fragrant carpets, enriched with shining mosses here and there, and with clintonia, pyrola, moneses, and vaccinium, weaving hundred-mile beds of bloom that would have made blessed old Linnaeus weep for joy.

Lake McDonald, full of brisk trout, is in the heart of this forest, and Avalanche Lake is ten miles above McDonald, at the feet of a group of glacier-laden mountains. Give a month at least to this precious reserve. The time will not be taken from the sum of your life. Instead of shortening, it will indefinitely lengthen it and make you truly immortal. Nevermore will time seem short or long, and cares will never again fall heavily on you, but gently and kindly as gifts from heaven.

10

LAKE ANGUS MCDONALD AND THE MAN FOR WHOM IT WAS NAMED

Helen Fitzgerald Sanders
1910

Helen Fitzgerald Sanders (1883–1955) was a prominent Montana writer, best known for her three-volume history of Montana (1913) and for her novel, *The White Quiver*, about the Blackfeet people. Early in 1910, just before the designation of Glacier as a national park, she completed her book *Trails through Western Woods,* which describes the area that became Glacier (which she calls "Sin-yal-min"). She also delves into the history and culture of the Flathead Indian Reservation west of the park; it is described in several chapters, along with a history of Native Americans in the Glacier region. Sanders clearly found the area breathtaking—as attested by her frequent passages of poetic, emotional description—and she delved deeply into its history by talking with old-timers, both Native and European. Her descriptions of a steamboat trip on Lake McDonald and a horseback foray to Sperry Glacier (from the third, seventh, and eighth chapters of the book) illustrate what early tourism was like even before the national park was established.

It should be noted that the origin of the name "Lake McDonald" is still in dispute. Local historian Jack Holterman commented in 2006, "There are several theories about the name McDonald, but the most probable and popularly accepted story derives the name from Duncan McDonald...the son of Angus McDonald." Duncan McDonald apparently camped at the lake in 1878 and carved his name in a tree; later settlers called the lake according to the name they found.

Within the range of Sin-yal-min, which rises abruptly from the valley of the Flathead to altitudes of perpetual snow, in a ravine sunk deep into the heart of the mountains, is Lake Angus McDonald....

The prospect is a magnificent one as the roadway uncoils its irregular, tawny length from rolling hills into the level sea of green where only a year or two ago the buffalo grazed in peace. Beyond, the jagged summits of Sin-yal-min toss their crests against the sky, their own impalpable blue a shade more intense than the summer heavens, their silvered pinnacles one with the drifting cloud. A delicate, shimmering thread like the gossamer tissue of a spider's web spins its length from the ethereal brow of the mountains to the lifted arms of the foothills below. The pass becomes more difficult, the growth thickens. Among the trees broad-leafed thimble berry, brew berry and goose berry blossom and bear; wild clematis builds pyramids of green and white over the bushes; syringa bursts into pale-starred flower; and a shrub, feathery, delicate, sends forth long, tender stems which break into an intangible mist of bloom.

Suddenly out of the tangled forests, a sheet of water, smooth and clear, appears, spreading its quicksilver depths among peaks that still bear their burden of the glacial age. And in the polished mirror of those waters is reflected the perfect image of its mountain crown. First, the purplish green of timbered slopes, then the naked, beetling crags and deep crevasse with its heart of ice. A heavy silence broods here, broken only by the wildly lonesome cry of the raven quavering in lessening undulations of tone through the recesses of the crags. Two Indians near the shore flit away among the leaves, timid as deer in their native haunts. Such is Lake Angus McDonald, and yonder, presiding over all, shouldering its perpetual burden of ice, is McDonald's Peak. Strangely beautiful are these living monuments to the name and fame of a man, and one naturally asks who was this Angus McDonald that his memory should endure in the eternal mountains within the crystal cup of this snow-fed lake?

The question is worth the answering. Angus McDonald was a Highland Scotchman, sent out into the western wilderness by the Hudson Bay Company. There must have lurked in his robust blood the mastering love of freedom and adventure which led the scions of the House of McDonald to such strange and varied destinies; which made such characters in the Scottish hills as Rob Roy and clothed the kilted clans with a romantic colour totally wanting in their stolid brethren of the Lowlands. In any event, it is certain that Angus McDonald, once within the magic of the wild, flung aside the ties that bound him to the outer world and became in dress, in manner of life and in heart, an Indian. He took unto himself an Indian wife, begot sons who were Indians in colour and form and, like his adopted people, he hunted upon the heights, moved his tipi from valley to mountain as capricious notion prompted, and finally made for himself and his family a home in the valley of Sin-yal-min not far below that lake and peak which do honor to his memory. Physically he was a man of towering stature, standing over six feet in his moccasins; his shoulders were broad and he was very erect. His leonine head was clad with a heavy shock of hair, and his beard, during his later years, snow white, hung to his waist. His complexion was ruddy, his eyes clear, blue and penetrating. A picturesque figure he must have been, clad in full buckskin leggins and shirt with a blanket wrapped around him. He was known among the Indians and whites through the length and breadth of the country about, and no more strange or striking character quickened the adventure-bearing epoch which we call the Early Days.

As he was free to the point of lightness in his nature, trampling down and discarding every shackle of conventionality, he was likewise bound but nominally by the Christian creed. He believed in reincarnation and his one desire was that in the hereafter, when his soul should be sent to tenant the new body, he might be re-born in the form of a wild, white horse, with proud, arched neck and earth-scorning hoofs, dashing wind-swift over the broad prairies into the sheltering hills.

So it seems fitting that McDonald's Peak and Lake should remain untamed even as their namesake; that the eddying whirlpool of life should pass them by and that in their embrace the native creatures should live and range as of yore. And may it be that within those shadowy gorges, remote from the sight and hearing of man, a wild, white horse goes bounding through the night?

LAKE MCDONALD AND ITS TRAIL

In the northern part of Montana, towards the Canadian border, the Main Range of the Rocky Mountains has been rent and carved by glacial action during ages gone by, until the peaks, like tusks, stand separate and distinct in a mighty, serrated line. No one of these reaches so great a height as Shasta, Rainier or Hood, but here the huge, horned spine rises almost sheer from the sweep of tawny prairie, and not one, but hosts of pinnacles, sharp as lances, stand clean cut against the sky. Approaching the range from the East, in the saffron glow of sunset, one might fancy it was wrought of amethyst, so intense and pure is the colour, so clear and true the minutest detail of the grandly sculptured outline. Within the ice-locked barriers of those heights live glaciers still grind their passages through channels of stone; down in shadowy ravines, voiceful with silver-tongued falls, lie fair lakes in the embrace of over-shadowing altitudes. The largest of these lakes, McDonald, is the heart of a vast and marvelous country, the center of many trails.

The road to Lake McDonald winds along the shores of the [Middle Fork of the] Flathead River for half a mile or more, skirting the swift current now churned into white foam by rapids, then calm and transparent, revealing the least stone and tress of moss in its bed, in shades of limpid emerald. Leaving the river, the way lies through dense forests of pine and tamarack, cedar and spruce, and so closely do the spreading boughs interlace that the sun falls but slightly, in quivering, pale gold splashes upon the pads of moss and the fragrant damp mold which bursts into brilliant orange-coloured fungus and viciously bright toadstools. Each fallen log, each boulder wrested from its place and hurled down by glacier or avalanche, is dressed in a faery garb of moss and tiny, fragrant shell-pink bells called twinflowers, because two blossoms, perfect twins, always hang pendent from a single stem as slender as spun glass, and these small bells scent the air with an odour as sweet as heliotrope. Within the forest dim with perpetual twilight, one feels the vastness of great spaces, the silence of great solitudes.

Suddenly there bursts upon one, with all the up-bearing exhilaration of a first sight of the sea, a scene which, once engraved upon the heart, will remain forever. The trees part like a curtain drawn aside and the distance opens magnificently. The intense blue of the cloudless sky arches overhead, the royal waters of the lake flow blue and green with the colours of a peacock's tail or the variegated beauty of an abalone shell; sweeping upward from the shores are tall, timbered hills, so thickly sown with pine that each tree seems but a spear of grass and the whole forest but a lawn, and towering beyond, yet seeming very near in the pure, white light, is a host of peaks silvered with the benediction of the clouds—the deathless snow. The haze that tints their base is of a shade one sometimes finds in violets, in amethysts, in dreams. Indeed, these mountains seem to descend from heaven to earth rather than to soar from earth towards heaven, so great is their sublimity.

As one floats away on the lake the view changes. New vistas open and close, new peaks appear above and beyond as though their legion would never come to an end. Straight ahead two irregular, rugged mountains with roots of stone emplanted in the water rise like a mighty portal, and between the two, seeming to bridge them, is a ridge called the "Garden Wall." The detail of the more immediate steeps grows distinct and we see from their naked crests down their timbered sides, deep furrows, the tracks of avalanches which have rushed from the snow fields of Winter, uprooting trees and crushing them in the fury of the mad descent. A long, comparatively level stretch, not unlike a gun sight set among the bristling, craggy summits, is the "Gunsight Pass," the difficult way to the Great St. Mary's Lakes, the Blackfeet Glacier and the wonderful, remote region on the Eastern slope of the range. Huge, white patches mark glaciers and snow fields, for it is within these same mountains that the Piegan [Sperry Glacier] and many others lie. And as we drift on and on across the smooth expanse of water, the magic of it steals upon our souls. For there is about the lake a charm apart from the beauty of the waters and the glory of the peaks; of spirit rather than substance; of soul-essence rather than earthly form. That mysterious force, whatever it may be, rising from the water and the forest solitudes and descending from the mountain tops, flows into our veins with the amber sunshine and we feel the sweeping uplift of altitudes heaven-aspiring that take us back through infinite ages to the Source which is Nature and God.

The good old captain of the little craft weaves fact and fancy into wonderful yarns as he steers his launch straight for the long, purplish-green point which is the landing. To him no ocean greyhound is more seaworthy than his boat, and he likes to tell of timid tender-feet entreating him to keep to shore when the lake was tumultuous with storm, and how he, spurning danger, guided them all safely through the trough of the waves. He keeps a little log wherein each passenger is asked to write his name. The poor old man has a maimed hand, his eyes are filmy with years and his gums are all but toothless, but it would seem that nature has compensated him for his afflictions by concentrating his whole strength in his tongue. He knows each landmark well, and gravely points out to the credulous traveller the highest mountain in the world; calls attention to the 18,000 fathoms of lake depth whence no drowned man ever rises, and other marvels, each the greatest of its kind upon the circumference of the globe. There came a day soon after when the lake chafed beneath a lashing gale and the little craft and her gallant captain were dumped ingloriously upon the beach. But accidents happen to the best of seamen, and the launch, after a furious expulsion of steam, and much hiccoughing, was dragged once more into her place upon the wave.

Although there is evidence that Lake McDonald was long ago frequented by some of the Indian tribes, it was not known to the world until comparatively recent times. There are two stories of its discovery and naming, both of which have a foundation of truth. The first is that Sir John McDonald, the famous Canadian politician, riding across the border with a party, cut a trail through the pathless woods and happening to penetrate to the lake, blazed his name upon a tree to commemorate the event, thus linking his fame with the newly found natural treasure. The old trail remains—probably the virgin way into the wilderness. The second story—which is from the lips of Duncan McDonald, son of Angus—runs thus: He and a little band of Selish were crossing from their own land of the Jocko into the country of the Blackfeet which lies East of the Main Range, to recover some ponies stolen by the latter tribe, when they came in view of this lake hitherto unknown to them. Duncan McDonald, who was the leader or *partizan*, as the French-Canadians say, blazed the name "McDonald" upon some pines along the shore. It matters little who was actually the first to set foot on these unpeopled banks, but it is a strange coincidence that the two pathfinders should have borne the same name.

The purplish-green point draws nearer, log cabins appear among the trees, each one decorated with a bear skin hung near its door. This is a fur trading center as well as a resort of nature lovers, and upon the broad porch of the club house is a heap of pelts of silver tip, black and brown bear, mountain lion and lynx, and from the walls within, bighorn sheep and mountain goats' heads peer down. The trappers themselves, quaint, old hunters of the wilderness, come out of their retreats to trade. But even now their day is passing. With the advent of outside life these characters, scarcely less shy than the game they seek, move farther back into uncontaminated solitudes. They are the last, lingering fragment of that old West which is so nearly a sad, sweet memory, a loving regret.

ABOVE THE CLOUDS

Of all the trails in the McDonald country, there is none more travelled, or more worthy of the toil than that which leads to the Piegan glacier. From the moment we stand in expectant readiness in the little clearing behind the log cabins comprising the hotel, a new phase of existence has begun for us. So strange are the place and the conditions that it seems we must have stepped back fifty years or more, into that West whose glamour lives in story and song. Strong, tanned, sinewy guides who wear cartridge belts and six-shooters, load grunting pack-horses and "throw" diamond-hitches in businesslike silence. When at last all is ready, the riders mount the Indian ponies or "cayuses"— Allie Sand, the yellow cow pony; Babe, the slumbrous; Bunchie, but recently subdued, and Baldy, nicknamed "Foolish" because of the musical pack of kettles, camp stoves and sundries that jingle and jump up and down upon his back, lightening the way with merriment for those who follow. With a quickened beating of the heart, the good cheer and Godspeed of friendly voices ringing in our ears, we take leave of the last haunt of civilization and strike out into the virgin solitude of heaven-aspiring peaks.

As the feeling of remoteness smites the spirit when we pass beyond the railway station of Belton and follow in creaking wagons the shadow-curtained road to the lake, so now it returns with stronger impulse, calling to life new emotions begotten of the Wild. The world-rush calms into the great stillness of untrodden places, the world-voices sigh out in the murmuring breeze, the petty traffic of the cities is forgotten in the soulful silence of the trees. And out of this newly found affinity with the Nature forces, the love of adventure thrills into being, together with the fine scorn of danger and the resolve to do that which we set out to do no matter what the cost or the peril. Here the "white feather" is the greatest badge of dishonour, and he who fails through cowardice to win his goal is a man among men no more. This spirit is the faint, far-off echo of the hero-bearing days of the early West.

Our guide is a stocky, little man of soldierly bearing, clad in khaki suit and cow-boy hat, whom his fellows call "Scotty." He is brown with exposure, smoothly shaven, and his keen, blue eyes are slightly contracted at the corners from the strain of peering through vast distances—a characteristic of men who follow woodcraft and hunting. He rides ahead silently but for a rebuke to the slumbrous "Babe," such as, "Go on, you lazy coyote," or a familiar, half-caressing remark to Bunchie, the ex-outlaw, who is his favourite. Indeed, he, like most men who have ridden the range, has the habit of talking to the ponies as though they knew and understood. And who can be sure they do not?

The forests begin as soon as the bit of clearing is passed, then single file the little cavalcade moves on through huckleberry fields, purplish-black with luscious, ripe berries, where bears come to feed and fatten, where, also, thirsty wayfarers stop to eat the juicy fruit. The pines clasp branches overhead in a lacy, broken roof whose pattern of needle and burr shows in dark traceries against patches of blue sky remote and far beyond. A thick, sweet shadow dappled now and again with splashes of yellow sun tempers the air which presses its cool touch upon our brows. On either hand a dense, even lawn of tender green fern and mist-maiden covers the earth and through the silence sounds the merry clamour of a stream. It ripples gaily along between wooded banks, breaking into little crests of foam upon the rocks, showing through the glassy medium of its waters, every stone and pebble of its speckled bed polished and rounded by ceaseless flowing. The horses splash through the creek and upon the opposite side begins anew the delicate lawn of mist-maiden and fern, so freshly, tenderly green with the pale greenness of things that live away from the sun, so ephemerally exquisite as to embarrass coarse, mortal presence. It is a spot fit for fairies to dance upon; fit for wood-nymphs and white hinds to make merry in; fit for the flute-like melody of Pan to awake to dancing echoes as he calls the forest sprites unto high revelry.

A forest ranger joins us. He is tramping to the Gunsight Pass with his axe upon his shoulder and his kit upon his back to repair the trail to the Great St. Mary's Lakes.

The shades of brown and green, the shadow threaded with an occasional strand of gold, are livened by crimson patches of Indian Paint Brush, blue-bells, white starry lilies called Queen's Cups, trembling feathers of coral pink, sun-yellow and white syringa. Beneath the overhanging verdure, around and upon the mossy rocks, the ever-present twin-flowers open their delicate petals and sweeten the air, and from clumps of coarse grass rise cones of minute white blossoms, the bear-grass, one of the most curious of the mountain flowers. This ranger knows the common names of nearly all the plants, and at every turn new varieties spring up. He stops to gather each kind of bloom until we have a great bouquet—a *potpourri* of all the floral beauty of the multitudes that people our path.

The way is very fair, ministering to the senses; troops of new, forest forms and colours pass before the eye, the mingled sweets of the flowers, the pungent mould and balsam of spruce and pine breathe sensuously into the nostrils, and the fingers of the wind caress and soothe as they pass. Through the voiceful silence, sounds that are on the borderland between fancy and reality thrill for a moment, then are lost in the grand chorus of trees and rushing rivers. A stream of volume and velocity flowing through a deep gorge falls twice in its downward rush. These two falls, the Wynona and Minneopa, flash great, white plumes among steeps of green forest.

With sharp descent and stubborn climb, the trail, that seems the merest thread, untangles its skein and leads, at length, into a small basin partly enclosed within sheer, naked rock-walls, whence three delicate silver streams trickle down and join the creek that waters a little park. Beyond, the peaks loom up masterfully, sheathing their icy lances in the clouds. High over the lip of the mighty rock-wall, rising like the giant counterpart of an ancient battlement, lies the glacier. Up that precipitous, overhanging parapet we must make our way, but where the footing or how the ascent is to be won, fancy cannot fathom, for it would seem no living thing save a mountain goat, a bighorn sheep or an eagle could scale this stronghold of Nature. Across the basin, where there is a gentler slope, the mountain side is dotted with groups of tall, spire-like pines. The level meadow is grassy and shaded with small spruce of the size of Christmas trees. And in this peaceful spot, girt with grim, challenging steeps, the tinkle of the stream sounds pastorally sweet, while the more distant and powerful roar of the three tumbling streams chants a solemn undertone to the merry lilt.

Here the camp is made. A fire crackles gaily and our tents are pitched beneath the trees. Suddenly a shadow falls—dimly, almost imperceptibly. The sun has gone. It is only six o'clock in mid-summer, but so lofty are the barrier-heights that even now we are in a world of shade—shade of a strangely luminous kind, hinting of ruddy lights that are obscured but not quenched. Through the quiet, echo the whistle of the marmot, the metallic whirr of contentious squirrels going off like small alarm clocks, and the mellow, drowsy note of bells ringing to the rhythmic crop of browsing ponies. So the long beautiful twilight settles over the mountains until the sounds are stilled save the tinkling bells and the water-voices singing their ceaseless song. The forest sleeps. Long, mystical fancy-bearing moments and tens of moments pass, and something of awe closes down with the gloaming. Then through the dim, monkish grey shadow pulses a red-gold stream of light that runs in long, uneven streamers across the face of the grim, dark walls, transfiguring them into radiant shapes of living golden-rose. In that effulgence of glory, lost peaks gleam for a second out of the dusk and vanish into nothingness again, snowy diadems flash into being and fade like a dream. The life-blood of the day ebbs and flows, sending out long, slender fingers to trace its fleeting message on the rocks, then with a deepening, crimson glow it flickers and is fled. Night settles fast and the flare of the camp fire, shedding its spark-spangles in brilliant showers, reclaims one little spot from the devouring blackness. It is a magical thing—this campfire, and the living ring around it is an enchanted circle. Perhaps its warmth penetrates even to the heart, or perhaps the bond of human fellowship asserts itself more strongly when only the precarious, flamboyant fire-light, leaping and waning, throwing forth a rain of sparks, or searing grey with sudden decline, separates our little group from utter desolation. Whatever the charm may be, it falls upon us all, and with eyes fixed on the ember-pictures or raised to the starry skies, we listen to tales of the long ago and of a present as unfamiliar as the past. The reserve of our guide is quite broken and he tells in a low, reminiscent voice of wonder-spots in the range—for he knows its every peak and gorge—of the animals that dwell in its solitary recesses and of how the Piegan Glacier got its name.

The Piegan Indians are a branch of the Blackfeet tribe, and in the early days they were almost as noted horse raiders as the Absarokes who flourished near the Three Tetons, in the country of the Yellowstone. Back and forth across the passes they came and went in their nefarious traffic, secure from pursuit among the horns of these lonely heights. The vicinity of the eternal ice-fields, probably this little basin itself, sheltered the shadowy bands, and thus the glacier became known by their name. Still, you may look in vain on the maps for Piegan Glacier; you will find it called Sperry instead. The old name was discarded for that of a Professor who spent some weeks exploring its crevasses and under whose supervision a corps of college students spent a part of one summer's vacation, building the glacier trail. Yet there are those who love the old names as they love the traditions for which they stand, and to them the glacier will forever bear the time-honoured title of these Indians who have long since disappeared from its solitudes.

As the hours pass we draw from our guide and story-teller something of himself. Little by little, in fragmentary allusions and always incidentally, during that even-tide and the days following, we learn thus much of his life. He was born in those troublous days of Indian fighting on the frontier, shortly after his father, an army officer, was ordered out on campaign against the Sioux. When he was but a few weeks old word came to his mother that her husband had been killed, and she, sick and heart-broken, died, leaving besides this infant one other boy. The two children were left to the care of the officers at Fort Kehoe [near Miles City in eastern Montana], but they were separated while both were so young that they did not realize the parting nor remember each other. Our guide became the ward of a lieutenant who had been a friend of his father. He played among the soldiers and Indian scouts at the Fort until he came to the age when he felt the desire to learn, then he went East to school, afterwards to college, always returning in the summer to ride the range or to lose himself in the mountains. And when the college days were done that old cry of the West, that old craving for the life that knows no restraint nor hindering bonds, beckoned him back inevitably as Fate. Again and again he had gone forth on the world's highway, once to serve in Cuba in the war with Spain, where in a yellow-fever hospital he met for the first time his older brother, who even then was dying of the pestilence, but always he returned to the freedom of the wilderness. He is a type in himself, who belongs to the time of Lewis and Clark, rather than to this century—a man who lives too late. And there is about him, for all his carefree indifference to the world, something of indefinable pathos. He is quite alone—he has no kinsfolk and few friends. He is a man without a home but the forests, who has renounced human companionship for the solitudes, without a love but the mountains, to whom the greatest sorrow would be the knowledge that he might never look upon them again.

A cloud, heavy with rain, drifts across the sky, and big, cool drops splash with a hissing noise in the fire, upon our upturned faces, upon the warm, flower-sown earth which exhales, like incense, the odours of sun-heated soil and summer shower. The bright flames deepen to a blood-red glow and ashes gather like hoar frost on the cooling logs and boughs. The circle around the fire disperses to seek the narcotic gift breathed by the pines, sung as a lullaby by the voices of trees and streams.

The start for the glacier is made while the day is young. Pack horses and camp are left behind and with the guide leading the way, the tortuous climb is begun. Sheer as those rock-walls seemed to be, there is a footing for the careful ponies, as from narrow ledge to ledge they turn and zigzag up the mountain-face; and naked as those steeps appeared, they are animated with frisking conies and marmots, and hidden among the stones are rarely exquisite flowers. Here the mountain lilies grow, blossoms with brown eyes in each of their three white petals, covered with soft, silvery fur which makes them seem of the texture of velvet. These lilies are somewhat similar to the Mariposa lily of the California Sierras. The ground-cedar, a minute and delicate plant; strange varieties of fern and moss, and everchanging, unfamiliar flowers appear as we ascend, until, wheeling dizzily hundreds of feet above the basin upon the slight and slippery trail, with things beneath dwarfed by distance into a pigmy world and things above looming formidably, the increasing altitude shears the rocks and leaves them bare and grim. The air grows sharp with icy chill, [and] great billowy, low-trailing clouds drag over the mountain-tops, down the ravines and float in detached banners in free spaces below. Broad stretches of snow lie ahead. The painstaking ponies pick their way across them, for it is fifteen feet down to solid ground. Sluggish streams creep between banks crusty with old ice, and pretty falls, broken into lacy meshes of foam, cascade down a parapet of rock and baptize us as we pass. In this spot the stone wall has been worn into a grotto where the water plays as in a fountain. From every little fissure ferns dart their long green lances and feathery fronds, and the rocks are grown over with moss.

From our eyrie we look down into a small lake called Peary's, sunk within dark and desolate cliffs, shattered and ground down into fantastic forms. It is but partly thawed and its cold, blue-green centre is enclosed in opaque, greenish-white ice and drifts of snow. Indeed snow is everywhere in broken drifts—in the furrowed mountain-combs and along the level in smooth white stretches. Close to the margin of the ice-sealed shores is a grotesque, sapless, scrubby vegetation, as strange in its way as the brilliant-hued waters or the rocks that impress us with huge antiquity and elemental crudeness, as though we stood face to face with Earth's infancy, close in the wake of ebbing, primeval seas. But for all the savage roughness and arctic chill this is a scene to cherish and remember—the blue cup of heaven, flecked with a thistledown of clouds, the black menace of shivered rock-crests, the dazzle of the snow and the darkly beautiful waters that are neither blue nor green yet seemingly of both colours, held fast in the circle of cold, pale ice.

Above this lake, down an overhanging wall, are more little falls, indeed the whole country is interlaced with them as though the life-blood of the mountains flowed in silver veins upon the surface. Within the hollow over the stone barrier lies Nansen's Lake, even more frigid in its ice-sheath, more palely green in the little patch of water which the sun has laid bare. And although the mountains soar tremendously, yet ever and anon the course lies upward over the frowning brows, over the very crowns of the Range, until the high peaks, stripped of atmospheric illusion, stand stark and naked to the gaze. There is in this sudden intimacy with the fellows of the clouds, the veiled lords of upper air, an awe which we feel before powers incomprehensible.

At last the trail ceases; overhead are cliffs no horse could climb. The guide ties the ponies, and with a stout rope clambers ahead up a smoothly sculptured parapet. We follow him and find ourselves on a bleak waste which leads to a small basin, strewn with great boulders and lesser rocks, dark and of the colour of slate. Growing upon these rock-heaps are masses of flowering moss starred by tiny pink buds and blossoms, or white spattered with the crimson of heart's blood. And now the guide begins to whistle—a long, plaintive note which is answered presently by a similar sound and a shrill, infantile treble, cheeping, cheeping among the stones. Then from the security of her home a Ptarmigan, or Arctic Grouse, hops into the open with her family of five chicks jumping on her patient back, and tumbling, the merest puffballs, at her feet. She chirps softly to them, proud and dignified in her maternity, ever watchful of her pretty little brood. She is dressed in Quakerish summer-garb of mottled grey, the feathers covering her to the utmost extremity of her toes. Once the winter snows descend, these birds become as white as the frigid regions which they inhabit. Ordinarily they are very wild, but this little mother, knowing only friendliness from human visitors, comes forth trustfully with her beloved young, suffers them to be handled and caressed and she, herself, with wings dropped in the semblance of a pretty courtesy, jumps into the hand of the guide, and from that perch feeds daintily on the pink and white buds of the moss, as fragilely lovely as the snowflakes to which they appear strangely akin. Indeed, the bird, the flowers and the environing snow all seem more of the cloudland than of the earth.

But there is a sequel to the story of this little grouse, which is, unhappily, a tragedy. Not long after she greeted us, giving an air of friendliness to the forbidding, wind-swept rocks, a Tyrolese came hunting through the mountains. He made his camp near the home of the Ptarmigan and her little ones, and one day when the guide came calling to her there was no answer but the empty whistling of the wind. He called again and again; he searched among the crags and the rock-heaps, then he came upon the ashes of a camp-fire and the mottled feathers and silken down of the Ptarmigan and her chicks. She had been betrayed at last by her trustfulness, and she and her brood had been cruelly sacrificed to the bloodlust and appetite of that enemy of poor dumb things—the man with the gun.

From the mossy basin of the Ptarmigan we climb with ropes up a broken escarpment and there upon the very lip of the glacier are blossoms so unearthly in form and colour as to seem the merest ghosts of flowers. One is a dark, ocean-blue bell and another an ashen-green thing furred over with a beard as soft and colorless as a moth's wing. From this eminence a stormy, wind-tossed little lake, the Gem, flashes angrily-bright waters beneath snow splashed, wonderfully stratified peaks, and there, through a gateway in the mountains, spreading out in a vast plateau of white, lies the glacier, undulating in frozen waves like a polar sea. Even under its shroud of snow one can trace its course by the seams and wrinkles of a congealed current. It is flanked on all sides by the savage, beetling peaks marshalled in endless ranks like the spears and unsheathed lances of war-gods in their domain midway between earth and heaven. Out across the death-white pallor of snow, in the death-chill of the ice-fields, we strike out slowly, cautiously, for the surface of the ice, now hidden by snow, is cleft by crevasses even to the mountain's core, and a misstep, a fall into their depths, would be doom. Far away over the white stretches, a gaunt, spectral coyote watches our painful progress. On and on we go by a tusk-like peak, the "Little Matterhorn," and ever on to a point where the giant panorama unfolds its mountain-multitudes, its barricaded lakes, and the echo breaks into a chorus that peals out as though each separate crest were possessed of a brazen tongue. These grimly naked heights, split and rent with elemental shocks and the resistance to huge forces, are the cradle of the lightning and the thunder-bolt, the citadel whence the storm-hosts ride down on blackwinged clouds upon the world. And even now phantom troops of clouds come gliding up out of the moist laps of the valleys, out of lakes and streams, passing in shifting wraith-shapes over the mountains, spreading their filmy scarfs across the sky until the livid expanse of snow, showing colourlessly in the grey light, brings to one a vivid picture of the ice-age, of a frozen world and the cold, pitiless illumination of a burnt-out sun.

Fine, pricking points of snow cut with the sharpness of needle-thrusts; the wind whips through the bleak gaps in the Range and over the glacier, gathering cold and speed as it comes. A chilling numbness deadens our feet and hands. So, wind-buffeted, storm-driven, with the trumpeting gale in our ears, we turn back from the kingdom where Winter is unbroken, and descend through alternate shadow and sun into the blooming beauty, into the golden Summer that swims in the world below, whence snow and cold are only hinted of in a white-breasted, mountain-kissing cloud.

11

FROM *AVALANCHE*

Albert L. Sperry
1938

Dr. Lyman B. Sperry was a Midwestern physician interested in geology when he first visited northwestern Montana on the newly completed Great Northern Railway. As a geologist, he was fascinated by the prospect of undiscovered glaciers in the United States—until Pumpelly's exploratory trip, it was assumed that glaciers did not exist in the Rockies. Sperry, after whom the largest glacier in the park was named, reported his experiences in a lecture and an article in the magazine *Appalachia* in 1896. A fuller account was given by his nephew, Albert L. Sperry (who accompanied his uncle in 1894, 1895, and 1897), in a book written late in his life, *Avalanche* (1938). Not only did the Sperrys explore the Avalanche Lake area and the glacier above it, but they also used local guides to penetrate the nearly trailless wilderness in the northern part of the region, eventually camping at Granite Park and going as far as a pass overlooking the Belly River region. This chapter includes excerpts from Albert Sperry's book, in which he describes a near-disaster above Avalanche Lake and the party's further explorations.

The next hour nearly changed my plans and might have made me a haunting voice echoing down that basin for centuries to come....In coming off the Matterhorn near the snow line there was lots of shale rock which no one knew was loose. The rock rested upon a sheet of ice not very deep below and as we clambered along the last shelf, I jumped down a few feet onto that shale and in a flash, it started. It was a mile to the edge of the rim wall and all down hill. Kelly shouted, "Get on your back," and Frank hollered, "Roll," and then they exacted silence from the others. I kept silent. A mountain problem had arisen and they knew what might happen. The shale kept gathering momentum and every few rods another city lot joined on and my feet were sinking into the mass and I soon knew that I must get on top of it or be swallowed up in it. I laid upon my back and using that Alpine stock [alpenstock] as a pry rolled and rolled towards the edge of the moving mass as fast as I possibly could and at about fifty feet from the edge of the rim wall I was on solid ground and heard that mighty crash instead of being a part of it. It would have been a cheap funeral for me with an eternal monument thrown in.

My clothes were torn and I was somewhat scratched. I waited an hour or so more for the party to come down. I had a fast ride with accelerating speed every second of it. The Doctor [Professor Sperry] started his avuncular observations just as soon as he hove in sight and Kelly stopped him short by saying, "Excuse me, Doctor, but that will be enough from you, for he used his head and he is here—not under millions of tons of rock." Kelly was provoked at the Doctor, for I had suddenly become initiated into the mountaineers guild.

We had accomplished all that we could about the glacier for that summer and the Doctor was now at liberty to entertain his guests so by common consent we went North along the Indian trail....The horses needed forage so we pressed on to Granite Park where there was horse feed.

I want to inject another pair of characters right now. There was a streak of copper running northwest through this section and some one had opened a copper mine far up in the mountains, known as "The Lady Collins Mine". She was a self contained individual quite able to look after herself and no one knew whether it was hers or someone else's money that was doing the mining. No mountaineers made free with her or her business, for she had a manager who was one more character in the mountains. Immense in stature, face of great determination, a hearty laugh, and a shock of curly hair marked him as abundantly able to attend to Lady Collins' investments. The story was that he had shot the wrong man in a love affair and that his presence here and absence from there was necessary. No one molested him. There were some stories about his drinking heavily at times. One day Lady Collins and this man were in a skiff on Lake MacDonald and in some way the man sunk to the bottom of the Lake never to rise again. No one asked any questions and no innuendoes were indulged in and none are here intended. It was simply an incident in a country where every man's business was his own and not that of others. The mine never paid out, for the world does not yet need copper which is so far distant from where it can be smelted as such ore is bulky and cannot be transported at a profit from such out of the way places.

Frank [likely Frank Geduhn, an early homesteader] had a mountain lion skin which was nine feet from tip to tip on the cabin floor and I called his attention to it and said, "Who got the big cat?" He said, "I did because I had to get it, not because I wanted it." That meant something so when opportunity presented itself, I said, "Let's talk about the big cat." He was relaxed then and in a mood to tell the story and he knew that he would get no hated hero worship from me. This was the incident. For convenience in getting venison, which was the cheapest meat supply available, the boys had put out what is known as a "salt lick" in a shielded clearing not over half a mile up the slopes. It was a nice clearing with lots of natural feed in it and surrounded by timber. There was a big rock on the west side of it behind which the killer could lie with the sun at his back at evening when they generally went up there. It was a carefully planned butcher shop for all of them. I went over the ground with Frank one evening not to get a deer but just to have him act out his story. He had gone up of an evening for a deer and lay behind the big rock in the edge of the timber, but no buck, doe, or fawn wandered that way. They did not always come. Perhaps the local supply was small or maybe the does were tending their fawns and it is never quite certain just where a buck may be even though the deer is a semi-domestic animal and likes to hover near settlers. Frank did not realize that the sun was so far down and would drop behind the mountains at one jump and that darkness was but a few minutes away. He gazed intently on the salt lick through the dusk and suddenly by some instinct, and not by any noise he heard, he turned his head and there was the soft-pawed cat not thirty feet away, creeping up to him. He snarled when Frank turned but did not retreat. To have wasted a shot in the semi-darkness would have meant a fight, so Frank retreated towards the clearing by backward steps hoping to get into the light so that he could see the sights on his rifle barrel. Frank backed a step, the cat came forward a step, Frank backed another step and the cat came forward another step, and it was like a dress rehearsal for a play with a slow moving dance in it, Frank back, cat forward, Frank back, cat forward, Frank back, cat forward for what seemed miles to him but probably was not in fact over a hundred feet. Then came the crisis. The cat had decided that this was to be a battle to the death and no shout turned his purpose. Finally when about the only place for a decision in his favor was reached, Frank pulled up his rifle in the dim light and the cat made his spring. It was all over in a second and the cat lay dead at his feet with a bullet straight through its head. It pays to shoot straight. Here is the real climax to the story. He said that he had heard about hair standing on end and never believed it and still thought he might not believe it, but he said, "You know I never took my hands from that gun barrel, I never passed under any bush, I never felt any breeze, I never scraped anything with my head, I never moved that gun barrel from off that cat, but MY HAT WAS ON THE GROUND AND MY HAIR was straight up and down and that is that". The nine foot skin was a tribute to a man who really knew how to handle himself in a pinch....

The best angler in the whole lot came up to me the next morning and casually said, "Mrs. Snyder wants some fish and would you like to go", and we were soon started in a skiff to pull over the four miles to the waterfall in the creek at the head of Lake MacDonald....We pushed right into the creek's mouth for he said, "I want a big Dolly Varden [bull trout] for dinner". He steered the skiff onto a shelving rock on the opposite side of the stream from the one frequented by tourists and, when the boat was beached, he told me to use about a hundred yards of line and work the one and two pound mountain trout against the swift current and that our side of the stream was beyond the reach of the other side and was alive with trout. He was correct and no keener pleasure could ever come to any fisherman than came to me. My creel was full in a short time. He stepped into the brush and pulled out a peeled and dried hemlock shoot about a dozen feet long and about a half inch in diameter which he had cached there. It would hold a bucking broncho. That the rod was no experiment was plain to be seen. It was a well-proven instrument for taking the big Dolly Vardens which loitered around the foot of that sixteen foot waterfall. He pulled out of his pocket a line, sinker, and a hook, then baited it with a chunk of venison about the size of a robin's egg and climbed up to the side of the waterfall, and sat upon a rock and cast his bait into that swirl. He rolled cigarette after cigarette and smoked in silence. Whenever I pulled one in, he smiled at me. I was fisherman enough to keep quiet. Across the stream a lawyer from Kalispell landed an eight pounder on a twelve ounce fly rod after a forty-five minute battle and he was happy. I thought the lawyer would "lose his case" and watched Spider, who shook his head once in a while, as much as to say "he won't land him" but evidently the eight pounder was well hooked and had no chance to break away. I thought that this lawyer did better than I could have done, for he let him run down stream and kept his line taut and did about all the things an angler would do to keep his fish; but the old Dolly Varden was smart and he would cross run the stream and kept making mad dashes against the current to loosen the line. He used every defensive art known to wise oldsters in the fish kingdom, but the lawyer brought him to creel and every onlooker was pleased. If that lawyer had been anything but a true sportsman, he would have gone after another big one, but he took his prize and left the stream. Spider knew how to wait and never made a gesture of impatience. He did not spit upon the bait or do any voodoo stunts or palaver about what he was going to do; he simply kept close watch to see that the bait was on and dragged it over the right ground knowing that the Dolly Vardens were there and would feed before long. His deliberation was like Bobby Jones making a putt on a golf green. I had fish enough for almost any sized table that noon but no Dolly Varden. That was Spider's prerogative. I saw the jerk and the gaff he made and saw the taut line moving the length of the rod and knew that the fish was on. Then Spider threw his fag away and rose to his feet, and with a swing of the hemlock shoot the fish was skidded onto a shelving rock. In an instant Spider had leaped that sixteen feet and landed upon the rock on top of the fish with his fingers in its gills, and then his feet slipped on the moss and slime and he and the Dolly Varden disappeared in the pool. When he came up, he had him by a grip that could never slip. He scrambled out and laid his fish in the brush, took his homely tackle apart, cached the hemlock shoot in its hiding place and calmly said, "Let's go so Mrs. Snyder can cook him for dinner". My fish were put in a cool place for the next day for this was "Dolly Varden" day. Mrs. Snyder stuffed that thirteen pound beauty with noodles and basted it up with twine, and after sticking strips of bacon, cloves and all sorts of condiments which she knew how to apply, on and around the fish, she put him in the oven. No better feast than that dinner with its slices of pink meated trout stuffed with the delicious dressing, was ever served to kings. Spider refused to take any, until all had been served in abundance, upon the ground that he could have them at any time. The mountaineers were courting patronage in a tactful way.

Shepard's nephew from Detroit, Michigan, had joined on for his first trip in the mountains and of course he was impressed by Avalanche Basin. He was a jolly fellow, and we two rented a 30-30 Savage rifle from someone and decided to carry it on alternate days and get some hunting, if it worked out that way. Naturally our opportunities came the day the other fellow had the rifle. We called him [the nephew] Louie and he was great fun for the guides and Lou, just as all tenderfeet are. I belonged to the guides lodge, and could laugh with them instead of being laughed at, as I had once been. Louie had a box of cigars which he was quite free with, and we all wondered just how long he would stick to them. Smoking and climbing do not mix for tenderfeet. It was about a mile back across the flats from our camp to Monument Falls on the rim wall, but at evening when the air was still and the waters were flush on account of the melting during the day, it seemed only a few steps away. Louie had his supper, lighted a cigar and guessed he would step back there and see those Falls. If it was anyone's duty to stop him—it was Shepard's, but he kept still.

In a very few minutes he came back all out of breath, with no cigar in his mouth, and sat down with the rest of us. He said the falls were beautiful, and that he never realized that such wonders existed, and praised everything and said that he was having a wonderful trip; but he shortly sought his bough bed.

Everyone smiled, but nothing was said that evening, but the next day when we were alone and I felt better acquainted with him, I asked him about the Falls. He saw the point and said, "I may as well come clean and tell you. I got out there a few rods in the brush and ran almost on top of a big bear feeding in the huckleberries and did I run back? That's was why I was puffing; I haven't seen those falls yet". He did not know that the bear was probably as startled as he was. We saw to it that he saw the falls towards evening when they were flush. He gave his cigars to the guides, and said that he guessed he would stop smoking for a while.

It was on that leg of the journey that we met an Indian riding a pony with some sort of a firearm under the side of his saddle, and a grouse hanging from its pommel. He was wearing moccasins and had a bright red bandana handkerchief around his head. The Doctor, who understood the Indian sign language, raised his hand and said, "How." The Indian replied in the purest of English, "Good afternoon, gentlemen. It is a beautiful day" and rode majestically on. That was some surprise, but as soon as the Indian was out of hearing, Lou told the Doctor "that man is Horace Clark, a graduate of Yale, who reads Latin and Greek, and speaks all the languages." His sister, at about that time, was Superintendent of Public Instruction for the State of Montana. Horace had a world of his own which was anywhere within a hundred miles of his home on the east side of the Range. He could be found anywhere, at any time. He lived wherever he might be, and was a self-sufficient man.

PART III

VISITORS

Glacier National Park has attracted casual visitors since the 1880s and '90s, the days of hunting expeditions on the east side and of the first hesitant tourists (such as Carrie and Robert Strahorn) arriving on the new railroad. Once the park was established, tourist facilities were soon developed, primarily through the influence of the Great Northern Railway and its president, Louis W. Hill. These early visitors were often writers, including Mary Roberts Rinehart, best known as the author of popular mystery novels but also an energetic traveler, explorer, and angler. Historian Agnes C. Laut also described the park in its early days, and Dorothy M. Johnson recalled visiting the park with a group of young women in the 1930s. Other writer-visitors made their mark as well, including the popular poet Vachel Lindsay (author of "The Congo"), whose backcountry exploits are well described later in this volume by his friend Stephen Graham. Lindsay came to the park and wrote a volume of poetry called *Going-to-the-Sun*, named after the prominent mountain above Upper St. Mary Lake. Lindsay also saw the Glacier landscape with the eyes of a poet-mystic in his later book of prose and poetry, *Going-to-the-Stars*. This poem, "The Bird Called 'Curiosity,'" is from *Going-to-the-Sun* (1923):

> Round the mountain peak called "Going-To-The-Sun,"
> In Glacier Park, a steep and soaring one,
> Circled a curious bird with pointed nose
> Who led us on to every cave, and rose

And swept through every cloud, then brought us berries,
And all the acid gifts the mountain carries,
And let us guess which ones were good to eat.
And even when we slept his sharp wings beat
The weary fire, or shook the tree-top cones,
Or rattled dead twigs like a fairy's bones.
The vulgar bird, "Curiosity"! When we
Were tired, and lean, and shaking at the knee,
We put this bird in harness. He was strong
As any ostrich, pulled our packs along,
Helped us up over the next annoying wall,
And dragged us to the chalet, and the tourists' resting hall.

And when once more we were young, well-fed men,
He beat the door to call us forth again.

12

FROM *FIFTEEN THOUSAND MILES BY STAGE*

Carrie Adele Strahorn

1911

About 1893, Carrie Adele Strahorn (1854–1925) came to Lake McDonald in the company of her husband, Robert E. Strahorn, whom she called "Pard." Robert was an employee of the Union Pacific Railroad, charged with finding resources and opportunities—and publicizing them—to benefit the railroad through increased passenger and freight traffic, land sales, and other commercial ventures. He published at least seven books on the "resources and attractions" of Idaho, Washington, Montana, Colorado, and Wyoming between 1877 and 1888. In defiance of approved practices for female behavior at that time, Carrie traveled with him. They wintered together in Omaha and explored the West in the summers.

Carrie was a keen observer and kept detailed journals. Even after the couple settled on the East Coast in the 1890s, she continued to work on revising her writings for publication. Finally, in 1911, G. P. Putnam's Sons published *Fifteen Thousand Miles by Stage: A Woman's Unique Experience during Thirty Years of Path Finding and Pioneering from the Missouri to the Pacific and from Alaska to Mexico*, with seventeen paintings and dozens of pen-and-ink illustrations by the great Western artist Charles M. Russell. Carrie, in fact, spent the summer of 1910 in a rented cabin on Lake McDonald, visiting Russell at his summer place and pressing him to complete the drawings.

When the Strahorns first arrived at the remote railroad stop of Belton (now West Glacier, near Lake McDonald) with their friend Horatio Kelsey, they found accommodations well below their expectations. They boarded with one of the first settlers in the area, Charley Howe, who had supposedly brought all his earthly belongings over Marias Pass in a handcart. A few days later, Robert went on to the wild railroad town of McCarthyville on the Middle Fork of the Flathead River and found it even worse than Lake McDonald.

Despite her racism and class superiority, all too common in that period, Carrie's curiosity and her humor—sometimes cutting and ironic, but often droll and delighted—enliven her description of Lake McDonald and the region, one of the first written accounts of the area by an outsider. She fished, climbed mountains, and boated the rivers, and she apparently maintained her inquisitive spirit and sense of humor throughout. She was also capable of parody, as her send-up of Victorian travel conventions demonstrates.

At that time, hunting and logging were still legal, as were homesteading and land sales. Four years after the Strahorns' first visit, a bridge was constructed over the Middle Fork of the Flathead River and the area was designated a forest reserve, with tourist facilities at both ends of the lake and a steamboat plying between.

CAMPING OUT—LAKE MCDONALD, ETC.

To roam the bosky woods at will
To fish beside the brook,
Will fill your soul with joy until
It comes your turn to cook.

There is no lovelier spot in all the West than Lake McDonald in western Montana, but it lay hidden in glacial shadows many years after the railway passed near it before any attempt was made to make the lake accessible.

We had been repeatedly misinformed about the route but would not give up without one more effort to get there. Officials of the Great Northern Railroad Company gave ample assurance of a stage line from Belton over to Lake McDonald where they also said there were good hotel accommodations.

Rolling away from the crowded city the cool breezes from the Mississippi, coupled with the quiet life of its borders, were soothing in effect, but it was not until spinning over the Rockies that we felt the desired change and could imagine the laughing eddies of every creek full of trout just waiting for the fly.

Belton was called only too soon and hours of reminiscence were blended into our new experiences. We were dropped off in time to see our baggage rolling down a steep embankment, and before we could get our breath the train was off like a flash, while every hope on earth seemed to fade as the rear car vanished in the distance. After all the assurances given us in St. Paul there was not even a platform and we slid down the grade with as little dignity as our baggage and with no chance to get aboard again before the train was off. Making inquiries for the stage office, etc., we were given the ha, ha. One man stared and grinned until Pard said he was demented. That stirred the grinning man's metal somewhat and he said, "No, stranger, I hain't no fool nor there hain't no stage to Lake McDonald and there hain't no road nuther."

Further urging developed the facts that it was half a mile to the river, no bridge over the river, and a poor trail full of fallen trees for two and a half miles "tother side of the river" to the lake.

Two men were finally found to take us across the Flathead River and show us the beginning of the trail. The craft was only a scooped-out log and five passengers greatly overloaded the dangerous pirogue. We were repeatedly cautioned not to make any movements to influence the canoe, and I fairly held my breath for fear we would not balance. But with all care possible there was a critical time when it seemed as if we would be rolled over into the swift turbulent whirlpools which resented our intrusion. Several attempts were made before a landing was secured and the dim trail pointed out. We watched our boatmen recross the river and wished we too were safely back on the other side, then resolutely turned our faces into the black heart of the dense forest.

At the first little opening where we could see God's smile in the blue sky through the treetops, we sat down on a log to express our feelings toward those Great Northern officials who had so grossly misrepresented conditions and led us into such a wilderness with night closing about us.

Horatio Kelsey, a Connecticut manufacturer of axe handles and suchlike useful implements, was so overcome by the magnitude of the trees that he lost sight of all discomforts in making estimates on how many handles a tree would make and the cash value of every tall sentinel. Pard and I were not interested in axe handles in general, but we wanted to swing an axe over the pay of at least one Great Northern official.

It was friend Kelsey's maiden trip to the great West and he accepted every adventure with all the exuberance of a boy with his first red topped boots. The merry twinkle in his eye told how he viewed the present dilemma, but had he lost his temper and growled over the situation I am sure we would have thrown him in the river.

To be in the open air and scent the sweet pine was a joy in itself and in spite of the hard trail a glad shout broke the silence when Lake McDonald lay before us in all its scenic opulence. For twelve miles it stretched its mobile length at the base of glacier-bearing mountains muffled on the lower slopes with dense green forests. The snow caps kissed the sky that spread its rosy blushes over the surface of the water, and the long shadows of the dying day were folding the peaceful nooks in the mysterious robes of night, while the moon hung low from a cloudless sky.

The "fine hotel" we were to find at the lake consisted of a log cabin about fifteen feet square, with parlor, bedrooms, dining-room, kitchen, and pantries all in one room. There was but one bedstead and that was home-made with boards a foot wide laid lengthwise six inches apart; over these boards were some deer skins but no springs, or mattress, or feather bed to disguise the hard side of the boards. A blooming red drapery hung from the ceiling around the bed and this private apartment was assigned to Pard and myself after I declined much urging to share it with the landlord's wife who was a native daughter of our continent.

Between the red curtains and cook stove was the bed of the host and hostess, with only a blanket between them and the floor, but their sleep was as sound and sonorous as if they had been in the most luxurious quarters. Close by on a large pile of deer skins was friend Kelsey. The whole cabin vibrated with every breath he drew, and when he expelled the air from his lungs it came with a "phew" as if he were blowing a fog horn, but at all events he was fortifying himself for whatever the morrow might bring. In the only remaining corner, on the floor, was a sturdy frontiersman, a regular boarder and lodger while building a cabin for himself in the nearby woods.

When the morning light broke through the column of busy mosquitoes that had been on duty the whole night, we gladly pulled our bodies out from between the boards and hastened into the bright warm sunshine on the lake shore.

But ye gods of the rod—what fishing! Hands trembling with joyous excitement knotted the lines and hooks most exasperatingly, but soon many colored flies were dancing on the ripples and scarcely would a fly touch the gleaming water ere it was seized by a hungry trout who started at once on its race for life. Its run was only equaled by the blood in the fisherman's veins. The whole world was forgotten and lost in the mad joy of the hour, and there was not a day in all the summer that followed so full of like excitement and rich success. A two- or three-pound trout can make more sport in a minute on the end of a good line fastened to a five-ounce rod than one can forget in a lifetime.

When our own camp equipment was brought in life was an ideal of nomadic bliss, and in spite of the discomforts and dangerous experiences of that first trip to Lake McDonald it became a favorite camping ground when there was a real bridge across the river and a stage running to the lake, about seventeen years after our first effort to reach the place.

One morning when everybody was soundly sleeping, Charley Howe, resident guide and our genial host as well, called out in an agonized whisper to "Get out o' the back side of the tent quicker 'n lightnin'; biggest elk in the mountains takin' water at the lake." Then he added most impatiently, "Oh! durn it, hurry up." He was so used to sleeping in his clothes that he had no patience to wait for a man to pull on his trousers.

He already had the tent pins pulled at the back of the tent and Pard rolled out with his rifle and a heart thumping with buck fever. "Oh, blast it! what are you waitin' for; shoot. Quick now," cried the guide and a true shot rang through the air, the buck plunged into a thicket, and a moment of dismay followed. The guide spoke assuringly and said: "Guess you've got 'im," and they followed hurriedly into the woods with apprehension dragging at Pard's heels. But the great elk had fallen stunned as he reached the thicket and taking the guide's trusty knife Pard hurried to put the poor beast out of misery. He had no sooner thrust the knife through the skin than he was turned in a complete summersault with the knife flying far away and the rifle out of reach. The unexpected onslaught was like a direful nightmare. The razor-like hoofs of the frenzied animal were already over him with his eyes like coals of fire glittering from his mad suffering. It seemed as if Howe was an eternity coming to the rescue— but his shot rang true and the animal fell in a limp mass upon poor Pard. The incident was almost a repetition of the experience in Yellowstone Park, but this time the animal required a second ball to bring him down.

The incident gave the men the hunting fever and nothing but bear, big black, cinnamon or grizzly, would do. They went direct to the wild haunts, some ten miles distant, of a famous grizzly who was the terror of prospectors, trappers, and campers in a wide region round about. They killed a deer the first afternoon, and after a big feast fixed up their lunches and equipment for a daylight start the following morning and turned in to sleep the sound sleep of the o'er tired and dream the dreams of conquerors. Some hours later they were aroused by the running and snorting of the stampeded ponies, and in the dim light of the expiring campfire were horrified to see Mr. Grizzly, of the proportions of an elephant, starting off with the only sack of flour. By the time they could reach their guns he had vanished, leaving only a white trail of the escaping flour, which they followed off into the black forest until it was obliterated by a snowstorm. Returning wet, tired, and disgusted, they found the ponies gone, with every ounce of food even to the lunches they had so carefully put up, and the remains of the deer and the syrup in the can licked up clean. There was nothing left to do but finish up bruin in their most eloquent literary style, shoulder their guns and camp equipage, and sneak sadly back to Lake McDonald afoot. Any one who wants a fight on short notice needs only to softly mention the incident in the presence of any of the participants.

Pard had to go outside for some needed supplies and he headed for the nearest place, which was McCarthyville, where he found a few straggling huts and tents that made up that hurrah town. He went to the most pretentious structure having a tavern sign and found the usual combination of barroom, dance hall, and kitchen on the ground floor. Lying on the end of the bar was the open register wherein he wrote his name and asked for a room. A very large, red-faced man informed him in a supercilious way that he had nothing left but the bridal chamber, which was spoken for, but if they didn't come mighty quick he would let the room go.

Assurances that he could get along with something less luxurious than the bridal chamber brought forth the frank suggestion that he "didn't look it." The proprietor further suggested that he "might as well have the best the country afforded." During this colloquy he [Pard] noticed a trio of very tough citizens taking special interest in his autograph, hearing one of them say in a disappointed way that "He is one of them there smart Alecks that don't purpose to let you know who he is." This was not the first time attention had been called to his peculiar chirography and he would have relished the joke exceedingly had he felt a little more at ease as to the tendencies of the critics.

Now McCarthyville was not as safe as a New England village; in fact it was noted all over the western half of the Union as being a trifle the roughest place on a Rocky Mountain rail route. A necessary adjunct to rapid railway construction, it sprung up in a night and disappeared with the same celerity. An army of railway graders, woodsmen, track layers, and railway operatives made it a supply point, which it remained while the Great Northern was being built. Toughs of every type congregated from all over the West to add terror to the settlement, and incidentally rob or kill, in order to secure their share of the wealth that the great work was putting into circulation. It had been a dull day when McCarthyville didn't afford a killing or a lynching, therefore it is gratifying to know that, in some cases at least, the right parties inhabit the lonely graveyard, which is now one of the most conspicuous and doleful reminders of those flush days.

Pard looked the town over somewhat nervously and returning asked mine host whether he was to have the bridal chamber. He answered cheerily, "Yes siree: they can't expect me to hold a room like that on an uncertainty. A dollar please. That's right; now go up-stairs to number 49 and make yourself to home. Can't miss it; first room to the right at the head of the stairs; you'll find light and everything all right; if you don't, jest ring."

Pard climbed up a narrow rickety stairway and found a long, low, dimly lighted room with canvas roof. Three rows of rough board bunks ranged the entire length of the room, each bunk having its number painted on the head-board in large figures, number 49, the "bridal chamber," not differing from the rest. It was grim, coarse, McCarthyville humor. The bunk had a thin straw pil-low, one blanket for a mattress, and one for a cover. The night was cold and frosty and Pard got in between the blankets without undressing.

A few others had already retired and were singing nasal melodies in var-ious keys and the notes swelled—until more than fifty were sleeping as best they could with the night revelry ringing in their ears. Pard was suddenly star-tled by something passing along over his body like a man's hand tugging at his blankets. He soon discovered it was the landlord leaning over him and trying to pull off the covering.

Anticipating robbery or something worse his revolver was wheeled like a wink into the man's face. Then came a muttered call not to shoot and the same voice added that it was so awful cold he must get a blanket from somebody and he shuffled down the aisle until he could strip some poor devil of his blanket, which he rolled himself in with a snore of content and grunted himself to sleep.

When Pard came back to camp he said if any one else had to go on a like errand he better grease himself so he could be sure of slipping out of McCar-thyville alive.

The climbing of the glacier mountains adjacent to Lake McDonald, and canoeing on the Flathead and Kootenai rivers, stopping in the primitive lit-tle towns of Columbia Falls and Kalispell, completed our explorations around Lake McDonald for that year.

When we were ready to leave Lake McDonald, Mr. Howe said that he and his man would take us by boat.

"What," I cried, "do you mean to take us in those little boats through those wild rapids down the outlet of this lake to the Flathead River then up to the station?"

"Oh, yes," he replied with aggravating coolness, "it's only 'bout four mile or so."

One may love adventure, ride the cow catcher of an engine, go in a bucket down a long tramway, or try snowshoes on a mountain trail, but to chance one's life like that seemed like daring fate, and there seemed a certainty of some one being a hero or perishing in the attempt before the day was over.

It would not do to show the white feather so early in the season and I made a grand effort to swallow the intruder in my throat, then called out merrily that it would be glorious sport. The echo fell upon my own ear like a minor chord but no one seemed to notice it and preparations were begun for the departure.

At the head of the outlet of the lake the boats were turned stern down and as the men wished to fish, a bag of rocks was dropped overboard and dragged at anchor to retard progress over the rapids. It was a bang on the bank, a dash on the rocks, shooting a rapid, plunging through cascades, a whirl under the willows, or a crush between logs, one after another in rapid succession, as we were buffeted like feathers on the angry waters. At last the boats shot into a quiet pool near the confluence of the two streams and there was one that said "Amen" though the trip was but half over.

While making a cast of the flies from along the shore in these seductive waters the gentlemen became separated and a fearful tragedy was narrowly averted. Fred James, of Chicago, in frantic endeavors to land two big trout at the same time slipped on the smooth spray-covered boulders, turning completely around in his fall, and was found by Pard, just in the nick of time, lying helplessly on his back, his portly form wedged tightly between two rocks, with head and shoulders downward in the icy current.

The boatman surprised us by saying the gentlemen would have to walk the rest of the way but he and his assistant could take the boat with baggage and "the woman" all right. It was easy to see the relief and pleasure it was for the gentlemen to be out on their feet and their encouraging remarks to me from the forks of the river would have made a good sized book. We were soon in the whirlpools. With a real giant in strength and nerve standing in each end of the boat to pole the craft, we slipped into the middle of the stream, then darted here and there to find the smoother currents; but as the banks came nearer together the waters grew more turbulent and progress could only be made by madly rushing into the fiercest of the cataracts. Ever and anon one or the other of the men was above his waist in the water; they would leap out to lighten quickly one end or the other of the boat that it might rise over some huge rock. At times the boat and its load would be drenched as it dipped and rolled and was tossed about as a child would toss a ball.

It was no child's play, however, to take a boat safely through such rapids and, in spite of the boatmen saying they were used to it and rather liked it, it was with a glad heart that I stepped on land in full sympathy with the Bostonian who returned from an ocean trip and said that he would forevermore stay on "terra cotta." But right here let me say that if any reader wishes to enjoy to the limit boating and fishing on one of the finest mountain streams in the world let him entrust himself to the safe guidance of Charley Howe on Flathead River.

The point on the railroad was only a switching station, but as the men were drenched through they felt the need of a fire to dry their clothing before proceeding further. The man in charge of the section house said he had a stove but had just received a telegram to have the stove ready to be taken up by No. 9 when it came along and he expected it every minute. "Of course," he humorously added, "if you build a fire in it, you are five to one and I can't help myself."

The suggestion was quickly followed. In a wondrously few minutes the stove was flaming red and when No. 9 blew its long whistle the boys chucked in more wood and kept it blazing. The conductor of No. 9 came in with a mouth full of bad words and demanded the stove. They told him to take it right along; there it was and no one was going to hold it. The men were dodging about the room less than half clad, turning one article and another in the drying process, and having such sport in their efforts that the conductor of No. 9 went out with a growl equal to an old grizzly but not half as dangerous, and only the grumbling wheels of the freight train smothered his mutterings as it went on its way without the stove.

13

FROM *THROUGH GLACIER PARK*

Seeing America First with Howard Eaton

Mary Roberts Rinehart
1916

Between 1906 and 1940, Mary Roberts Rinehart (1876–1958) was one of the most popular writers in the United States. She was especially known for her murder mysteries and has been called "the American Agatha Christie," though her work actually precedes Christie's by well over a decade. Rinehart authored dozens of novels and short stories, many of which appeared in popular magazines of the day. She was also a war correspondent during World War I and an outdoor enthusiast who loved camping and fishing. In 1915, she joined a horseback trip in Glacier organized by Howard Eaton, proprietor of the most famous dude ranch in the country. The forty-two "dudes" spent about three weeks in Glacier and rode from East Glacier over a series of trails to Many Glacier, then over Gunsight Pass to Lake McDonald. This chapter includes an excerpt from her account of that trip, *Through Glacier Park*.

FALL IN

It was rather a picturesque party. Those who had gone up from the Eaton ranch in Wyoming—a trifle of seven hundred miles—wore their riding-clothes to save luggage. Khaki was the rule, the women mostly in breeches and long coats, with high-laced shoes reaching to the knee and soft felt hats, the men in riding-clothes, with sombreros and brilliant bandannas knotted about their throats. One or two had rather overdone the part and were the objects of good-natured chaffing later on by the guides and cowboys.

Not very long before, I had been to the front in Belgium and in France. I confess that no excursion to the trenches gave me a greater thrill than the one that accompanied that start the next morning from the Glacier Park Hotel to cross the Continental Divide. For we were going to cross the Rockies. Our route was three hundred miles long. It was over six passes, and if you believe, as I did, that a pass is a valley between two mountains, I am here to set you right.

A pass is a bloodcurdling spot up which one's horse climbs like a goat and down the other side of which it slides as you lead it, trampling ever and anon on a tender part of your foot. A pass is the highest place between two peaks. A pass is not an opening, but a barrier which you climb with chills and descend with prayer. A pass is a thing which you try to forget at the time and which you boast about when you get back home. For I have made it clear, I think, that a horseback trip through Glacier Park, across the Rockies, and down the Pacific Slope, is a sporting proposition. It is safe enough. Howard Eaton has never had an accident. But there are times…

Off, then, to cross the Rocky Mountains—forty-two of us, and two wagons which had started early to go by road to the first camp: cowboys in chaps and jingling spurs; timorous women, who eyed rather askance the blue and purple mountains back of the hotel; automobile tourists, partly curious and partly envious; the inevitable photographer, for whom we lined up in a semicircle, each one trying to look as if starting off on such a trip was one of the easiest things we did; and over all the bright sun, a breeze from the mountains, and a sense of such exhilaration as only altitude and the West can bring.

Then a signal to fall in. For a mile or two we went two abreast, past a village of Indian tepees, past meadows scarlet with the Indian paintbrush, past—with condescension—automobile busses loaded with tourists who craned and watched. Then to the left, and off the road. The cowboys and guides were watching us. As we strung out along the trail, they rode back and forward, inspecting saddles, examining stirrups, seeing that all were comfortable and safe. For even that first day we were to cross Mount Henry, and there must be no danger of saddle slipping.

Quite without warning we plunged into a rocky defile, with a small river falling in cascades. The shadow of the mountain enveloped us. The horses forded the stream and moved sedately on.

Did you ever ford a mountain stream on horseback? Do it. Ride out of the hot sun into a brawling valley. Watch your horse as he feels his way across, the stream eddying about his legs. Give him his head and let him drink lightly, skimming the very surface of the water with his delicate nostrils. Lean down and fill your own cup. How cold it is, and how clear! Uncontaminated it flows down from the snow-covered mountains overhead. It is living.

THE SPORTING CHANCE

The trail began to rise to the tree-covered "bench." It twisted as it rose. Those above called cheerfully to those below. We had settled to the sedate walk of our horses, the pace which was to take us over our long itinerary. Hardly ever was it possible, during the days that followed, to go faster than a walk. The narrow, twisting trails forbade it. Now and then a few adventurous spirits, sighting a meadow, would hold back until the others had got well ahead, and then push their horses to the easy Western lope. But such joyous occasions were rare.

Up and up. The trail was safe, the grade easy. At the edge of the bench we turned and looked back. The great hotel lay below in the sunlight. Leading to it were the gleaming rails of the Great Northern Railway. We turned our horses and went on toward the snow-covered peaks ahead.

The horses moved quietly, one behind the other. As the trail rose there were occasional stops to rest them. Women who had hardly dared to look out of a third-story window found themselves on a bit of rocky shelf, with the tops of the tallest trees far below. The earth, as we had known it, was falling back. And, high overhead, Howard Eaton, at the head of the procession, was sitting on his big horse silhouetted against the sky.

The first day was to be an easy one—twelve miles and camp. "Twelve miles!" said the experienced riders. "Hardly a Sunday morning canter!" But a mountain mile is a real mile. Possibly they measure from peak to peak. I do not know. I do know that we were almost six hours making that twelve miles and that for four of it we led our horses down a mountain-side over a vacillating path of shale. Knees, that up to that point had been fairly serviceable, took to chattering. Riding-boots ceased to be a matter of pride and emerged skinned and broken. The horses slid and stumbled. And luncheon receded.

Down and down! Great granite cliffs of red and blue and yellow across the valley—and no luncheon! Striped squirrels hiding in the shale—and no luncheon! A great glow of moving blood through long-stagnant vessels, deep breaths of clear mountain air, a camera dropped on the trail, a stone in a horse's foot—and no luncheon!

Two o'clock, and we were down. The nervous woman who had never been on a horse before was cinching her own saddle and looking back and up. The saddle tightened, she sat down and emptied her riding-boots of a few pieces of rock. Her silk stockings were in tatters.

"I feel as though my knees will never meet again," she said reflectively. "But I'm so swollen with pride and joy that I could shriek."

That's what it is, partly. A sense of achievement; of conquering the unconquerable; of pitting human wits against giants and winning—a sporting chance. You may climb peaks in a railroad coach and see things as wonderful. But you are doing this thing yourself. Every mile is an achievement. And, after all, it is miraculously easy. The trails are good. The horses are steady and sure-footed. It is a triumph of endurance rather than of courage.

If you have got this far, you are one of us, and you will go on. For the lure of the high places is in your blood. The call of the mountains is a real call. The veneer, after all, is so thin. Throw off the impedimenta of civilization, the telephones, the silly conventions, the lies that pass for truth. Go out to the West. Ride slowly, not to startle the wild things. Throw out your chest and breathe; look across green valleys to wild peaks where mountain sheep stand impassive on the edge of space. Let the summer rains fall on your upturned face and wash away the memory of all that is false and petty and cruel. Then the mountains will get you. You will go back. The call is a real call.

Above the timber-line we rode along bare granite slopes. Erosion had been busy here. The mighty winds that sweep the crests of the Rockies had bared the mountains' breasts. Beside the trails high cairns of stones were piled, so that during the winter snow the rangers might find their way about. Remember, this is northwestern Montana; the Canadian border is only a few miles away, and over these peaks sweeps the full force of the great blizzards of the Northwest.

The rangers keep going all winter. There is much to be done. In the summer it is forest fires and outlaws. In the winter there are no forest fires, but there are poachers after mountain sheep and goats, opium smugglers, bad men from over the Canadian border. Now and then a ranger freezes to death. All summer these intrepid men on their sturdy horses go about armed with revolvers. But in the fall—snow begins early in September, sometimes even in August—they take to snowshoes. With a carbine strung to his shoulders, matches in a waterproof case, snowshoes and a package of food in his pocket, the Glacier Park ranger covers unnumbered miles, patrolling the wildest and most storm-ridden country in America. He travels alone. The imprint of a strange snow-shoe on the trail rouses his suspicion. Single-handed he follows the marks in the snow. A blizzard comes. He makes a wikiup of branches, lights a small fire, and plays solitaire until the weather clears. The prey he is stalking cannot advance either. Then one day the snow ceases; the sun comes out. Over the frozen crust his snowshoes slide down great slopes with express speed. Generally he takes his man in. Sometimes the outlaw gets the drop on the ranger first and gets away.

During the winter of 1913 one of these rangers was frozen to death. He was caught in a blizzard, and he knew what was coming. When at last he sat down beside the trail to wait for death he placed his snowshoes points upward in the snow beside him. He sat there, and the snow came down and covered him. They found him the next day by the points of his snowshoes.

The snow melts in the summer on the meadows and in the groves. But the peaks are still covered, and here and there the trail leads through a snow-field. The horses venture out on it gingerly. The hot sun that blisters the face seems to make no impression on these glacier-like patches, snow on top and ice beneath. Flowers grow at their very borders. Striped squirrels and whis-tling marmots, much like Eastern woodchucks, run about, quite fearless, or sit up and watch the passing of the line of horses and riders, so close that they can almost be touched.

Great spaces; cool, shadowy depths in which lie blue lakes; mountain-sides threaded with white, where, from some hidden lake or glacier far above, the overflow falls a thousand feet or more; and over all the great silence of the Rockies! Nerves that have been tightened for years slowly relax. There is not much talking. The horses move along slowly. The sun beats down. Some one, shading his eyes with his hand, proclaims a mountain sheep or goat on a crag overhead. The word passes back along the line. Also a thrill. Then some wretched electrical engineer or college youth or skeptical lawyer produces a pair of field-glasses and announces it to be a patch of snow.

Here and there we saw "tourist goats," rocks so shaped and situated as to defy the strongest glass. The guides pointed them out and listened with silent enjoyment to the resulting acclamation. After that discovery, we adopted a safe rule: nothing was a goat that did not move. Long hours we spent while our horses wandered on with loose reins, our heads lifted to that line, just above the timber, which is Goatland. And the cry "A goat!" and the glasses, and skep-ticism—often undeserved.

The first night out of doors I did not sleep. I had not counted on the frosty nights, and I was cold. The next day I secured from a more provident member of the party woolen pajamas. Clad in those, and covered with all the extra por-tions of my wardrobe, I was more comfortable. But it takes woolen clothing and bed socks to keep out the chill of those mountain nights.

One rises early with Howard Eaton's party. No matter how late the story-tellers have held the crowd the night before around the camp-fire, somewhere about five o'clock, Howard—he is either Howard or Uncle Howard to every-body—comes calling among the silent tepees.

"Time to get up!" he calls. "Five o'clock and a fine morning. Up with you!"

And everybody gets up. There are basins about. Each one clutches his cake of soap and his towel, and fills his basin from whatever lake or stream is at hand. There is plenty of water in Glacier Park, and the camps are generally beside a lake. The water is cold. It ought to be, being glacier water, cold and blue. The air is none too warm. A few brave spirits seek isolation and a plunge bath. The majority are cowards.

Now and then a luxurious soul worried the cook for hot water. They tell of a fastidious lady who carried a small tin pail of water to the cook tent and addressed the cook nervously as he beat the morning flapjacks with a savage hand.

"Do you think," she inquired nervously, "if—if I put this water on your stove, it will heat?"

He turned and eyed her.

"You see it's like this, lady," he said. "My father was a poor man and could n't give me no education. Damned if I know. What do you think?"

Before one is fairly dressed, with extra garments thrust into the canvas war-sack or duffle-bag which is each person's allowance for luggage, the tents are being taken down and folded. The cook comes to the end of the big tent.

"Come and get it!" he yells through hollowed hands.

"Come and get it!" is repeated down the line of tepees. That is the food call of an Eaton camp. Believe me, it has the butler's "Dinner is served, madame," beaten forty ways for Sunday. There is no second call. You go or you don't go. The long tables under the open end of the cook tent are laden with bacon, ham, fried eggs, flapjacks, round tins of butter, enameled cups of hot coffee, condensed milk, sometimes fried fish. For the cook can catch trout where the most elaborately outfitted Eastern angler fails.

The horses come in with a thudding of hoofs and are rounded up by the men into the rope corral. Watched by night herders, they have been grazing quietly all night in mountain valleys. There is not much grass for them. By the end of the three hundred-mile trip they are a little thin, although in good condition. It is the hope of the Superintendent of the Park and of others interested that the Government will soon realize the necessity for planting some of the fertile valleys and meadows with grass. There are certain grasses that will naturalize themselves there—for instance, clover, blue-joint, and timothy. Beyond the first planting they would need nothing further. And, since much of the beauty of this park will always be inaccessible by motor, it can never be properly opened up until horses can get sufficient grazing.

Sometimes, at night, our horses ranged far for food—eight miles,—even more. Again and again I have watched my own horse nosing carefully along a green bank and finding nothing at all, not a blade of grass it could eat.

With the second day came a new sense of physical well-being, and this in spite of a sunburn that had swollen my face like a toothache. Already telephones and invitations to dinner and tailor's fittings and face powder belonged to the forgotten past. I carried over my saddle and placed it beside my horse, and a kindly and patronizing member of Howard Eaton's staff put it on and cinched it for me. I never learned how to put the thing on, but I did learn, after a day or two, to take it off, as well as the bridle and the red hackamore, and then to stand clear while my buckskin pony lay down and rolled in the grass to ease his weary back. All the horses rolled, stiff-legged. If the saddle did not come off in time, they rolled anyhow, much to the detriment of cameras, field-glasses, and various impedimenta strapped thereon.

ALL IN THE GAME

Day after day we progressed. There were bright days and days when we rode through a steady mist of rain. Always it was worth while. What matters a little rain when there is a yellow slicker to put on and no one to care how one looks? Once, riding down a mountain-side, water pouring over the rim of my old felt hat and pattering merrily on my slicker, I looked to one side to see a great grizzly raise himself from behind a tree-trunk, and, standing upright, watch impassively as my horse and I proceeded. I watched him as far as I could see him. We were mutually interested. The party had gone on ahead. For a long time afterward I heard the crackling of small twigs in the heavy woods beside the trail. But I never saw him again.

It is strange to remember how little animal life, after all, there seemed to be. There was plenty, of course. But our party was large. We had no chance to creep up silently on the wild life of the park. The vegetation was so luxuriant in the valleys. Beyond an occasional bear, once or twice the screaming of a mountain lion, and the gophers and marmots, we saw nothing. There were not many birds. We never saw a snake. It was too high.

There was one young woman in the party to whom things were always happening—not by her own fault. If there was a platter of meat to be dropped, it fell in her lap. And so I remember that one day, the coffee having been made at a luncheon stop, the handle came off the coffee-pot and this same young woman had an uncomfortable baptism.

But it was all in the game. Hot coffee, marmalade, bread and butter, cheese, sardines, and the best ham in the world—that was luncheon. Often there was a waterfall near, where for the mere holding out of a cup there was ice water to drink. The horses were not unsaddled at these noonday stops, but, having climbed hard all morning, they were glad to stand in the shade and rest.

Sometimes we lunched on a ledge where all the kingdoms of the earth seemed spread out before us. We sprawled on rocks, on green banks, and relaxed muscles that were weary with much climbing. There was much talk of a desultory sort. We settled many problems, but without rancor. The war was far away. Here were peace and a great contentment, food and a grassy bank, and overhead the trail called us to new vistas, new effort.

There were days when we reached our camping-places by mid-afternoon. Then the anglers got their rods and started out for trout. There were baths to be taken in sunny pools that looked warm and were icy cold. There were rents in riding-clothes to be mended; even—whisper it—a little laundry work to be done now and then by women, some of them accustomed to the ministrations of a lady's maid at home. And there was supper and the camp-fire. Charley Russell, the cowboy artist, was the campfire star. To repeat one of his stories would be desecration. No one but Charley Russell himself, speaking through his nose, with his magnificent head outlined against the firelight, will ever be able to tell one of his stories.

There were other good story-tellers in the party. And Howard Eaton himself could match them all. A hundred miles from a railroad, we gathered around that campfire in the evening in a great circle. There were, you will remember, forty-two of us—no mean gathering. The pine and balsam crackled and burned, and overhead, often rising in straight walls around us for thousands of feet, were the snow-capped peaks of the Continental Divide. Little by little the circle would grow smaller until at last only a dozen choice spirits remained for a midnight debauch of anecdote.

I have said that the horses ranged wide at night. Occasionally they stayed about the camp. There was one big horse that was belled at night. Now and then toward dawn he brought his ungainly body, his tinkling bell, and his satellites, the other horses, into the quiet streets of tepee town. More than once

I have seen an irate female, clad in pajamas and slippers, with flying braids, shooing the horses away from her tent in the gray, cold dawn, and flinging after them things for which she vainly searched the next morning.

RUNNING WATER AND STILL POOLS

I had taken West with me a fly book and a trout rod, and I meant to use them. Now and then, riding along the trail, we met people who drew aside to let us pass, and who held up such trout as I had never dreamed of. Or, standing below a waterfall, would be a silent fisherman too engrossed to more than glance at our procession as it wound along.

But repeated early attempts brought me not a single strike. Once in my ardor I fell into an extremely cold lake and had to be dried out for hours. I grew caustic about the trout. Then somebody, with the interests of the park at stake, said that he would make up a party and see that I caught some trout. He would see that I caught something, he said, if he had to crawl into the lake and bite my hook himself.

So we went to Red Eagle Lake. There are trout in that lake; there are cut-throat trout weighing four pounds. I sat in a boat with a man who drew one in. I saw two college boys in their undergarments standing up to the waist in ice water and getting more large trout than I knew were in the world. I ate trout that other people caught. But they were bitter in my mouth.

I threatened to write up Glacier Park as being a fishing failure. The result was calamitous. Earnest-eyed fishermen spent hours in rowing me about. They imperiled my life, taking me into riffles; they made me brave pneumonia and influenza and divers other troubles in the determination that I should catch a mammoth fish. And nothing happened—nothing whatever. Once a man in the boat hooked a big one and it ran under the boat. I caught the line and jerked the fish into the boat. That was the nearest I came to catching a large cutthroat trout at Red Eagle Lake. Later on—but I haven't come to that yet.

I lay that night at Red Eagle in a tent on a bed built of young trees driven into the ground and filled with balsam branches. A pack-horse had carried up the blankets and pillows. It was a couch for a queen. In the forest a mountain lion screamed like a woman, and at two o'clock in the morning one of the college boys got up from the cook tent where he was sleeping, and said he thought he would go fishing!

As I look back, that was a strange gathering at the fishing-camp at Red Eagle—so very far from anything approaching civilization. There was a moving-picture man and his outfit, there were the two college men, there was the chief ranger of Glacier Park. There was a young couple from New England who were tramping through the park, carrying their tent and other things on their backs. They were very young and very enthusiastic. I suspected them of being bride and groom, although I did not know, and the most vivid recollection I have is of seeing the young woman washing their camp-dishes in the cleanest, soapiest dishwater I had seen since I left home. And there was a cook who is a business man in the winter, and who made excellent soda biscuits and talked books to me.

That night, around the camp-fire, there were more stories told. The college boys—"Pie" Way, the Yale pitcher, was one—related many marvelous tales. They said they were true. I hope so. If they were, life is even more interesting and thrilling a thing than I had believed. If they were fiction, they had me beaten at my own game.

The next day was lowering and cold. I spent the morning trying to get fish, and retired sour and disappointed when every one else succeeded and I failed. Sometime I am going back to Red Eagle Lake, and I shall take with me a tin of coral-colored salmon eggs—a trick I learned from George Locke on the Flathead River later on. And then I intend to have my photograph taken with strings of fish like bunches of bananas around me.

THE CALL

As the days went on there was a subtle change in the party. Women, who had to be helped into their saddles at the beginning of the trip, swung into them easily. Waistbands were looser, eyes were clearer; we were tanned; we were calm with the large calmness of the great outdoors. And with each succeeding day the feeling of achievement grew. We were doing things and doing them without effort. To some of us the mountains had made their ancient appeal. Never again should we be clear of their call.

To those of us who felt all this inevitably in the future would come times when cities and even civilization itself would cramp.

I have traveled a great deal. The Alps have never held this lure for me. Perhaps it is because these great mountains are my own, in my own country. Cities call—I have heard them. But there is no voice in all the world so insistent to me as the wordless call of the Rockies. I shall go back. Those who go once always hope to go back. The lure of the great free spaces is in their blood.

We crossed many passes. Dawson Pass was the first difficult Rocky

Mountain pass I had ever seen. There was a time when I had thought that a mountain pass was a depression. It is not. A mountain pass is a place where the impossible becomes barely possible. It is a place where wild game has, after much striving, discovered that it may get from one mountain valley to another. Along these game trails men have built new paths. Again and again we rode through long green valleys, the trail slowly rising until it had left timber far below. Then at last we confronted a great rock wall, a seemingly impassable barrier. Up this, by infinite windings, back and forward went the trail. At the top was the pass.

"I'm getting right tired," said Charley Russell, "of standing in a cloud up to my waist."

Each new pass brought a new vista of blue distance, of white peaks. Each presented its own problems of ascent or descent. No two were alike. Mountain-climbing is like marriage. Whatever else it may be, it is always interesting.

There was the day we went over the Cutbank Pass, with instructions to hold our horses' manes so that our saddles would not slip back. I shall never forget my joy at reaching the summit amid the horror that followed when I found I was on a rocky wall about twenty feet wide which dropped a half-mile straight down on the other side to a perfectly good blue lake.

Triple Divide. The trail had just been completed, and ours was the first party after the trail-makers. I had expected to be the first woman on the top of Triple Divide, but when I arrived, panting and breathless and full of the exaltation of the moment, two girls were already there sitting on a rock. I shall not soon recover from the indignant surprise of that moment. Perhaps they never knew that they had taken the laurel wreath from my brow.

Triple Divide is really the culminating point of the continent. It is called Triple Divide because water flows from it into the Gulf of Mexico, into the Pacific Ocean, and into Hudson Bay.

There was the day when, on our way to Gunsight, we rode for hours along a trail that heavy rains had turned into black swamp. The horses struggled, constantly mired. It was the hardest day of the trip, not because of the distance, which was only thirty-five miles, but on account of the constant rocking in the saddle as our horses wallowed out of one "jack pot" into another—jack pots, I presume, because they are easy to get into and hard to get out of!

There was some grunting when at the end of that day we fell out of our saddles, but no complaining. That night, for the first time, the Eaton party slept under a roof at the Gunsight Chalet, on the shores of a blue lake. The Blackfoot

Glacier was almost overhead. It was the end of a hot July, but we gathered around a fire that evening, and crawled in under heavy blankets to the quick sleep of fatigue.

One more pass, and we should be across the Rockies and moving down the Pacific Slope. The moon came up that night and shone on the ice-caps of the mountains all around us, on the glacier, on the Gunsight itself, appropriately if not beautifully named. As far up the mountain-side as the glacier our tired horses ranged for grass, and the tiny fire of the herder made a red glow that disappeared as the night mist closed down.

No "Come and get it" the next morning, but a good breakfast, nevertheless: a frosty morning, with the sun out, and the moving-picture man gone ahead to catch us as we climbed. There was another photographer who had joined the party. He had been up at dawn, on the chance of snapping a goat or two.

As we began the last descent, the party grew silent. It was the last leg of the journey. A day or so more and we should be scattered over the continent on whose spine we were so incontinently tramping. Back to civilization, to porcelain bathtubs and course dinners and facial massage, to stays and skirts, to roofs and servants and the vast impedimenta of living.

Sperry Chalet and luncheon. No more the ham and coffee over a wood fire, the cutting of much bread on a flat stone. Here were tables, chairs, and linen. Alas, there was a waitress who crumbed the table and brought in dessert.

Back, indeed, with a vengeance. But only to the ways of civilization itself. All afternoon we went on, descending always, through the outriders of the forest to the forest itself. Dusk came, dusk in the woods, with strange soft paddings of unseen feet, with a gray light half-religious, half-faëry, that only those who penetrate to the hearts of great forests can know.

"It makes me think of death," someone said in a low tone. "Just a great shadow, no color. Nothing real. And silence, and infinite distance."

Then Lake Macdonald. We burst out of the forest on a run. The horses had known, by the queer instinct of horses, that just ahead would be oats and a corral and grass for the eating. They broke into a canter. The various things we had hung to ourselves during the long, slow progress over the mountain rattled and banged. We hung on in a kind of mad exultation. We had done it. We had crossed the Continental Divide, the Lewis Overthrust, whatever geographers choose to call it.

The trail led past a corral, past a vegetable garden such as our Eastern eyes had seldom seen. Under trees, around a corner at a gallop. Then the Glacier Hotel at Lake Macdonald, generally known as "Lewis's."

Soft winds from the Pacific blew across Lake Macdonald and warmed us. Great strawberries were ripening in the garden. Our horses got oats, all they could eat. In a pool in front of the hotel lazy trout drifted about.

There was good food. Again there were people dressed in civilized raiment, people who looked at us and our shabby riding-clothes with a disdain not unmixed with awe. There was fox-trotting and one-stepping, in riding-boots, with an orchestra.

There is little of the old West left. Irrigation, wheat, the cutting-up of the Indian reservations into allotments, the homesteader, all spell the end of the most picturesque period of America's development.

Not for long, then, the cow-puncher in his gorgeous chaps, the pack-train winding its devious way along the trail. The boosting spirit has struck the West. Settlements of one street and thirteen houses, eleven of them saloons, are suddenly becoming cities. The railroads and the automobiles, by obliterating time, have done away with distance. The old West is almost gone. Now is the time to see it—not from a train window; not, if you can help it, from an automobile, but afoot or on horseback, leisurely, thoroughly.

14

FROM *TENTING TONIGHT*

A Chronicle of Sport and Adventure in Glacier Park and the Cascade Mountains

Mary Roberts Rinehart

1918

In 1916, Rinehart returned to Glacier with her husband ("the Head") and their three teenaged sons, whom she calls "Big Boy," "Middle Boy," and "Little Boy." They were accompanied by a motion picture photographer, a still photographer, and a mysterious man called "Bob," who seemed to be a sort of director/producer of the expedition. This time, with hired guides, they explored the North Fork region of Glacier and, after arduous trail clearing, managed to get a wagon with two wooden boats on board to a put-in point on the North Fork of the Flathead River near the Canadian border. There they began what may have been the firstever descent of the North Fork by boat. Rinehart's chronicle of their adventures, *Tenting Tonight*, was published by Houghton Mifflin in 1918.

THE BIG ADVENTURE

Getting a pack-outfit ready for a long trip into the wilderness is a serious matter. We were taking thirty-one horses, guides, packers, and a cook. But we were doing more than that—we were taking two boats! This was Bob's idea. Any highly original idea, such as taking boats where not even tourists had gone before, or putting eggs on a bucking horse, or carrying grapefruit for breakfast into the wilderness, was Bob's idea.

"You see, I figure it out like this," he said, when, on our arrival at Belton, we found the boats among our equipment: "If we can get those boats up to the Canadian line and come down the Flathead rapids all the way, it will only take about four days on the river. It's a stunt that's never been pulled off."

"Do you mean," I said, "that we are going to run four days of rapids that have never been run?"

"That's it."

I looked around. There, in a group, were the Head and the Big Boy and the

Middle Boy and the Little Boy. And a fortune-teller at Atlantic City had told me to beware of water!

"At the worst places," the Optimist continued, "we can send Joe ahead, in one boat with the 'movie' outfit, and get you as you come along."

"I dare say," I observed, with some bitterness. "Of course we may upset. But if we do, I'll try to go down for the third time in front of the camera."

But even then the boats were being hoisted into a wagon-bed filled with hay. And I knew that I was going to run four days of rapids. It was written.

It was a bright morning. In a corral, the horses were waiting to be packed. Rolls of blankets, crates of food, and camping-utensils lay everywhere. The Big Boy marshaled the fishing-tackle. Bill, the cook, was searching the town for the top of an old stove to bake on. We had provided two reflector ovens, but he regarded them with suspicion. They would, he suspected, not do justice to his specialty, the corn-meal saddle-bag, a sort of sublimated hot cake.

I strolled to the corral and cast a horsewoman's eye on my mount.

"He looks like a very nice horse," I said. "He's quite handsome."

Pete tightened up the cinch.

"Yes," he observed; "he's all right. He's a pretty good mare."

The Head was wandering around with lists in his hand. His conversation ran something like this:—

"Pocket-flashes, chocolate, jam, medicine-case, reels, landing-nets, cigarettes, tooth-powder, slickers, matches."

He was always accumulating matches. One moment, a box of matches would be in plain sight and the next it had disappeared. He became a sort of match-magazine, so that if anybody had struck him violently, in almost any spot, he would have exploded.

Hours went by. The sun was getting high and hot. The crowd which had been watching gradually disappeared about its business. The two boats—big, sturdy river-boats they were—had rumbled along toward the wilderness, one on top of the other, with George Locke and Mike Shannon as pilots, watching for breakers ahead. In the corral, our supplies were being packed on the horses, Bill Shea and Pete, Tom Sullivan and Tom Farmer and their assistants working against time. In crates were our cooking-utensils, ham, bacon, canned salmon, jam, flour, corn-meal, eggs, baking-powder, flies, rods, and reels, reflector ovens, sunburn lotion, coffee, cocoa, and so on. Cocoa is the cowboy's friend. Innumerable blankets, "tarp" beds, and war-sacks lay rolled ready for the pack-saddles. The cook was declaiming loudly that some one had opened his pack and taken out his cleaver.

What did we wear, that bright morning when, all ready at last, the cook on the chuck-wagon, the boats ambling ahead, with Bill Hossick, the teamster, driving the long line of heavily packed horses and our own saddlers lined up for the adventure, we moved out on to the trail?

Well, the men wore khaki riding-trousers and flannel shirts, broad-brimmed felt hats, army socks drawn up over the cuff of the breeches, and pack-shoes. A pack-shoe is one in which the leather of the upper part makes the sole also, without a seam. On to this soft sole is sewed a heavy leather one. The pack-shoe has a fastened tongue and is waterproof.

And I? I had not counted on the "movie"-man, and I was dressed for comfort in the woods. I had buckskin riding-breeches and high boots, and over my thin riding-shirt I wore a cloth coat. I had packed in my war-bag a divided skirt also, and a linen suit, for hot days, of breeches and coat. But of this latter the least said the better. It betrayed me and, in portions, deserted me.

All of us carried tin drinking-cups, which vied with the bells on the pack-animals for jingle. Most of us had sweaters or leather wind-jammers. The guides wore "chaps" of many colors, boots with high heels, which put our practical packs in the shade, and gay silk handkerchiefs.

On the east side of the Park I had ridden Highball. It is not particularly significant that I started the summer on Highball and ended it on Budweiser. Now I had Angel, a huge white mare with a pink nose, a loving disposition, and a gait that kept me swallowing my tongue for fear I would bite the end off it. The Little Boy had Prince, a small pony which ran exactly like an Airedale dog, and in every canter beat out the entire string. The Head had H—, and considered him well indicated. One bronco was called "Bronchitis." The top horse of the string was Bill Shea's Dynamite, according to Bill Shea. There were Dusty, Shorty, Sally Goodwin, Buffalo Tom, Chalk-Eye, Comet, and Swapping Tater— Swapping Tater being a pacer who, when he hit the ground, swapped feet. Bob had Sister Sarah.

At last, everything was ready. The pack-train got slowly under way. We leaped into our saddles—"leaped" being a figurative term which grew more and more figurative as time went on and we grew saddle-weary and stiff—and, passing the pack-train on a canter, led off for the wilderness.

All that first day we rode, now in the sun, now in deep forest. Luncheon-time came, but the pack-train was far behind. We waited, but we could not hear so much as the tinkle of its bells. So we munched cakes of chocolate from the pockets of our riding-coats and went grimly on.

The wagon with the boats had made good time. It was several miles along the wagon-trail before we caught up with it. It had found a quiet harbor beside the road, and the boatmen were demanding food. We tossed them what was left of the chocolate and went on.

The presence of a wagon-trail in that empty land, unvisited and unknown, requires explanation. In the first place, it was not really a road. It was a trail, and in places barely that. But, sixteen years before, a road had been cleared through the forest by some people who believed there was oil near the Canadian line. They cut down trees and built corduroy bridges. But in sixteen years it has not been used. No wheels have worn it smooth. It takes its leisurely way, now through wilderness, now through burnt country where the trees stand stark and dead, now through prairie or creek-bottom, now up, now down, always with the range rising abruptly to the east, and with the Flathead River somewhere to the west.

RUNNING THE RAPIDS OF THE FLATHEAD

It was now approaching time for Bob's great idea to materialize. For this, and to this end, had he brought the boats on their strange land-journey—such a journey as, I fancy, very few boats have ever had before.

The project was, as I have said, to run the unknown reaches of the North Fork of the Flathead from the Canadian border to the town of Columbia Falls.

"The idea is this," Bob had said: "It's never been done before, do you see? It makes the trip unusual and all that."

"Makes it unusually risky," I had observed.

"Well, there's a risk in pretty nearly everything," he had replied blithely. "There's a risk in crossing a city street, for that matter. Riding these horses is a risk, if you come to that. Anyhow, it would make a good story."

So that is why I did it. And this is the story:

We were headed now for the Flathead just south of the Canadian line. To reach the river, it was necessary to take the boats through a burnt forest, without a trail of any sort. They leaped and plunged as the wagon scrambled, jerked, careened, stuck, détoured, and finally got through. There were miles of such going—heart-breaking miles—and at the end we paused at the top of a sixty-foot bluff and looked down at the river.

Now, I like water in a tub or drinking-glass or under a bridge. I am very keen about it.

But I like still water—quiet, well-behaved, stay-at-home water. The North Fork of the Flathead River is a riotous, debauched, and highly erratic stream.

It staggers in a series of wild zigzags for a hundred miles of waterway from the Canadian border to Columbia Falls, our destination. And that hundred miles of whirlpools, jagged rocks, and swift and deadly cañons we were to travel. I turned around and looked at the Family. It was my ambition that had brought them to this. We might never again meet, as a whole. We were sure to get to Columbia Falls, but not at all sure to get there in the boats. I looked at the boats; they were, I believe, stout river-boats. But they were small. Undeniably, they were very small.

The river appeared to be going about ninety miles an hour. There was one hope, however. Perhaps they could not get the boats down over the bluff. It seemed a foolhardy thing even to try. I suggested this to Bob. But he replied, rather tartly, that he had not brought those boats at the risk of his life through all those miles of wilderness to have me fail him now.

He painted the joys of the trip. He expressed so strong a belief in them that he said that he himself would ride with the outfit, thus permitting most of the Family in the boats that first day. He said the river was full of trout. I expressed a strong doubt that any trout could live in that stream and hold their own. I felt that they had all been washed down years ago. And again I looked at the Family.

Because I knew what would happen. The Family would insist on going along. It was not going to let mother take this risk alone; it was going to drown with her if necessary.

The Family jaws were set. *They were going.*

The entire outfit lowered the wagon by roping it down. There was one delicious moment when I thought boats and all were going over the edge. But the ropes held. Nothing happened.

They put the boats in the water.

I had one last rather pitiful thought as I took my seat in the stern of one of them.

"This is my birthday," I said wistfully. "It's rather a queer way to spend a birthday, I think."

But this was met with stern silence. I was to have my story whether I wanted it or not.

Yet once in the river, the excitement got me. I had run brief spells of rapids before. There had been a gasp or two and it was over. But this was to be a prolonged four days' gasp, with intervals only to sleep at night.

Fortunately for all of us, it began rather quietly. The current was swift, so that, once out into the stream, we shot ahead as if we had been fired out of a gun. But, for all that, the upper reaches were comparatively free of great rocks.

Friendly little sandy shoals beckoned to us. The water was shallow. But, even then, I noticed what afterward I found was to be a delusion of the entire trip.

This was the impression of riding downhill. I do not remember now how much the Flathead falls per mile. I have an impression that it is ninety feet, but as that would mean a drop of nine thousand feet, or almost two miles, during the trip, I must be wrong somewhere. It was sixteen feet, perhaps.

But hour after hour on the straight stretches, there was that sensation, on looking ahead, of staring down a toboggan-slide. It never grew less. And always I had the impression that just beyond that glassy slope the roaring meant uncharted falls—and destruction. It never did.

The outfit, following along the trail, was to meet us at night and have camp ready when we appeared—if we appeared. Only a few of us could use the boats. George Locke in one, Mike Shannon in the other, could carry two passengers each. For the sake of my story, I was to take the entire trip; the others were to alternate.

I do not know, but I am very confident that no other woman has ever taken this trip. I am fairly confident that no other men have ever taken it. We could find no one who had heard of it being taken. All that we knew was that it was the North Fork of the Flathead River, and that if we stayed afloat long enough, we would come out at Columbia Falls. The boatmen knew the lower part of the river, but not the upper two thirds of it.

Now that it is over, I would not give up my memory of that long run for anything. It was one of the most unique experiences in a not uneventful career. It was beautiful always, terrible occasionally. There were dozens of places each day where the boatmen stood up, staring ahead for the channel, while the boats dodged wildly ahead. But always these skillful pilots of ours found a way through. And so fast did we go that the worst places were always behind us before we had time to be really terrified.

The Flathead River in these upper reaches is fairly alive with trout. On the second day, I think it was, I landed a bull-trout that weighed nine pounds, and got it with a six-ounce rod. I am very proud of that. I have eleven different pictures of myself holding the fish up. There were trout everywhere. The difficulty was to stop the boat long enough to get them. In fact, we did not stop, save in an occasional eddy in the midst of the torrent. We whipped the stream as we flew along. Under great boulders, where the water seethed and roared, under deep cliffs where it flew like a mill-race, there were always fish.

It was frightful work for the boatmen. It required skill every moment. There was not a second in the day when they could relax. Only men trained to river rapids could have done it, and few, even, of these. To the eternal credit of George and Mike, we got through. It was nothing else.

On the evening of the first day, in the dusk which made the river doubly treacherous, we saw our camp-fire far ahead.

With the going-down of the sun, the river had grown cold. We were wet with spray, cramped from sitting still and holding on. But friendly hands drew our boats to shore and helped us out.

THE SECOND DAY ON THE FLATHEAD

In a way, this is a fairy-story. Because a good fairy had been busy during our absence. Days before, at the ranger's cabin, unknown to most of us, an order had gone down to civilization for food. During all those days under Starvation Ridge, food had been on the way by pack-horse—food and an extra cook.

So we went up to camp, expecting more canned salmon and fried trout and little else, and beheld—

A festive board set with candles—the board, however, in this case is figurative; it was the ground covered with a tarpaulin—fried chicken, fresh green beans, real bread, jam, potatoes, cheese, cake, candy, cigars, and cigarettes. And—champagne!

That champagne had traveled a hundred miles on horseback. It had been cooled in the icy water of the river. We drank it out of tin cups. We toasted each other. We toasted the Flathead flowing just beside us. We toasted the full moon rising over the Kootenais. We toasted the good fairy. The candles burned low in their sockets—this, also, is figurative; they were stuck on pieces of wood. With due formality I was presented with a birthday gift, a fishing-reel purchased by the Big and the Middle and the Little Boy.

Of all the birthdays that I can remember—and I remember quite a few—this one was the most wonderful. Over mountain-tops, glowing deep pink as they rose above masses of white clouds, came slowly a great yellow moon. It turned the Flathead beside us to golden glory, and transformed the evergreen thickets into fairy glades of light and shadow. Flickering candles inside the tents made them glow in luminous triangles against their background of forest.

Behind us, in the valley lands at the foot of the Rockies, the horses rested and grazed, and eased their tired backs. The men lay out in the open and looked at the stars. The air was fragrant with pine and balsam. Night creatures called and answered.

And, at last, we went to our tents and slept. For the morning was a new day, and I had not got all my story.

That first day's run of the river we got fifty trout, ranging from one half-pound to four pounds. We should have caught more, but they could not keep up with the boat. We caught, also, the most terrific sunburn that I have ever known anything about. We had thought that we were thoroughly leathered, but we had not passed the primary stage, apparently. In vain I dosed my face with cold-cream and talcum powder, and with a liquid warranted to restore the bloom of youth to an aged skin (mine, however, is not aged).

My journal for the second day starts something like this: "Cold and gray. Stood in the water fifteen minutes in hip-boots for a moving picture. River looks savage."

Of that second day, one beautiful picture stands out with distinctness.

The river is lovely; it winds and twists through deep forests with always that marvelous background of purple mountains capped with snow. Here and there, at long intervals, would come a quiet half-mile where, although the current was incredibly swift, there were, at least, no rocks. It was on coming round one of these bends that we saw, out from shore and drinking quietly, a deer. He was incredulous at first, and then uncertain whether to be frightened or not. He threw his head up and watched us, and then, turning, leaped up the bank and into the forest.

Except for fish, there was surprisingly little life to be seen. Bald eagles sat by the river as intent on their fishing as we were on ours. Wild ducks paddled painfully up against the current. Kingfishers fished in quiet pools. But the real interest of the river, its real life, lay in its fish. What piscine tragedies it conceals, with those murderous, greedy, and powerful assassins, the bull-trout, pursuing fish, as I have seen them, almost into the landing-net! What joyous interludes where, in a sunny shallow, tiny baby trout played tag while we sat and watched them!

The danger of the river is not all in the current. There are quicksands along the Flathead, sands underlain with water, apparently secure but reaching up clutching hands to the unwary. Our noonday luncheon, taken along the shore, was always on some safe and gravelly bank or tiny island.

The [second] day had been gray, and, to add to our discomfort, there was a soft, fine rain. The Middle Boy had developed an inflamed knee and was badly crippled. Sitting in the drizzle beside the camp-fire, I heated water in a tin pail and applied hot compresses consisting of woolen socks.

It was all in the game. Eggs tasted none the worse for being fried in a skillet into which the rain was pattering. Skins were weather-proof, if clothes were not. And heavy tarpaulins on the ground protected our bedding from dampness.

The outfit, coming down by trail, had passed a small store in a clearing. They had bought a whole cheese weighing eleven pounds, a difficult thing to transport on horseback, a wooden pail containing nineteen pounds of chocolate chips, and six dozen eggs—our first eggs in many days.

In the shop, while making the purchase, the Head had pulled out a box of cigarettes. The woman who kept the little store had never seen machine-made cigarettes before, and examined them with the greatest interest. For in that country every man is his own cigarette-maker. The Middle Boy later reported with wide eyes that at her elbow she kept a loaded revolver lying in plain view. She is alone a great deal of the time there in the wilderness, and probably she has many strange visitors.

THROUGH THE FLATHEAD CAÑON

The next morning we wakened to sunshine, and fried trout and bacon and eggs for breakfast. The cook tossed his flapjacks skillfully. As the only woman in the party, I sometimes found an air of festivity about my breakfast-table. Whereas the others ate from a tarpaulin laid on the ground, I was favored with a small box for a table and a smaller one for a seat. On the table-box was set my graniteware plate, knife, fork, and spoon, a paper napkin, the Prince Albert and the St. Charles. Lest this sound strange to the uninitiated, the St. Charles was the condensed milk and the Prince Albert was an old tin can which had once contained tobacco but which now contained the sugar. Thus, in our camp-etiquette, one never asked for the sugar, but always for the Prince Albert; not for the milk, but always for the St. Charles, sometimes corrupted to the Charlie.

I was late that morning. The men had gone about the business of preparing the boats for the day. The packers and guides were out after the horses. The cook, hot and weary, was packing up for the daily exodus. He turned and surveyed that ghost-forest with a scowl.

"Another camping-place like this, and I'll be braying like a blooming burro."

On the third day, we went through the Flathead River cañon. We had looked forward to this, both because of its beauty and its danger. Bitterly complaining, the junior members of the family were exiled to the trail with the exception of the Big Boy.

In one of the very greatest stretches of the rapids, a long straightaway, we saw a pigmy figure, far ahead, hailing us from the bank. "Pigmy" is a word I use generally with much caution, since a friend of mine, in the excitement of a first baby, once published a poem entitled "My Pigmy Counterpart," which a typesetter made, in the magazine version, "My Pig, My Counterpart."

Nevertheless, we will use it here. Behind this pigmy figure stretched a cliff, more than one hundred feet in height, of sheer rock overgrown with bushes. The figure had apparently but room on which to stand. George stood up and surveyed the prospect.

"Well," he said, in his slow drawl, "if that's lunch, I don't think we can hit it."

The river was racing at mad speed. Great rocks caught the current, formed whirlpools and eddies, turned us round again and again, and sent us spinning on, drenched with spray. That part of the river the boatmen knew—at least by reputation. It had been the scene, a few years before, of the tragic drowning of a man they knew. For now we were getting down into the better known portions.

To check a boat in such a current seemed impossible. But we needed food. We were tired and cold, and we had a long afternoon's work still before us.

At last, by tremendous effort and great skill, the boatmen made the landing. It was the college boy who had clambered down the cliff and brought the lunch, and it was he who caught the boats as they were whirling by. We had to cling like limpets—whatever a limpet is—to the edge, and work our way over to where there was room to sit down.

It reminded the Head of Roosevelt's expression about peace raging in Mexico. He considered that enjoyment was raging here.

Nevertheless, we ate. We made the inevitable cocoa, warmed beans, ate a part of the great cheese purchased the day before, and, with gingersnaps and canned fruit, managed to eke out a frugal repast. And shrieked our words over the roar of the river.

It was here that the boats were roped down. Critical examination and long debate with the boatmen showed no way through. On the far side, under the towering cliff, was an opening in the rocks through which the river boiled in a drop of twenty feet.

So it was fortunate, after all, that we had been hailed from the shore and had stopped, dangerous as it had been. For not one of us would have lived had we essayed that passage under the cliff. The Flathead River is not a deep river; but the force of its flow is so great, its drop so rapid, that the most powerful swimmer is hopeless in such a current. Light as our flies were, again and again they were swept under and held as though by a powerful hand.

Late the afternoon of the third day we saw our camp well ahead, on a ledge above the river. Everything was in order when we arrived. We unloaded ourselves solemnly out of the boats, took our fish, our poles, our graft-hooks and landing-nets, our fly-books, my sunburn lotion, and our weary selves up the bank. Then we solemnly shook hands all round. We had come through; the rest was easy.

On the last day, the river became almost a smiling stream. Once again, instead of between cliffs, we were traveling between great forests of spruce, tamarack, white and yellow pine, fir, and cedar. A great golden eagle flew over the water just ahead of our boat. And in the morning we came across our first sign of civilization—a wire trolley with a cage, extending across the river in lieu of a bridge. High up in the air at each end, it sagged in the middle until the little car must almost have touched the water. We had a fancy to try it, and landed to make the experiment. But some ungenerous soul had padlocked it and had gone away with the key.

We lunched that night where, just a year before, I had eaten my first lunch on the Flathead, on a shelving, sandy beach. But this time the meal was somewhat shadowed by the fact that some one had forgotten to put in butter and coffee and condensed milk.

However, we were now in that part of river which our boatmen knew well. From a secret cache back in the willows, George and Mike produced coffee and condensed milk and even butter. So we lunched, and far away we heard a sound which showed us how completely our wilderness days were over—the screech of a railway locomotive.

Late that afternoon, tired, sunburned, and unkempt, we drew in at the little wharf near Columbia Falls. It was weeks since we had seen a mirror larger than an inch or so across. Our clothes were wrinkled from being used to augment our bedding on cold nights. The whites of our eyes were bloodshot with the sun. My old felt hat was battered and torn with the fish-hooks that had been hung round the band. Each of us looked at the other, and prayed to Heaven that he looked a little better himself.

15

THE TWO MEDICINE
OR WHITE MAGIC LAKES

Agnes C. Laut
1926

Agnes C. Laut (1879–1936) spent most of her youth in Winnipeg, Manitoba. She eventually moved to the United States, settling in New York State, but remained a loyal Canadian; many of her thirty-odd books focus on the history of western Canada and the United States. In 1925, she was invited to join a Great Northern Railway excursion, the "Upper Missouri Historical Expedition," which erected statues to notable explorers at several sites along the route of the railroad. This journey spawned her book about the history of the area as well as *Enchanted Trails of Glacier Park*, from which this hymn of praise to the Two Medicine Valley is drawn. Laut's prose style may seem old-fashioned and histrionic to the modern reader, but her love of the place is sincere.

Here, then, to the Medicine or Mystery Lakes came the wise men of the Blackfeet to settle early tribal disputes. One can visualize the old scene—the mooseskin tepees, the primeval forest before the fires worked desolation here, the Indians fishing on the margin of the blue tarn, the stillness broken only by the raucous cry of the eagle, or the shrill sentry warning of the osprey hawk nested on the top of some blasted tree, the little "tent pin" gophers erect on hind legs surveying the camp from brush trail, the hoary marmot uttering a lone whistle from a pile of rocks, the shy deer, now in reddish fawn-colored coat, peering furtively from the underbrush, with a bound into the thicket as the single file Indian riders come padding in to the camping ground, the small chip fires— the big log fire is called "fool whiteman fire"—scenting the shadow-filtered atmosphere with an odor of resin, then the shadows of the "medicine-men" dressed in beaded white buckskin round the council fire, calming tense nerves by whiffing the peace pipe in a circle toward the setting sun before beginning their deliberations.

What were they disputing, I wonder? Was it the oncoming white men, the irresistible firearms, the disappearance of the buffalo, of which skeletons have been found as deep in the mountains as these very lakes?…In the '80's, thousands starved to death because they were too proud to acknowledge their plight of destitution; and now the Blackfeet number on the American side of the border only two thousand six hundred people.

You pause at the Trick Falls (now called Running Eagle Falls; see frontispiece), where the white waters seem to emerge from the cliffs as if an Indian Moses had struck them, and the short walk limbers out cramped muscles, though I marveled how women in satin slippers and silk stockings could endure the stone bruises on their bulging toes or the mosquitoes where strong shoes and wool golf hose would have meant immunity. Then subtly you had become aware of a presence—the tall pines had encircled you from the time you left the first lake. The trail ahead became an aisled passageway shot with bars and beams of gold light. The ferns began to tremble as if in expectation of something beautiful. There was "the voice of many waters." When the car lunged down and crossed the brook, you no longer saw a ribbony creek. There were laughing blue and white waters bubbling over a pebbly bottom in a great hurry, lipping and babbling in a vocal white-fret of lace. If you know mountains you will know the signs—these waters came through stones, the stones of a moraine jumble of rocks damming up an approaching stream in some deep alpine tarn.

Then the car emerges from the aisled pines and spruces and there bursts on you in all its beauty the real Two Medicine Lake—the upper tarn—a sapphire blue set amid buff and green and yellow and red mountains sheer as a wall, sharp as a spire. I am not going to name the mountains. You will find them in any guide book; but I beg of you to take out your field glasses and study those moving spots of white far up on the ledges that look as narrow as a knife.

"Snow, by gum, snow!" cried the bull-voiced tourist; but if he had used his brains and a field glass, he would have seen that the spots of white were not snow patches but mountain goats driven up the precipice by the ravening timber wolf and now stealing shyly out to drink at those sparkles of water, which are trickles of upper falls, or to browse on heather and moss and lichen that would feed no other four-footed creature but the mountain goat and sheep. Look again, and look hard; for it is four o'clock and the filtered shadows are falling in a curtain of blue haze and in an hour these lofty majestic spires will fold them in panoplies of dusky indigo pricked by diamond stars in a hazy network. The long shadows are already etching across the lake; so that you see a perfect replica of each peak in the water below as in the heavens above, and know why the Indians called these Medicine or Mystery Lakes. Their curtains are falling and closing like the shadow of a mysterious death. Look quickly. There is much to see if you have eyes. There is an old pine gripping the rocks with guy-rope roots, that has fought life against frost and hurricane for—how long? You can't count the whorls of annual growth; for the pine branches have all been torn from the trunk by the winter gales except one last top spar still waving a flag of triumph to the demons of winter storms. It stands like a beleaguered thing, the last of the surviving warriors of a forest washed out when these mountains were seas. And then at its foot is something more tender— a poor little dwarfed groundling evergreen, flattened, beaten, crouched, hanging to the naked rock with taut finger-roots. Will the rocks toss it down to a watery death, or will it burst and hurl the rocks down—where a long slide of shale shows what happens in the wild storms of winter, when Thor's hammer deals redoubled blows on the monuments of an eternity? There is a lisping and whispering of the waters as the day thaw slacks, that is almost eerie if you know what they are saying.

The archeologist is rushing to get quarters in the Chalet. The geologist is getting out his burlap bag and hammer. A fisherman is paddling in from the lake with a great string of trout on a willow and the usual wonder yarn of "the big fellow that got away." And thanks be to the gods of these Mystery Lakes, they can never be fished out. First, the Government keeps them stocked with the finest mountain trout in the world. Next, the jumble of marine rocks at the entrance to the river keeps the fish not only in the lakes but protected from marauder fish which would devour the eggs and the young. There are falls in all these upper tarns, which can never be ascended by any cannibal fish. Then the ooze of forest humus and glacial silt supplies an ideal feeding-ground for the midge and fly and insect to support the trout; and last and most important of all, the season is so short—two months at times, four at most—that the white man "fish hog" can never exhaust the lakes. The regulations set less than twelve fish as the most a fisherman may catch in a day; and fish less than six inches long must be thrown back at once.

A great many people summer at the Chalet here; and a more secluded spot could not be found on earth. This, too, is a tree lodge, with all the comforts of a home; and though it were visited by a thousand tourists a day—which it isn't— the surrounding forests are so dense and the mountain trails to the passes so good, that by taking a lunch and only sleeping in the Chalet at night, one can be in forest as deep and undisturbed as Rackham's eerie drawings of "Alice in Wonderland"; and it is a wonderland, every foot of it. It seems impossible to believe you are only fifteen miles away from a railroad to the great cities. Where forests are deep and the compass of the sun is shut out, the warning is unnecessary that you should keep on the plain, well-cut posted trail. Bears and wolves are numerous here, so numerous that if you go scouting in the underbrush and neither osprey hawk nor squirrel gives you warning, you may hear the snorting grunt of a bruin not ten feet away; but wild animals do not frequent man-smelling trails, and don't molest you unless you molest them. All the same, paste these two warnings in your hat—(1) Keep on the trail; for the Park does not allow you to carry firearms. (2) If you hear an osprey hawk, or a squirrel scolding furiously—hop for the trail; for these two sentries of the wilds are the best danger signals in the world; and their eyesight is sharper than yours. The next day I met a young hiker who had ignored the first warning. She heard a "woof" and didn't stay. It was a brown bear. Once, in Jasper, I ignored the second warning because I was limbering up axle joints after a nine-mile walk, all down grade and very steep. I didn't hear the "woof" but I later met the gentleman. He was dressed in black fur and asking for the bacon in our camp....

At the lake, there is a rush of sightseers to ensconce themselves in the little launch that will carry them two or three miles to the head of the lake, where another short walk will reveal more waterfalls; and all the time you are advancing up the sapphire lake the mountain walls seem to be folding, folding round you—barring out the cares of the world, accepting you in sacred initiation to their celestial temples.

I did not go up to the Second Falls this time. I wanted to be alone to listen. Again the typical lady with the tight satin slippers and silk stocking and narrow skirt, which wasn't slit but would be presently—trotted off up the darkening wood trail to "do" the Falls. I was left alone. There was the sharp crash of rock from some upper ledge, where, in the eternal battle between groundling juniper and adamant rock, the little finger-roots had dislodged their enemy and sent a great stone bounding down. There was the jump at some watergnat of a trout, which would have paled the largest fisherman lie. The thrush came out of shy hermitage and uttered his threnody to dying day. The vesper sparrow from somewhere back in the tangle of criss-crossed sunbeams and incense-steaming resinous pines twittered his plaintive ditty to the night breeze playing the harp in the needles of the pines. A woodpecker came out in his red cap and hammered the cinnamon barks for a juicy worm salad. There was a riffle of wind that set the waves whispering. The hum of a night-hawk's wings cut the air with the zoom of a far aeroplane, and then came down very cautiously, the merrymaker of these northern woods—he is always cautious coming down, but quick as a streak of light going up; a Douglas squirrel—that wingless flyer, that arrow, that dart of red life, that sentry on watch for all danger, that friend of man and gay little scold of householders among the pines. I suspect he was out for a salad of chocolate cones and green needle-tips. He popped up and looked at me and cracked a nut and sat up on his hind legs and asked me plainly as a squirrel could speak—"What are you doing here? Don't you know there are big brown bears and timber wolves that say 'woof'?" Then a scolding "skur-ur-ur—spit-fire—spit-fire—here comes a skirted biped with black satin for paws—how can she crack nuts with those paws"; and the lady with the black satin pumps slumped back into the launch....

"I've had enough—I haven't a toe those rocks on the road didn't aim and hit! And mosquitoes?—say!"—she was slapping from knee to ankle—"I'm like that unbowed head in what-do-you-call-that-fellow's poems—all bloody from head to heel. I'm just positively rising in welts and bumps all over the size of a bun— oh, pest, take that!"—and she dealt a welt that would have flattened a man, let alone a mosquito—"Gracious, my feet feel"—What, I asked myself, and what I am sure that squirrel asked himself was—

Did she see the mountains?

Whether she saw the luminous floods of color among the upper peaks, or felt the hush of the flushed alpine glow in the sunset, or heard the rivers now lowering their jubilate of noonday to the last faint notes of a music divine—the mountains were working their White Magic on her just the same. They were obliterating sense of care. They were obviously curing all symptoms of lethargy. If a few little needle-stings did puncture her periphery, the ozone was expelling fatigue poisons, cleaning out sluggish lungs and clearing a tired brain.

16

CAREFREE YOUTH AND DUDES IN GLACIER NATIONAL PARK

Dorothy M. Johnson
1975

Dorothy M. Johnson (1905–1984) was one of the American West's finest writers. Born in Iowa, she grew up in the little railroad town of Whitefish, not far from the western entrance to Glacier. A prolific author of articles, essays, short stories, and novels, Johnson wrote the stories on which were based three notable films: *The Man Who Shot Liberty Valance, A Man Called Horse,* and *The Hanging Tree.* Late in life, she authored a number of whimsical reminiscences for *Montana The Magazine of Western History,* including this piece, somewhat shortened, on early tourism in the park. This version was published in Johnson's collection, *When You and I Were Young, Whitefish* (1982).

A funny story about Glacier National Park concerns the visit of the famous author, Mary Roberts Rinehart, in 1917, when the Park was in its infancy. (It was established in 1910). The mountains and glaciers had been there a long time, but the national park hadn't. The Rinehart party traveled in style, with the famous Eaton guides, packers and horses. There was champagne, too, and what is more, the famous lady wrote a book about the trip. It was entitled *Tenting Tonight,* and it brought the area to the attention of a lot of people who hadn't heard about it before.

One night, while getting ready for bed in her tent, the celebrated lady author punctured her air mattress with a hatpin. That's all there is to the story, but it gets funnier with the passage of time. A hatpin? What on earth was she doing with a hatpin on a camping trip? Did she plan to use it to defend herself from bears? No, in those days ladies always wore hats and did their hair high, and it took a couple of hatpins to keep the hat anchored. At the time it happened, a lot of slightly jealous people who weren't rich enough to travel with an air mattress laughed merrily and figured that small accident served an Eastern dude just about right.

My first experiences with social strata, rich people and Eastern dudes, were all in Glacier Park. We unrich Westerners were suspicious of the whole lot of them. We looked down on them because we thought they looked down on us. But they didn't even *see* us, which made the situation even more irritating. Years later, when I lived in a big Eastern city, I learned not to see strangers; it is a necessary protective device where there are too many people. But in the uncrowded West, in *my* country, it's bad manners, and on the trail it's proper to acknowledge the existence of other human beings by saying hello.

My early memories of Glacier National Park, whose western entrance is some twenty-six miles from Whitefish, are less about the breath-taking mountain scenery than about the vast social chasm between Eastern dudes and us who lived around there. We were especially doubtful of famous people. For outdoor wear, rich Easterners were costumed by Abercrombie and Fitch or the equivalent.

Once, trudging along a trail, some of us met Irvin S. Cobb. We loved his stories in the *Saturday Evening Post*, but that was *his* world; what was he doing in ours? (There was no mistaking him; he was the homeliest man I ever saw, with a face like a frog).

Mr. Cobb was carrying fishing equipment, and his shirt and pants had well-pressed creases instead of wrinkles. He wore high laced boots of off-white leather. Those boots endeared him to us. They were scratched and worn and water-stained. They had taken him through rough country and into mountain streams. We knew right away that this was no dude. We judged that even though he was an Easterner and world-famous, Irvin S. Cobb was acceptable in our world. In Western slang, he'd do to ride the river with.

All this was long before you could drive casually through Glacier Park on your way to somewhere else. You couldn't drive casually *anywhere* in western Montana then; the roads were too bad, where they existed at all.

So Park visitors, including us locals, went by train, and since the journey was expensive, those from far away tended to settle down and stay for several weeks at one or more of the hotels, which the Great Northern Railway owned. This was a sensible arrangement. The railroad generated a lot of summer passenger traffic by promoting Glacier as an unspoiled playground full of scenic wonders and, having got the dudes out there, provided food and lodging on which, presumably, it also made a profit. The temporary hotel help was recruited from the University of Minnesota.

By 1960, most people no longer came by train, so in December of that year the Great Northern sold its hostelries to Donald Hummel, a businessman of Tucson, Arizona. He operated them under the name of Glacier Park, Inc. (A couple of years after that I got into an argument with a feisty lady about who owned those hotels. I couldn't convince her that they had changed hands. What she knew, she knew, and she couldn't bear contradiction. The funny thing about this argument was that it took place in Tangiers, Morocco, while we were eating cous-cous in the elegant Rif Hotel. This just goes to show that some tourists will fight about anything anywhere. She wouldn't speak to me for the rest of the tour, all the way back to Madrid).

Back in the days when East was East and West was West and the twain met briefly and suspiciously in Glacier Park, we went from Whitefish to Belton (now West Glacier) on the train, in hiking clothes and carrying our possessions in back packs. Lots of people back-pack there now; it is the "in" thing to do. But in my time it wasn't fashionable—it just showed that we couldn't afford to stay or eat at the Lewis Hotel, now called Lake McDonald Lodge.

From Belton we walked to Apgar and there boarded a big motorboat that took us to the hotel at the head of Lake McDonald. If we were really economizing, we hiked all the way—about ten miles. There was a road that far.

Then we roughed it, and most of what we did was probably illegal, but the statute of limitations must have expired since then, so it's all right to confess it now. There may have been some campgrounds; I don't remember them. I do remember that one rainy night five of us, including my mother, crawled into a barn that had a loose board on the back and slept on the hay. We all slid during the night, and the roof leaked, so we woke up in the morning at the bottom of the hay pile with our feet in a puddle.

Another night we managed to get into a dance pavilion and slept on the hard floor. I had contracted a bad sunburn three or four days before by floating around on a raft on Whitefish Lake all one lovely afternoon. The burn was beginning to peel, the straps of my pack had rubbed some skin off my shoulders, and when I complained about having the equivalent of stand-up fish scales on my back, some wag in the party suggested that I was no doubt sprouting wings and a little discomfort was only to be expected, as when a baby gets a new tooth.

We weren't supposed to sleep where we slept or to cook where we cooked, but we were fairly experienced woodsmen, and we didn't get caught. We used wood that was already down and dead, and we were experts at completely extinguishing our little cooking fires. (Some thirty years later, using a modern portable gasoline stove at a modern, legal campground, I came close to setting Glacier National Park afire, but that's a later story). Once we found a huge edible mushroom of the puffball type, sliced it and fried it like steak—it made a fine meal for the whole bunch of us.

Being curious about how the rich dudes from the East fared at the hotel, a couple of us peered through a dining room window one night. Some of those ladies wore low-topped, long-skirted *satin* evening dresses! Out in the wilderness, mind you, roughing it in the Rocky Mountains! Ah, the hardships suffered by the daring adventurers who spent the summer in Glacier National Park, instead of back in Newport where things were civilized.

Some of them did have great adventures and were out-going enough to admit it. One day, a middle-aged woman in an elegant hiking costume came running out to the boat dock at the hotel calling, "Cahl! Cahl!"

A young man who was about to go swimming answered, "Yes, Mothah?" (Translating this cleverly from Eastern to Western dialect, I figured out that his name was Carl and hers was Mother. We treat the letter R with more respect). Mothah was simply ecstatic—she had picked half a pint of huckleberries growing wild in the woods. Cahl was polite about it.

Meanwhile I watched to see how Cahl would react when he hit that water; I had just got out of it, regretting having got in, and was trying (while my teeth chattered) to understand how water that cold could remain fluid. It was liquid glaciers.

I rather expected that Cahl, being a dude, would collapse when he hit that cold water and would probably never come up. But he emerged in a thrashing crawl and swam clear around the dock to prove he could do it—and maybe because people were watching. I began to suspect that "Easterner" was not synonymous with "softy." He didn't go in again, though. Neither did I.

Next day (after sleeping on that dance pavilion floor) our hardy little band set out for Sperry Chalets. The rich went on horses, with a guide. We went on foot, six miles that seemed straight up. We grew thirstier and thirstier, and nobody had had the wits to bring a canteen. Most of the way we were tormented by the sound of rushing water—nice cold water in vast quantities, gushing through a narrow stream bed down below at our right, not far away but totally inaccessible. Between us and it there was a vertical drop down a cliff. We chose to go thirsty rather than court disaster by trying to get a drink. And somewhere along the way I got mad.

"I don't want to see Sperry Glacier," I announced bitterly. "I don't give a hang about *any* glacier. I am going to stay right here and enjoy my sunburn and listen to the creek and be thirsty, and you can pick me up on your way back. Good-bye."

And there I stayed, and on they went after some argument. They were gone for some hours. They didn't reach the glacier, 9 miles from the Lewis Hotel, but they did get to Sperry Chalet and brought back pictures to prove it.

I lay there propped against a log, stubborn as Achilles before the walls of Troy, and after a while the branches in a tree above me began to look mighty like a bobcat or perhaps a small mountain lion. I didn't move. I was the prototype of the petulant teen-ager. Let him leap, I thought. And will they be sorry when they find my blood and bones scattered all over the trail! The big cat dissolved into tree branches.

After an endless time, my companions returned, limping, but acting as if they had enjoyed the trip, which only made me madder. They had had a lovely drink of water up at the chalets—but they had also contracted some blisters in their boots. They had not tried to reach Sperry Glacier.

In the summer of 1952, my mother and I were living in Whitefish again. I had a longer look at the Park, in comfort, by car, for a whole week. My companion was Catherine A. Burnham (hereinafter known as Kay), a long-time friend and former neighbor in New York. This was my very first experience in vacationing by car. For the fifteen years I had worked in New York I didn't have or need one. We could take anything we might possibly want—how nice! How different from the miseries of back-packing years before! And I was pretty naïve about the facilities available, in spite of having studied *Guide to Glacier National Park* by George C. Ruhle.

What I borrowed and packed would have taken us on an expedition into the Gobi Desert—bedding (never needed at the cabins and hotels we used), five gallons of gas (totally unnecessary), knapsacks, flannel shirts, winter pajamas (we did need them at Sperry), food, dishes, cooking equipment, a thermos bottle and a library: Mr. Ruhle's *Guide, Immortal Poems of the English Language*, and *How to Know the American Mammals*. The American mammals we met, mostly small rodents, seldom stood still long enough for us to find the right page in the book. A week before we reached Many Glacier, a ranger had shot a grizzly there, but it had been removed, and anyway if I meet a bear I won't need to look in a book to figure out that it's not a chipmunk.

The fact was that I didn't know any more about seeing Glacier Park by car

than Kay did. But I drove, which made me captain, and Kay, who was a lieutenant in the Naval Reserve, was the crew. She dropped the anchor—every time
we stopped on a grade, she leaped out and put a chunk of rock where it would
keep the car from rolling.

Glacier Park with roads and a car was a lot different from the way I remembered it way back then. And we were prosperous enough to buy our way under
a roof every night—none of this sneaking into places where we weren't supposed to be. We traversed the cliff-hanging Going-to-the-Sun Highway along
the Garden Wall, where Kay enjoyed the spectacular scenery—tall trees are
so far below that they look like grass. (The only time I ever see the scenery up
there is when someone else is driving). We made a short stop at Logan Pass,
where there were facilities that a friend of mine called Going-to-the-John Chalet, enjoyed snowbanks and wild flowers, and rented a cabin at Rising Sun
cabin camp.

We had no cooking facilities, so we unpacked our groceries at a public
campground and undertook, with unwarranted self-confidence, to build a
cooking fire. Wood was provided—in such big heavy chunks that we agreed a
receding glacier must have left it there.

Our axe was ineffective, but we haggled off some bits, which Kay arranged
hopefully in a stone fireplace while I unlimbered a one-burner gasoline stove
as a backup device. The people who lent it to me had given me two lessons in
operating it, but I flunked my final. I pumped the stove with great determination, held a match to it, and almost burned up Glacier National Park. The
flame, which should have been short and blue, was tall and yellow. If anyone up
in Alberta noticed northern lights to the south that evening, it was that flame
they saw. After I knocked the stove off the log, the flame blazed horizontally.
One thing I must say for that stove: even enveloped in fire, it didn't explode.

I went shrieking off to the nearest occupied campsite and encountered a
heroic fellow who raced back with me and tamed the stove. He even made
Kay's wood fire burn—our frying pan of pork chops wasn't even warm. He was
an awfully nice man, our rescuer. If I were a hot-shot reporter I would have
found out more about him, but all I knew when the emergency was over was
that he wore a red shirt and came from California.

[After a brief visit to Waterton Lakes National Park in Canada, our] next stop
was at Many Glacier, where—like dozens of other awe-struck visitors—we sat
in the hotel lobby and stared across a lake at a most spectacular mountain.

How convenient, to have such a view where you can gaze at it in comfort! One man seemed to be defying that mountain silently to take one step toward the hotel, just one, and he'd fix it. We suspected that the view was the reason for putting the hotel there.

From there we went on a hike to Grinnell Lake, conducted by a Park naturalist. The hike was easy—most of it was by boat. One ride took us to the end of Swiftcurrent Lake and another along Josephine Lake. We were relieved to find that passengers didn't have to portage the launch. Someone had thoughtfully provided a boat for each lake.

After a side trip to Browning, outside the Park, to see the Museum of the Plains Indian, we went back to the west side, to that haunt of my childhood, the former Lewis Hotel, by this time renamed the Lake McDonald Lodge. What a difference the years had made! Nobody wore formal clothes to dinner any more, you couldn't tell Easterner from Westerner, and we were all just travelers together, having a good time. Here, the next morning, we set out bravely for Sperry Glacier, taking our necessaries in knapsacks and leaving our other baggage locked in the car.

But this time we traveled like rich people, on horseback. Our party included five horses, a guide, and a man who led a packhorse. We arranged the night before to set out at 8:45 A.M. Our guide comforted us in the bleak gray morn by saying that we didn't really have to start then. It might rain, he said. We had assumed that, once plans were established, the horses would be stamping indignantly in the lobby at precisely the time agreed upon. It turned out that those horses hadn't been indignant about anything for years and wouldn't have cared if we had called off the trip entirely. There were times, in the next few hours, when we wished they had tried to talk us out of it.

It didn't really rain on the way to Sperry Chalets but we got wet anyway, because the brush along the way was dripping. Wet clouds sagged down from the mountain peaks.

My horse developed a freak stunt when we started to ford a stream. He went into reverse. Nobody had ever told me what to do in a case like that. I know how to start and stop a horse and how to shift him into high gear if he has one, but what do you do with a horse that goes backward? For a while it looked as if I'd have to head him downhill in order to make him go up it.

How fine it would be, Kay and I kept telling ourselves, to get to the chalet. How nice to sit before a roaring open fire among jolly, athletic mountain climbers, bubbling with youthful zest as they dried their socks before the leaping flames and made the rafters ring with song as they raised glasses high. This thought cheered us upward and onward.

So did our guide. He approved of us because we were going up to a glacier. "People have got too soft," he fretted. "Used to be they hiked or rode all over—there're a thousand miles of trails in the Park. Now it's all cars, cars, cars, and they won't make no effort to go nowhere, they expect us to bring the glaciers down to them."

When, at last, we saw the chalets perched high above us on a cliff, we knew how stout Cortez felt, silent upon a peak in Darien, and how the Pilgrim Fathers welcomed their first glimpse of Massachusetts. We felt that our triumphant arrival should be greeted with a great burst of music—something by Wagner, accompanied by the full Metropolitan Opera orchestra and the costumed chorus in full cry, waving spears.

Instead we got immediate cups of hot coffee, which was more to the point.

There were no healthy, jolly mountain climbers drying their socks by an open fire. Sperry Chalets had oil heaters—the oil was toted up on packhorses—because it wouldn't do to hack down the forest primeval for firewood. It's part of the scenery. The only potential mountain climbers were the not terribly jolly Glacier Girls, Kay and Dorothy, and we weren't feeling *very* healthy. My right hip was slightly dislocated, and Kay said her solar plexus squeaked.

Still, riding was better than walking.

All my life I have worried about being late. So I had carefully planned that we would get to Sperry the day the chalets opened, before they became crowded. We did arrive on opening day—July 1—and this was an awful mistake. It was still winter up there, with lots of snow and vast sheets of ice. Some days ahead of us, four women and a boy who were going to run the place had arrived. They were all dying to make us happy. Every time they saw us, the ladies gave us a snack, and there were substantial meals as well. The boy spent his waking hours trying to make the oil heater work in our sleeping quarters. We had expected to stay two or three days, but a look at the snow and ice and rain-clouds persuaded us otherwise.

"Let's get up to that glacier and get it over with," said Kay grimly. "It's three miles, the guide book says."

We never made it. So early in the season, nobody had cleared the trail. Wading through snow with ice water running under it is different from riding a horse that does the wading. There was a broad, steep slope ahead, a talus slope where broken rocks had slid down the mountain in a great swoop. The trail across that swoop was visible in places, but the walking was worse than on the level because of snow patches with slippery bear grass underneath. We crossed two of the patches at considerable risk to life and limb and then sat down to consider the immediate future. We really needed a bulldozer, some ropes, a regiment of trained mountain troops, and more stamina. We had nothing to lose by changing our minds. Mine was changed before we crossed the first snow patch. The second one converted Kay. Feeling that we had some rights as that season's pioneers, we named the snow patches Burnham's Folly and Johnson's Doom.

"A girl could get her pretty neck broke here," Kay remarked, looking down into the abyss. We teetered perilously back to the chalet for hot coffee and dry socks. Then from the porch we looked down through gray clouds toward Lake McDonald, six moist miles away, and sighed.

With my elbows on the railing I recited, "The blessed damozel leaned out from the gold bar of heaven; she had three lilies in her hand, and the stars in her hair were seven."

This didn't cheer us up. I was wearing wet wool slacks and two wool shirts over winter underwear, and with that rig lilies would have been inappropriate.

Kay remarked wistfully, "Now I know how a kitten feels at the top of a telephone pole. How soon can we get out of here?"

"We can phone down and have the man with the horses up here by noon tomorrow or earlier," I suggested.

"I'd rather walk and get it over with," Kay decided, but she agreed that we'd better wait until morning.

It didn't rain *all* the time we were at Sperry. For a while it hailed instead. After a bountiful supper we were sitting by the oil stove in the sleeping chalet, moodily greasing our shoes, when a clatter on the porch made us jump. Three mountain goats were staring in at us. They ran, with Kay after them; she peered cautiously around the corner of the building to find them peering cautiously back at her. For the rest of the evening they played ring-around-the-chalet, clattering the length of the porch and peeking in the window.

Since those goats are up there anyway, with time on their hands (or hooves), why couldn't they have broken a trail for us to the glacier? But no, they waste their time playing childish games and staring through windows at startled ladies who are trying to get into their winter pajamas by the oil heater and wondering whether five Hudson's Bay blankets will be enough. (With six, you can't turn over).

Next morning, for a change, the sun was shining. Not much, but some, just to prove it could. The management offered enough breakfast for twelve people, but we prudently ate enough for only four or five.

The trip down, on foot, took four hours. Now and then we peeled off a layer of wool as we advanced into the temperate zone. I told Kay how elegantly people had dressed for dinner at that hotel back in the years when I couldn't afford to eat there but peeked in the window like a mountain goat.

When we arrived, we were going to look like a couple of tramps. Somehow we managed to work up quite a rage about a purely imaginary conversation that would take place if the management didn't like our looks at lunchtime. Our car was there, our baggage was there, we had been there two nights before; we were not going to get all slicked up for lunch, because we were hungry. No such conversation took place. Nobody cared how we looked. Aw, shucks. How times had changed in Glacier National Park!

We were relieved not to meet our guide again, because our failure to reach Sperry Glacier had put us into the category of tourists he didn't like, those who expect the glaciers to come down to the road to be looked at. And why shouldn't they? Glaciers do move, although not very fast. They're big; they can just shove things out of their way. And furthermore, they know the country. We did our best. Let *them* co-operate a little....

PART IV

CHARACTERS

Parks attract people of vivid personalities—loners, wanderers, travelers, storytellers, jokesters, singers, and craftspeople. Stories about these folks abound and give the national park a human presence, a life, which complements the wilderness setting. The character sketches that follow exemplify Glacier's power to draw unique people: Louis Hill, the railroad president who overspent his budget for tourist facilities in the park; ranger-turned-poacher-and-outlaw Joe Cosley; legendary cowboy artist Charles M. Russell, whose summer cabin on Lake McDonald became a gathering point for visitors from all over; and Josephine Doody, the "bootleg lady of Glacier Park." One of the most colorful was dude wrangler, campground caretaker, and cowboy poet Jim Whilt, the "Poet of the Rockies," who in the span of thirty years published several books of rhymed verse and a collection of anecdotes titled *Giggles from Glacier Guides*. This poem, "The Outside Trail," is from his 1951 collection, *Mountain Echoes*:

> The trails of the park are many,
> They lead almost anywhere
> And the ones who are lucky to take them
> Forget every sorrow and care.
>
> Some lead far up to the ice fields,
> And some follow the mountain's rim.
> Sometimes one travels and travels

'Til the sun in the west has grown dim.
Some follow the streams where the meadows
Are ablaze with the wild flowers sweet,
While some climb high in the passes
And look at the world 'neath their feet.

While some lead deep in the forest
Where you scent the odor of pine.
When I ride these trails of beauty,
I feel that the whole world is mine.

17

LOUIS HILL'S DREAM

Glacier National Park in 1915

Dave Walter
1985

Son of James J. Hill (the so-called Empire Builder), Louis W. Hill Sr. (1872–1948) became president of the Great Northern Railway upon his father's retirement in 1907. Working behind the scenes, Louis encouraged Congress to pass the enabling act that established Glacier National Park; President Taft signed the bill into law on May 11, 1910. Almost immediately after, Louis Hill—outdoorsman, sportsman, violinist, and landscape painter—set to work to establish tourist facilities that would hopefully earn a profit while encouraging passenger traffic on the railroad. To this day, the speed with which roads, trails, hotels, chalets, tent camps, and other facilities were built is astounding. By 1915, a network of accommodations was in place and tens of thousands of summer visitors began exploring the park. Former seasonal park employee Dave Walter (1943–2006), who wrote many articles and books about Montana history as the research director for the Montana Historical Society, contributed this study of Louis Hill's work to the magazine *Encounters*, published by the Science Museum of Minnesota in St. Paul in 1985.

When Glacier National Park was established 75 years ago Louis W. Hill, Sr., beamed. Finally the president of the Great Northern Railway Company had a nationally recognized scenic attraction on his main line. Glacier Park created an opportunity that Louis Hill had no intention of squandering.

Since the Great Northern had completed its transcontinental line in 1893, it had competed with the Northern Pacific Railroad for freight and passenger traffic in the Northwest. But the Northern Pacific held two distinct advantages: It was a land-grant railroad, with extensive property holdings in the West, and it passed just north of Yellowstone National Park, a fact which enabled it to book tourists from the East and the Midwest onto its main line. The Great Northern countered the land-grant advantage by extensively promoting agricultural and commercial settlement along its route. With the establishment of Glacier National Park, it finally could offer tourists an alternative to Yellowstone.

In fact, the settlement and development which had occurred in the Glacier Park area prior to 1910 was largely the result of the Great Northern Railway. This rugged, mountainous section was virtually inaccessible before the construction in 1892 of the Great Northern main line around what would become the southern boundary of the Park. With rail line access, settlers began to filter into the mountain valleys west of the Continental Divide, particularly around Lake McDonald, near the Great Northern station at Belton (West Glacier).

The railroad—ever eager to explore and encourage the development of commercial possibilities along its line—sent Carleton College professor Lyman B. Sperry to the McDonald Valley to search for glaciers (1894–1895). The company also encouraged the writings of George Bird Grinnell, who effusively described the alpine beauty along the east side of the Divide. Although both Louis Hill, Sr., and his father, James J. Hill, maintained a low profile during the effort to have Glacier made a national park (1907–1910), each realized that the park would be a tremendous asset to the railroad's passenger traffic.

Even after he became the president of Great Northern in 1907, Louis Hill remained in the long shadow cast by his illustrious father. The creation of Glacier Park offered Louis the chance to develop a project that would be wholly, distinctly his own. And he seized that opportunity with enthusiasm and tenacity, throwing the substantial resources of the corporation into the project.

What Hill envisioned was a public park, catering to the well-heeled, recreation-minded tourist who was transported to and from the Northern Rockies on his railroad. The motif would be European, similar to that of the Swiss Alps. The transportation system similarly would be European, meshing rail, road, trail, and boat trips. This transportation network would link a series of chalet-style hotels, lodges, and camps spread throughout the picturesque, mountainous east side of the Park. The Great Northern tourist would enjoy some of the nation's most majestic scenery in comfort and style.

The Department of the Interior and the Glacier Park administration embraced Hill's plan with enthusiasm, for several reasons. First, the park was effectively severed by the Continental Divide, and Park headquarters were situated on the west side, at Lake McDonald. If the Great Northern would assume the development of the remote east side, some of the pressure would be relieved from the federal government.

Second, Congressional appropriations for Glacier were woefully inadequate for the federal government to accommodate the increasing number of visitors to the new park. Thus, the railroad's opening of the east side would allow park management to concentrate on west-side facilities. Third, the Great Northern constituted a reliable business organization, with proven construction experience and substantial financial resources. The alternative to the Great Northern's visitor transportation and accommodation system was development by individual contractors operating on a shoestring budget. The tourist would be better served by the railroad's network.

Almost miraculously, Louis Hill developed his communication, transportation, and accommodation network on the Park's east side in three years (1912–1915)—despite an effective construction and tourist season of less than six months each year. By 1915 the Great Northern's basic facilities were in place. They were built, maintained, and operated either directly by the railroad's Glacier Park Hotel Company or indirectly by contract operators, supported by the railroad.

The system was most impressive. Midvale Station was renamed Glacier Park Station (now East Glacier), and here the tourist disembarked from the Great Northern's "Empire Builder" to confront the massive Glacier Park Hotel, modeled after the Portland, Oregon, Forestry Building. This rustic log hotel complex was the kingpin of the system. From here the visitor could travel by horseback, bus, and lake launch to smaller Swiss-style chalets at Two Medicine Lake, Cut Bank Creek, two sites on Upper St. Mary Lake, McDermott [now Swiftcurrent] Lake (Many Glacier), and Goathaunt [at the south end of Waterton Lake]. Alpine chalets near Sperry Glacier, Gunsight Pass, and Granite Park could be reached by foot and on horseback.

Many of the roads and trails on the east side had been built and were maintained by the Great Northern Railway, occasionally with reimbursement from federal appropriations. And the whole system was linked by the company's own crank-phone lines, on which supplies were ordered, tourist accommodations reserved, and emergencies handled. The Great Northern network provided accommodations in the park for 12,385 visitor-nights in 1915, *excluding* tourists staying in the huge Glacier Park Hotel in East Glacier. About one-half of these visitor-nights were logged at the newly opened hotel at Many Glacier.

Louis Hill directed the planning, construction, operation, and maintenance of the entire Great Northern investment on Glacier Park's east side. He developed the theme of Glacier as the "Switzerland of America" in the architectural style of all the buildings, in the alpine attire of his staff, and in the employment of certified Austrian mountaineers to guide climbers from the hotels. In the 1920s he carried the European theme further, by erecting large bells on several of the mountain passes, to be rung by hikers reaching the summits.

The substantial expense involved in establishing this network on the east side was justified by the increased numbers of rail line tourists. Visitation to the park had risen by more than 650% between the 1910 season and the 1915 season. The popularization of the auto was responsible for a bit of this increase. A much larger percentage was the result of Louis Hill's advertising campaign to promote vacationing in Glacier National Park. Tying it to his "See America First" promotion, Hill directed the advertising blitz to the East and Midwest. The results proved effective: Of 9,400 out-of-state visitors to the park in 1915, almost one-third came from New York, Illinois, and Minnesota.

A major component of the Great Northern's advertising campaign focused on the Blackfeet Indians as the "Indians of Glacier National Park." Before long, the Blackfeet were driving tourists around in open buses, having their photographs taken before the majestic mountains and Great Northern hotels of Glacier, representing the railroad and the Park in promotional trips throughout the nation, and camping on the lawn of the Glacier Park Hotel in East Glacier, demonstrating native crafts. The Great Northern created a tie between the Blackfeet and Glacier that would only be strengthened by the portraiture of Winold Reiss and the popularization of Indian names for Glacier Park features.

The visitor to Glacier National Park in 1915 enjoyed Louis Hill's dream almost as much as did the Great Northern president himself. The modern tourist can capture a measure of that dream, for several of Hill's hotels and chalets are still in operation—and *all* of the scenery remains intact. The dream continues.

18

THE LEGENDARY JOE COSLEY

Jerry DeSanto
1980

Joe Cosley (1870–1944)—Park Service ranger, trapper, poacher, fugitive—remains one of the great legendary characters of Glacier National Park. As long-time ranger and historian Jerry DeSanto (b. 1928–2017) explains in this article, Cosley was charismatic, elusive, and mysterious throughout his life. A writer himself, Cosley elaborated on his own legend in a few pamphlets and poems, as well as in his own self-descriptions and stories; most of the quotes in this article are from a posthumously published pamphlet, *A Short Story of Joseph E. [sic] Cosley, Trapper, Guide, Soldier and Student.* He was especially linked with the Belly River country in the northeastern corner of the park, which he knew, everyone agreed, "like the back of his hand."

DeSanto himself was a beloved ranger in the park for many years. Often called "the last of the old-time rangers," he served as the ranger in charge of the North Fork area (where he survived a severe mauling by a grizzly), but he also spent much time in Belly River. He devoted a good part of his retirement years to researching and writing about the history of Glacier. This article is excerpted from *Montana The Magazine of Western History.*

In August of 1910, Major William R. Logan arrived in Belton, Montana, to take charge of the newly-established Glacier National Park, and to appoint the first crew of park rangers. The new rangers he chose were old hands in the mountains: hunters and trappers and prospectors, and a few who had been rangers when the area of Glacier Park was administered by the Forest Service. They were local residents who already knew the dim trails and remote valleys of the wilderness park for their own reasons. In some cases, Major Logan applied a principle still revived occasionally, that "it takes a poacher to catch a poacher." One such choice, and the most colorful of the seven original Glacier rangers, was forty-year-old Joseph Clarence Cosley.

Joe Cosley had already spent at least fifteen years in and around Glacier. A skilled trapper, he knew the haunts of the beaver and the marten, and he trapped in valleys rarely visited even today. An expert rider and packer, he took great pride in the appearance of his horses and equipment. The trails and passes he routinely traveled, in winter as well as summer, remain challenges to contemporary hikers. He sought to leave his mark on Glacier, from carving "JC" on dozens of trees to grandly naming mountains and other landforms for himself.

Above all, Joe Cosley worked to create his own legend. He cultivated exotic dress, ascribed his flowery speech to a nonexistent college education, claimed aristocratic birth that put his rough life into high relief. If the colorful character of his imagination overshadows his real feats, one gathers that Cosley wouldn't mind—as long as people still tell Cosley stories.

Cosley was born near Lake Huron, Ontario, in 1870. His father, Stephen, was a commercial fisherman and trapper and his mother was either Cree or Chippewa with a good education for the times and place. Cosley himself usually denied any Indian blood, although in one account he said he was of Chippewa descent and he is often mentioned in contemporary accounts as the "Indian trapper Cosley" or the "half-breed Cosley."

The story of his early days is vague and much of this is because of the wild tales Cosley himself told to newspapers during his later years. Following an interview in 1939, the *Edmonton Bulletin* reported that he was "from an aristocratic family whose beautiful mansion was situated at Saratoga, N. Y." In a posthumous story, the *Lethbridge Herald* said he was a "college graduate who always wore ear-rings." The truth is that the Cosley family moved to a homestead near Blind Rivers, Ontario, soon after Joe was born. The children received their education there, probably at a convent school, and this was undoubtedly the extent of young Joe's formal education.

Cosley's prose style was wildly colorful and this contributed to his reputation as well-educated. In 1894, he and a companion were roaming through the mountains and their adventures brought forth an outburst of vivid description.

> Excessive joy in our patent need came to our long desponding spirits and we sprang to the packs without delay and with vigor....It was about time that such a haven of blessedness opened in our existence, for we were drenched to the skin, copiously drenched, and shivered till our teeth chattered with the cold.

He was also a poet of sorts and anyone who could create rhymes on sentimental subjects, as Joe did, must have been regarded as at least a college graduate by his rough companions. In a poem entitled *Proposal*, he wrote:

Ah lovely maiden, kind and true,
Through these lines I appeal to you;
Pause, Oh pause along the path of life
Thou queen of loveliness, and become my wife.

His suit was rejected, but hunters and trappers would certainly have been impressed by the author's "education."

Cosley left home at his father's death, and after a few years of wandering showed up in Montana around 1890. In later stories, he described some of these early years with tales of adventure that were good copy for urban newspapers. An article in the *Edmonton Bulletin* in 1939, for example, described Cosley as "one of the toughest Indian fighters since Daniel Boone," and there is a dramatic account of his duel on horseback with Lone Hand, a Sioux warrior.

They both fired and missed, then rode at each other with Bowie knives. Cosley won but it was said it took a year for his wounds to heal. He still has a scar above his right eye. This was in 1890 when Sitting Bull fought his last battle at Wounded Knee.

The same newspaper had run an article six years earlier in which Cosley only "reminds one of the 'Injun fighters' of history and fiction." In this story, his exploits in World War I are recounted and there is no mention of Indian fighting. The true story of these years is likely to be far less thrilling. Cosley probably drifted through the western United States from job to job, acquiring rudiments of the outdoor skills he later mastered. Many years later, he recalled that he was a cowboy on "the plains of Montana" in 1890, and he must have seen much of the Old West, from Arizona to Montana, in those early years.

This rough and exciting life appealed to young Joe and the legend of the Indian fighter began to grow. His long hair and mustache with the pointed goatee are in the Buffalo Bill fashion and his later feats of trick riding and shooting were first learned in those years. By the time he came to Montana, then, he was ready and eager to take on the mountains and winters with all the thrills and hardships of the wilderness. But his later stories of aristocratic heritage, college education and fighting Indians are only fictions of an aging and overly-enthusiastic imagination.

In 1890, Lt. George P. Ahern led a detachment of soldiers to the headwaters of the Belly River, over the pass on the Continental Divide that now bears his name, past Lake McDonald and down the Flathead River. The soldiers were forced to build a trail over Ahern Pass. Their crossing by pack train is one of only two ever recorded. Cosley may have been along as a packer or assistant since there is mention of "Crossley, a half-breed" in the party. If this "Crossley" was Joe Cosley, this is the earliest record of his presence in the park area. Even if this were not Cosley, the real Joe shortly was to use Ahern Pass many times. Although Ahern Pass is the quickest route to the McDonald country from Belly River, as Lt. Ahern, Joe and many other early travelers realized, it is rarely used today since the trail has not been maintained for many years.

Although Joe may not have been with Ahern, he can definitely be placed in the Glacier Park country in the mid-1890s. At that time, prospectors were working through the northern Rockies and a few minor leads had been located in the park area. Until a final agreement was made with the Blackfeet Indians in 1896, the country east of the Continental Divide was off limits to mineral exploration, and although some surreptitious prospecting was carried on in east slope valleys, most early work was done west of the divide. Early interest centered on the area around the headwaters of Mineral Creek (a tributary of McDonald Creek), where, along a small feeder stream that now bears his name, Joseph Kipp located a claim in the early 1890s. Here he built a cabin, and in about 1894, he hired Joe Cosley and J. M. Wallerbeck, nicknamed "Porcupine Jim," to improve his claim.

Cosley and Porcupine Jim began their journey on horseback at Blackfoot on the newly completed Great Northern mainline and may have reached Kipp's cabin by traveling up the Belly River and over Ahern Pass. Here, in September, they found themselves in a place "fearfully wild in its nature" and abounding in grizzly bears and mountain lions. But Indian summer came on and, under its spell, the two led a pleasant life, materially aided by a bumper crop of huckleberries, an abundance of game and good forage for the horses. Cosley wrote of "beautiful glades [with] plants in full bloom" and the "variety of sweet flowers." "We certainly enjoyed our new paradise," he wrote, "upon which the great sun poured down its radiant beams through a clear sky." Chickadees sang as if it were summer and Joe "could only attribute this untimely strain to their progenies of trivial mind[s] who knew no better."

Their idyllic life came to a rude end. Returning to camp after a day's work, they found the cabin burned to the ground and with it, their food, blankets, coats and cash. "I no longer held an especially agreeable interest in the climatic condition or the beauty which it imparted to the verdant land," Joe wrote. The next morning they began a trek to Lake McDonald, for additional supplies, probably via Mineral Creek and McDonald Creek. Making the round trip in four days, they returned for another ten days of assessment work just as a snow storm "set in with threatening foreboding."

While the storm raged, they argued over the route out of the high country and with morning and three feet of snow, they decided to leave immediately. Rejecting the route over Ahern Pass as too dangerous in the new snow, they headed north "down an unknown canyon for better or for worse." After slipping and sliding down the bluffs and cliffs that separate Flattop Mountain from the Waterton River valley, they found old trail blazes that led them to a trapper's shack at the edge of a meadow. On the table in the cabin was a note: "To anyone coming this way, may use our cabin to his convenience for the night. John G. Brown." On the shelves were books and "stationery of the choicest kind" and pens, ink and pencils. Cosley surmised that Brown was "evidently a writer of manuscripts."

After a trip of several days that took them to Waterton Lake, along its west shore, past Cameron Falls and across the flat on which Waterton Townsite now stands, they met John G. Brown at his home near Knight's Lake.

This was "Kootenai" Brown, the first white settler in what is now Waterton Lakes National Park, and later the first superintendent of that park. Kootenai and Joe became fast friends and Joe modeled himself in many ways after his acknowledged hero. Joe described Kootenai at their first meeting.

> He was a small man, agile in movement and quick eyed. A Stetson buckskin sombrero crowned his head—a bright red rose and a few green leaves painted on the under right-side of the brim. He wore a voyageur's red sash, long fringed, hanging loosely at his side; a brocaded silk muffler about his neck, cowboy style. He had long hair that fell gracefully in wavelets over his shoulders. A gray mustache, terminating in points and slightly curved upward. He had the appearance of a typical frontiersman.

Soon after, Cosley adopted the Kootenai look in both dress and hair style, and was as deeply impressed by what he called the "weight" of his new friend's intellect. Kootenai Brown was able, said Joe, to discuss "doctrines of Christian faith in the middle ages" and he was "versed…in the spirit of Scholasticism. Withal he was a queer fish! A great hunter; a good masher. A man who interspersed Latin quotations and classic oaths begotten of Oxford with the usual Western formula of embellished expressions."

Kootenai Brown had never seen Oxford and his knowledge of Medieval theology was nil, but he had just enough learning to impress and teach the 24-year-old Cosley. Joe imitated Kootenai in many ways. Not only did he adopt the red rose and green leaves on the underside of his hat brim, but he took to wearing a colorful sash, sported long hair, and grew a mustache and goatee in the Buffalo Bill-Kootenai Brown tradition. And he may have begun to think and act like Kootenai, as his overblown writing style indicates. Joe, it seems, liked to combine the wildness and freedom of the frontier life with the culture and learning of another society.

From the 1890s on, Joe spent most of his time in northern Montana and southern Alberta, with trapping as his main livelihood. It was in the late 1890s that he started carving his name and date on trees scattered through his trapping grounds. Some say this was his defiant way of telling the Law where he had been and others, more romantically, say it was merely an "old Cosley custom…there will be J.C. as long as the trees last, in deep and inaccessible places of the western forests, and along the mountain trails." "Cosley trees" are still found in Glacier National Park. One near Cosley Lake is well known, another is near the Belly River Ranger Station and another was recently cut down and hauled to Park Headquarters as a historical curiosity. Others are known to exist in out-of-the-way places in the North Fork country of the Park.

In the 1890s, Joe was probably at his best as a snowshoer and a trapper. Stories are told of how he traveled all day at a trot, leaving tracks five feet apart. According to Julia Nelson, a Mountain View writer, Joe would set out on his trapline with less than thirty pounds of supplies, "mainly tea, salt, and beans, and his snowshoes, revolver, and .22 automatic." He had a winter route that covered 200 miles of foothills and mountains. Along the way he usually slept in the open or in dugout shelters, and one he may have used, along Boundary Creek in Glacier Park, is still recognizable.

Joe's trapline covered some of the best marten country left in Montana, when marten pelts were in great demand. It is a Cosley tradition that he shot the martens with his .22, skinned them out on the spot, and ate the carcasses as his only food on winter trips. This is an exaggeration, but he undoubtedly did use the carcasses for food and he seems to have shot more martens than he trapped. For a traveler like Joe, shooting the animal was a quicker and easier way of getting his furs and food, but he had to hit them with a perfect shot to avoid damaging the pelt.

Joe made good money trapping but he squandered it on fancy clothes and equipment. He was especially proud of his saddles, spurs and other tack, and he must have spent a good part of his earnings on such items as silver-mounted spurs permanently attached to his riding boots. He was also a photographer and, like his idol Kootenai Brown, "a writer of manuscripts." In one way or another, he probably managed to be broke in the fall but flush in the spring. But what a life it must have been for him! Full of health and strength, skilled in the ways of the wilderness and close to the nature he knew and loved, he was living completely the life of his choice.

The Belly River claims were taken up following reported discoveries of surface petroleum. These claims extended up the Belly River from the international boundary all the way to the head of Glenns Lake along one fork to Elizabeth Lake along the other. The first claims were located in 1902 and Joe appears in the records both as one of the earliest locators and as a claimant. Other claimants included Frank Liebig, Frank Geduhn, and Dan Doody, early Forest Service rangers. Several local merchants and other residents were active in the Swiftcurrent [Many Glacier] mining and oil exploration, but apparently little or no oil was produced and the only evidence of activity that can still be found is a casing that projects from the ground near the forks of the Belly River. The oil seeps of the early years are now, as they were then, mineral licks used by elk, deer and other animals. The most heavily-used and most odoriferous is the lick within sight of the Belly River Ranger Station on a fork of Gable Creek.

Although Joe Cosley had certainly been in the Belly River before 1902, he probably dated his close acquaintance of it from this time. A rough wagon road was punched through from Canada in about 1902 and one branch ended at Cosley Lake on the Mokowanis River (west fork of the Belly River). The other branch dwindled off near Dawn Mist Falls, after fording the Belly River just upstream from the site of the present ranger station. Joe must have pioneered these roads and, according to local legend, he also built two cabins that are now in ruins.

Up until a few years ago, the National Park Service used the road to supply the ranger station and in earlier, less-sensitive times, rangers and tourists drove trucks and cars right to the station. The Cosley Lake branch is rarely used now and is almost grown over. Both cabins are off the beaten track—one along an unnamed creek near the head of Glenns Lake. Joe first used these cabins as trapping headquarters, then Forest Service rangers used them on patrol up until 1910, and again Joe used them as Park Service stations from 1910 to 1914.

Belly River became Joe's haunt....This may have been the time that he began, "with characteristic ego," naming topological features such as Mount Cosley or the Pyramid of Cosley (now either Cosley Ridge or Pyramid Peak) and Cosley Lake (changed to Crossley by later mappers but changed back to Cosley Lake by still later mappers). He also drifted around picking up various odd jobs and it may have been Joe who showed up as a cook on the North Fork Railroad survey in 1909. This Joe, identified as "Joe Crosly, a half-breed Indian...was an excellent cook, he was one of the dirtiest cooks I have ever encountered and one was never sure what he was eating." This doesn't sound particularly like Cosley, but the next lines do. "He was a picturesque fellow— always a red sash for a belt. I can see him yet backed up to the campfire with his face lifted to the stars, reciting 'The Wreck of the Julie Plant[e].'" Later, this picturesque cook "borrowed" some horses—much to the displeasure of the writer.

Joe Cosley worked for the Forest Service off and on from 1900 to 1910 and, when not working, spent much time in what is now the northeast corner of Glacier Park and in the country along the North Fork of the Flathead. In a group photo of the Blackfeet National Forest rangers taken at Olney in 1910, he is present and is identified as Jos. C. Cosley. With his uniform, he also wears a stiff-brim Stetson, a bandanna, and what looks like a red sash around his waist. There were other colorful characters in this group, including Fred Herrig, a Roosevelt Rough Rider and ranch hand, who was [a] ranger up in the North Fork before 1910. Herrig was a big man who rode a huge white horse and he was usually accompanied by two Russian wolfhounds. His saddle was silver-mounted and he wore a pair of pearl-handled revolvers. Some others in the picture are Frank Liebig, the first ranger at Lake McDonald, and North Fork homesteaders Theo Christensen and Jack Wise.

Joe Cosley's Park Service comrades in those early days in Glacier were remarkable and genuine. There was Albert Reynolds, also known as "Dad" and "Death-on-the-Trail." The nickname "Dad" was due to Reynold's age (in 1910, he must have been about 60) and his full gray beard and mustache. The origin of "Death-on-the-Trail" is unknown, but it may have indicated the way Reynolds wanted to go out....In that year, a party of tourists met him at Granite Park with his son Dexter and Ranger Frank Liebig. A newspaper clipping of this trip noted that the party was "led by Ranger Reynolds, who could climb like a mountain sheep."

When Reynolds first came on as a Park Ranger in 1910, he was assigned briefly to Kintla and then to Waterton. At Waterton, he battled successfully to ward off logging interests in the Waterton valley and he commuted to the ranch of his friend, Kootenai Brown, to pick up and send off his mail. On one of these trips in February of 1913 he fell ill at Kootenai's ranch, after being out in bitterly cold weather, and soon after died of pneumonia at a hospital in Pincher Creek, Alberta. He missed his end on the trail, but not by much.

In the early days of the park, a ranger's primary duty was protection. Today, protection usually signifies protection of the visitor; in 1910 it meant guarding the park's resources. At his assigned post in the Belly River area, Joe kept an eye on the few miners who were permitted to continue their developments. His other duties included trail maintenance, guiding visitors and predator control. Joe must have been constantly busy with these official duties, but there is little doubt that he found plenty of time to prowl around in the park and to visit in nearby Canadian and American communities.

Cosley, always noted for his exploits, experienced a brush with death in 1912. According to the Superintendent's Report for that year,

> Ranger Cosley, under date of July 6, when returning to his station after a conference at headquarters, attempted Ahearn [*sic*] Pass. While crossing the pass a snow-covered ledge broke off and he narrowly escaped with his life. The horse he was riding and his pack horse were instantly killed, falling hundreds of feet into the canyon beneath.

Another account of the same incident claims that Joe was actually returning from a July 4th celebration in Browning, which seems more in character for him than a conference at headquarters. This was the pass first crossed by Lt. Ahern in 1890 and there is an outside chance that young Joe was with that party. Tradition has it that there has been only one other successful crossing on horseback—that by R. H. Sargent of the Geological Survey and packer Frank Valentine in 1902.

One of the best-known Cosley stories dates from about 1913. Joe bought a diamond ring for a Canadian girl, putting out the extravagant amount of $1500 for it. The girl, sometimes described as a rich widow, soon grew tired of both Joe and the ring and returned the gift. A disconsolate Joe buried the ring in a tree somewhere in the Belly River country. The legendary part of the story is that the ring is still there and whoever finds it is welcome to it. The truth is that Joe dug it out several years later to finance the purchase of trapping gear.

Joe was still on the rolls as a park ranger in March 1914 and drew $83.33 as his pay for that month. In August, he volunteered for the Canadian Army, thus ending his rangering days. A story is told that when Joe hurriedly left for the army he abandoned his cabin (probably the one near the head of Glenns Lake) without packing, moving things out, or even taking the dishes off the table. Joe must have been a man of instant decisions.

Ever since his army days Joe had skirted the law by trapping illegally in both Canada and the U.S. Rangers from Glacier Park and wardens from Canada's Waterton Lakes National Park supposedly "stalked him constantly and unsuccessfully for years" and Joe is said to have told one ranger that he would kill him if he found him on certain trails. In those days, rangers and wardens spent all year at remote stations and patrolled constantly. In 1927, Glacier superintendent J. Ross Eakin wrote Assistant Director Horace M. Albright, making it clear what the first priority was for Park rangers: "At Glacier a Ranger's duty to the exclusion of everything is to patrol his district." It was just a matter of time before Joe would be caught despite his experience and skill. In 1929, he slipped, resulting in the best-known story in the Cosley repertory and the end of Joe Cosley as a familiar figure in the Glacier Park country.

On a spring day in 1929, Belly River Ranger Joseph F. Heimes noticed that a beaver dam had flooded the wagon road that led from Canada into his station. Upon investigation, he found a camp along the river about three quarters of a mile from the international line. Beaver hindquarters were smoking over a fire, muskrat hides were packed away between blankets and, although no one was there, it was evident that the trapper would return by nightfall. Sensing a chill coming on, Heimes hiked to his station to report the matter by park telephone and to don his winter underwear. Returning to the camp, he found the trapper cooking his supper. Although he had never met Cosley, Heimes recognized him and immediately confronted Joe with his violation. Cosley said he would not be taken in, that he was going the other way into Canada. Heimes stiffened and threatened to beat Cosley with a club if he must. At a standoff in the darkening wilds, the two men settled down to what must have been a long and unpleasant night. Cosley tried to bribe Heimes with his watch, but it was no use. In the morning, they set out for Belly River Station, seven miles upriver.

Along the trail Heimes had to chase down Cosley several times as the poacher tried to escape; each time a scuffle ensued with Heimes threatening the older Cosley with a club. Finally reinforcements arrived—a Park Ranger and a Canadian warden. The foursome continued on to Belly River Station, taking with them Cosley's rifle, muskrat hides and traps as evidence. The next day they went over Gable Pass, where they met up with another ranger at Kennedy Creek and then drove to East Glacier to spend the night. The following day they boarded the train for West Glacier and Park Headquarters.

After Cosley had traveled four days and three nights following his apprehension by Joe Heimes, the Park Commissioner found him guilty of poaching, and fined him $100 and confiscated his gun, traps and hides. Friends paid Joe's fine and he was turned loose. He hitched a ride to the end of the road— then near Logan Creek, twenty miles from Park Headquarters—hopped on his snowshoes and headed for Belly River.

His route lay past Granite Park, over Ahern Pass, down the Belly River past Helen and Elizabeth Lakes and the Belly River Station and on into Canada. On the way, he picked up the rest of his camp including a few beaver hides. Although he walked only thirty miles, it was a hard trip, especially at that time of the year and at his age; Joe was now fifty-nine years old. Meanwhile, Heimes and another ranger took the train to East Glacier, were driven to Canada and then headed into Belly River on foot. They intended to stop at Cosley's camp and collect the remaining gear. "We arrived where his camp had been," wrote Heimes, "and there wasn't a sign of it left. All tracks had been carefully erased and everything had completely disappeared."

About Joe's capture, George C. Ruhle, Glacier's Chief Naturalist in 1928, wrote:

> Joe Cosley, the poacher, was nothing short of being a most remarkable character; a half-breed Indian of Chippewa extraction, he was a six-footer of splendid physique....At the time of his capture, Cosley's facial appearance was anything but invitation to anyone for an encounter. His protruding teeth and blown cheeks gave him a particularly vicious and ugly appearance; by sight, there could be no doubt that he was a bad actor. It was quite a shock by contrast to hear this unsightly individual speak in a voice of softest timbre with choice diction and pleasing pronunciation.

In his last known letter, Joe wrote that he was feeling good, eating three big meals a day and enjoying Edmonton life. It was February 1943. He had spent the winter in town for the first time in many years, and was certain that he was catching colds he would not have caught had he been out on the trap line. But he was interested enough to be writing his stories, and he seemed to be happy in the quietness of his room.

Joe set out on his last trip north that fall. Supposedly he said "what he never said before": "If I'm not back in May, send someone to look for me." When Joe did not appear in Edmonton in the spring of 1944 to claim his World War I pension checks, the authorities informed the RCMP [Royal Canadian Mounted Police] at Ile a la Crosse, Saskatchewan. In September, Constable J. McLeod and an Indian guide set out in search of Joe and were gone twenty days. They found what was left of him in or near his cabin, buried the remains and decided the cause of death was scurvy.

The triangular-shaped cabin where Joe spent his last winter had earlier been the scene, in 1939, of another trapper's death by scurvy. According to stories, this trapper had placed a curse on the cabin—a curse that was known to Joe. Joe's diaries were found with him and in his last entry, he had described how it had taken him all afternoon to reach a creek just fifty feet away. He must have died the following day, May 23, 1944. It is said that his last written words were "I am steadily growing weaker....I can hardly write....I have reached the end." His diaries and other personal effects were presumably turned over to relatives—either a brother in Ontario or a sister in Michigan.

Most of those who knew Joe personally are gone, but he will never be forgotten in Glacier Park, where Cosley stories are standard park lore. Writing about the Joe Cosley he once knew, George C. Ruhle called him "a fabulous hunter, trapper, poacher and newspaper correspondent who distinguished himself in World War I. He was one of the first rangers in Glacier National Park and made the Belly River country his life haunt." Joe may have wished for a little more, but that is the gist of the story.

19

FROM *EXIT LAUGHING*

Irvin S. Cobb
1941

Irvin S. Cobb (1876–1944) was one of America's most popular writers and humorists during the first half of the twentieth century. A native of Paducah, Kentucky, Cobb became known as the "Duke of Paducah," in tribute to his charming reminiscences about his small-town boyhood. An acquaintance of cowboy artist Charles M. Russell, Cobb and his wife spent the summer of 1925 in a rented cabin in Glacier Park. Subsequently, he wrote several short stories set in or near Glacier that were published in the collection *Ladies and Gentlemen* (1927). The following sketch was published in his collection of humorous essays, *Exit Laughing*.

I think one of the happiest summers I ever spent was the summer we had a cottage on Lake McDonald in Glacier National Park. Charley Russell and Nancy Russell were in camp down at the foot of the lake, six miles below the cottage we had leased from John Lewis, proprietor of Lewis' famous hotel. When Charley wasn't painting a picture or modeling in clay or writing one of his designedly illiterate humorous sketches, he was likely to be sitting on our front porch at the edge of the water, where the Rockies were humping up their spiny backs like angry cats behind us, and across to the south was a view of the saddle in the mountains where the transcontinental trains dipped through. Sitting there one afternoon he held up to the light a pair of smeared and blurry glasses and said to his wife:

"Hon, why is it these here specks of mine always look like windows in a hen house?"

"When did you wash them last?" she inquired.

"Only yestiddy," he stated. "Or maybe the day before."

"Too bad you don't wash your thumbs at the same time," she snapped tartly. The Lady Nancy had a clever tongue of her own.

In a parched but breezy August a forest fire threatened the middle gateway to the Park. Every able-bodied adult at the entrance joined the fight of saving the splendid timber which clothed those notched foothills under the shoulders of the Great Divide. Day and night men worked to check the roaring, swirl-ing, mounting façade of flames; worked until all of them were black as sweeps and choked with resiny fumes, worked until some dropped in their tracks and might have burned to death had there been no volunteer rescue crews to drag them away. Under a false twilight of smoke, the women trudged back and forth in the defending lines, with sandwiches and coffee and drinking water and some of them carried first-aid kits for blistered faces and streaming eyes, and some risked their lives by venturing deep into the imperiled pinelands with rations for the front skirmishers.

A change in the wind saved the little settlement of Belden [Belton], on the state road piercing the main gap. The nearermost sparks were beaten out at the back side of the Russells' stable yard. That was how close a call the village had. On that last day the park rangers evacuated everybody in the colony and brought the lot of them up to Lewis'. Hundreds slept in the hotel that night, and strangers were stretched on pallets upon every spare foot of space on the floors of our cottage and temporarily homeless families were quartered in a double row of log cabins along the lake shore on beyond us.

The Russells, with their adopted son Jack, occupied one of these cabins. Just across the narrow footpath from them, a Belden transient, an itinerate pho-tographer by trade, was domiciled. Having been compelled to abandon his shop, this refugee arrived, it would seem, in a state of low spirits and, presum-ably to comfort himself, he spent practically the entire night practicing on a slide trombone which he had fetched along with him. The selection chosen to lighten his gloom was the hymn "Nearer My God to Thee," an appropri-ate choice, the governing circumstances considered. But since the saddened instrumentalist knew only the first bar of "Nearer My God to Thee," he played it over and over again a thousand times, and never seemed to get any nearer.

Next morning after breakfast I came along the trail between the twinned lines of cabins. Charley, worn by a sleepless night and with a murderous glint in his reddened eyes, was sitting on the slab doorstep of his cabin. He hailed me:

"Old Cobb," he said, "would you maybe like to buy one of these here slip horns at a bargain?"

"Well, now, Mr. Russell," I said, "you take me by surprise but on first thought I would say, with a reasonable degree of certainty, that at present I am not in the market for a slip horn."

"Better think it over," he said. "There's a man's hide goes with this one."

One of the most engaging of the near-by sojourners was an ex-cowman who had wandered afar from his native Panhandle, with a string of ponies. His father must have been somewhat of an extremist as a patriot, for he had named his four sons after four of the cities of his beloved state—Waco, Dallas, Austin and Tyler. Our neighbor was Dallas—Dallas Desbro. From him I purchased four travel-worn Texas ponies and for the season he threw in the use of bridles and stock saddles. I think he rather overcharged me but the Cobbs, like the elephant, never forget and in the fall before we left I got even with him. I gave him back the four plugs and left him stuck with them and winter coming on and the sucker crop gone from Glacier. It was indeed a fiendish revenge.

My steed was a reformed cowhorse, a steep-gabled high-ribbed structure which, being of a prevalent beige tone, would anywhere in the West inevitably be known as "Buckskin." But because of a certain attribute he shared with a lifelong comrade of mine, I rechristened him "Bob Davis"—he ate everywhere he could stop and stopped everywhere he could eat. In his youth, it was said, he had been a snaky and unpredictable animal, freely addicted to scolloping, sunfishing and swapping ends with himself. But the years were supposed to have sapped his enthusiasms.

One afternoon I decided to go for a ride on the government highway then building up toward the great ramparts of the towering Garden Wall. The remaining members of the household were otherwise engaged and so when I mounted Bob Davis and undertook to ride him out of the improvised corral behind our cottage, he balked; he didn't want to leave his three mates at the feed rack. I raked his corrugated withers with a pair of inefficient Central Park spurs and slapped him between two stubbornly cocked ears with my hat—and lo, he had left in his usually sedate system a few unexpended bucking gestures and, without warning, he arched his spine and sank his head and put them on, with intent pronto to pour me out of the saddle.

The first stiff-legged lunge jolted me so high aloft I could see distant peaks I never had seen before. I had ample time for deciding where I would come down, so I decided to come down somewhere on his upper plane surfaces. So I alighted on his rump, away back by his tail roots, and slid forward. And the next trip down I straddled his neck and slid backward; and next time after that I descended solidly in the center of him and I could feel some of his vital organs fetching loose from their moorings and seemed to hear these detached contents sloshing about inside of him. So to make a mutually painful story no more painfully prolonged than needs be, when he quit, with his quivering legs widely braced and his sides heaving like a captive balloon and his humiliated nose in the dust, I still was aboard.

All through this Charley had been perched on the top rail of the fence, intently eying the proceedings. Now he climbed down and calipered on his bowed legs over to where I sat, breathless but triumphantly enthroned, and he took my free hand and warmly he shook it and said:

"Old Cobb, you've been norratin' around that you're no fancy rider. Me, I claim after seein' this here exhibition, that you're better'n average. I admit your system is different from any I ever saw, but there ain't a way for any four-legged critter to beat it. I figger you must be part eagle. Why, you jest natchelly hover over a hoss!"

20

LETTERS FROM BULL HEAD LODGE

Charles M. Russell
1906–1926

The most famous and beloved summer resident of Lake McDonald during the first quarter of the twentieth century was the "Cowboy Artist," Charlie Russell (1864–1926). A native of St. Louis, Russell first came to frontier Montana in 1880 when he was sixteen. Supporting himself as a herder of sheep, cattle, and horses (in that order), he gradually developed his artistic talents until he became, along with Frederic Remington, the leading portrayer of cowboys, Indians, and the Old West, using watercolors, oils, clay, bronze, and any other material that lent itself to art.

In late 1905—five years before Glacier was designated a national park—Charlie and his wife Nancy bought a building lot on the shore of Lake McDonald near the tiny settlement of Apgar and hired local residents to build them a log cabin as a summer residence. Eventually they added an artist's studio/guesthouse and other outbuildings. The Russells spent every summer until Charlie's death at "Kootnaei Lodge" (so spelled, rather than "Kootenai"), later renamed "Bull Head Lodge" after the bison skull with which Charlie signed his paintings and sculptures. Charlie used the summers to relax, sketch, paint, ride horseback, and host vacationing friends and working artists; he also wrote wonderfully illustrated letters to people all over the country, recounting activities, joshing former visitors, and depicting the glorious scenery of the park.

One of these letters—addressed to "dude-wrangler," horseman, cowboy, and guide Mike Shannon—included a watercolor of a cowboy leading a group of mounted tourists to an overlook with the park's mountains in the background. The letter has unfortunately been lost, but Charlie's text survives with this statement of his love for wilderness and for the park:

> I think thairl be lots of people in the park this summer and as thair are still people who like to ride I hope you and your horses have all you can handle a machine will show folks the man made things but if people want to see Gods own country thave got to get a horse under them In spite of gasoline the biggest part of the Rocky Mountains belongs to God and as long as it dose thairl be a home for you and your kind to me the roar of a

mountian stream mingled with the bells of a pack trane is grander musick than all the string or brass bands in the world

Fifteen examples of Russell's creative artistry follow. As in the example above, Russell rarely used punctuation of any kind and his spelling was, to say the least, inventive.

Plate 1. Sketch of "Bulls Head Lodge," watercolor on birchbark, 1906. This sketch was apparently drawn soon after the original cabin was completed.

Plate 2. "Greetings from us all," watercolor on birchbark, sent to Albert and Margaret Trigg and their daughter Josephine, July 23, 1906. The Triggs were friends and neighbors of the Russells in the city of Great Falls, Montana, and frequently visited the Russells at Lake McDonald in the summer.

Plate 3. "Best Wishes to Mr. and Mrs. Calvert, Kootnaei Lodge," watercolor on birchbark, 1906. Charlie depicts himself rowing a boat and towing another on the lake, bringing supplies to the cabin during the Russells' first summer there. The Calverts were friends from Great Falls.

Plate 4. "Says the halk with a stare," watercolor on birchbark, August 1905, sent to Katharine and Robert P. Roberts. The Robertses were a young couple who were married in the Russells' home in Great Falls on August 9, 1905. The Robertses spent their honeymoon at a cabin rented by the Russells at Lake McDonald, and Charlie painted this scene for them. The text seems to read:

Says the halk [hawk] with a stare How maney are there In the glare of the sun I cant see but one said the owl Its a figureless sum tis two made one said the Fisher Add it and try figurs wont lie youl find it quite true twise one makes two says the Fisher Youl have to show me Iv seen two ones [make?] Three I see Says the Stork Its two said the Loon an a strong case of spune [spoon]

Plate 5. "In remembrance of August Ninth 1905 Lake McDonald from your friends at Kootnaei Lodge," watercolor on birchbark, 1906. A year after the wedding, Charlie sent this anniversary gift of a kingfisher at Lake McDonald when the young couple was visiting the Russells' new cabin.

PLATE 1

PLATE 2

Best Wishes
to
Mr. and Mrs. Calvert

"Kootnaei Lodge"

PLATE 3

PLATE 4

In remembrance of
August Ninth 1905
Lake Mc Donald
from your friends at
"Kootnaei Lodge"

PLATE 5

Plates 6–9. In this letter (water color and ink on paper, September 4, 1908) to Edgar to Edgar I. Holland, a friend and neighbor of the Russells in Great Falls, Charlie describes, tongue-in-cheek, the goings-on at Bull Head Lodge and addresses the Hollands' daughter Marion ("Little Sunshine") with a parodic tale based on the romantic literature of the day. He also refers to his "night watches," a medieval knight and a buckskin-clad Indian that Charlie had created from wood and scraps of material. He even teases Mrs. Virginia Holland about her pronunciation of "tomato." The letter reads:

Friend Holland

I have received sevral letters from you an I guess its time Im answering news are short up here an I havent seen Apgar for a day or two so I havent got much to right about tell Littel Sunshine the blood hounds have eat the last Ladrone blood raw an are now taking there seastia [siesta] an the Don after a firce struggle was swollod [swallowed] by an allagator. our hero spyed the reptile but to late an noting its sweled an after dinner look rased his trusty rifal an pirced its brane after another firce strugle it sank to the depth of the lagoon with its lothsum repast never to rase again after one long sad look our hero turned an sadly retraced his steps an marryed the widow under the spreding palms while the sweet voised pelicons sang the wedding march. things are verry quiet up here since the folks left there is onley seven of us now couting the two chickons an as bakon is getting scarce I belive they will not be with us long we have just returned from a trip to the [Sperry] glacier an had good wether an a fine time the wether since has been rany an cold up to the last fiew days it is now fine tell Miss sun shine that the lake is still warm in spite of the cold wether I hope Mrs Hollond is getting all the tomaters I mean tommotoes she wants people are leaving the lake every day for there homes an we will soone be getting ready our selvs one are two skunks have taken up quarters ender the house an seem to like the place al so a numbr of montian rats [pack rats] have mooved in an by the noise they make Iv a hunch my night watches are sleeping on gard as soon as dark comes the new comers goes to work all hands the skunks practis two seps [steps] and barn dances on the porch or in the kitchen the rats dont seem to like our roof all night long thair bussy making it over occasionaly stopping to gether up tooth brushes leaving rocks sicks [sticks] ore old bones in exchange they are traders who belive a fair exchange is no robery the great horned owl in the seaders [cedars] at intervals askes who no one knows so receiving no answer he keeps it up all night an at day brak flies away in disgust but returns the next night with the same question its to bad someone cant tell him well Holland as I cant think of aney more foolishness I will close with best wishes to you all

your friend
CM Russell

Plates 10–11. "Friend Bill [William H. Rance]," watercolor on paper, August 12, 1912. Bill Rance was one of Charlie's closest friends and was the proprietor of the Silver Dollar Saloon in Great Falls—Charlie's favorite hangout even after he quit drinking alcohol in 1908. Rance regularly shipped cases of "boose," as Charlie spelled it, to Bull Head Lodge for the enjoyment of the Russells' visitors. Here Charlie imagines himself tending bar on the shore of the lake for prosperous "sports" with fishing rods. He also reports a dance between a man and a "lady grizzley" that did not end well for the man (the park has no record of such an incident, by the way).

Friend Bill

I received the papers and also box [of beverages] an as I am not using aney myself I am thinking of opning a little open air joint most of the fellrs I see up here don't look like CoKaCola men Catch one of these long thirst leg weary fisherman with nothing but water to drink an hel buy red ink at your price an thank you for it. an with that high grade Joy juce of yours Bill I could have them writing home for money well Bill there aint much doing up here but I heard there was a man up on the mane range that mixed up with a lady grizzley an they pulled of the genuine grizzley bear dance they say the man wasent strong on round dances but he couldent refuse a lady an you know every bodys doing it an I guess before that dance closed he thought pritty near every body had done it to him. the folks that arrived after the ball dident find much, a belt buckle som buttens things a bear couldent use well Bill I will close with regards to yourself an the bunch

Your Friend
CM Russell

SEP 4
1908

Friend Holland

I have received serral letters
from you an I guess its
time   Im answering

news are short up here an
I havent seen Akgar for a day
or two so I havent got much
to right about .

tell Little Sunshine the blood
hounds have eat the last
Sadrone blood raw an are now
taking there seastia an the Don
after a firce struggle was swollod
by an allagator . oure hero spyes
the reptile but to late an noting
its sweled an after dinner look
rased his trusty rifal penetrated its
brane after another firce strugle it

PLATE 6

sank to the depth of the lagoon
with its lottisum repast never
to rase again
after one long sad book our
hero turned an sadly retraced
his steps an marryed the widow
under the spreding palms while
the sweet voised pelicons sang
the wedding march.
things are verry quiet up here
since the folks left there isonley
seven of us now conting the two
Cluekons an as bakon is getting
scarse I belive they will not be
with us long

we have just returned from
a trip to the glacier an had
good wether an a fine time
the wether since has been
rany an cold up to the last
birds days it is now fine
tell Miss sun shine that the
lake is still warme in spite
of the cold wether
y hope Mrs Holland is getting
all the tomaters I mean tommotoes

PLATE 7

she wants
people are leaving the lake
every day for there homes an
we will soone be getting ready
our selvs
one are two sknnks have taken up
quarters ander the house an seem
to like the place al so a number of
montian rats have mooved in an
by the noise they make Iv a
lunch my night watches are
sleeping on gard

as soon as dark comes the new
comen goes to work all hands
the sknnks practis two sepr arad
barn darnces on the porch or in tte

PLATE 8

kitchen the rats dont seem
to like our roof all night
long thair bussy making it over
occasionaly stopping to gether up
tooth brushes leaving rocks sicks
ore old bones in exchange
they are traders who belive
a fair exchange is no robery
the great horned owl in the seader
at intervals asks who no one
knows so receiving no answer
he keeps it up all night
and at day brak flies away in
disgust but returnes the next
night with the same question
its to bad someone cant tell
him
well Holland as I cant think
of aney more foolishness I will
close with best wishes to you
all Your friend
C M Russell

PLATE 9

Friend Bill
    I received the papers and
also box an as I am
not using any myself
am thinking of opning
a little open air joint
most of the fellrs
I see up here
dont look like CokaCola
men

Aug 12
1912

BOOSE FOR BOOSE
FIGHTERS
C M RUSSELL
CIGARS

FROM
Bill RANCE

catch one of these long thirst leg weary fisherman
with nothing but water to drink an hel buy red ink
at your price an thank you for it.
an with that high grade Joy juce of yours Bill I could
have them writing home for money

PLATE 10

well Bill there aint much doing up here
but I heard there was a man up on the
maine range that mixed up with
a lady grizzley   an they pulled of
the genuine grizzley bear dance
they say the man wasent strong
on round dances   but he couldent
refuse a   lady   an you
know   every bodys doing
it   an I guess before
that   dance closed he thought
pritty near every body had done it
to him, the folks that arrived after the
ball dident find much, a belt buckle som
buttens things a bear couldent use
    well Bill I will close
        with regards to yourself
          an the bunch
      Your Friend
        CM Russell

PLATE 11

Plate 12. "Friend Bob," watercolor and ink on paper, 1908, is addressed is addressed to Robert J. Benn, a prominent citizen and "booster" of Kalispell, Montana, who had visited Bull Head Lodge with his wife the previous summer. Russell refers to the recent removal of his gallbladder and appendix, as well as to an incident (probably exaggerated) in which he used his characteristic red sash to pull Benn up a cliff in the park. The text reads:

Friend Bob

we received the buffilo meat an it was shure fine we all enjoyed it verry much I am feeling fine since the Doctor trimed me but am still sum sore no dought Bob you will savy this sketch and if aney of thim flat heads [residents of the Flathead Valley? local Indians?] ask you why I ware a sash show them this picture who was it that saved the life of Bob the Booster it was me I guess yes where would Boby been if it headent been for that old red ge string as fathful as a dog B- G- [By God] yes Bob the Flat hed [Valley] would have lost its gratest booster if Id been with out my red sash thanking you for the buffilo an a happy new year to you both yours without the appendix

CM Russell

Plate 13. "I have just returned from the glasier Bill," watercolor and ink on paper, letter to William H. Rance, September 4, 1908. Like the previous letter, Russell probably exaggerates an incident on his trip to Sperry Glacier with Bob Benn. He also mentions the notorious outlaw Kid Curry (Harvey Logan), an acquaintance from his earlier years.

I have just returned from the glasier Bill they say the trail has been improved a lot since you were up that may be but it will need sum more fixen before the goats are troubled with autoes its a good trail for air ships they have a rope on the last clime now an when I got a holt it was mine all right an Kid Curry are no other hold up culd take it with all the guns in the state this is the nerest hevon ever I was an if the trail is the same all the way Il never make it its a sinch Il go south [that is, to hell

with best whishes to the bunch your friend
C M Russell

1908

Friend Bob
we received the
buffilo meat an it
was shure fine
we all engoyed it verry
much
I am feeling fine since the
Doctor trimed me but am
still sum sore
no dought Bob you will savy
this sketch an if aney of thim
flat heads ask you why I
ware a sash show them this
picture
who was it that saved the life
of Bob the Booster it was me
I guess yes where would Boby
been if it hadent been for
that old red ge string
as faithful as a dog B- G-
yes Bob the Flat hed would
have loste its gratest booster if Id
been with out my red sash
thanking you for the
buffilo an a happy
new year to you both
Yours without
the appendix
C M Russell

PLATE 12

I have just
returned from
the glasier Bill
they say the trail
has been improved
a lot since you were
up
that may be but
it will need sum
more fixen before
the goats are troubled
with autoes
its a good trail
for air ships
they have a rope
on the last clime
now
an when I got a
holt it was mine
all right an Kid
Curry are no other
hold up culd take
it with all the guns
in the state
this is the nerest
heven ever I was an
if the trail is the same
all the way Il never
make it its a sinch Il
go south
with best whishes to the
bunch your friend
C M Russell

PLATE 13

Plate 14. "Mr and Mrs John Lewis," water color on paper, August 11, 1918. The crowd of tourists in their "Western" outfits in this illustration may have been brought to the park by the prominent Wyoming dude ranch operator, "Uncle" Howard Eaton, who organized mammoth horseback trips for parties of one hundred riders or more (Mary Roberts Rinehart and Charlie Russell were part of the 1915 expedition). Russell's mention of the Little Missouri is a reference to Eaton's first dude ranch on the Little Missouri River, which flows through North and South Dakota. John Lewis was the owner and builder of the Hotel Glacier, near the head of Lake McDonald, which the Russells frequently visited. That hotel was known to most as the "Lewis Hotel"; it is now called Lake McDonald Lodge. Lewis often arranged for Russell to display his paintings and sculptures in the hotel. The letter reads:

> Dear Friends I left with out thanking you for the good time you gave me and my best half the above sketch will show that I dident sleep all the time I was at your cap these folks aint so fancy as the old time injun nor as wild as the cow puncher but for variety of anatomy they got injuns and cow folks skined to the dew claws. I cant back track Howard further than the bufalo range on the Little Missouri but if hes Uncle to all them nephews and neices I met at your camp some of his brothers must have been Bishops in Utah not buffalo hunters.
>
> with meny thanks from us both
> your friend
> CM Russell
>
> Dont forget you are coming to our camp and bring the three Bolingers"
> (see plate 19, below)

Plate 15. "Dudes," watercolor on paper, 1915. This sketch depicts a pair of marmots observing a long train of horseback riders during a time when horseback was the most popular form of travel in the park. It seems like one of the marmots identifies the human intruders as "Dudes." It exemplifies Russell's apprehensions about the effects of increased tourism on the park's animal life—and its tranquility.

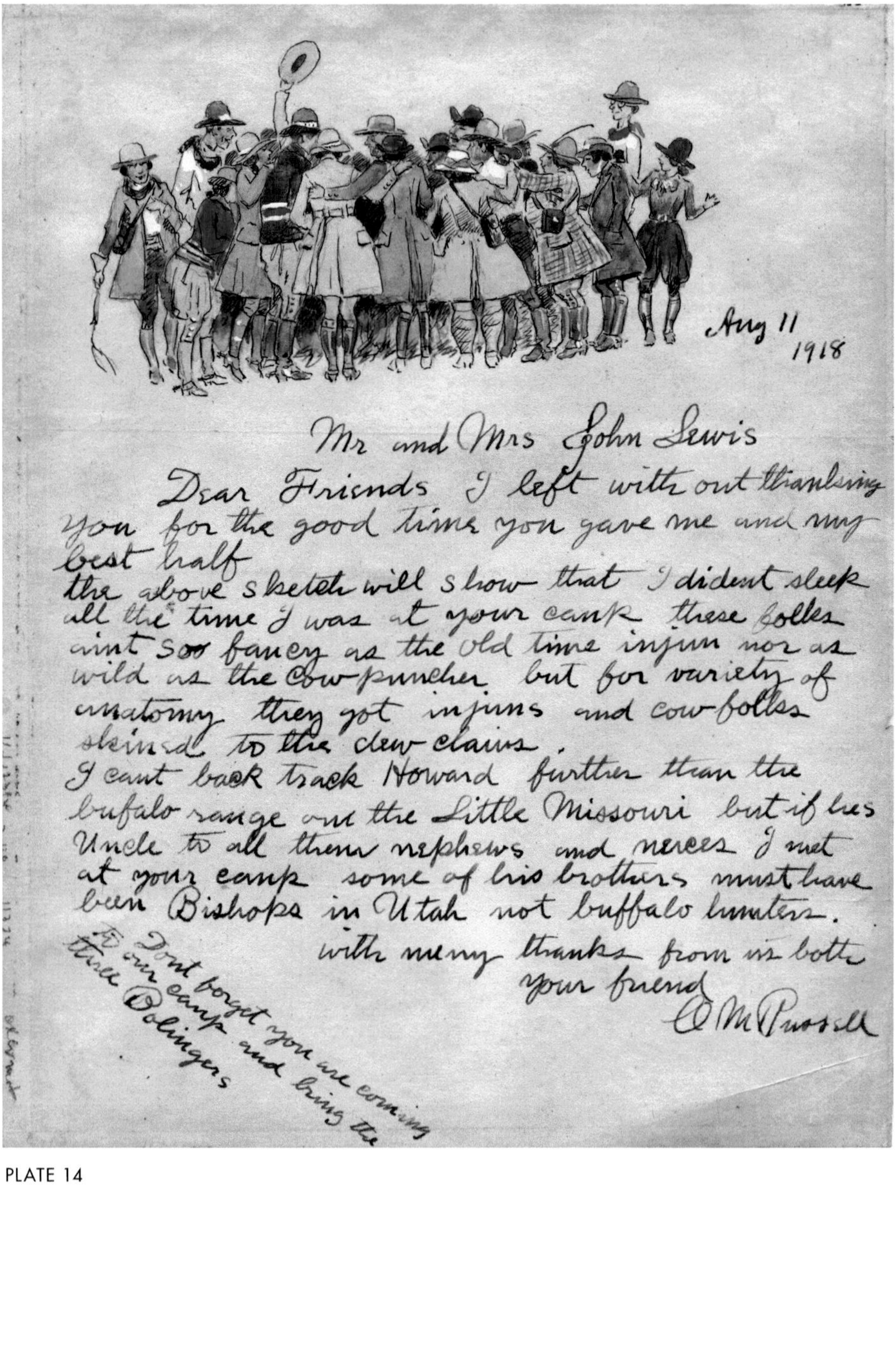

Aug 11
1918

Mr and Mrs John Lewis

Dear Friends I left with out thanking
you for the good time you gave me and my
best half
the above sketch will show that I dident sleep
all the time I was at your camp these folks
aint soo fancy as the old time injun nor as
wild as the cow-puncher but for variety of
anatomy they got injuns and cow folks
skined to the dew claws.
I cant back track Howard further than the
buffalo range on the Little Missouri but if hes
Uncle to all them nephews and neices I met
at your camp some of his brothers must have
been Bishops in Utah not buffalo hunters.
                        with meny thanks from us both
                                your friend
                                        C M Russell

Dont forget you are coming
to our camp and bring the
three Bolingers

PLATE 14

PLATE 15

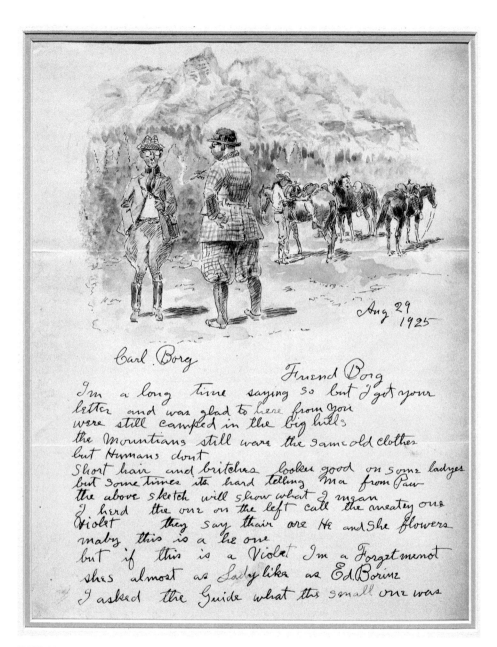

Aug 29
1925

Carl Borg

Friend Borg

I'm a long time saying so but I got your
letter and was glad to here from you
were still camped in the big hills
the Mountians still ware the same old clothes
but Humans don't
Short hair and britches looker good on some ladyes
but some times its hard telling Ma from Paw
the above sketch will show what I mean
I herd the one on the left call the meatey one
Violet they say thair are He and She flowers
maby this is a he one
but if this is a Violet I'm a Forget me not
shes almost as Lady like as Ed Borine
I asked the Guide what this small one was

PLATE 16

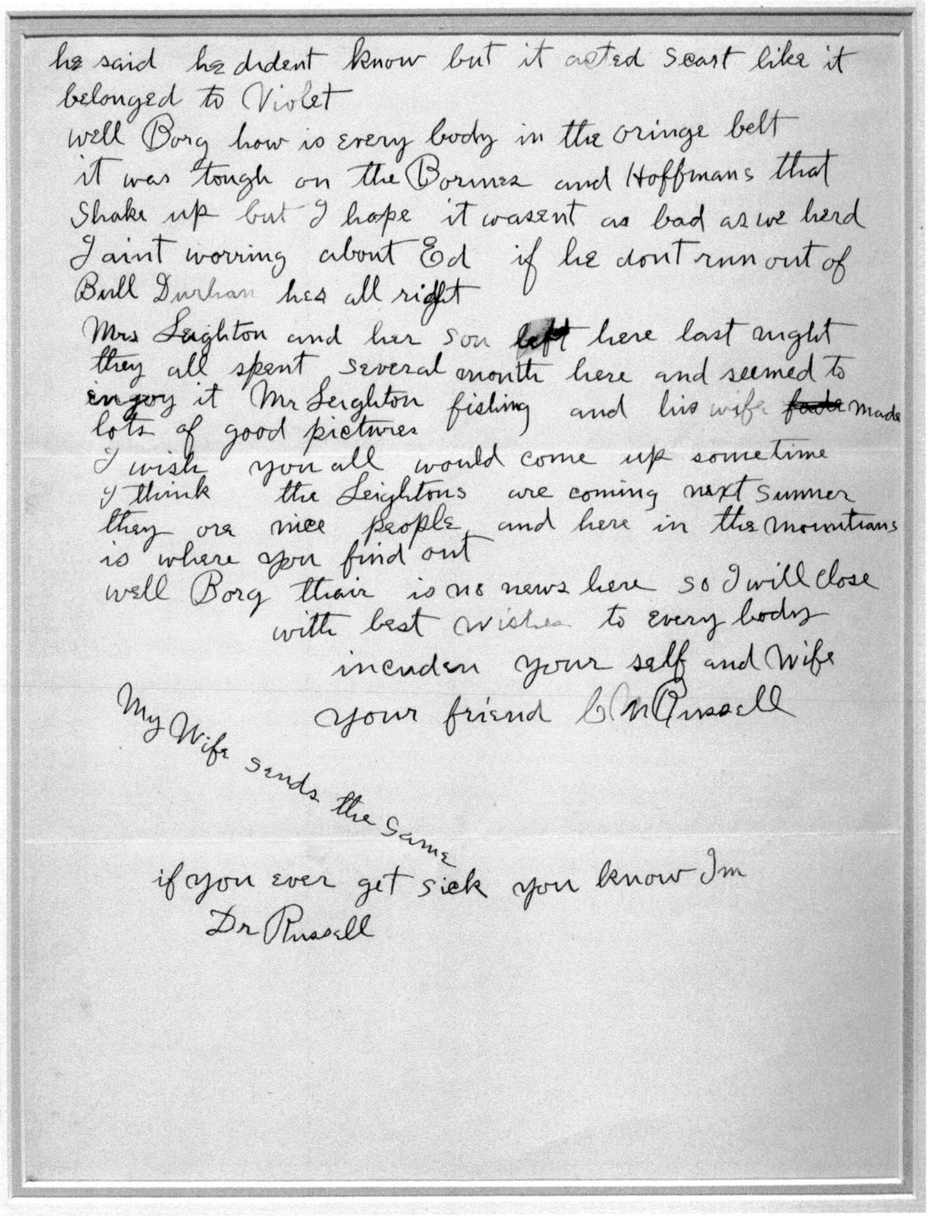

he said he didnt know but it acted scart like it
belonged to Violet

well Borg how is every body in the oringe belt
it was tough on the Bornes and Hoffmans that
shake up but I hope it wasent as bad as we herd
I aint worring about Ed if he dont run out of
Bull Durham hes all right

Mrs Leighton and her son ~~left~~ here last anght
they all spent several month here and seemed to
enjoy it Mr Leighton fishing and his wife ~~took~~ made
lots of good pictures
I wish you all would come up sometime
I think the Leightons are coming next summer
they ora nice people and here in the mountians
is where you find out

well Borg thair is no news here so I will close
              with best wishes to every body
                 incudin your self and wife
                 your friend C M Russell

My Wife sends the Same

if you ever get sick you know Im
      Dr Russell

PLATE 17

Plates 16–17. "Carl Borg / Friend Borg," watercolor on paper, August 29, 1925. Carl Borg was a prominent landscape painter (born in Sweden) and an acquaintance of the Russells. He spent winters in Southern California in the 1920s and finally built a house in Pasadena that was nearing completion when Charlie died of a heart attack in October 1926. Here Russell pokes fun at modern-day tourists and at changing fashion styles; he also refers to a number of artist friends in California—including Ed Borein, Samuel L. Hoffman, and Kathryn Leighton—and to a recent earthquake in that area. Charlie's final line refers to his having recently received an honorary Doctor of Letters degree from the University of Montana. The letter reads:

> Im a long time saying so but I got your letter and was glad to here from you were still camped in the big hills the mountians still ware the same old clothes but Humans dont Short hair and britches lookes good on some ladyes but some times its hard telling Ma from Paw the above sketch will show what I mean I herd the one on the left call the meatey one Violet they say thair are He and She flowers maby this is a he one but if this is a Violet Im a Forget menot shes almost as Lady like as Ed. Borine I asked the Guide what the small one was he said he dident know but it acted scart like it belonged to Violet well Borg how is every body in the oringe belt it was tough on the Borines and Hoffmans that Shake up but I hope it wasent as bad as we herd I aint worring about Ed if he dont run out of Bull Durham [tobacco] hes all right Mrs Leighton and her son left here last night they all spent several month here and seemed to enjoy it Mr Leighton fishing and his wife made lots of good pictures I wish you all would come up sometime I think the Leightons are coming next summer they ore nice people and here in the mountians is where you find out well Borg thair is no news here so I will close with best wishes to every body incuden your self and wife
>
> Your friend CM Russell
> My Wife sends the same
> if you ever get sick you know Im Dr Russell

Plates 18-19. "Miss Isabel Brown," watercolor and ink on paper, July 30, 1926. In this letter, Charlie responds to a get-well note from a teenaged Great Falls neighbor following his surgery to remove a goiter at the Mayo Clinic in Rochester, Minnesota. It's one of Russell's best attempts to portray the mountain goat, long established as the park's symbol. The letter says:

Dear Miss Isabel

I received your kind letter and was glad to here from you When I get aney thing in the mail thats not a bill it a safe bet its from a friend I got more letters while I was in Rochester than ever before in my hole life but not one from an under taker Miss Isibel My friends gave me nerve to go up aganst the knife I glad I went to Rochester but the best end of the trip was coming west as I said before I got letters from maney friends but yours was from my youngest friend to write a letter take time and young folks use a lot of that and whene they use aney of it on me I appreciate it wer all up at Lake MacDonald having a good time Im weak yet but am getting back slow

With best Whishes to you
Your Father and Mother
Your friend
CM Russell

Plates 20-21. "Dr. Philip Cole," watercolor on paper, September 26, 1926. Cole was a wealthy native Montanan who was then living near New York City and was a frequent purchaser of Russell's art. In this letter, Charlie reminds Cole of his Montana upbringing, refers to their mutual friend (the artist Olaf Seltzer), and comments on the loss of wild places and wild creatures. A month after this last of his illustrated letters was written, Russell, age sixty-two, died of a heart attack at his home in Great Falls. The letter reads:

Friend Cole

I just received your gift the books by Will James which I like verrey much when it comes to horses nobody can beat James thair is no other horse like our range horse and James savys every moove they make we have just returned from our mountian camp the big hills look very beautiful in thair fall clothing of maney Colers the above sketch is of a small band of elk we saw a fiew days before we left which I hope will remind you of the country you were born and raised in the camp you live in now can bost of man made things but your old hom is still the real out doors and when it coms to making the beautiful Ma nature has man beat all ways from the ace and that Old lady still owns a lot of Montana to show what

July 30
1926

Miss Isabel. Brown

Dear Miss Isabel

I received your kind letter and was
glad to here from you

When I get aney thing in the mail
thats not a bill   it a safe bet its
from a friend

I got more letters while I was in
Rochester than ever before in my hole
life   but not one from an
under taker

Miss Isibel   my friends gave me neive
to go up aganst the knife
I glad I went to Rochester but the best
end of the trip was coming west

PLATE 18

as I said before I got letters
from many friends
but yours was from my youngest
friend
to write a letter take time and young
folks use a lot of that
and where they use aney of it on
me I appreciate it
wer all up at Lake MacDonald haveing
a good time
I'm weak yet but am getting back
slow

With best wishes to you
your Father and Mother
your friend
C M Russell

September 26
1926

Dr Philip Cole

Friend Cole

I just received your gift the books by
Will James
which I like verrey much
when it comes to horses nobody can beat
James
thair is no other horse like our range
horse James savys every moove they make
we have just returned from our mountian
camp
the big hills look verry beautiful in
thair fall clothing of maney colers
the above sketch is of a small band of
Elk we saw a few days before we left
which I hope will remind you of the
Country you were born and raised in
the camp you live in now can bost
of man made things
but your old hom is still the real
out doors

PLATE 20

2

and when it coms to making the beautiful
Ma nature has man beat all ways from
the ace
and that Old lady still owns a lot of
montana
to show what I mean man made this
animal   but the old lady Im
takima   about made this one

I have made a living painting
pictures of the horned ox and
the life about him it took regular men
to handle real cows
I would starve to death painting the hornles
deformity
God made cows with horns to defend herself
and when a wolf got meat it wasent easy
often he was so full of horn holes he wasent
hungry
a weasel could kill the man one with out
getting a scrach
but I forgot Iv got no kick coming Iv
been trimed my self
but the medicine men at Rochester
ouely took from me things I dident need
and was glad to get rid of
I look and feel better but Im still very
weak
if you see Olaf Seltzer give him my
regards
I suppose by this time hes a real Newyorker
we have been having lots of snow but to day
it has cleard and I think the storm is over
we all send our best regards to you and
yours   Your friend
C M Russell

PLATE 21

Dec 25 1910

Friend Bob I got the buffalo all right and we both send thanks and wish you and Mrs Benn a Merry Christmas and a happy New Year your friend C M Russell

PLATE 21

I mean man made this animal but the old lady Im takina about made this one I have made a living painting pictures of the horned on[e] and the life about him it took regutar men to handle real cows I would starve to death painting the hornles deformity God made cows with hornes to defend herself and when a wolf got meat it wasent easy often he was so full of horn holes he wasent hungry a weasel could kill the man[made] one with out getting a scrach but I forgot Iv got no kick coming Iv been trimed my self but the medicine men at Rochester onely took from me things I dident need and was glad to get rid of I look and feel better but Im still verry weak if you see Olaf Seltzer give him my regards I suppose by this time hes a real New Yorker we have been having lots of snow but to day it has cleard and I think the storm is over we all send our best regards to you and yours

Your friend
CM Russell

Plate 22. "Friend Bob," watercolor on paper, December 25, 1910. Robert J. Benn was the proprietor of Benn's Buffet in Kalispell and a close friend of Russell (see plate 12). Benn participated in the annual roundups on the National Bison Range south of Flathead Lake, occasionally providing Russell with meat. In this letter, Russell thanks Benn in his usual whimsical way, at the same time providing us with one of his best self-portraits. The note reads:

Friend Bob I got the buffalo all right and we both send thanks and wish you and Mrs Benn a Merry Christmas and a happy New Year

Your friend
CM Russell

1. Edward S. Curtis: "Blackfoot Tipis." Edward S. Curtis was one of the pioneering photographers in the United States. He eventually published twenty volumes of photographs of Native Americans from all over North America. The Blackfeet were one of the first tribal groups he encountered, visiting them just east of the Rockies in the days before Glacier National Park was established.

VILLAGE OF THE KALISPEL

2. Edward S. Curtis: "Kootenai Duck Hunter." Though the Kootenai, like their neighbors the Kalispel and the Salish, were justly famous for their skills on water and their distinctive canoes, they also regularly crossed Glacier's mountain passes to hunt buffalo, which often put them in conflict with the Blackfeet.

3. Unknown photographer: "Wives Wanted," ca. 1901. These men—Bill Daucks, Frank Geduhn, Esli Apgar, and Dimon Apgar—were early residents of the village of Apgar at the foot of Lake McDonald. It is not clear today if the men were serious about seeking wives (the cats and dog suggest a kind of domesticity) or if the sign was a joke.

4. R. E. "Ted" Marble: Mary Roberts Rinehart and companions eating lunch, 1916, on McDonald Creek. Marble was based in Seattle but made frequent visits to the park and photographed widely. Rinehart, one of the most famous writers in America, made two visits to Glacier, in 1915 and 1916—*Tenting Tonight* chronicles her journey on the north Fork of the Flathead River.

5. T. J. Hileman: George Bird Grinnell—often called "the father of Glacier Park"—
and his wife, Elizabeth, on Grinnell Glacier, about 1926. Grinnell, the editor of
the New York magazine *Forest and Stream*, actively explored the St. Mary and
Swiftcurrent Valleys in the 1880s and was later deeply involved in drafting and
lobbying for the legislation that designated Glacier as a national park in 1910.

6. T. J. Hileman: Members of the Blackfeet tribe at the railroad depot at East Glacier, Montana, ca. 1925. Members of the Blackfeet Nation were recruited by the Great Northern Railway to meet arriving trains at Glacier Park Station (now East Glacier Park).

7. George S. Grant: "Lunchtime in Preston Park area, July 18, 1932." The preferred mode of travel in the early days of the park was horseback, and the guides—often derided by working cowboys as "dude wranglers"—brought box lunches and prepared coffee for their guests. Grant was the official photographer of the National Park Service at that time.

8. Unknown photographer: A guide leads a party across Sperry Glacier, probably between 1910 and 1920. Ropes were essential in case one of the party broke through a snow bridge over a crevasse.

9. Unknown photographer: "The Mountaineers on Tour—Wash Day," on the banks of a stream in the Two Medicine Valley. These women were part of a large contingent from the Mountaineers of Seattle. The club made several trips to Glacier and spent as much as three weeks traversing the park in the late 1910s and early 1920s.

10. George S. Grant: "Girls Camping at Two Medicine Campground, July 17, 1932." In this photo, some adventurous young women seem to be finishing breakfast and preparing for an excursion.

11. Unknown photographer: A visitor measures a snowbank on the newly built Going-to-the-Sun Road, probably about 1930. Haystack Butte (left) and the Garden Wall (center) dominate the background.

12. Ansel Adams: "Evening, McDonald Lake, Glacier National Park," 1941. One of the most famous photographers in America, Adams toured national parks in the West in 1941 under the sponsorship of the Department of the Interior. His photograph of Lake McDonald at sunset captures the remarkable mirroring of clouds, mountains, and water.

13. Unknown photographer: Blackfeet tipis on the shore of Lower St. Mary Lake. This encampment was probably sponsored by the Great Northern Railway to satisfy tourists' curiosity about the local Indians; the Blackfeet likely did not camp at this spot, preferring forested valleys.

21

BOOTLEG LADY OF GLACIER PARK

John Fraley
2008

John Fraley is a writer who has worked for Montana's wildlife management agency in northwest Montana for thirty years. His intensive research into the history of the Flathead Valley and the three branches of the Flathead River have led to numerous articles and books, including *Uncommonly Normal; A Women's Way West: In and around Glacier Park from 1925 to 1990*; and *Wild River Pioneers: Adventures in the Middle Fork of Flathead, Great Bear Wilderness and Glacier National Park*, from which this portrait is taken.

I am haunted by a woman who died long before I was born. Frontierswoman Josephine Doody was a quirky figure in the lore of the Middle Fork, and even after years of being driven to research her life, I still find her a mystery.

I became interested in Josephine's story one day in October of 1987 on a hike to Harrison Lake. I waded across the Middle Fork of the Flathead River, cut across the flats and found the Boundary Trail along the Glacier Park side of the river. At the junction of the Harrison Lake Trail, I first saw the remnants of the Doody homestead cabin and outbuildings.

The homestead fronts about a million acres of virtual wilderness. To reach it, you have to cross the clear, swift Middle Fork, which like all mountain rivers in Montana, rushes and ebbs with snowmelt and rainstorms. Rising above the homestead, up the Harrison Creek drainage, lie Harrison Lake and the glaciated peaks of Walton and Thompson. Whoever lived at this homestead had to have relished the backcountry and made an effort to separate themselves from civilization.

I was moved by the thought of someone living in this isolated meadow surrounded by heavy timber within one of the most remote areas of Glacier National Park. I felt compelled to find out more.

When I returned to Kalispell after that trip to Harrison Lake I asked Doris Huffine, a former resident of the Middle Fork, postmaster at Nyack, and a pioneer woman herself, about the homestead. She described the people who had lived there: her friend Josephine Doody and Josephine's husband Dan. She told me things Josephine told her that sounded bizarre and unbelievable, but knowing Doris's objectivity and memory, I felt they had to be true. To start sleuthing Josephine's story, I needed to follow up on the leads that Doris gave me.

Josephine Gaines was born somewhere in Macon County, Georgia in 1854. Her birth date isn't certain. In her obituary in January 1936, she is listed as 82 years of age, consistent with that birth date. But census records show she may have actually been born in 1848. So she either lied about her age, or the census takers back in Georgia got it wrong.

Josephine was a member of a well-off family who owned a plantation. She told Doris Huffine that she had been suckled by a slave lady. She had been educated in good schools.

She told Doris that as a girl, she had come west in the 1870s on a wagon train, traveling with a young man with whom she had probably eloped. She said that their party came upon a site where another party had been massacred by Indians. She was sickened by the sight of human heads stuck on posts.

After reaching Colorado, Josephine somehow lost her man and turned to prostitution in the saloons, dance halls, and brothels of the tough western frontier towns. Her wit, direct style, attractive features, and Georgia accent endeared her to the railroad workers and miners. But something went terribly wrong. Josephine shot and killed a man in Pueblo, beginning what would be a lifetime of conflict with the law. Josephine claimed self-defense, and lawmen scheduled a trial. But with help, she fled north on the rails before the trial could be held.

Josephine landed in the raucous town of McCarthyville in 1890 during the boom period of railroad construction over Marias Pass. Now in her thirties, men were still drawn to Josephine's shapely figure and pretty face. Sadly, out of desperation she became addicted to opium supplied by the Chinese railroad workers. So far, Josephine's thirty-odd years had been mostly filled with despair, admittedly brought about in part by her own bad choices.

But Josephine had shown time and again that she was a survivor. McCarthyville proved to be a perfect place for her to hide from the law and continue her "career" as a saloon girl (she later told Doris that she was a "dancer.") Her fiery personality was known and appreciated around the railroad camp. She also had a big heart and compassion for the men who paid for her services. Fed up with the treatment of sick railroad workers in the town's sorry "hospital," Josephine once threatened a railroad official at gunpoint, demanding that he hire a real doctor. She would always be known as someone who didn't hesitate to reach for a gun.

Finally, as the boomtown began to die, Josephine's luck changed. She met a local prospector and trapper who had traveled north from Colorado years earlier. Dan Doody worked for the railroad construction company and probably spent time in town doing business with Josephine. He fell for her and he wanted her all to himself. He was a few years younger than Josephine, but he figured he wasn't getting any younger, and women were scarce in the wilderness of Northwest Montana. He had claimed some land in Nyack Flats across the Middle Fork of the Flathead River and had built a cabin there. Dan thought that Josephine would fit in just right....

Dan knew that it wouldn't be easy to get Josephine out of McCarthyville, out of her opium habit, and into his cabin surrounded by wilderness. He knew what he needed to do and how to do it. He couldn't take the chance that Josephine would say no, so he kidnapped her.

One night he grabbed the small but wiry woman, who was high on dope, and tied her to a mule. Over the course of a few difficult days he was able to transport her along Bear Creek, down along the Middle Fork of the Flathead River and across Nyack Flats to his remote cabin and land about 25 miles northwest of McCarthyville.

At first, Dan thought that his plan to save Josephine and marry her had been a bad idea. Josephine raged at him and repeatedly said that she hated him. He had to lock her in a small cabin in order to break her of the addiction. Unpleasant weeks passed, but eventually Josephine admitted that Dan had saved her life. Josephine said that they got married that year but it must have been a "frontier marriage," because no official record of it exists.

Dan had taken action and found himself a woman. He had judged correctly to act quickly or be womanless. For the next seven years of her life on the homestead across the river, Josephine never saw another woman.

The railroad town below Marias Pass died after the rails were completed west to Kalispell. Only a few prospectors and trappers remained in the remote valley of the Middle Fork. The Doodys were the only people living on the far side of the river.

Josephine found that frontier life on the homestead suited her. Their 160 acres were surrounded by four million acres of wilderness, broken only by the thin rails of the Great Northern Railway located across the Middle Fork. They were separated from civilization, and had their own large tributary, Harrison

Creek, which entered the Middle Fork just upstream. Not far up the canyon was Harrison Lake. Westslope cutthroat, bull trout and mountain whitefish abounded in all these clean, cold waters. Grizzlies, elk, moose, deer, and fur-bearers roamed their land. All the bounty of this wilderness, everything they needed to live, was close at hand. They had this all to themselves. It's impossible today to imagine what this kind of freedom must have been like. Josephine especially liked to fish the clear waters of the Middle Fork for the cutthroat and bull trout. She developed a lifelong skill and love for catching and eating these vibrant native species.

Dan had designed the homestead buildings with a lodge function in mind, planning to outfit friends and hunters that he might attract from the railroad. In the main cabin a large square room dominated the interior. To conserve space, he fashioned two log alcoves along one side for beds, and another alcove for his beloved Airedale dogs. The Doodys used these dogs for protection and ran bears and mountain lions with them when they could. The cabins were located on the edge of a small clearing among the old-growth spruce, cedar and fir. Within a few years, Dan added a guest cabin and built a breezeway connecting the two structures. His illegal outfitting camp was now complete.

Josephine came to love the isolated life on the far side of the Middle Fork, but her past still haunted the couple's happy existence. Lawmen from Colorado were looking for her and telegraphing north to lawmen in Montana. Dan knew he could beat the lawmen because of his knowledge of the country, and because no trainman would ever give away Josephine's whereabouts.

Up the ridge across Harrison Creek, about a mile north of the homestead, Dan built a small, tight cabin. This cabin was hidden among the timber on the edge of a large cut bank nearly 1,000 feet above the Middle Fork and a long way from any water source. Clearly, this structure was more than a simple trapper's line cabin. It was built for comfort and for hiding. It measured fifteen feet square, with a stone fireplace fit into a corner. Josephine could look out its only window to the river floodplain below. It's rumored that she fled to this cabin or possibly another cabin upriver anytime law officers were rumored to be in the area looking for her.

The Doodys had the confidence of the railway men, and the train was the only practical way to reach the Nyack area of the Middle Fork. This made it nearly impossible for an officer to arrive unannounced and apprehend Josephine.

Dan hosted hunters from all over the country on his 160-acre homestead.

From his cabins, he could access millions of acres of wilderness where hunters could find deer, moose, elk, black bear and grizzlies. He didn't have to worry about rangers or game wardens.

Dan, who had worked on the railway at Marias Pass, was highly regarded by officials of the Great Northern Railway. Jim Hill, the prominent founder of the Great Northern, reportedly accompanied Dan on hunting and fishing forays to Harrison Lake. On one fall hunting trip Hill became injured and Dan had to rescue him, hauling him in a toboggan down to the river and across in a rowboat to a waiting train. In gratitude, Hill ordered trainmen throughout his company to stop whenever the Doodys needed a ride or anything else. Hill actually established a stop known as Doody Siding across from the homestead. The "siding" was in the middle of nowhere and was established solely for the Doodys and people visiting them. Hill would stop in his private coach, and Dan would take him and his guests across the river for a few days of hunting....

Major William R. Logan was hired as Glacier's first superintendent on August 8, 1910; in one of Logan's first acts as superintendent he asked Dan, one of the best-known mountain men in northwest Montana, to become a Glacier Park ranger. Dan accepted the appointment on August 12 and according to Park records appears to have been the very first Park ranger hired. His area included the entire Middle Fork of the Flathead drainage extending upstream to Fielding and Marias Pass.

Dan was joined by five more rangers: Billy Burns, Joe Cosley, Frank Doll, Frank Pierce, and Dad Randals. An official early photo shows the six rangers on horseback, with handlebar-mustached Dan staring at the camera from under a big-brimmed hat. Logan had chosen the best known, toughest mountain men familiar with each area of what was now a national park. The original rangers were independent but did not fit the strict mode of law officers. They had lived free too long for that.

Dan accepted the appointment, the prestige, and the limited pay of the position; but he didn't accept the government's designation for his part of the Middle Fork. He and Josephine went on hunting and trapping and hosting guests as if nothing had changed. They were going to live off the land they had pioneered for the last 20 years no matter what designation the government gave it. Dan believed he had a certain immunity. After all, he was now the ranger, and he surely wasn't going to turn himself in....

Dan's relationship with the Park Service deteriorated as his reputation for lawlessness grew. Despite his cavalier attitude towards the law, he managed to get himself reappointed as a park ranger seven times. Records show him gaining ranger appointments in 1910, 1911, 1912, 1913, 1914, 1915, and early 1916. He was "terminated" on March 15, 1916 for unstated reasons that were probably obvious to everyone.

Mountain lion hunting was a passion and an attraction for the Doodys, who kept Airedale dogs that were carefully trained to run and tree the big cats.… Unfortunately, [Josephine became] the victim of a lion hunt gone badly. One big male cat jumped down from the tree where it had sought refuge and attacked one of the Airedales. Josephine foolishly tried to help the dog, and the lion got a few licks in on her before it escaped. Josephine was scratched in the neck and face and bled profusely. From this she bore scars for the rest of her life.…

As the years went by, Josephine and Dan developed a high-value source of income that was perfectly suited to their remote homestead. The dictionary defines bootleg liquor or moonshine as "alcoholic liquor unlawfully made, sold, or transported, without registration or payment of taxes." You couldn't get a better description of what the Doodys did: they made it, they transported it across the river, and they sold it to the trainmen for distribution. And Josephine took particular pleasure in it. After all, the product was highly sought after by men. She could get good money for something that cost her almost nothing, and she could stiff the government, all at the same time. It had similar characteristics of her former profession, and in her mind, it was perfect.

Josephine's moonshine had the highest reputation for quality, produced from the rushing glacial waters of Harrison Creek. The Doodys had three stills housed in small log sheds scattered through the timber on their homestead and they produced gallons and gallons of the white lightning from their own special grain-mash recipe. Josephine sold it by the pint jar, quart jar, or gallon jug.

The railroad siding across the river provided the means for distributing the hooch. A train operator would halt the train (which would be a serious offense except at the Doody Siding, where it was winked at) and signal the number of quarts of moonshine by the number of toots on the train whistle. The transaction took place at a prearranged schedule, so that Josephine could have a supply ready in the timber across the river. The trainmen pulled the whistle, and soon a small figure would appear out of the timber and climb into a small rowboat. Josephine was expert at rowing with the bow pointed upstream so as not to lose ground in the current. If the river flow was too high, the sale would have to wait.

The train operators would grab the bow of Josephine's boat when it touched shore below the tracks. Josephine would exchange the mountain dew for cash or credit. Josephine would thank them in a melodious southern drawl, with a little good-natured banter thrown in. She knew how to handle men, of course. And according to those who knew her she could "talk like a muleskinner," which delighted the trainmen. Sometimes the trainmen left the train "parked" at the siding and had dinner at Josephine's, a practice that would have gotten them fired at any other stop along the Great Northern line. With the help and cooperation of the trainmen, the Doodys seem to have avoided being busted by the law for their relatively large-scale bootleg operation. There is no record of their being caught by a ranger or "revenuer" during the period that Dan was alive....

By 1919 Dan recognized that his heart was weakening fast, so he transferred the homestead deed to Josephine. A few years later he walked out of the main cabin one day to do chores but died of a heart attack instead.... Dan's 800-word obituary reflected his prominence as a mountain man, calling him "every inch a man" and "one of the best known men in northwest Montana." It mentioned his trapping, prospecting, outfitting, ranger service, and his friendship to railroad presidents and section men. "Scores of people" and "flowers in profusion" attested to his popularity....

For the next decade as she aged gracefully into her 70s, Josephine ran the homestead with a special efficiency. Her moonshine business flourished. She was a favorite with many of the Park rangers who patrolled around her 160 acres. And amazingly, she had a much larger dwelling built for herself, her friends, and visitors who came to fish and hunt. Obviously, she knew men well and was good at getting them to do what she wanted.

Chris Vale, who had worked for Dan, became Josephine's foreman and moved into the main dwelling with her when it was completed. The building contained two stories, with multiple rooms for guests and workers. Vale hosted fishing parties to Harrison Lake, but since rangers now occasionally patrolled across the river, the illicit hunting was scaled down and then eliminated....

Josephine's moonshining finally caught up with her in 1928, when her friends in the Park Service had little choice but to assist federal officers on a raid of her homestead. Rangers called these men "revenuers" or the "dry squad." In the ranger journal for the Nyack Ranger Station for Saturday, February 18, 1928, the ranger (not identified, but probably her pal Hugh Buchanan) described the takedown. The ranger had visited the deer feeding station and stopped to see Josephine on his way back to the ranger station. He had little choice but to cooperate with the federal men.

"I stopped at Mrs. Doody's on my way home and soon after leaving the house I met McDonald and two federal men. They wanted me as a witness as they said they were going to search the place. They talked with her a few minutes and then proceeded to a small cabin about 500 or 1,000 feet from the house and there found a padlock on the door so one of the men chopped it off and entered, finding a 50 gallon still and all that goes with it, 12 barrels of mash and 17-1/2 gal moon, and destroyed all but a sample. They found three deer hides which were behind the house or cabin which they told me they knew nothing, so I took them to headquarters. On the trail from the house to the boat landing they found two stills, one 25—and one 20 gal. About 50 feet from the boat under a log was a one gal jug of whisky making a total of 18-1/2 gal of moon."

Josephine maintained her friendship with the Hills of Great Northern fame. Louis Hill, Jim Hill's son and president of Great Northern, occasionally stayed at her place and fished Harrison Lake. Hill made sure that Josephine could get on the train in either direction any time she wanted. All she had to do was call her friend Bud at the switchboard in Belton, eight miles downriver, and let him know she wanted a train, either eastbound or westbound, to stop at Doody Siding. Bud would forward the message upriver to Essex Station if the train was coming from the east. Once, a new dispatcher named Ole confidently refused to order the train to stop at Doody Siding, saying "Nobody can stop a train like that." A more experienced trainman informed him that he would be fired if he didn't stop the train at the siding.

As she reached her late 70s, Josephine was bent and hunched forward at the shoulders....Josephine had to accept that she was getting too old to remain on the isolated homestead across the Middle Fork and all the work that went with it.

In 1931, Josephine reluctantly moved out of the homestead and across the Middle Fork to a small cabin along Deer Lick Creek, just a short distance from the railroad tracks and the road that ran along the river. For the first time in her life, Josephine, now 80, lived in a place that was accessible by car, at least from May to November....

Josephine kept 40 cats and cooked beans for them daily. Even in her 80s, Josephine went out of her way to help others. She kept a garden and gave potatoes and other food to Mrs. Wingate, who lived about a half-mile east of her little cabin. Mrs. Wingate had seven daughters and they were poor and hungry.

Josephine's health had been excellent for 82 years, but her hard life finally caught up with her in January 1936. The old woman contracted pneumonia and fell seriously ill.... The train was the only transportation in the Middle Fork canyon during winter. Eager to help, the Great Northern men on January 15 stopped the train one last time for Josephine. It was a snowy afternoon, with temperatures dipping below zero. Josephine was loaded on a makeshift stretcher and carried to the train. At Columbia Falls, Josephine was transferred to the "Dinky," a small, rattletrap passenger train, and then finally transported on to the hospital in Kalispell. She was unconscious when she arrived and never awakened, according to Velma Guy who came in to stay with her....

In contrast to her husband's prominence and large funeral, few people attended Josephine's funeral and her burial at the Conrad Memorial Cemetery.... She was buried next to Dan, but as I found out when I searched for it, her grave was never marked with a stone....

The homestead across the Middle Fork is still remote. The 160 acres haven't been altered, although different people hold a deed to some of the acres, and the Park Service now owns a portion. The homestead cabin, which was two shaky stories when I first visited it, is collapsing into the earth. Packrats, marten, mountain lions, grizzlies, elk and deer frequent the meadows and heavy timber around the homestead. The little moonshine root cellars can still be found. Nyack old-timers were confident that sealed moonshine jugs, abandoned and lost during revenuer raids, are still buried here and there around the homestead. Undoubtedly, there are secrets of other kinds buried there that Josephine never revealed.

FROM *GIGGLES FROM GLACIER GUIDES*

Jim Whilt
1935

National parks produce all kinds of folklore, from historical narratives to rituals to tall tales. Many of these are produced by park workers—rangers, maintenance workers, hotel employees. The wranglers—the cowboys who guide tourists on horseback trips—are an especially rich source of storytelling, and virtually every park in the West has local characters who tell exaggerated stories about, to cite a few Glacier examples, the fur-bearing trout of Iceberg Lake or the giant grizzly of Gunsight. One of Glacier's best-known wranglers in the old days was Jim Whilt, an old-time cowboy who became a "dude wrangler" in Glacier Park in the 1920s; later on, he got seasonal work with the park. When I met him in 1958 while on vacation with my parents and sisters, he was the caretaker at Rising Sun Campground. He told us some stories and sold us his little book, *Giggles from Glacier Guides*. It was copyrighted in 1935 and was, in 1958, in its tenth printing, having sold fifty-two thousand copies. Jim was also a cowboy poet—"the Poet of the Rockies," as he styled himself. Here are some examples of Jim's tall tales, many of which have a long heritage in American folklore.

So here in Glacier Park, God's own outdoors, God's and mine, myself and sixty others take the dudes over the trails and tell them some of the facts about this land of shining mountains for a period of three months. Then our work begins. We have to go over the entire park, shut off all the waterfalls, fold up the switchbacks, brand all the young sheep and goats, dig all the dens for the bears, teach the little fish to swim and plant them in different lakes and streams. The latter is a hard job, for in the fall the water is hard and digging the holes is an arduous task....

Hank McVey was the best fisherman the park had and he had one secret stream where he took most of his parties. There the fish were a foot long at birth and in the spring Hank had to go there and walk along the stream to keep the fish headed up. If one got crosswise it backed the water up so there was a flood. Bill

Heald was another very proficient guide. Whenever he had a dude who had never ridden, he always gave her a horse that had never been rode, so you see neither had any advantage over the other; he let them learn together.

In the spring my work starts as the snows are leaving, having to set out wild flowers over five miles of trails to Grinnell Glacier; various waterfalls have to be turned on and several rock gardens have to be planted. Some plants have to be put in where it is impossible to climb. For this I have two trained monkeys. Speaking of wild animals, we have the usual bear, deer, sheep, goat, etc., but we have the unusual also: the wampus, the high-behind, the side hill gouger and the Glacier whooper. The wampus has been very hard to catch, but by nailing a piece of cheese on the front side of a waterfall he is enticed there, but when he gets his feet wet he seeks a grassy spot, lays on his back and holds his feet up to dry. Soon he falls asleep, then Clair Kimbal, one of the hunter guides, who can tread as stealthy as any Indian, slips up behind and jerks a bow knot in his tail. The wampus, startled, runs down hill, pulling his tail between his legs like a dog that has been kicked, then thinking he is being pursued he looks back between his front legs, gets his head in the noose in the tail and chokes himself. The high-behind has hind legs that telescope so he can feed on any slope and keep his hind quarters higher than his head. As soon as he is scared he pulls up his hind legs and rolls over backward as far as he wishes to go. When he wants to stop he lets out his legs again and you can see him far down the mountain, peacefully grazing as before, hips much higher than his shoulders. He has never been captured, but Clair says if he can get the hum off the wings of a humming bird for bait he will sure have one to show the dudes next year.

The side hill gouger is another peculiar animal, legs longer on one side than the other, so he can only travel around the mountains one way. But the funny part of their existence is that some have the long legs on one side and some on the other and are known as the right and left hand gougers. There is only one case that I know of where a mother gouger who was left handed gave birth to a baby gouger that was right handed. The baby could not follow its mother, neither could the mother follow her offspring. So they took different ways around the mountain. Along the baby trail it looked like there had been a heavy shower, while the trail left by the mother resembled a heavy cloudburst, and it was all from the tears they shed.

The Glacier whooper is an animal no one seems to know much about as he lives a life of seclusion and seldom ventures out from his den. When he does he is very cautious and is equipped with a long tail which has a large broom on the end. He sweeps out all his tracks so it is impossible to follow his trail and no one knows from where he comes or whither he goeth.

Here in the high lakes fed by the glaciers and from the field of perpetual snow, the water never gets warm, always remaining about two degrees above freezing. People who bathe in them have fur lined bathing suits and the fish that are found in these lakes have short, thick fur instead of scales. Their food consists of a small worm which grows in the decaying ice, and you have to find the worms before any fish can be taken. Most lakes have a limit of ten fish per person per day, but no limit is placed on the fish that wear fur....

There is a real park vocabulary, for no one is known by his right name. For example, guides are "dude wranglers," bell hops are "pack rats," bus drivers are "gear jammers," cooks are "dough smokers," waitresses are "garbage heavers," chambermaids are "sheet snatchers," laundry girls are "bubble queens," and clerks are "pencil pushers," while the dishwashers are "pearl divers."

PART V

ADVENTURERS

Glacier National Park, like all extreme pieces of topography, attracts the adventurous, the ambitious, and—let's face it—the foolhardy. Accidents do occur, but the sense of wonder that comes from Glacier's backcountry—its rivers, mountains, lakes, and trails—more than makes up for the danger and discomfort of wandering in rugged terrain. Some adventurous souls—such as Doug Peacock, Doug Chadwick, Andy Russell, and Norman Clyde—were willing to take personal risks for that feeling of discovery. Others—like Stephen Graham and his friend, the poet Vachel Lindsay—were clearly unprepared for their encounter with the wilderness but survived anyway. Graham has provided us with a bone-chilling account of their adventure. Often unmentioned and unnoticed, park employees patrol the backcountry as well, maintaining facilities, checking on the safety of hikers and backpackers, and occasionally fighting forest fires.

In the early days of the park, particularly during the Great Depression, poaching was a huge problem, as many locals treated the protected area as a giant meat locker. During Prohibition, whiskey smuggling from Canada presented more problems. Rangers patrolled regularly, using snowshoes in the winter, and often faced danger from both the weather and the intruders. Their refuges were a series of log cabins built in remote areas, cabins used by trail crews and backcountry rangers today; they are still referred to as "snowshoe cabins."

In January 1930, Assistant Chief Ranger G. N. Paige published the following poem, "Winter Patrol in Glacier Park." It's a good example of folk poetry or vernacular poetry, intended for a local audience and describing local incidents.

It was published in a little mimeographed publication for park personnel, *Glacier Nature Notes.*

Have you ever put in a winter
      Where the wind always seems to blow,
Sweeping down from the bleak mountain passes,
      And most every day brings more snow;
In a cabin set back in the timber
      Somewhere near the Canadian line;
With white peaks of the Rockies as guide post
      While patrolling thru forests of pine?

Four log walls: they are barren of pictures;
      Just two windows; a snug fitting door;
There's a cot, and a table, and cook-stove,
      And tin dishes you've used once before.
All the meals are of sour dough for hot cakes,
      Or vegetables brot in a can,
Or dried prunes, navy beans, ham and bacon,
      That were packed in ere winter began.

You snowshoe twelve miles to the mail-box
      Where weekly the stage passes by;
The stage horses find it tough going
      Thru snow that is piled shoulder high;
You receive a whole arm-load of papers,
      A week's issues all come in one bunch,
So that night you are reading past midnight
      To try to get caught up at once.

While the cold settles down in the logs
      With a snap like a pistol's shot,
While the mercury drops and keeps dropping,
      While the good little stove glows red hot.
In morning the creeks are all frozen,
      Oh, that's most important, indeed!
For you chop thru the ice to the bottom

To get all the water you need.

You must snowshoe all over the district
       To make sure that all poachers stay out,
And you follow the tracks in the fresh snow
       To study what has been about.
You soon learn that all troubles and trials
       Are not fastened on people along,
That each little beast of the woodland
       Has some troubles and trials of his own.

Here a rabbit was running for dear life,
       For a marten did want him for lunch;
Here's a deer that was jumped while twas feeding;
       Here three coyotes came by in a bunch.
It's the old story told in the woodland,
       That the fittest are those that survive,
And winter's the season of seasons
       That the weak must pass o'er the divide.

You come home all tired out in the evening;
       Stand the snowshoes alongside the door;
And you think that this cabin's a blessing
       When the long day's journey is o'er.
When the fire's again brightly glowing,
       There's nothing much else left to do,
But to wait for the coffee-pot's singing,
       And my! Smell that Mulligan stew.

If you've ever put in such a winter,
       Tho at times you have found it quite tough,
You have proved to yourself and your fellows
       That you're made of about the right stuff.
There are others with lives far more easy,
       With parties and dances and shows,
But give me the snug snowshoe cabin
       In the woods where the free wild wind blows.

23

CLIMBING RED EAGLE

Stephen Graham
1922

In the early 1920s, Vachel Lindsay (1879–1931) was probably the most popular poet in the United States. A charismatic figure on stage, he gave readings all over the country, characterizing his work as "singing poetry." His most popular poems, published in 1914 and 1915, were "The Congo" and "General William Booth Enters into Heaven." On a reading tour of England in 1920, he renewed his acquaintance with the journalist and writer Stephen Graham. Graham (1884–1975), son of a prominent Scots literary family, left school at an early age but learned Russian and wrote more than thirty books, many of them socially progressive books about the "new" Russia then coming into being. In 1921, he and Lindsay journeyed together to Glacier, where they embarked on one of the most hair-raising cross-country excursions ever reported in the park. Beginning at Glacier Park Station (East Glacier Park), the pair improvised a course through the wilderness. As Graham wrote in *Tramping with a Poet in the Rockies* (1922), "We…set out next morning with blankets and provisions and steered a north-westerly or west by north-westerly course by our compasses, abjuring trails and guides" (16). During and after their tramp, Lindsay wrote poems (see pages 87–88) and later published a small book of poetry about their journey, *Going-to-the-Sun* (likely 1924), as well as a book of prose and poetry, *Going-to-the-Stars* (1926). This excerpt, from Graham's *Tramping*, conveys the sheer adventure (or foolhardiness) of these forty-ish adventurers as they made their way over Red Eagle Mountain on the south side of Upper St. Mary Lake.

We journeyed through the primeval forest without a trail to guide us, through the jagged, thorny, tumultuous pine wilderness. It was not so easy for Lindsay, whose legs are shorter than mine, but he took it as a game of banter leader and moved forward doggedly into the openings I made. We were glad to take advantage of the thousands of wild-smitten trees which lay dead, piled at every angle and piled on one another.

We climbed upward for miles on the white, smooth, dead timber of fallen trees, balancing and jumping, transferring from trunk to trunk, and clambering over the immense stars of upturned roots. We were rewarded at length by a view of the rocks above the tree line and of a tumbling cascade. This was in the direction we required and we made for it and lunched by the cascade become rivulet, and then climbed all the afternoon by rock stairs to the snow.

At six beside a "bride-veil waterfall," we had supper. Above us was an amphitheatre of red rocks and ruined slate and it seemed but a small climb to the top of the mountain. The gradient was steep and there were large quantities of loose stones. We climbed without intermittence until 9 o'clock at night, and as one top was nearly conquered another top seemed to be added. The amphitheatre receded upward to heaven.

How arduous it was and at times how risky! Massive stones on which we relied to place our feet proved to be only passengers like ourselves upon the mountain and at a touch from us resumed their downward track, clashing and smashing from rock to rock. We came to steep banks of shale which moved *en masse* with the weight of our bodies and we lay flat on them and slid with them unwillingly and fearfully. Nevertheless we did make great progress upward, and if we did not conquer the mountain on which we were we at least conquered some peaks that were behind us. We entered the society of the mountains. The mighty eminences and august personalities of the southward view came into our ken.

The sun went down, the shadows below us deepened, the snow banks multiplied themselves in number, and their outlines and suggestiveness intensified as the valley whence we had arisen lost its trees and changed to a vast blank abyss. Our unfailing wonder when we sat down on a stone to regain our lost breath was the multitudinous terrain of awful, wrathful mountain peaks which in indescribable promiscuity had climbed the horizon wall to stare at us.

Vachel confessed to being dizzy and dared hardly look downward whence we had come. He preferred to look upward, and it was always "three more dashes and we'll be there," though instead of three we made thirty.

Our mountain at length seemed to show the last limits and to be crowned by a sort of Roman wall. We came in view of a long, serried, level grey rock which ran evenly along the mountain brow like a fortification, and in the midst of it was a way of stone steps and a gap. I got up through the hole in the wall and hauled up Lindsay's pack after me, and he followed.

But when we got on top it was flat, but it was not the top. We lay full length there and ate raisins and looked upward over another field of shale and loose boulders, and a cold wind as from the Pole swept across. We watched the first stars appear and talked of finding a sheltered ledge somewhere and sleeping on it or at least waiting on it till morning. But secretly we still had a strong hold on hope. Mountain tops are only to be conquered, and we would not give in.

"The other sky beyond the mountain ridge is on tiptoe waiting for us," said I.

It should be explained that the mountains here are nearly all "razor-edges." When you have climbed sheer up to the top you have to climb sheer down the other side. Plateaus and table mountains are rare.

The mountain "cirques" and ridges actually cut the great sky in two and you can only join the two pieces of it at the top.

However, when, after another forty minutes of picking our way upward, we did actually reach the summit no new sky greeted us. Indeed, I shrank back aghast from the dreadful view that I saw. For the mountain swept downward in long, swift and severe lines into a funnel of Erebus darkness. We stood perched at a gigantic height above the world, and it was black night with an abyss both behind and in front of us.

You could stand on top of the mountain and see the two dreadful views, on the one side scores and fifties of wrathful, staring mountains and on the other a purgatorial abyss for lost souls.

We dared not start a descent so we slept on the top of the mountain. I lay on a narrow ledge and slumbered and waked. And Vachel, who was hypnotised by the abyss, would not lie down for fear he might fall off or might get up in his sleep and jump. So he sat like a fakir the whole night long, looking unwaveringly on one fixed spot.

"Our friends all lie in their soft beds with their heads on pillows of down," I thought, "far away in the valleys and across the plains, in snug, comfortable homes, and we lie on rocky, jagged edges on the very top of a great mountain, far from human ken."

We seemed as much nearer the stars as we were further away from mankind. Venus was like a diamond cut out of the sun, and she lifted an unearthly splendour high into the sooty devouring darkness of the night. In other parts of the sky the meteors shot laconically in and out as if on errands for the planets. Cold winds ravaged the heights, but they did not roar. For the forests were far away. And there was no sound of waters—only the long slow threatening roll and splurge of loose rocks continually detaching themselves from the heights and slipping downward to perdition.

I lay and I lay, and Vachel sat unmoving and we heard, as it were, the pulse of the world. We did not see humanity's prayers going up to God. We only saw the stars and the night.

> If you join the mountain-peak club
> You'll notice the old members stare at you,
> Call you silently a parvenu, interloper, upstart.
> Upstart you are, of course,
> But never mind, you've got a rise in the world.
> No use trying to outstare the mountains
> Sitting in their arms-chairs [sic], nursing their gouty feet.
> Be a social climber still,
> Aspire higher,
> And be put up as soon as you can
> For the club of Heaven's stars.

DOING THE IMPOSSIBLE

Blessings for dawn and the rosy lights and for the cloudlessness of the morning! Had mist enshrouded us we should have had to have remained high up on the slippery knife-edge of the mountain till the mist had passed. We were able to descend, cautiously, cautiously, for three hours in a trackless precipitous zigzag to the red peak of a lower mountain and a high snow-bound lake, where we made a good fire and made coffee with our last coffee, and lay down again and slept. Then we washed in the snow and ceased to be old weather-beaten tramps and recaptured our yesterdays and our youth, and Vachel began to sing again and our knapsacks felt lighter, as indeed they were, for we had eaten up all the rations, even the iron rations.

Then we walked to the [St. Mary] valley of the Sun-Mountain adown the rocks of a continuous cascade. The descent to the snow-bound lake and the red peak had seemed impossible, and we essayed the impossible again. It was not merely a polite walk downstairs. Every step that we took was a problem. We used our hands and the strength of our wrists as much as our feet and the tension of our ankles. Constantly were we faced with fifteen to twenty-foot drops on to narrow ledges, where a balance must be kept when we alighted.

No doubt I am by nature a mountaineer and hillsman, half a Highlander, at least, and Vachel's genius is the genius of the plains. I am an antelope and he is a bear, we tell each other.

"You lead," says Vachel. "Where the antelope will go the bear will follow after him, but the antelope will not follow the bear."

So he followed downward, and we took the most abominable chances of breaking our legs or our necks—we had to take them. Then presently we came to what seemed a full forty-foot sheer drop of foaming water—an impossible descent, you would say, for all the grasp and grip in it was water-washed and water-smoothed by ages of water—impossible, impossible. But no, face it, think it over, it can be managed. O caution, caution! Trust yourself to the Almighty Protector and grit your teeth!

Timidity fought daring all the way down. We sat once or twice, and regarded the view. One thing was certain: we could not climb back to the places we had come from. If we did not continue downward we had to remain where we were.

We did things which one does not do without guides and ropes and the paraphernalia of mountaineering, and when we got down to the tortured fissured rocks below the cataract we looked up whence we had come and said again to ourselves, "Impossible, impossible!"

And as in going up the mountain the winning of the summit was continually deferred, so in descending to the valley we only conquered one steep mountain slope to be presented with another steep mountain slope and another series of terraces and another impossibility.

Perhaps no one ever came this way over the mountains unless it was some adventurous Indian, but even Indians do not venture where horse cannot go. I remember as one of the most remarkable passages of our descent an hour we spent in a subarboreal channel shut out from the light of day, a jagged downward plunge where the stream fell away in darkness while in voluminous curves the thick sallow roofed it in. We made a hanging descent, clinging to handfuls of branches of sallow and swaying and sagging and drooping, and then touching rock with a dangling foot, and then clutching another lower bunch of branches and letting ourselves down again, downward, downward.

But it all ended well, for we came at last to sheets of sliding shale and then to a spacious forest. And we had been saved from all mischance, and the silence which danger had gradually imposed on us was broken.

"Bread, beauty, and freedom is all that man requires," cried Vachel, "and now I'll translate it into fire, water, and a place to sleep."

These we found, and one by one the stars discovered us when they peeped through the branches of the lofty pines. They saw us where we lay now far away below, stretched out beside the embers of our fire and luxuriating in its warmth like cats.

We boiled a pot of black currants and wild gooseberries and we ate it to the last berry, though, as the poet said afterwards, it was a quart of concentrated quinine. And we made a rosy layer of wild black-currant candy in the frying-pan which was not allowed to remain long unconsumed. We had no food in our knapsacks, only a little sugar, but we counted ourselves happy though hungry because we had been up on top of a great mountain and had come down.

"A joy to the heart of a man is a goal that he may not reach," says Swinburne. And a greater joy still is the joy of reaching it. That is what we have been doing all day.

"Call it 'Doing the Impossible' and thinking well of ourselves," adds the poet....

24

WANDERINGS AFOOT

Norman Clyde
1929

Norman Clyde (1885–1972) was one of the most famous American mountaineers of the twentieth century. He claimed dozens of first ascents throughout the American West and was best known for his prodigious exploits in the Sierra Nevada of California. He frequently embarked on long treks through the mountains, climbing peaks that appealed to him, usually going alone. Unlike many contemporary mountaineers with their "go light" ethic, Clyde carried an enormous pack loaded down with whatever pleased him—ropes, tools, canned goods, camping gear. In fact, some referred to him as "the pack that walks like a man." For many years, he also led Sierra Club trips throughout the West, helping novices learn hiking, camping, and climbing. Prickly and opinionated, he was eventually relieved of those duties by the club.

In 1923, Clyde came to Glacier and—according to later accounts—climbed forty-two mountains in forty-three days, often in rain, snow, and lightning. The following year, he accompanied a large Sierra Club contingent; this time, his instructional duties reduced his peak bagging to a total of only twenty. A later trip with the Sierra Club resulted in six new peaks and many repeats. He is credited with at least a dozen first ascents in Glacier, including Mt. Wilbur, whose sheer east face dominates the Swiftcurrent Valley. In 1929, at the request of Morton J. Elrod, then chief interpreter, Clyde consented to write descriptions of his climbs for the benefit of Glacier Park personnel. These were published in a monthly mimeographed journal called *Nature Notes from Glacier Park* (later the title was changed to *Glacial Drift*), and they clearly show Clyde's high-quality classical education. Here is one description, first published in November 1929, of his ramble through the remote Red Eagle Valley.

On the third day I abandoned the Cut Bank Trail and followed a dim, unused one up Red Eagle Creek toward its source. This beautifully turquoise hued stream winds through a heavy forest of fir and spruce. The trail was overgrown with shrubs and tall herbs, and numerous trees had fallen across it. Evidently it had been used but little for years. Here and there were foot-prints of elk and also those of a large bear that had recently passed along it. Several miles upstream the first meadows were encountered. The trail seemed to vanish in the marsh and the willows with which they were overgrown, but after fording a stream several feet in depth, it was found in the forest, a short distance above. It became somewhat monotonous as it wound along mile after mile through the heavy stand of fir, when suddenly it emerged from it and a scene of startling beauty came suddenly into view. Directly ahead was a meadowy expanse bounded by a cirque wall hundreds of feet in height over which a snow white cascade dashed and the melodious sound of its falling water was wafted through the verdant solitude. The scene was a sequestered one of rare charm: the forest below, cliff and crag above, while roundabout were flowery meadow and willowy marsh.

After stopping for a short time in a luxuriant meadow surrounded by beautiful, spiry spruce trees standing singly and in small groups, I continued on my way up a badly overgrown trail that zigzagged up a steep slope until it finally surmounted a limestone cliff. Here, on the rim of the upper cirque, the outlook was broad and inspiring. Five hundred feet below was the broad, heavily verdured floor of the lower cirque. Swinging around it in a great horseshoe were cliffs of limestone and argillite, from which rose many rugged peaks. The most conspicuous of these was Split Mountain with an almost vertical face and narrow truncated summit. In the upper cirque, gently sloping meadows, clothed with grass and sprinkled with alpine flowers, undulated upward toward crags and peaks at its head. As it was growing late I pressed on toward Red Eagle Glacier. After traveling for some time, I came to some exquisite meadows a short distance below the glacier where flowers of unusual delicacy and beauty of tinting grew in profusion. The castilleia, the wild heliotrope, the bryanthus, the cassiope and the anemone adorned the green sward with a wealth of delicate blossoms. Many small brooks glided through the meadows, some clear as crystal, some milky white from glacial flour. Dwarfed and twisted growths of alpine fir and spruce clothed scattered hillocks of morainal material. Almost the only sounds heard were those of streams falling over the ledges below and occasionally a sharp crack from the glacier a short distance above. The upper cirque was soon enveloped in deep shadow, but Split Mountain and neighboring peaks glowed with a brilliance that gradually deepened as the sun went down, and then faded into darkness.

Camp was made on the lee of a mound clad with a thick growth of fir. As

I was lounging beside the dying embers of a small fire a short time after sunset, I heard a slight sound and upon turning my head, saw a flock of wild goats deploying around the hillock. There were a dozen of them; old females rendered unusually grotesque by the dangling masses of wool that hung from them in long disheveled shreds; slighter, trimmer females and young, frolicsome kids. They continued to come toward me, gazing at me in a mystified but unalarmed manner, until some of them were only a few yards away. As I rose to my knees to photograph them, they became suddenly frightened and hurriedly loped away in their ungainly fashion, to some nearby ledges from which they peered down with amusing curiosity.

On the following day I contemplated an ascent of one or more of the neighboring peaks. Mt. Logan, the highest of those at the head of the cirque, appeared to be unscalable from its nearer side. Immediately to the west of it is an unnamed mountain that forms a striking pyramid. By crossing a small glacier and scaling a broken portion of the cliff I gained the saddle between the two mountains. From there I easily made the ascent without incident except that several wild goats scrambled along the ledges, dislodging miniature avalanches of stones as they did so. Although the peak was relatively low, it commanded a superb panorama. Thousands of feet below lay Nyack Creek with its great trough-shaped valley. Across it the lofty and striking form of Mt. Stimson, its rocky summit projecting far above the green mantle of evergreens that clothe its lower slopes, rose six thousand feet above the floor of the valley. Still more impressive was Blackfeet [Blackfoot] Mountain, its dark summit protruded from a white robe of glaciers from which numerous milky streams cascaded down the walls of a great cirque to the verdant valley several thousand feet below. After enjoying the view for some time I descended to the saddle and there climbed a chimney leading to the crest of the main ridge of Mt. Logan. This I followed to the summit. There an immense panorama extended in every direction. Sublimely rugged and awe-inspiring was the long array of peak after peak along the main axes of the range. Especially imposing were the towering summits of Blackfeet Mountain and Mt. Jackson with their girdle of gleaming glaciers. The sky was a deep blue and bright sunshine bathed the mountains. Silence pervaded the atmosphere except for the sound of cascades dashing down cliffs and now and then a piercing report from a rending glacier.

In the descent I followed a winding course eastward around the mountain, keeping to the ridge that led toward Blackfeet Glacier. A pair of mountain sheep bounded ahead occasionally stopping to look back. Before proceeding far, I swerved to the right, climbed down a rather precipitous cliff, glissaded across a steep portion of the glacier and then climbed to a pass above camp. The cliff below was perpendicular but I knew that somewhere along it there was a chimney that could be descended. Although the sun was already low, Almost-A-Dog Mountain rose to the left of the pass and the opportunity for another scramble proved too alluring to resist. While approaching the summit I encountered several embarrassing places on the narrow shelves along the side of the mountain. On account of the shaly character of the rock, a rope was useless and a single slip would probably have resulted in a plunge of a thousand feet. Eventually I came to a great gash in the ridge. The highest point of the mountain was beyond it. As it seemed impossible to circumvent it at that time of day I reluctantly retraced my steps. A magnificent bighorn leaped up nearby, stood for a few moments silhouetted against the evening sky and then bounded down the mountainside. Upon reaching the chimney above camp again, after a short search I discovered a negotiable chimney, descended it, and hastened across the meadows, reaching camp as night settled down over the mountains.

The next morning I approached Almost-A-Dog Mountain from another angle. Upon nearing the summit, a storm seemed imminent, but unwilling to be disappointed again I sprang from shelf to shelf and soon reached it—a narrow ragged ridge about forty yards in length. Storm clouds were hurrying in various directions, one apparently bearing directly toward the peak on which I was standing. I therefore hastily threw up a cairn and was soon on my way down to the saddle east of the mountain. However, the storm passed by and continuing along the ridge I reached Little Chief Mountain and ascended it. The view obtained was an enthralling one. Five thousand feet below lay the beautiful Lake St. Mary, surrounded by mountains both picturesque in form and fascinating in color. The eye was delighted by the bold outline of Going-to-the-Sun Mountain, standing out like the prow of a great battleship, directly across the lake; the spire-like peaks of Fusillade and Reynolds Mountains along the main crest; the stalwart form of Citadel Mountain tapering gradually to a narrow, flat top, and numerous others scarcely less striking. The red and green hues of the argillite, the gray and buff tones of the limestone; the white of the hanging glaciers; the turquoise shades of the expanse of the lake and the deep green of the coniferous forest that densely clothed all the lower levels, formed a color symphony of wonderful beauty.

Evening found me again in camp.

25

A FOREST FIRE EXPLOSION

H. T. Gisborne

1929

Forest fires have plagued Glacier National Park, like other large forested areas in the West, for centuries. New philosophies of fire management are beginning to recognize the essential role of fire in clearing mature forests, providing sunlight and nutrients, and creating feeding grounds for animals. During most of the twentieth century, however, fire was considered an enemy wherever it occurred, and massive resources (including involuntary recruitment of firefighters) were expended on trying to control fire, often without success. This account of the Half Moon Fire of 1929 describes a massive blowup on Desert Mountain, just four miles from Belton (West Glacier), across the Middle Fork of the Flathead River from the park. The author is Henry Thomas Gisborne, a native of Vermont who did wildfire research for the U.S. Forest Service in Missoula. This account appeared in a collection called *Western Prose and Poetry* (1932), edited by Rufus A. Coleman, then an English professor at the University of Montana.

Newspaper accounts of large forest fires in the northern Rocky Mountain region frequently refer to "runs," "blow-ups," and occasionally to "explosions" of the fire. Many Federal, State, and private timber protective organization officers, and some unfortunate homesteaders, have seen these fires "blow-up" and "explode," but either because the incident was attended by so much grief and worry, or because the spectacular features were obscured by the necessity of being somewhere else, few of these men have attempted to describe the event.

When Montana's largest man-caused fire, the 90,000-acre Half-Moon conflagration, ran this summer (1929) from Teakettle Mountain to Belton and Glacier Park Headquarters in one afternoon it left a trail of desolation which will ruin that twelve-mile auto drive for thousands of autoists for many, many years. No visitor to Glacier Park can escape that blot on one of Montana's beauty spots. Homesteads, ranches, and small sawmills were reduced, not to heaps of ashes, but to mere traces of light and dark ashes, small patches of fused china and glassware, twisted metal bedsteads, bent drive shafts, and cracked engines and saws. Several families lost all that they had struggled throughout life to acquire. The region lost the soft green forest that made it beautiful, and that supplied the materials and the chance for labor which made life possible.

At the Dessert [Desert] Mountain forest-fire lookout station, four miles south of Belton and 3,000 feet above it, the man on duty made fast time down the nine-mile trail to Coram Ranger Station when the head of this fire came roaring toward his mountain. But the natural wind channel, formed by the gorge of the Middle Fork of the Flathead river, drew the center of devastation past him temporarily. Two days later, on August 23, 1929, we went back to the top of Dessert to obtain measurements of atmospheric temperature, humidity, and wind, and to note for comparison the behavior of the fire in different timber types on different slopes and exposures according to the prevailing weather. Forest protective organizations ought to know at all times for all parts of their properties what fire behavior to expect according to their current weather measurements. With such knowledge it should be possible to give the utmost protection when the danger is greatest, and to spend the least money when the danger is least.

We arrived at the lookout station about noon and after making a first series of weather measurements I went north the half mile along the ridge top to Belton Point, a secondary observation station. From this point the north face of the mountain drops two thousand feet in one mile, the contours running east and west, to the gently rolling and flat topography meandered four miles away by the Middle Fork of the Flathead river.

At that time the southern flank of the fire was still over a mile from the base of the steep north end of the mountain. Perhaps six miles of front were visible, the rest hidden by soft swirls of big columns of smoke. I knew no attack was being made along this line at that time, all available men and equipment being concentrated around the town of Belton and around Park headquarters, with fire on all sides of them, trying first to save these most valuable properties. Altho the front below me was beginning to boil actively in the green timber, as a result of the rising temperature and wind and decreasing afternoon humidity, it was not yet crowning extensively. And with the light wind coming from the southwest, diagonally opposing the advance toward the south, I thought it was safe to go down to the spring, some 800 feet in elevation and thirteen switchbacks by trail, below Belton Point and on its eastern slope.

The trip to the spring and back to the lookout station, with a five gallon backpack, was completed just in time for the four o'clock weather measurements. It seemed preferable, however, to make these on Belton Point, closer to the fire and where the front, which was now very active, could be seen more extensively than from the main station. This was a sad decision, because it resulted in no measurements whatever.

The lookout, Mr. Tunnell, who had been cleaning up the cabin while I went for water, decided to go with me to Belton Point. As we walked toward it smoke was boiling up from the north end of the mountain in a tremendous pillar towering thousands of feet above our 7,400-foot station. Just as when one looks up from the sidewalk at the base of a sky-scraper the top is out of view, so the top of this column of smoke was hidden by its sides even tho we were over half a mile from its base. For some unknown reason the customary roar of such rapidly rising masses of smoke, gas, and flame was not present in this case, nor did I notice it later when the mile wide whirling "explosion" developed and swept in under us. It was obvious, nevertheless, that the fire front which had been over a mile from the base of the mountain an hour ago was now going to reach Belton Point before we could, or at least before we would.

Like all truly massive movements the great pillar of smoke belching from the north face of the mountain seemed to move slowly. Black bodies of unburned gases would push their fungoid heads to the surface of the column, change to the orange of flame as they reached oxygen, and then to the dusty gray of smoke. Huge bulges would grow slowly on the side of the column obliterating other protuberances and being in turn engulfed. We could see beautifully, as the atmosphere between the fire and us was kept clear by the light southwesterly wind. There seemed to be no danger as the mountain of smoke leaned appreciably with this breeze, and leaned away from us. We went forward about two hundred yards.

Such a spectacle, even as it enlarged one's heart enough to interfere with normal breathing, made us wish for the presence of others to enjoy the thrill. We stopped to take two pictures, one of the soft and apparently slowly boiling smoke column to the north, and one to the northeast out across the two-mile-wide canyon that slashes north and south between Dessert Mountain and the range tipped by Pyramid Peak. Down there lay the valley in the shadow of death, but altho even the poor photograph portrays it, we did not realize what was to happen in the next few minutes.

Drifting across the north and opening end of this canyon dark, dirty, sinister curtains of smoke kept out the clean sunlight and reduced all objects to a dull gray-brown color. From the northwest shoulder of the mountain across the trough belches of flame would rip thru the smoke surface with a light of a hideous color never used by Maxfield Parrish. The high cirque forming the head of Kootenai Creek on the eastern slope, across the divide from us, was burning out in one brief instant. All the colorful beauty of the Alpine flora surrounding two lovely little lakes nestled high up in the home of the ptarmigan was being turned to deathly ashes. For perhaps half a minute the flames leaped hundreds of feet above the rocky ridge top, followed by billows of dull, funereal smoke as a mountaineer's paradise became a Hell's Half Section.

Even as I snapped these two photographs we noticed that the wind velocity was increasing. One glance at the boiling inferno north of us and we saw the reason. The southwest wind, sweeping gently as it was around the northwest shoulder of Dessert Mountain, was striking the periphery of a rising mass of hot gas and smoke. The result was the beginning of a whirling, clockwise motion, with the deep canyon east of us acting to draw the center of suction into it.

Suddenly, yet it seemed slowly—the movement was so massive—the curtain of smoke across the mouth of the canyon bulged at about our level, perhaps two thousand feet above the creek bottom. The bulge moved south, up the canyon, and as it moved it dipped deeper and deeper until it touched the creek, turned toward the southwest and up the slope toward us, turned west, then northwest, and then north away from us and toward the northern tip of our mountain and the center of great heat. The map shows this revolving mass was more than a mile in diameter.

Most of this we saw over our shoulders as we sprinted south along the open ridge-top trail to the lookout cabin. As we dashed in the door to snatch our packsacks with what clothes we had not unpacked from them, we saw a second whirl developing. As we came out the door, hurriedly adjusting our shoulder straps, the new revolution swept majestically up the creek, up the slope under the lookout cabin—but a full quarter of a mile below us, turned west, northwest, and north, and obliterated the spot from which we had taken our pictures.

Then came the finale, the explosion, the display that should terminate any really spectacular show. The suction of this rising mass of heat drew the air across our ridge with a velocity that bounced me up against the lookout house as I stood there gaping. This clean, cold, and therefore heavy air literally tore across the ridge and down the eastern slope to remedy the vacuum and to ignite the waiting torches. Like a mile wide and crystal clear wedge it drove in under the solid whirl of superlatively hot smoke and lifted it fifty or sixty feet, so that we could again see the entire slope from ridge top to creek bottom. As the oxygen in this fresh air reached the trees, brush, windfalls, and grass which had been superheated by the big whirls everything burst into flame at once. According to the map about two square miles of surface area, over 1,300 acres, were devastated by these two whirls in a period of possibly one or two minutes.

Ordinarily the front of a forest fire advances like troops in skirmish formation, pushing ahead faster here, slower there, according to the timber type and fuels, but maintaining a practically unbroken front. Even when topography, fuels, and weather result in a crown fire the sheet of flames leaps from one tree crown to the next, changing green forest to black ruins at a relatively slow rate, from one-half to one mile an hour, according to two measured runs on the Sullivan creek fire. "Blow-ups" begin when such "runs" commence to throw spots of fire ahead of the advancing front, the spots burning back to swell the main front and thereby adding appreciably to the momentum of the rising mass of heat. Men have been able to race out to safety from in front of many ordinary runs and crown fires. Some men have escaped and some have been trapped by blow-ups. But when square miles of forest are, in the course of a few seconds, blanketed by a smothering, blistering whirl of heat so great that the temperature of all animal and vegetable materials is raised far above the ignition point yet cannot burn for lack of sufficient oxygen, then, when the oxygen comes, a true explosion results.

Two days later, entering the canyon east of Dessert Mountain from its northern end, to blaze a trail in to the now slowly burning front and to select a safe site for a fire camp, I found the body of a young grouse. Sitting erect where it had been actually scared stiff by the terrifying whirl of death sweeping into its canyon home, it was facing toward the direction from which the great heat had come. Undoubtedly too frightened to fly, the little bird's muscles had hardened in paralysis. Even the neck and head were still alertly erect in fear and wonder. The beak, feathers, and feet were seared away. The perfectly balanced body still sits there; one of thousands of such monuments to man's carelessness.

About eight feet farther up the blackened slope a pine squirrel, sometimes called "Happy Jack," lay stretched out at full length. The burned off stubs of his two little hands were reaching out as far ahead as possible, the back legs were extended to the full in one final, hopeless push, trying, like any human, to crawl just one painful inch farther to escape this unnecessary death.

26

FROM *GRIZZLY COUNTRY*

Andy Russell
1982

Andy Russell (1915–2005) was a writer, hunting guide, and rancher who lived most of his life in the foothills just east of Waterton Lakes National Park in Alberta. Deeply knowledgeable about animal behavior and mountain ecosystems, Russell wrote nearly a dozen books, including *Trails of a Wilderness Wanderer: True Stories from the Western Frontier (2000), Horns in the High Country*, and *Andy Russell's Adventures with Wild Animals*. His book *Grizzly Country* deals with hunting grizzlies—first with guns, later with cameras—and includes precise observations on grizzly habits and habitat. In these excerpts from chapters 7 and 9 of the book, he recalls the early days in his home country and the remarkable encounters with grizzlies that he had along the way.

Our ranch was by a small lake cradled among folded hills, part of a vista of aspen and cottonwood parks in the lee of Drywood Mountain, which stood over us with massive shoulders humped up close to its rounded dome as though frozen in an endless shrug of patient endurance.…Behind and beyond the outside range were mile upon mile of tumbled peaks and twisted canyons, making an almost trackless and uninhabited wilderness reaching from Glacier Park north to the arctic, and from our door to the fruit-growing country of British Columbia, two hundred and fifty miles to the west.

We met old mountain men, colorful in dress and speech, who still clung to their primitive, free life and spurned the comforts of civilization. There was "Kootenai" Brown, an Englishman fugitive from a shooting scrape in far-off India, where he shot a fellow officer in a duel over a woman. He came to the Waterton Lakes country about 1860 and was one of the first white men allowed to stay in Blackfoot country by those warlike tribesmen. He was a trader and hunter at first, and later he became the first superintendent of Waterton Lakes National Park, in which office he died. There was Joe Cosley, a college-educated half-breed Indian who trapped and hunted widely through the mountains. He was a quiet-spoken man, a deadly shot with both rifle and pistol, and apart from being a great hunter, he was something of a naturalist and journalist. His name still appears clearly on a giant aspen not far from our door, where it was scratched with his lonesome-heart insignia in 1922.

There was Henri "Frenchy" de Reviere, son of a French aristocrat and nephew of a cardinal of the Roman Catholic Church, who was likely the most efficient hunter and trapper of grizzlies I ever knew. He had deserted as a young man from the French Navy in New Orleans and made his way north and west to finally settle with a warm-hearted Scotch-Cree woman in this country.

Neither last nor least there was George Gladstone, Frenchy's brother-in-law, who was the son of a Hudson's Bay man and a direct descendant of the famous British politician of the same name. George was a natural-born wilderness comedian and raconteur with a rich fund of stories he would tell with great glee at the slightest excuse. A happy bachelor with absolutely no fear of anything walking on two legs or four, he had a sense of the ridiculous that towered. He loved youngsters, and they invariably loved him. Nothing pleased him more than to sit with young folk sprawled at his feet and tell them a story. Sometimes the story would have done justice to Baron Munchausen, and sometimes they were true. We were forever left wondering where truth left off and fabrication began—a minor detail, for the tale was inevitably uproarious. George was an irresistible version of a Rocky Mountain Uncle Remus. One story he often told, illustrates his fun-loving nature and is even stranger for being true.

One fall George was employed as guide by a couple of hunters from Duluth, Minnesota. They were away back in the mountains one bright day hunting along some skyline ridges high above timberline when George spotted a grizzly. The big bear was digging for a marmot, and only his hind end was projecting from the small mine he had excavated. He was a long way off, and the only possible approach was to cut a circle and come in against the wind over a ridge crest above him. So George led the way over a mountain shoulder with the hunters toiling at his heels for more than an hour across one steep canyon and gully after another. Finally they climbed up the back of the ridge where the grizzly had last been seen.

Was the bear still there? Breathless from exertion and mounting excitement, the hunters trailed George up to a lookout point of rock and peered over. About a hundred fifty yards downslope the grizzly was still engrossed with business at the bottom of the hole, his furry rump projecting ever toward the sky. Nobody with a shred of sense shoots a grizzly in the south end when he is heading north; so they waited in ambush for their trophy to back out into full view. The hunters were slowly dying of acute suspense. George, meanwhile, calmly studied the animal through his binoculars. Suddenly George stood up and softly announced, "You boys get set. I'm going down and give him a good kick!"

Before either of the dudes could open his mouth or move, George put his hands in his pockets and blithely sauntered down toward the grizzly—not even bothering to take his rifle. To their popeyed horror he strolled up behind those big hindquarters and planted a rousing kick on them. Nothing happened. The bear was stone dead.

Wiley George had spotted bluebottle flies swarming on the grizzly's fur and immediately had known the truth. The opportunity for a joke was too good to miss. After he had managed to calm himself and the jelly had somewhat receded from the hunters' knees, they proceeded to examine the grizzly.

The bear had dug deep trying to dislodge the marmot from under a subterranean boulder, but the little animal's fortress proved impregnable. Although the grizzly could get close enough almost to touch it, he could not quite reach his prospective lunch. Under such circumstances a grizzly is quite likely to lose his temper,…and this one must have worked up an apoplectic rage. Herculean efforts to haul the boulder out of its bed, coupled with a burst of temper, had apparently caused some kind of internal hemorrhage; for the bear's head lay in a puddle of blood and his paws were still holding the boulder. No evidence of any external injury could be found.

Regardless of story content, the natural acting that went along with the telling of such stories leaves me painfully aware of my shortcomings in describing the natural talent of such wilderness elocutionists—a vanishing breed, for radio and television has largely killed the art. Certainly their stories opened vistas of adventure to their listeners—especially to small boys and to this one in particular. Small wonder that my fascination with the wilds grew by leaps and bounds until I could think of little else.

This preoccupation must have been noticeable, for I have not forgotten a bit of advice George Gladstone gave me one day in one of his rare moments of absolute seriousness. "You will be good in the mountains," he told me. "Go learn what they have to tell you. It is the way your moccasins are pointed, and you will be happy."

This I was eager to do, and as it does to all young people, the process of growing up seemed very slow to me. Dad and mother both loved to hunt and fish, but never at the expense of neglecting their work—a virtue neither of their sons inherited. A crack shot in his own right, dad schooled us early in the correct use of firearms. Going hunting with him was an occasion to be looked forward to for weeks, even when we were still too small to hold a gun.

Guns were never far from anyone's reach in those days. Sport shooting was purely a by-product of hunting for meat and protecting livestock from preying grizzlies. Sometimes it seemed as though the bears resented our intrusion into the portals of their mountain strongholds and went to some length to show it. Certainly, at that time they were bold, and many were the flurries of excitement when they raided the cattle. Once a big grizzly climbed into a homesteader's corral in the dead of night and massacred his milk cow within easy hearing distance of the owner. The homesteader, Alex Campbell, a misplaced British sailor with a good deal of courage and recklessness, ventured forth with a shotgun and a coal-oil lantern to avenge the untimely death of his cow. Everyone agreed his luck was not all bad, for he failed to close with the bear. Next day George Cairns, an adjoining neighbor, trailed and killed this grizzly.

For all their brashness the big bears rarely raided buildings. On the one occasion when this occurred, the incident took place under somewhat extenuating circumstances in the village of Waterton Lakes National Park, a few miles to the south.

Late one fall a particularly bold grizzly made an appearance in the village, where he proceeded to raid garbage cans at night. The Park residents were accustomed to shooing black bears out of their way, but they had no desire to fall over a grizzly some night in the dark. Forthwith a delegation went to the superintendent demanding the bear's removal.

The superintendent was of British army stock, a spit-and-polish type who ruled exactly by the book of regulations and did not believe that laws were written for the direction of wise men and the eminence of fools in their administration. The rulebook said clearly and emphatically that no animal within a national park shall be hunted, killed, or otherwise molested. So he looked down his prominent patrician nose in some disapproval and quoted the book verbatim, ending his peroration with: "By Jove! It just can't be done, don't you know. Completely contrary to regulations. Impossible to consider such a notion!"

The delegation departed muttering under their breaths, while the grizzly went his unsuspecting way. Some days passed, and then came a night with stormy, gusting winds blowing snow squalls down off the peaks. It was as dark as the inside of a cow.

As was their custom, the superintendent and his wife left home early that evening to play bridge with friends. Some enterprising character, unrecorded by history, chose that opportunity to smear a bucket of honey all over the back door of the official residence.

It is safe to say that the superintendent had no suspicion of this development; for he did not return until nearly midnight and was horrified to find his home occupied by a large, well-fed grizzly. The animal had shattered the rear door in his enthusiasm for honey and so gained entrance to the larder of winter supplies. There he proceeded to enjoy a variety of fare, the likes of which he never dreamed existed. In the course of his feasting he ripped open a hundred-pound sack of flour and a twenty-pound pail of syrup, then he happily tramped the mixture all over the place. The house was a complete shambles.

The worthy official lost no time in sending word to the nearest warden, who lived on the far side of the village. "Come quickly! There's a blawsted grizzly in my house!"

The warden, one McFarland, an inscrutable western type whom nothing could excite except perhaps the dismal expression of an empty bottle, arrived in due course. He came weaving through the storm, carrying a dim coal-oil lantern in one hand and a very dilapidated Winchester in the other. The rifle, the only official weapon in the Park, was an ancient .30-30 carbine, battered and rusty. Its magazine would not function, the trigger was broken, and the only way it could be fired was to load it single-shot fashion and then slip the hammer off the ball of the thumb.

By this time the grizzly had prudently decamped into the forest, leaving his big fresh tracks in the snow. Several people who had arrived to commiserate with the superintendent as well as to enjoy both the excitement and his discomfiture tried to dissuade the indomitable McFarland from following the bear. But he was of a rather unreasonable frame of mind and went weaving off through the pines to be swallowed in the gloom. Ten minutes went by, twenty minutes—half an hour—and then the single boom of the rifle away off on the mountain. Those waiting, watching, and holding their breaths as they listened for some further sign of Mac's well-being were not particularly cheered by the lonesome howling of the wind.

Then there appeared a swaying dot of light glimmering through the timber, and McFarland emerged, just as inscrutable and unhurrying as when he left.

He went up to the superintendent, steadied himself, and managed to focus his eyes long enough to report: "Your grizzly is dead."

"Dead!" exclaimed that unbelieving official.

"Christ yes!" reiterated the gruff-voiced Mac. "Deader'n hell!" Whereupon he turned on his heel and wove off toward his cabin.

Subsequent investigation next morning proved this to be true. The grizzly was lying inert at the far end of his tracks with a neat bullet hole at the butt of his ear. How close McFarland had to get to administer the quietus with such a weapon in the dim light of a lantern is anybody's guess, and he never said. At any rate Mac assumed immortal status among bear hunters, for the story is still told around mountain campfires.

FROM "ALONG WILDERNESS TRAILS"

When I first saw the country along the upper reaches of the north fork of the Flathead River in southeast British Columbia, it was wild and grand. We came from the east by pack train over the Continental Divide on the historic South Kootenai Trail, a great Indian and fur trade route of the old days, used so much by so many horses that it was worn into a dozen terraces where it dropped sixteen hundred feet in the first mile off the steep western slope. It was the kind of place where anything could happen to a pack and sometimes did.

On occasion Bert Riggall would stop the pack outfit on the summit overlooking the vast panorama of peaks and the depths of the canyon below, whereupon he would announce to our guests with a flourish that we would now tie all the horses together, nose to tail, with the last one anchored to a tree; and when all was ready, we would chop down the tree to get them all going in the right direction at once as they slid. Even if he was only making some lighthearted fun, he was not so far from wrong.

In wet weather that particular portion of trail is about the closest thing to a prolonged otter slide imaginable, and it is no joke when absolutely dry. Upon reaching the bottom of the first long pitch into the canyon by the most reckless use of gravity, it goes straight up the opposite side with typical Indian disregard of contours and horse flesh, to hang itself precariously on ledges and lose itself in the brush. Then it plunges in a most irresponsible fashion for another mile into the main valley of Kishaneena [Kishinena] Creek. There it winds down the valley, resting from its exertions, past waterfalls, rapids, and gorges, through meadows and forest. It tangles itself mischievously in stiletto-thorned clumps of wild hawthorn brush here and there, and it gives the pack horses nervous fits when it goes through chains of beaver dams in the lower reaches of the valley.

Here it goes through some of the most magnificent natural parks in the mountains, where great western larches tower a hundred fifty to two hundred feet against the sky, and we rode stirrup deep in grass and flowers. In June rare and lovely yellow orchids lift their rich-throated blooms in thick clumps beside mouldering logs to add an exotic touch to this mountain heaven. At every step our horses crushed blooms beneath their feet, and we lay on them at night in camps where the muted rush of streams and the soft murmur of the gentle Pacific breeze lulled us to sleep.

We rode past curious moose and herds of elk. We saw the flashing flags of whitetail deer as they scampered from the sound of the Swiss bells. Goats gazed solemnly down at us from the crags. Grizzly and black bear tracks flattened the soft loam of the trails with their broad pads. Sometimes mule deer came right into our camps, drawn by the smell of salty, sweat-soaked leather. Once I woke in the small hours of morning to find a buck with his massive antlers filling the open front of the tent as, salt hungry, he ate the laces out of my boots. Hardly a shot had been fired in that country for fifty years, and it held about as much game then as it did when white man first saw it.

Upon coming to the International Boundary, we left the old trail to turn directly west along the open cut of the forty-ninth parallel. This man-made line between two great countries is a monument to peace, unguarded by guns along its entire four thousand four hundred miles, and proof that men of different nations can live as friendly neighbors.

Leaving the Kishaneena, the trail went up and up to the top of a high, timbered ridge and then took us down in a long, steep swoop into Alder Creek. Again it soared up another steep slope, where sometimes a dozen times in a mile we immigrated from Canada to the U.S. and back again as we switchbacked to find an easier grade for our loaded horses.

On the timbered crest of the summit between Alder and Sage Creeks the whole length and breadth of the upper Flathead Valley lay exposed—huge, sprawling, and fading into the bluish distances to the west and north. Flanked on the west by the rugged limestone peaks of the McDonald Range and on the east by the main range of the Rockies, it was a rolling ocean of green and deep, hazy blue, five days wide and seven days long by pack train. With the silver loops of the river showing here and there down its middle, it was so beautiful that a man's breath caught in his throat just looking at it.

It was pretty, smiling country, but it could show its teeth in a different humor, too. Parts of it were easy to travel, but through the main valley and the many side valleys dropping into it there was every kind of hazard from soft, quaking muck to steep rock.

Much of it was old burn, blanketed with dead logs lying from four to twelve feet deep and thick with second-growth lodgepole pine. In the worst of the *brulé* travel by pack train was utterly impossible. Here it was only possible to go on foot by walking logs. On such exploration trips about the only time we came to the ground was to eat and sleep. Where logs upwards of a hundred feet long and three to five feet thick at the butts are lying strewn three or four layers deep, the way is no place for daydreaming. In places it was even too tough for moose to get through, and when deadfall timber gets that bad, it is purely awful.

In most stretches of the valley we could use the horses, although it often meant days of chopping and sawing to clear the way. Even then the pattern of our detours was like a maze, where one could see his destination a rifle shot away and it would take hours to reach it.

The down timber was well sprinkled with standing dead trees—tall, bleached-out ghosts of the old living forest merely balanced on their roots that long since had failed to function as anything but props. Traveling among these with a long string of loaded horses was something we carefully contrived to arrange on calm days. Sometimes I woke at night bathed in the cold sweat of a nightmare wherein I dreamed of being caught out in such country in a wind with the pack outfit.

It was relatively windless down along the main valley, where the big dead timber stood the thickest, but sometimes a passing line squall or thunderstorm would set up sufficient thermal drafts to rock the big dead trees past their angle of balance. The tall spire of the trunk would then pause for a long moment as though reluctant to take that final plunge, and there would be a rising swish of sound culminated by a great crash as the log hit, smashing everything under it, sometimes splintering itself and often throwing debris for many yards. If the tree missed a man, there was still a good chance of his being hit by flying splinters and dead limbs. Either way the results could be final.

I remember being caught out once in such a place with six heavily loaded pack horses in the dusk of late evening, when a big thunderhead blew past a mile or so up the valley. Although we missed the hail and the rain, we got caught in the wind along its turbulent perimeter, and then the big trees began coming down. One snag—a bone-hard Douglas fir about two feet thick—fell across the trail in front of us, and another fell behind us, pinning us down like we were in a corral with all the gates locked. As the wind howled like a banshee in the weather-checked wooden tombstones all around us, there came the earth-shaking splintering crashes as the trees fell. It was a frightful place to be, and we were practically helpless to do anything about it. Out there in the dark, with the wind's tortured wailing and the logs crashing down, it sounded like a prelude to being suddenly squashed like a bug. I cannot remember ever being more frightened in my life.

Yelling at the horse wrangler bringing up the rear of the string to get off his horse and under something big, I dived from my saddle and lay flat under a three-foot fire-killed fir. All I could do for my horses was hope they would be lucky. When it was over and everything became still about half an hour later, we crawled out to find the horses standing patiently—all unscathed. I distinctly recall that my scalp felt sore from the prolonged extreme tension.

We were within a quarter mile of the open flats, but it took hours to clear a way through and around the debris blocking our trail. One does not blithely attack fire-killed logs, even with a razor-sharp axe. When we finally jingled into camp at 3 a.m., dawn was breaking. We unpacked, turned the horses loose, and fell into our sleeping bags utterly exhausted.

Upon arriving in the valley on that first exploratory expedition years ago, we dropped leisurely down the last long slope to the banks of the river. There in the midst of a clearing well grown with small trees and dotted with old stumps was an old, abandoned log building with doors ajar and windows staring blankly through empty sashes like sightless eyes. It was the old customs house on the wagon road coming up from Montana to no particular destination in Canada. It marked a past era of human occupation near the turn of the century, when coal prospectors teemed in the valley, aflame with the anticipation of a bonanza from its great coal deposits. But even more coal was then discovered in Crowsnest Pass along the railroad a few miles to the north, which burst the Flathead bubble, leaving little to mark its passing but a mouldering cabin or two smelling of pack rats in a couple of stillborn villages, where a few rotting oak stakes in the encroaching rabbit jungle of new pines still marked off the lot boundaries of the proposed towns.

A couple of abandoned wooden oil derricks of a somewhat later oil-drilling prospect stood as a silent threat of what was to come. But largely speaking, the whole valley had been reclaimed by the wilderness. It was unoccupied except for two or three trappers and a small customs house of later vintage located across the river to keep tabs on summer visitors.

As though to prove the wilds were reclaiming their own, a big grizzly scat lay within ten yards of the old customs house door. Indeed, from one end to the other and from the deepest deadfall patches to the rugged shoulders of the high peaks, this was grizzly country, where we were to have many adventures with the big bears. Such adventures often came unannounced and unexpected. There was, for instance, my discovery of a bear bridge across the river.

It happened near a camp we made on a ten-week trip with a group of geologists making a survey of the area. At the head of a big pool on a bend of the river flanked by giant spruces, a huge log spanned the stream just at the tail of the rapids coming in from above.

We arrived at the place in the middle of the afternoon. When the tents were all set up and the camp ready for a prolonged stay, there was still plenty of time to catch some trout for supper; so the cook and I went fishing in the pool. I waded upstream in the shallows at the tail of it to cast upstream with my fly-rod, while he took his ancient steel telescope rod and ensconced himself in the middle of the log. With his back comfortably supported by the broken-off snag of a big limb, he baited his hook with a piece of bacon and let it float down into the pool. In no time we both had good fish on.

I fought a fat cut-throat trout down into the shallows and beached it on a little gravel bar. When I looked up, I saw the cook unceremoniously horsing its twin brother up onto the log.

Killing the fish and hanging it on a string, he looked self-satisfied and half-asleep as he lowered his bait back into the river. Then the jungle growth of dogwood and willows on the bank at the butt of the log shook and quaked as a big grizzly ambled out on it. The bear came about two steps out over the water before he discovered the cook blocking the way. He stopped dead with about the most comical expression of astonishment and sheer disbelief that a bear was ever known to wear on its face.

Meanwhile the cook was utterly oblivious of the fact that he had company on the log. The grizzly made the first move by executing a most spectacular belly-flopping dive into the swift water on the high side of the log. He lit with a huge splash and began to swim powerfully, but strong as he was, the current swept him down almost under the log. The cook roused himself to see what had fallen into the river behind him. His reaction upon finding a grizzly almost within touching distance was sudden and almost disastrous. He started for the bank, but his feet slipped and he came within a whisker of falling into the river with the bear. Fighting desperately for traction, he fell down three times in about as many seconds without moving away from the spot. Accomplishing miracles of recovery of balance every time he slipped, he looked like some sort of strange, giant, fledgling bird threatening to fall out of the nest. Eventually he reached the bank, partly on his feet and partly at a sort of gallop on his hands and knees. In the meantime the grizzly came out on the gravel bar across the river, threw a disgusted look at the cook, and galloped into the timber.

When the cook came crashing and banging through the undergrowth down to my end of the pool, he found me rolling helplessly on the gravel bar holding my sides. Somehow he failed to see anything funny about the whole thing just then, and he went stomping off to the tents.

There are three versions to this story: mine, the cook's, and the grizzly's. Naturally I have never heard the bear's version, but likely it is just as funny as the other two.

Later, upon examining the log, I found it thickly pocked by bear claws. It was a regular bear bridge undoubtedly used by every bear in that portion of the valley at one time or another.

Sometimes I am very sure that bears have a well-developed sense of humor. Certainly they seem to create situations about as comical as anything can get. About a week after the cook's adventure on the log I saw another comedy of the wilds.

I was out scouting some new country on foot and had had a rough morning crossing a stretch of bad burn, where the logs were lying like straws and the second-growth lodgepole pine was as thick as the hair on a dog. I came out on a little benched meadow by the river about noon, feeling a bit the worse for wear and ready for something to eat. Old rotten logs and stumps were scattered on the meadow, and among these the wild strawberries were growing so lush and thick it was impossible to walk without squashing them. In ten steps my boot soles were wet and red.

I am somewhat addicted to strawberries—any kind of strawberries. Surely no fruit can come near the strawberry for pleasurable eating. But whatever horticulturists have done for the size of the tame ones, nothing can match the flavor of the wild ones. Without moving from one spot, I got down on my hands and knees and ate a pint or two. Then I crawled into the shade of a little spruce to eat the sandwiches the cook had put up for me, cool off with a drink at a little spring nearby, and proceeded to have another feed of strawberries for dessert. Full to the ears, I lay back against a log in the shade to contemplate the trials and tribulations of being a guide.

I was only about half awake when a slight movement on the edge of the willow-grown riverbank caught my eye. Before I could raise my binoculars for a look, a grizzly stepped up into full view. He was a big shaggy bruin with old winter hair still clinging to his back and shoulders in patches. His head was shed off slick and smooth, but around his neck he still wore a collar of old fur, all tattered and unkempt, making him look like a hobo who, for want of money or by dint of just plain laziness, was still wearing a part of his winter clothes. He acted like one, too. He was feeding on the wild strawberries, eating them leaf, stem, and all, in about as lazy a fashion as could be imagined.

He did not walk very briskly but mooched along, indolent in the sun, as though the effort of putting one foot ahead of the other were almost more of a responsibility than he cared for. At one spot he lay down on his belly to eat around the base of a big stump, hitching himself along without even getting to his feet. Then he crawled over the log that had fallen from it and lay draped like some kind of big animated rug across it while picking berries on the other side. Upon coming down off the log, he rolled over on his side for a nap. Through my glasses I could see the berry juice glistening on the bottoms of his big feet.

But the sun was too hot for him. He came up on his feet and angled across the meadow toward me, and again he lay down in the shade of some little spruces with his nose pointing my way and not more than a hundred yards from where I sat. Through my glasses every whisker of his craggy countenance was visible, his eyes half-shut, and now he looked more like a fat, lazy old hobo than ever.

Perhaps fifteen minutes passed before I heard the querulous chirping of an excited chipmunk somewhere near the bear. A search with the binoculars finally located him on top of a section of dead log lying with its butt overhanging the river bank and its broken tip about three feet ahead of the bear's nose.

The little animal was in a perfect ecstasy of excitement, curiosity, and alarm. With his jerking tail seeming to trigger his tiny barks, he appeared to be propelled against his will out along the log closer and closer to the snoozing behemoth. This nightmarish development seemed to galvanize the little animal's terror. Here and there on his mesmerized journey he started as though to streak for safety; but inevitably his fascination turned him back toward the bear. If living dangerously was intoxicating to this chipmunk, then he was on a real bender.

As he progressed closer and closer to the grizzly, his spasmodic actions speeded up until finally he was sitting on the broken end of the log looking down into the bear's face. The grizzly seemed not to know that the little animal existed. It was a feeling not mutually shared; for now the chipmunk's chirps were almost lifting him off the log, and his tail was snapping back and forth like a whiplash.

Both animals were clear and sharp in the field of my glasses, and I saw the bear's ribs swell in a great breath. When he expelled it in a gusty sigh, the chipmunk seemed to be blown from the log three feet into space. He was running frantically in the middle of his jump, and when he hit the ground, he was streaking for cover over the lip of the bank with a long, quavering string of panic-stricken chirps. The grizzly roused himself to look after his departing visitor and then dropped his head back on his paws.

A moment or two later a little twister of breeze crossed the flat to give my scent away. Instantly the grizzly leaped up with a horrified sniff, as though something had set fire to the seat of his ragged pants, and went barreling over the bank of the river, going whoosh-whoosh-whoosh every jump clear across the river. It was about as comical as anything in the wilds can be.

PART VI

ANIMALS

The wild animals of Glacier are an eternal source of fascination for visitors, from the mountain goats and bighorn sheep of the heights to the moose and whitetail deer of the lowlands. Ground squirrels and other rodents are everywhere, the basis for the food chain. But it is the carnivores that get the most attention, from bobcats to cougars, weasels to wolverines, foxes to wolves, and, of course, bears, both black and grizzly.

Glacier's wilderness provides an ideal lab for the study of rare mammals, including cougars (pumas or mountain lions), bighorn sheep, mountain goats, and such rarities as lynx and wolverine. Bears—the grizzly in particular—are especially interesting to scientists, perhaps because they are so much like us. They are omnivorous, mobile, able to roam at will and eat what they please. They are at times playful, courageous, lovingly parental, fierce, temperamental, and just plain goofy. They also attack and injure—and sometimes kill—humans, almost always if they're surprised by hikers, if they have cubs, or if they are defending a food source. But sometimes there is no good explanation. And so the bear becomes the main subject for stories in Glacier Park, whether accurate, exaggerated, or total hearsay. One of the great twentieth-century American poets, Maxine Kumin (1925–2014), considered the bear and its mysteries in her poem, "In the Park," published first in 1988:

> You have forty-nine days between
> death and rebirth if you're a Buddhist.

Even the smallest soul could swim
the English Channel in that time
or climb, like a ten-month-old child,
every step of the Washington Monument
to travel across, up, down, over, or through
—you won't know till you get there which to do.

He laid on me for a few seconds
said Roscoe Black, who lived to tell
about his skirmish with a grizzly bear
in Glacier Park. *He laid on me*
not doing anything. I could feel his heart beating against my heart.
Never mind *lie* and *lay*, the whole world
confuses them. For Roscoe Black you might say
all forty-nine days flew by.

I was raised on the Old Testament.
In it God talks to Moses, Noah,
Samuel, and they answer.
People confer with angels. Certain
animals converse with humans.
It's a simple world, full of crossovers.
Heaven's an airy Somewhere, and God
has a nasty temper when provoked,
but if there's a Hell, little is made of it.
No long-tailed Devil, no eternal fire.

and no choosing what to come back as.
When the grizzly bear appears, he lies/lays down
on atheist and zealot. In the pitch-dark
each of us waits for him in Glacier Park.

27

GRIZZLY ENCOUNTERS

Don Burgess
1980

Don Burgess spent over twenty summers building and maintaining trails and bridges in Glacier Park and the national forests of western Montana and northern Idaho. A former NEH (National Endowment for the Humanities) teacher/scholar of the year for his work as an English teacher at a tribal high school on the Flathead Indian Reservation in western Montana, he also served as hunting editor for *Bugle*, the magazine of the Rocky Mountain Elk Foundation. He has published numerous articles and essays on hunting and conservation in the northern Rockies. Burgess now works as a freelance writer and spends his spare time hunting, hiking, and watching over his flock of chickens. This article originally appeared in a somewhat different form in *Montana Magazine*.

Happily for those of us who love spending time in the back country (including, and even especially, those parts of it that are home to grizzlies), it is possible to avoid close, potentially painful encounters with bears most of the time. Even when contact does occur, there is usually no conflict. However, the outcome of any human-grizzly encounter—aside from those in which grizzlies are intentionally pursued by capable hunters, researchers, or game managers—depends largely on the disposition of the bear. And the mood of a grizzly can be extremely varied and unpredictable. Some grizzlies, sometimes, can be disarmingly "friendly" while others can sometimes be downright malevolent.

During the summer of 1977, a grizzly bear in Denali National Park, Alaska, approached several groups of hikers and campers over a period of several days. Unarmed, in compliance with the no-firearms-in-the-park rule, and carrying no pepper spray—which was not widely available at that time—the hikers abandoned their camps, discarded their packs, and backed away, hoping the bear would take those offerings and not harm them.

The bear ignored the tents and packs and made straight for the people instead. In each instance the bear seemed merely curious about the often fear-paralyzed humans, observing them closely, nuzzling their legs and touching them with its forepaws, then wandering away.

In the summer of 1976 a grizzly in Glacier National Park, Montana, exhibited a darker yet equally enigmatic side of the grizzly's collective persona. As three hikers—a man and two women—passed through a brushy area on one of Glacier's trails, intentionally making noise to avoid surprising a bear, this grizzly clearly responded to their heads-up by taking cover alongside the trail and ambushing them as they went by.

The bear leapt out, knocked the man down and then lay down on top of him. One of the women ran back down the trail and the other started up a tree. Smothered and helpless under the bear's weight, playing dead was a relatively easy decision for the man, but the sour smell of the bear's body nauseated him, and when it began to chew on his shoulder, inflicting deep and painful wounds, he thrust with his legs and pushed himself out from under it.

The grizzly ignored the man and turned its attention to the woman who was trying without success to climb the tree. Running to the base of the tree, the bear grabbed her lower leg in its jaws and pulled her down, tearing a long gash in her calf. She landed in a sitting position, face to face with the bear, which looked her in the eye, almost quizzically, then turned and walked back to the man, who was still lying where the bear had left him, still playing dead. The grizzly squatted beside the man's face, deposited a pile of excrement, and left the scene.

Hundreds of grizzly encounters, most of them much less dramatic, occur in grizzly country each year. Each is etched deeply on the memory of the people who experience them. Each moment in the presence of a grizzly is unique and electrifying. Close encounters are the subject of many a campfire tale, capable of stirring the blood with every retelling.

The stories that follow, describing some of my own and others' experiences with grizzlies while working and living in Glacier National Park in the late 1960s and early '70s, tend to confirm that the big beasts are simply unpredictable. That sometimes disconcerting quality, and the fact that they can essentially do as they please with human beings, adds an extra measure of drama and excitement to outdoor adventures in grizzly country.

Six of us climbed toward the glacier with shovels in hand, clearing rocks from the trail. As we entered a group of trees someone shouted "Bear!" The rest of us turned to look where he pointed, and saw two grizzlies staring down at us from behind a fallen tree 30 yards above the trail. We removed our hardhats, banged them with our shovels, and shouted, thinking the noise would drive the bears away. They continued to stare at us, apparently unperturbed. We stopped our noise and stared back in silence. Their probing, fearless gaze made us uneasy. Not knowing what else to do, we resumed our noise-making. The bears turned simultaneously and shot up the mountainside, away from us, with great bellows, blasts of air rushing from their lungs. Their hind legs tore up the earth and sent a shower of dirt and sticks and stones down the slope.

The next day part of the crew returned to the area with dynamite to open the trail where it crossed a steep snowfield below the glacier. They placed the charges and were preparing to set them off when they noticed three grizzlies sliding on their rumps down another snowbank above them. The men detonated the dynamite, sending up a huge shock wave and plume of snow. The bears continued to play on the snow as if nothing had happened.

Eating my lunch beside a creek, I saw a group of bighorn ewes and lambs staring down at me from a scree slope way up the mountain on the other side of the creek. I waved at them, wondering why they found me so interesting. Finishing my lunch, I laid back against the trunk of a tree and watched the sheep, puzzled that they were still there, still staring. Then it occurred to me that they must be looking at something else. I scanned the slope below them and looked slightly to my left just in time to see the broad rump of a grizzly slowly disappear into a shadowy stand of trees just across the creek from me.

We were throwing a Frisbee outside the bunkhouse as darkness fell. The disc sailed into the trees and when I went to pick it up, I found a still-hot pile of bear dung looking like chunks of heavy rope filled with long, half-digested grass fibers. I peered into the darkness beneath the trees, hair rising on the back of my head.

That night a grizzly—perhaps the one who watched us play—visited the incinerator in which we burned food scraps and other garbage. It stepped in some spilled diesel fuel at its base, and the next morning we found the oily prints of its forepaws six feet up the walls, along the window ledges of the bunkhouse.

Hardly a foot of the log cabin's outer walls was unscarred by the teeth and claws of bears. The windows were shielded by iron bars. The door was studded from top to bottom with iron spikes driven through from the inside to protrude six inches on the outside. One year a bear had gotten in by tunneling beneath a wall, and spent the winter.

As four of us trail workers turned out the lantern and went to bed on the cabin's bunks and cots after a day's work in mid-September, we laughed about the latch on the inside of the spiked door: a piece of bent wire with one end wrapped around a nail in the door and the other end hanging loosely in the eye of a fence staple driven into the door frame.

When we began to hear faint, soft thuds, perhaps footfalls, around the perimeter of the cabin, we thought about that latch some more. Someone whispered "What do you suppose that is?" Someone else turned on a flashlight. Two of us slipped quietly from our sleeping bags and leaned axes against the wall beside our beds.

The mysterious sounds became monotonous and unthreatening, and soon we slept. But at some point we were all awakened by a loud, sharp "crack" of breaking wood. We groped for our weapons and held onto them, whispering to each other just enough to confirm we'd all heard it and were all awake. We gripped our axes, breathing quietly, listening, for several long minutes. Soft thuds and thumps continued around the edges of the cabin, and eventually lulled us back to sleep.

In the morning we opened the door and found the ground covered with wet, trackless snow. Thin slabs of it had slid off the cabin's metal roof, and we realized that this must have been the source of at least some of the continual thudding sounds we'd heard. Then someone noticed a foot-long splinter of wood, painted green on two edges, lying on the bare floor of the covered wooden porch. The splinter matched perfectly, tooth-marks and all, with a fresh, ragged gap five feet up the edge of the green doorframe.

A companion and I were out walking one black and overcast night. We crossed the bridge across the Middle Fork at West Glacier and slid blindly down a steep bank onto the gravel bar below the bridge. Threading our way by feel through clusters of willows, we made our way toward the water. We stopped when we heard it lapping among the small stones at our feet, and the heavy rush of it a few yards out. Backing away, our feet found a low ridge of gravel and we brushed it with our hands for glass or sharp stones or sticks before sitting down.

No light shone among the houses on the bluff across the river. No cars passed over the bridge. Our eyes were useless, but our senses of touch, hearing and smell seemed greatly enhanced. We talked quietly for a while, and when the cold gravel became uncomfortable we stood up. My friend laughed about something, and suddenly there was an explosion of air from very near us in the willows, and a shower of gravel rattled against the steel girders of the bridge. Small stones clattered among the willows around us.

The night was instantly quiet again, except for the rush of the water flowing beneath the bridge. We crept back across the gravel bar, climbed up to the road, and crossed the bridge back to the town. The next morning I went back and looked down from the bridge and saw the tracks of a grizzly in a sand spit beside one of the abutments, near the base of the steep bank we'd climbed down. Tourists crossed the bridge by the carload, heading for the interior, looking for wildlife.

The dust in the rutted road at the top of the bluff took the imprint of my hand as butter would, showing the lines in my palm. Beside my outstretched hand the pawprint of a grizzly held every dimple and scar and crack, the fine-grained texture of its sole and toepads. I noticed a black beetle crawling across another bear footprint just a few inches away, and saw that the trail of the beetle led back to—and had been obliterated by—the pawprint beside my hand. Unless the beetle had paused a while for a rest, these tracks were not more than a couple of minutes old.

The tracks indicated that the bear must have heard us, and come down the road across the burnt ground just far enough to allow a brush-shielded view of us as we struggled noisily up the slope through a mess of fallen, fire-blackened lodgepole. The tracks turned abruptly but casually back on themselves and we followed them toward the wall of green timber at the upper edge of the burn, and toward the main North Fork/Polebridge road that was our destination.

Fifty feet from the edge, we saw where the grizzly had stepped out onto the road from a small island of brush and trees that had escaped the flames. Three full-cropped ravens rose heavily from the undergrowth. They did not croak, and even their wingbeats seemed deliberate and quiet as they disappeared over the edge of the bluff. The smell of carrion came to us as we passed downwind of the thicket. We looked at each other, then at the tracks of the bear. Unable to think of options, we went on up the road and into the timber at what we hoped was a calm and respectful pace. Noise seemed inappropriate. The bear already knew we were there.

The road became a tunnel curving through dark woods; there was no vehicle track, no sign of recent human use. Perhaps twenty yards into the tunnel, we saw that the bear had left the road and veered off into denser timber. Our young dog had been walking beside us, but here she leaped off the road and trotted eagerly, head and ears up, toward where the bear had gone. I ran after her, grabbed her up and held her muzzle. From the thicket came a quick blast of expelled air. I carried her back to the road, and we got out of there fast.

I remember feeling especially alive in the last hundred steps to the main road, when it seemed that the danger had passed. Every breath of air seemed cool and sweet.

My wife and I made camp on a narrow strip of gravel along the shore of a lake ringed by trees. Rain began to fall as we finished setting up the tent, and we went inside and crawled into our sleeping bags after preparing and eating a hasty meal. The night was perfectly black, the sky utterly shrouded by thick rain clouds. When we left the tent to urinate before going to sleep, our flashlights penetrated the mist and rain just far enough to illuminate the wall of trees behind the tent.

Before sleep could come we heard a sound that was at first barely distinguishable from the rain on the tent and the wind in the trees. My wife whispered to me, and I whispered that I heard it, too: the sound of some- thing stepping very deliberately and slowly on loose gravel, a *crrrrrrreshh— crrrrreshh—crrrreshh* sound, as of soft paws being set down and weighted, rolling forward, lifting, coming nearer and nearer.

I reached for the pistol beneath my pillow, rolled onto my back, then lay still with the pistol in my hand, resting it outside the sleeping bag and across my chest, holding my breath as the sound went past our heads and around to my side of the tiny A-frame nylon tent. My muscles tensed and rivulets of cold sweat ran down the sides of my chest.

For a few moments we heard nothing. Then something pushed the fabric of the tent downward on my left side and pressed against my lower leg, then withdrew. After many long minutes of silence, except for the wind and rain, we fell asleep.

Several small, hastily-lettered signs around the Visitor Center at Logan Pass warned of the presence of a grizzly in the area. We learned the bear had last been seen crossing a wide meadow half a mile away. My two companions were eager to take pictures of the bear, and we set off immediately to see if we could find it.

We reached the deep, wide cleft where Reynolds Creek runs down through the open alpine country, and stopped to scan the area below us. A hundred yards to the east, the creek split around a small grassy island, and there beside the stream was the grizzly. As we watched through binoculars and camera lenses, the bear leaped into the shallow water, stretched out on its belly and rolled vigorously from side to side. Then it stood and lunged out of the water and onto the island, where it shook itself like a huge dog, sending a brilliant spray into the air. Backlit by the rising sun, the bear's wet hide gleamed golden brown. Its supreme vitality and beauty took our breaths away. At the same time, its quickness and power and proximity made us shrink and tremble a little.

My friends' cameras clicked steadily. The grizzly rolled in the tall grass and stood and shook again. Then, suddenly, it froze. Its head rose, nose pointing straight up, then turned our way. As the bear stared straight at us, my friends lowered their cameras. We began to shrink back from the edge of the cleft. The bear jumped into the water and loped upstream alongside it until it was directly beneath us, then turned our way and disappeared behind the curve of the slope. We turned and walked fast away from the edge, wanting to run but knowing that running might only encourage the bear to chase us—and that if he wanted to catch us he could do so with ease.

To our left stood a rock outcropping about ten feet high. To our right ran a line of trees no taller than the rocks. The roof of the Visitor Center showed above the trees, some six hundred yards away. It might as well have been six hundred miles. The bear came up behind us and then swerved off to our right, passing us easily in a loose, long-striding gallop, tossing its head like a big playful St. Bernard. We kept up our fast walk, feeling absurd, as the bear veered to the right and disappeared among the stunted trees.

An hour later, as we climbed a nearby snowfield, we heard two rifle shots from below. The bear lay still near the Visitor Center parking lot, its heart blown open by a tiny piece of copper and lead from a ranger's rifle, while the tourists who'd thrown it sandwiches and cookies travelled onward.

28

THE BLACK GRIZZLY

Doug Peacock
1990

Doug Peacock served two tours of duty as a Green Beret medic in Vietnam. When he returned to the United States, experiencing combat flashbacks and what today we would call post-traumatic stress, he sought the wilderness and eventually came to Glacier, where he worked as a seasonal fire lookout at Scalplock Mountain in the southern part of the park and at Huckleberry Mountain on the west side between 1976 and 1983.

He was working in grizzly country. The trails to fire lookouts often run through brushy woods and alpine meadows, appealing grounds for grizzlies who there find favorite foods, from glacier-lily bulbs to pine nuts to ground squirrels. Huckleberry-rich areas especially see lots of traffic in the fall as the bears fatten up in preparation for winter.

Peacock spotted many bears from his fire lookouts and he eventually began exploring their home turf. His method was direct: he carried only basic camping gear, brought no food or scent-laden toiletries, ate off the land, and did everything he could to remove "man scent." Packing a 16mm movie camera on a tripod, he walked into the places where he had seen grizzlies, prepared for anything. He emerged with wonderful footage of grizzlies tending cubs, playing in ponds, carrying out their daily lives—some of the best footage ever shot of grizzlies in their natural habitat. But as many bear-related tragedies attest, going into grizzly country alone is terribly dangerous and not recommended for anyone.

Doug Peacock is a passionate defender of wilderness, wildlife, and intact ecosystems. He is probably best known as the model for the character George Washington Hayduke in Edward Abbey's novel *The Monkey Wrench Gang* (1975). Peacock himself has written five books, including *Walking It Off: A Veteran's Chronicle of War and Wilderness* (2005), a memoir about Edward Abbey and his post-Vietnam long-distance treks in the American Southwest and Nepal.

In this excerpt from *Grizzly Years: In Search of the American Wilderniss*, Peacock describes a Glacier Park bear that he calls the Black Grizzly, a bear with an attitude.

THE BLACK GRIZZLY
SEPTEMBER (1980s)

The leaves of the bushes along the narrow game trail had been knocked off, telling me that there had been considerable traffic, most of it bears. I was moving slowly, weighed down with the big Trailwise [backpack] full of 16-mm camera equipment and enough camping gear for a week. The only thing I was short on was food: like the bears, I would live for the next six or seven days on huckleberries. Between the upper branches of the towering larch and spruce, survivors of the last two cycles of forest fire, wedges of a distant hillside flashed by, mottled in brilliant red and yellow. Fall had already touched the high country.

I waded across a tiny creek and filled my three gallon canteens, since the upper reaches of this small mountain range were poorly watered and the few cool spring holes were favorite bedding spots for grizzly bears. The brush along the creek, mostly alder and dried stalks of cow parsnip, was trampled and broken by the recent passage of many animals. I started upstream, leaning into the brush more cautiously, making just enough noise to forewarn any bear napping in the creek bottom. I skirted the muddy edge of a marshy area, reading the tracks of a moose, a large black bear, and at least five different grizzlies who passed though in the previous ten days. It looked like a sow with two cubs, a subadult, and a huge adult grizzly. I would be glad when I climbed up out of this brush onto the ridge top.

The timber opened onto the tail of an old avalanche scar. The bushes of the nearest ravine moved and a fat brown bear, glistening with silver-tipped guard hairs, moved into the sunlight. I wasn't sure if I recognized him. This area attracts a lot of large grizzlies and it's hard to tell them apart.

The grizzly was too far away to see me. I turned and struck off down an even more obscure game trail, leaving an obvious boot track in the fork not taken out of ancient habit, pulling myself up by bushes and alder trees for twenty minutes, then topping out on a narrow open, rocky ridge top.

I stopped before a huge huckleberry scat, wondering if I knew the proportionately large bear who had dropped it. There were only three or four animals that size, and one of them was the Black Grizzly.

A sound startled me. I froze and leaned my better ear into the wind. A brash bawling drifted along the timbered valley, coming from the upper reaches of the basin. Again the cry shattered the mountain stillness. The sound seemed to be moving toward me, down the small drainage. I glassed the openings and avalanche chutes for movement. Nothing. I dropped my pack and crawled to the edge of the ridge, scanning the creek bed at the bottom of the small valley. I heard the rhythmic crunch of brush under the weight of a large animal running.

A medium-size brown grizzly rushed into an opening in the timber three hundred yards below me, spun, and reared. A second later two brown cubs ran underneath her. It was the family I had seen from the lookout the previous week. She and the cubs turned and bolted into the trees. Just as they passed below me, one of the cubs, unable to keep up with his mother, let loose a panicked and mournful cry. What they were running from I could only guess, though it was probably another bear. Whenever bears congregate, first-year cub mortality can range up to about a third. The litter size of bears at the Grizzly Hilton is low: over a six-year period, more than fifty grizzly families averaged 1.3 to 1.4 cubs and yearlings per productive female. Generally, it should be about two. The bulk of the cubs are likely killed by other grizzlies, and the Black Grizzly probably figures significantly in this.

I realized I was sitting in a small saddle grizzlies used to cross from one drainage to another. Last year I had gotten into trouble there: I had set up my tripod and camera to film close-ups of mountain ash berries, and just as I was about to run the Bolex, I heard movement in the brush below me. Seventy feet away across the open slope was a brown grizzly and her small cub. They had not seen or smelled me, but they continued nibbling huckleberries and were headed straight for me. At that range, any sudden movement would make the sow charge, so I had no choice but to stand my ground and let the family know I was there. I turned on the Bolex. If I was going to get my ass chewed, I wanted it on film. The sow had fed on when the noisy camera started. The cub looked imploringly into his mother's face. Within a heartbeat she turned in the direction of the metallic clicking, gnashing her teeth and popping her jaws. Without moving or taking my eye away from the viewfinder, I began talking to the grizzly in what I hoped was a soothing tone.

The sow reared and looked right at me. She dropped back to all fours and took little steps in my direction. I kept on babbling. Still moving her mouth, the bear looked back toward the trees. She didn't know what to do any more than I did. I rewound the Bolex for another twenty-eight-second run, and the two bears wandered across the open slope to my right. Once more the sow rose on her hind legs. Through the viewfinder I watched the brown backsides of grizzlies bounce through the bear grass.

One close call in that saddle was enough. Now I moved in case the sow and her two cubs decided to use this gully again. I grabbed my pack and the tripod and pushed on up the ridge, climbing to a level just below the highest summits. Finally I reached a saddle overlooking a tiny tarn with a larger, deeper valley that fell off to the north. I set up on a flat ridge, restricting myself to an area about thirty feet square to minimize disturbance to the grizzlies. I had been coming here since 1975. I always returned to the same place so that the few grizzlies who had detected my presence could predict where I would be and what I would be doing.

I took the pair of big navy glasses from my pack and began searching the slopes. Although it was the hottest part of a warm September day, the grizzlies were active. A big brown sow and two fat blond yearlings browsed in the shadows just upslope from the tarn. Up the hill 150 yards, a pair of four-year-old silvertips fed together. They might have been a previous litter of the brown sow, but I am never sure about relationships where there are so many bears. Below me, in the timber covering the bottom of the drainage, I caught dark movement in the shadows. I glassed the thicket of spruce and fir. A huge dark brown head popped into the sunlight. I breathed a sigh of relief: it was not the Black Grizzly but a familiar big brown boar. He was bedded, waiting for the shadows to fall before he ventured forth to feed.

The brown bear ignored the family of yearlings who, nonetheless, avoided violating the boar's "individual space," the distance within which a bear would charge or otherwise defend his territory. Grizzlies are not territorial, the way wolves are, but they do have a preference for certain seasonal ranges and share these forage areas with other bears. Grizzlies are secure and tolerant on day beds. I have seen the big brown boar allow smaller bears to pass within fifty feet while he was bedded.

Meanwhile the trio browsed rapidly downslope toward the shallow pond. I dug into the pack for the old Bolex, set it on the tripod head, and screwed on a 300-mm lens. The bears rolled over the last brush and into the open, walking over a jumble of deadfalls toward the water. As the grizzly family neared the tarn, the yearlings' usual taut discipline broke. They threw themselves into the pond, beating the water with their paws and leaving brown mud trails as they stirred up the bottom. The sow cautiously scented the air, then walked out on a bleached log and dove into the water. The two yearlings flailed away at each other with their paws from either side of another snag. They bit each other's ears and nipped like wrestling puppies. The mother joined them and all three bears rolled in the froth and spray.

The sow tried to disengage herself and was attacked from the rear by one of her yearlings. She shook the smaller bear off and crawled out onto a log. Despite her playfulness, she remained alert. It was only a matter of minutes before foreign odors would drift through the valley: smells of ornery male grizzlies and, then, the stench of man.

Suddenly she scented the air and bolted with the yearlings close behind. Racing across the open ground, she circled once in an attempt to locate the scent, then lumbered over the tangle of deadfalls with the muscles of her flank rippling. Through the viewfinder of the Bolex, I watched her flight, feeling regret, awe, and admiration. The air currents were fickle here, blowing over the ridges, curling into the basins, and diffusing in every direction. Some trace of human odor had reached the sow. I screwed up. I should have noticed the cold air flowing off the ridges.

Feeling remiss, I decided to visit the Grizzly Hilton before I stirred things up any more. The Grizzly Hilton is simply the clump of trees I make my camp in—a thicket of fir lying on a little knoll apart from the ridge-top game trail the bears sometimes use. There was no berry habitat in the immediate vicinity, and I had never seen sign of any grizzly bedding where I camped. It's about as bear-free as any place can be that's crawling with griz.

With the afternoon sun behind me, I climbed the highest local summit, sat, and glassed the shrub fields. Nine bears were visible on the distant slopes: two family groups with a single offspring each and five other adults. The shadows lengthened. Two more grizzlies came off their day beds to begin feeding as the air cooled. One subadult fed too close to a larger bear that made a short charge to drive off the youngster. Usually these grizzlies behave more like bison: a dominant animal browses his way in and the subordinate bear merely moves on a bit.

But all this was happening at a considerable distance away: it lacked the intimacy of the ridge below the Hilton, where you sat in the middle of a great sea of ebbing and flowing grizzlydom. My observation post below the Grizzly Hilton was the center of a great wave of bear activity. Animals rolled down one slope into the basins displacing the grizzlies already there, who, in turn, passed over my ridge and down into the opposite basin—causing another wave of bears to break.

I walked down the high ridge and crawled into the Hilton at dark. I listened to the sounds of elk bugling until I fell asleep. At daybreak, I dressed and started down the ridge toward my observation post. I heard large rocks rolling down the mountain. The big brown bear I had seen yesterday was digging on the far slope under a fir tree. He tugged at roots and threw the dirt out in clouds. He seemed to be digging a den. I suspected that this bear denned around here, since I had often seen him in the area late into October feeding on mountain ash berries. Grizzlies may den repeatedly in a single small area, but they usually dig a new den every year.

The bear dug on until the sun hit him, then retreated to a clump of trees and bedded. I walked over the ridge and peered down into the deep basin to the north. A fan of avalanched snow still lingered in the shaded bottom. A sharp, high-pitched trumpeting broke the stillness: a bull elk, late in his rut. A few minutes later I heard brush breaking and an eight-hundred-pound bull elk with a magnificent rack of antlers stepped to the edge of the snow, where a small pond of water filled a sump. He strode into the water, lowered his head, and slashed the surface with his antlers and hooves. After five minutes of battle, he ceased warring on the tiny wallow and strutted down the basin.

Just as the elk reached the trees I saw the peculiar gait of a lanky, dark grizzly. It was Happy Bear, whom I first came to know in 1976 when he was a skinny four-year-old. Now he was about my age in bear years, one foot already in the grave. Happy Bear is the most playful solitary bear I know. Once I filmed him sitting in the tarn contemplatively blowing bubbles in the muddy water and biting them. Then he attacked the water, like the elk, beating it with his paws and slashing the surface with his jaws.

Happy Bear ambled across the basin, lumbering in the stiff, swinging gait that made him so easy to recognize. He walked up to the snow patch and sniffed at the scat of another grizzly. Suddenly he leaped in the air as if stung by a bee, careening and prancing up and down the anvil of whiteness like a baby buffalo. Leap for joy, grizzer bear! Happy Bear approached another caviared pile of berry scat with feigned seriousness only to repeat his magic dance. He shook his head like a shaggy ox and leaped in tight circles. I filmed him leaving the show, prancing across the tiny sedge meadow into the brush.

I watched [a] grizzly family feed throughout the remainder of the afternoon, until shadows fell and the big brown grizzly came back out. Happy Bear failed to reappear. I saw a sow with a single light-colored cub in the north basin, feeding up the slope in my direction. Not wanting to disturb them, I climbed the steep ridge to the Grizzly Hilton, allowing the bears to use the ridge in peace. I sat just below my camp glassing the basins in the fading light. Just at dark, a big black grizzly appeared at the snow patch.

The wind whipped the tent fly. I could not hear a sound over its scream, and that made me nervous. The Black Grizzly had arrived, and the time of secure camping and sound sleeping was over. I pulled the wool cap off my ears and listened to the wind in the trees. Now and then I thought I heard something moving in the brush, but I was never sure. I was completely helpless, dependent upon the whim of the most unpredictable and powerful animal I knew. Drops of wind-driven rain exploded against the tent. The din of wind and rain lulled me to sleep. I dreamed of white bears until a change in the sounds outside woke me up. The wind died and the thud of rain on the tent softened: it was snowing. I burrowed deeper into my sleeping bag, only dimly remembering that the previous afternoon I was sitting shirtless in the sun. The snow meant the huckleberries would freeze and drop off their bushes in three or four days, and this congregation of grizzlies would begin to disperse, a process that would accelerate as the season advanced, markedly hastened by the badass presence of the Black Grizzly. I wondered where he was. That curiosity kept me awake until daybreak.

I shook the snow off the tent flap and peered out. A four-inch blanket of snow covered everything. The morning was gray but at least I was not in a cloud. I could get some spectacular movie footage today. Moving off the edge of the knoll, I glassed the basin below. The big brown grizzly dug at his den again. The day before, winter seemed a long way off. Obviously the brown grizzly knew something I didn't.

The Black Grizzly worried me. He was the one animal up here who regarded me as a subordinate. All the other grizzlies treated me much as they did other, more dominant bears and ran away most of the time. A few, including the den-digging griz, showed neither fear nor aggression and stood their ground. The Black Grizzly, on the other hand, charged and ran off other bears. He hadn't charged me because I hadn't given him a chance. The big brown griz and the Black Grizzly seemed to be the two top animals in this group of thirty or so bears, and they had a pact. I'd seen them feed within 150 yards of each other as peacefully as cattle, though the brown bear deferred slightly to the Black Grizzly in leaving him the prime berry areas.

By late afternoon the snow melted and I had not seen a thing. I started breaking down my camera, getting ready to return to the Hilton, when I heard movement in the brush below me to the north. The sow with the dark patch on her hump, from the previous night, and her small, light-colored cub walked onto the false hellebore–studded meadow near the snow field. The cub leapt and nipped at its mother, who wanted no part of the play. She was clearly nervous. The cub paused to graze on the low sedges growing on the wet flats below the snow, then ran to catch up to the sow, who had started climbing the long ridge between me and the Grizzly Hilton. She would pass over the saddle just in front of me. I did not want to disturb the grizzly family, but I did not want to be stuck on the ridge after dark either. I decided to let the bears pass over the ridge first, then slip by them and climb the rest of the way to the Hilton. If I was careful, they would not get my scent.

Darkness was falling and the grizzlies had not hit the ridge top yet—they had stopped to feed on huckleberries. I was waiting in the shadows when my heart skipped a couple of beats: below, in the meadow, stood the Black Grizzly, nibbling sedge. I hoped he would stay down there. I already had two grizzlies between me and my camp, and it would be dark in forty-five minutes.

The Black Grizzly crossed the meadow with his usual disdain for scents and worlds beyond his immediate one and started browsing his way up the side of the ridge. He climbed rapidly and was halfway up the ridge when it dawned on me that he was going to catch up with the grizzly family feeding just below me. I was going to be stuck there in the dark with a sow, her cub, and the Black Grizzly between me and my sleeping bag. I edged off to the side of a steep-sided ridge to get a better view. The Black Grizzly browsed a hundred feet or so below the sow; neither bear seemed aware of the other. I considered dropping off the back side of the ridge and trying to circle around the three bears, but I would never make it; the steep brush was nearly impenetrable.

Suddenly there was a roar, and I heard a huffing and the sound of animals running through the brush. The sow broke into the open a hundred feet in front of me and raced across the saddle. The tiny cub struggled with the brush, running at her heels. I could hear the intake and exhalation of each breath with each stride. They contoured along the rock outcrop below the ridge, oblivious of my presence, running for their lives before the Black Grizzly, who tore up the slope and burst over the ridge top. He galloped like a racehorse and moved just as fast. The sow and cub flew below the small cliff. The cub fell a couple of yards behind and I could make out a high-pitched coughing, a panicky sound as if the little bear knew it had but seconds left to live. The Black Grizzly gained ground until his jaws were but a yard from the cub's hindquarters.

At the last second the sow spun on her heels, allowing the cub to slip under her as she braced for the crush of the huge grizzly with a chilling roar. The boar bellowed back, and they locked jaws. The Black Grizzly slashed with his teeth.

The sow parried and warded off the attacking jaws of the bigger bear. The cub retreated to a rock thirty feet above and stood there bawling. The boar leapt forward and knocked the smaller sow off balance, forcing her to expose her vulnerable flank. The huge male lunged and seized the female by the neck. She yelped in pain, throwing her head against the bigger bear, and broke the grip of his jaws. The sow quickly recovered. She held her own.

I could see no blood, though both bears must have been wounded by then. They alternately slashed and parried, then stood nose to nose roaring amplified growls, the likes of which I had never heard in nature. The Black Grizzly slowed his attack. Abruptly he changed tactics and lunged once again for the throat of the sow. She leaned into the attack; they locked jaws and rose to their hind feet like circling wrestlers. They broke and dropped to all fours, roaring and bellowing into each other's snouts.

The face-off stabilized as the Black Grizzly gave up trying to kill the sow. The last roars rumbled through the valley. Though a little shaken by the proximity of the battle, I managed to run a few feet of film.

The smaller of the two carnivores backed slowly up the hill, still growling with the hair on her neck straight up. The Black Grizzly roared again, his head slightly lowered, his ears flattened back. She inched away from him a few feet at a time and turned her head to the side—a sign she was done fighting. He read it and turned away almost regretfully. The battle was over.

I was in a predicament. It was almost dark and I was perched on a knife-edged ridge with steep, impassable brush on either side and nowhere to go but up to the Grizzly Hilton. Between me and the Hilton, one hundred and fifty feet away, stood the baddest bear in the mountains, now at his ugliest after an inconclusive fight.

I let my instincts loose: I had no choice but to face down the great grizzly. Any failure of confidence could be fatal. I picked up two large brown bags that had been covering my camera and held them at arm's length. I was wearing a black sweater; both black and dark brown grizzlies were often big males. The Black Grizzly turned just off the crest of the ridge a hundred feet away and pretended to feed. He still had not seen me.

I made my move. Slowly I inched up the ridge and spoke. "Hey, grizzer bear, it's only me, good old Arapaho. Sure hate to bother you." The words were irrelevant, but tone and posture were everything. The grizzly reared and spun. He took a huge breath, exhaled like a sounding whale, then dropped to all fours facing me. I continued inching toward him, my arms outstretched holding the silly garbage bags, talking nonsense with my head cocked off to the side. The grizzly clicked and gnashed his teeth. I stopped at fifty feet and the bear advanced stiff-legged toward me. His ears were flat back against his head. I was finished. "I'll make it up to you, griz, honest." At fifteen feet away the great bear stopped, his head lowered. There was something in his eyes that I would never quite put my finger on. The Black Grizzly turned his head to the side, almost sadly, spun gracefully on his rear feet, and ambled off into the brush leaving me alone on the ridge top.

Only half believing my good fortune, I wasted no time. I slid by the spot where the bear disappeared and shot up the ridge to my hilltop camp. By the time I got there it was dark. I leaned into the darkness listening for sounds and caught myself shaking uncontrollably....

Normally I build no fires at the Grizzly Hilton because I don't like to spook the bears, but that night a fire was my only defense against the roaming bear I had just escaped. I worked fast, kindling a tiny blaze a few feet from my hidden tent. The fire bolstered my shaky nerves, and I stepped to the edge of the hill. Somewhere, down in the darkness, was the unmistakable sound of a big animal moving through the brush. I listened breathlessly. The Black Grizzly was coming uphill. I stoked up the fire and gathered beargrass plumes. I made a torch of them, but the stalks burned poorly. I added branches and got the whole thing flaming. I heard the snapping of brush just over the edge of the knoll. Again, I had no choice but confrontation. Walking to the brink of the hill, I heard the grizzly moving not forty feet downslope. I spoke softly, telling the bear I was sorry that I had invaded his territory, thanking him, and assuring him I would move on. Waving the flaming plumes and branches in the air, I saw the small eyes shine red for a second. They blinked off and disappeared into the darkness. I heard the huge bear slowly move through the bushes back down the hill. I went back and huddled by the fire.

Half an hour passed, maybe more. I was beginning to think the bear would leave me in peace when I heard thrashing in the shrub field on the other side of the knoll. Again I gathered firebrands and walked to the edge of the steep drop-off. I stared into the darkness and heard the angry grizzly fight his way up the hill. When he got thirty feet away, I threw a burning branch down the slope. The bear stopped. I waved the brands in the air and said, "Hey, Black Grizzly, it's me again. Why don't you give me a break?"

Silence. I peered into the blackness, seeing nothing. The torch had almost burned down, leaving me unprotected. The big bear slowly withdrew down the mountain. An hour later I heard him probe the third side of the pyramid-shaped hill. The scene was repeated.

The wind rose, bringing dim sounds of dark shapes to my ears. The snapping of a twig carried to the fire, and my head jerked toward the black trees, finding nothing. It must have been midnight. I could not remember being so tired. I could not afford to fall asleep. I tried to keep my mind moving. My thoughts drifted, landing on the irony of meeting my end at the jaws of my favorite beast. For a moment I could imagine the flickering fire reflecting the hint of a smile on my face. It vanished as I heard another branch break.

By about two in the morning, peace returned to the mountains, broken only once by bugling elk in a distant basin. I dozed by my tiny fire, waking every half hour to rekindle a small blaze. Gray dawn broke in the southeastern sky. With each moment the daylight spread and my confidence returned. Still I had to get out of these hills, past the Black Grizzly.

I picked up my binoculars and walked to the edge of the knoll where I could see down into the basin. A couple of hundred yards to my right the brown grizzly with her two lovely blond yearlings ate berries. She sniffed the air and trotted away from me. Shit, she got my scent. The bears ambled through the steep brush, then picked up a near-vertical bear trail leading to the bottom of the basin.

In the trees near the edge of the sedge meadow I saw a dark shape. The Black Grizzly stepped into the open and began grazing. The sow and her two yearlings continued dropping down the steep trail. Just as they hit bottom, the big boar lifted his head and saw the family a hundred yards away across the flat. Without pausing, he charged full tilt over the log-filled meadow. The sow and her young turned, scrambled back up the steep game trail, and climbed above a rocky outcrop out on a low cliff. The Black Grizzly stopped at the foot of the hill and looked up, allowing the family to reach safety on the cliffs.

Another close one.

I was upset with myself. I had almost run those little bears into that black bastard and got them killed. That's it, I'm leaving as soon as he beds. I was angry at the Black Grizzly for being such a cantankerous son of a bitch, but he was just being a bear. I was a blundering nuisance who was not doing the bears a bit of good.

I returned to the Hilton and broke camp, deciding to take a walk in the opposite direction to give the bear time to bed down.

Overhead, a jet trail bisected the single patch of blue sky. It probably was an air force jet out of Great Falls carrying a full payload, ready for the Big One, finger on the switch.

I lay back on the grass and looked up. Those buttons, the wonders of technology, had safely removed us from the evolutionary realities that we had once faced along with the grizzlies. Future pathfinding would be in space—the last frontier, as they say. We were out there right now trying to discover what had already been lost here. Orbiting satellites were being used both to keep tabs on our commie terrestrial enemies and to radio-track collared grizzly bears who seem to be wandering.

Back on the ridge above the Grizzly Hilton, I held onto a fistful of beargrass, firmly tethered to the earth. Fuck space. There was no way in hell I could imagine the Black Grizzly straying from home. There was no doubt in my mind who was really lost.

I hiked back to camp in the afternoon to finish packing up. The bears should have been bedded by now. I approached the Grizzly Hilton and stopped short. Something was wrong. Down stuffing covered everything. My cache of gear had been pulled down from the tree and the contents scattered. My sleeping bag was torn to shreds. I found my dirty brown T-shirt chewed to pieces. The bear had eaten everything that smelled of me.

I packed up the remains of my camp, threw it in the backpack, and started down the ridge. I glassed the timber just below the basin and caught a flash of the black bear on his day bed. He was so arrogant he did not even bother hiding in the timber like other bears. I could see half of his enormous body stretched out in the open.

I approached my observation post with apprehension. Two of my one-gallon water canteens lay on the ground crushed by the grizzly's jaws. The camera and the tripod were knocked over. The foam sound blimp had been chewed off Gage's old Bolex, which, outside of a few canine dents, was undamaged.

I stuffed my pack with damaged equipment, trembling slightly out of mixed rage and fear. I walked the ridge to the spot directly over the Black Grizzly's day bed. I pried loose the biggest boulder I could find and rolled it down the slope, crashing into the timber. The great bear lifted his head and looked up at me. A piercing cry shattered the silence as I roared at him. He yawned and his head disappeared again into the thick trees. I turned and slipped on down the ridge, leaving the bear and the mountains behind.

29

PREDATOR PUMA

Pat Hagan
2006

Pat Hagan has worked at Glacier as a seasonal naturalist for nearly thirty years. Naturalists are the uniformed personnel who give campfire talks, take visitors on trail walks and hikes, and provide information at visitor centers and even parking lots about the park's animals, plants, and geology. Hagan has collected many humorous anecdotes about his park experiences, often with tourists, which he published in a little book called *Seasonal Disorder: Ranger Tales from Glacier National Park.* Some of his writing might best be viewed as tall tales set against the backdrop of Glacier National Park, with perhaps a bit of fictionalizing thrown in.

There are few creatures in the animal kingdom that captivate the imagination like the mountain lion. As a predator it has few rivals, unless you include Hugh Hefner or Woody Allen. With its stealth, cunning, and charisma, the mountain lion holds us enthralled. But mountain lions are elusive, and not many of us actually have an opportunity to view one. Seeing a mountain lion is something precious and rare, sort of like finding a polite person in Paris, France.

Mountain lions (frequently called catamounts, panthers, cougars, pumas, and, occasionally, Nikes) are predators—meat eaters. Their diet consists of deer, elk, moose, and, if available, those little cocktail weenies. Like many members of the cat family, mountain lions are nocturnal, or active at night, and so much of their life remains a mystery. And their lives will continue to be a mystery as long as mountain lion researchers conduct their work during the day. Researchers have avoided working nights for various reasons, ranging from "It is difficult to write notes in the dark" to "It is difficult to write notes in the dark with this big cat on my chest."

Years ago, I had the pleasure of volunteering a few months of my precious time at a remote cabin in the North Fork region of Glacier National Park. Most people only dream of enjoying the solitude of a cabin in the middle of nowhere. Instead, each day they slave away at their 9-to-5 job, counting paperclips, chatting over coffee, and fantasizing about their escape into the freedom of the wild. But for me it was no fantasy, I was actually THERE…because I didn't *have* a job.

The one-room cabin where I was stationed was built around 1900. The old log structure was situated in a small meadow used as a recreational facility by some of the resident deer. Hauling gear from the car to the cabin was about a quarter-mile trek, and I had so much gear I needed to make several trips. The deer were not disturbed by my activity in the least. They continued to frolic, playing games of "eat the flower" and "follow the butterfly," as I lugged provisions. I had left suburbia and entered a Disney fantasy.

The windows of the cabin were barred with iron and barbed wire to protect the cabin's contents from pesky forms of wildlife, such as mountain lions, grizzlies, wolverines, and campers who have run out of instant oatmeal. In front was a small porch that overlooked a lake. Downwind was the bathroom equipped with all the modern conveniences, such as a hole, a splintered wooden seat, corncobs, and a small amount of chlorinated lime. I thought the outhouse was kind of fun, in a primitive sort of way. But on future trips I'd forgo the rustic pleasures and bring some toilet tissue, two-ply.

My first morning, after a warm spring rain, I decided to take a six-mile hike up to the head of the lake and check out the backcountry campground. Since I was a lowly volunteer, I wanted to show the "powers that be" that I had some initiative. Besides, I wanted to see if the outhouse at the other end of the lake had any toilet paper to swipe.

As I was walking up the muddy trail, numerous deer tracks reminded me that I wasn't alone in my wilderness world. Signs of deer were everywhere: scat (a scientific term meaning "Shoo! Go away!"), tracks, and plant limbs that had a ragged appearance due to feeding. Although a novice in these woods, I knew that where there are deer, there are also predators. Fearing that there was a predator ready to separate me from my viscera, I became acutely aware of my surroundings; my personal radar was turned on and set on high. Sounds that normally went undetected seemed amplified; my eyes picked up on odd colors and things that seemed out of place; subtle movements quickly drew my attention. I kept sniffing for strange scents. If animals were going to eat me, first they had to invade the protective umbrella of my heightened senses. Then, quite suddenly, I felt a squishing sensation oozing from either side of my right foot. I had stepped into some warm—I believe the scientific word for it is—poop, and I also made a mental note to check the warranty on my personal radar.

I took off my backpack and hunkered down to inspect the poop. I pulled out my field guides, pored over the pages, and found out, with certainty, that this discovery wasn't a ruby-throated hummingbird or a glacier lily. After consulting a book on tracking, I narrowed the substance down to mountain lion poop. I was thrilled—and a little scared.

Knowing that I was walking in the same vicinity as a mountain lion put a spring in my step. I was about a mile from the backcountry campground and, due to said spring, I made it in three paces.

Seeing the campground made me feel more secure. After walking six miles and finding no apparent traces of humans, this backcountry site was quite a relief. Signs of humanity were everywhere. The trees had been thinned, there were leveled areas for tents, and an outhouse loomed as large as a skyscraper. All these signs of human occupancy slowed my heart's frantic pace.

Feeling somewhat courageous again, I decided to have a look about the campground. I inspected all the tent sites individually, hoping to find signs of upright animals. A short examination of the whole area told me I had the whole valley to myself. Not so much as an old piece of garbage or a tent peg could be found. There were no tracks in the fresh mud, human or otherwise. The only prints to be found in the muddy campground were mine.

Soon, I realized that I was in the same area as the outhouse, or as we like to say euphemistically in the Park Service, a "comfort station." There is a law of nature that states that how badly one needs to use the comfort station is directly proportional to how close one is to the actual relief site. A great distance means no great need; a close distance, however, has some urgency attached. I'm not one to break laws, especially laws of nature, and I needed some comfort. Besides, maybe I could acquire the much-needed toilet paper.

As I walked toward the comfort station, I hit the side of my head with the heel of my right hand just to see if I could jump-start my faulty radar. I could almost hear it turn on with a chug and a sputter, and if someone else had been around, they might have been able to hear it too.

Radar on. Check. Sniff and sample the air—nothing; check. Listen for unusual sounds—nothing; check. Look for tracks near the outhouse—nothing; check. Enter outhouse; check. Discontinue air sampling, quickly; check. Look for toilet paper; *be damned sure and* check. Obey laws of nature; check. Relax and shut off radar; check.

Naturally, I was much relieved upon coming out of the outhouse. Good thing, too. As I was zipping up my fly, I looked down into the mud. Directly in front of my boot, about a foot away, there was a large set of distinctive, four-toed tracks: mountain lion. Muddy water could be seen *seeping into* and filling up the imprints. Fresh! If I hadn't, only seconds ago, been following the laws of nature, I would certainly be following them now.

In a desperate attempt to activate my radar, I started frantically hitting my head again. The air was still and silent, but the tracks, which circled the out-house, indicated a mountain lion—here—*NOW!* I scanned the nearby trees, the top of the biffy, all around. My heart rate steadily increased.

I thought to myself, "When would be a good time to leave?" Under the circumstances, "NOW!" seemed to be a reasonable answer. I started back the six miles, toward the safety of the cabin, when I realized that my fresh tracks leading up to the campground had been stepped on by the same four-toed tracks. The mountain lion had followed me up to the campsite.

Getting back to the cabin was the longest, most difficult hike I have ever experienced. My entire body shook with fear. I couldn't rely on my defective radar to protect me from an animal whose survival is based on stealth. Then I remembered something I read about protecting yourself from mountain lions: If one encounters a menacing mountain lion, one should look directly at it…make eye contact. I had to continuously scan the entire area. But since I had no idea from which direction the mountain lion would come, I had to check all possibilities and rotate 360 degrees. So, flushed with adrenaline, I hiked by pirouetting, like a whirling dervish, the entire way back to the cabin. Let's see him walk in my footsteps now!

I stopped only once, and that was to check on a French couple hiking the same trail. They must have seen something coming down the trail, possibly the mountain lion, that caused them considerable alarm. They leaped off the trail as I came spinning toward them. Due to the language barrier, I couldn't tell what they were trying to communicate by rotating their index fingers around their ears. It could have been French sign language.

Once back at the cabin, I threw myself on the soft green grass and waited for my heart to stop racing and for the world to stop spinning. The cabin, the trees, and one resident deer were all revolving around me at an incredible rate. Pirouetting a trail for six miles is great aerobic exercise, but it can make one just a little dizzy. After a short time, the world ceased to spin and returned to normal. As I sat up in the cool breeze, I ran a hand across my sweaty brow and looked ahead. My blood froze. Ten feet away, a mountain lion crouched, ready to spring upon me as though I were stuffed with catnip. After spinning down that trail, I was stuffed with absolutely nothing. A fact the mountain lion should have noticed as he followed me.

As the mountain lion faced me, I became mesmerized by the pale, yellow-green depths of its eyes; the pupils grew larger and larger. Its claws sunk into the soft soil. Like a Looney Tunes character, I could see the large cat envisioning me as some oversized cocktail weenie. And what a weenie I was.

I watched the tawny cat's haunches wiggle in anticipation of the deadly pounce. As the tensed feline leaped, a scream escaped from my lips. It was so high that no one actually heard it. (Though, strangely, far away some wolves broke into a howl.) I sat frozen, watching this mountain lion sail, slow-motion, through the air, while I sat forcing air out through my gaping, silent orifice. I was still soundlessly screaming, too. I closed my eyes. I heard the cat land. A guttural snarl. I heard a strange bleating sound. I felt nothing. No pain. No pain.

It had just attacked one of the resident deer.

It was over quickly for the deer. It was over quickly for me, as a witness. Very nimbly, and with strength that belied its size, the cat dragged the carcass away into the trees. Just like that—it was over.

Sweating and shaking, I hauled myself out of the grass. My quivering bones wouldn't totally support my weight, and I staggered over to the cabin. I was dizzy again. I threw open the door, saw my bed, and collapsed. A few more steps, and I would have actually landed on the bed. The floor felt cool on my face. I closed my eyes and drifted, mercifully, into slumber.

The next morning I awoke, still on the floor. The sunlight that streamed through the barred windows bounced off a little puddle of drool on the floor, reflecting directly into my eyes. I pushed myself off the floor and got up on my feet. One advantage of sleeping on the floor is that making the bed takes no time. I wiped the drool up with a hankie. I squinted toward the light. It was a bright sunny day. It held a lot of potential.

As I moved, my muscles responded slowly and felt stiff, calling to mind yesterday's events. I made myself some instant oatmeal and gingerly walked down to the lake. At the shore, I faced the sun and felt the warm reflections off the water illuminating my face. The sun was well over the peaks, and I knew I had slept in, but I didn't care. I looked out over the lake, which was as smooth as polished glass. I thought about the previous day. The big thrill. I had finally seen my first mountain lion! My feet started to shuffle. I couldn't help it; I started to dance. At the water's edge, I happily twirled about like a whirling dervish.

30

FROM *A BEAST THE COLOR OF WINTER*

The Mountain Goat Observed

Douglas H. Chadwick
1983

Douglas H. Chadwick (b. 1948) is a prolific writer and student of the natural world. Based in the Glacier Park area, Chadwick is a long-time contributor to *National Geographic* magazine and the author of many books, including *True Grizz: Glimpses of Fernie, Stahr, Easy, Dakota, and Other Real Bears in the Modern World* (2013) and *The Wolverine Way* (2012), studies of grizzly bears and wolverines in and around Glacier. The selection below is from a book-length study of Glacier's mountain goats, the "white climbers". Like most of Chadwick's work, it involves endless hours of observation and a thoughtful—and personal—consideration of animal behavior.

It was on a high pass through the Continental Divide that I first met the billy I called Gore, and learned about mountain goat society by taking a personal part in it. F. Fraser Darling, whose study of red deer in Scotland during the 1930s was a marvelous piece of pioneering in the field of animal behavior, wrote in his introduction to *A Herd of Red Deer*, "I still go on the principle that if you are watching the higher animals, watch them as if they were human beings of a different civilization or culture, and if you are watching human beings observe them as if they were animals. Your anticipation of the next move will not be far wrong." Gore was the one who brought this message home.

I called him Old Gore at first. He was, and remains, the biggest billy I have ever seen. His hooves were getting on toward the size of a bull elk's, and his horns were long and exceptionally thick. When I got my first close look at those horns I discovered from the number of rings near the base of them that Old Gore was less than five years of age, a young giant with years of growing left.[1]

Along with two to three dozen other goats, Gore spent the warm months in and around this particular pass in Glacier. It is a traditional summering spot for the climbers. The cliffs are laminae of blue-grey limestone, and red, olive green, and cream-colored argillite. They are bounded by permanent snowfields and crevasse-striped glaciers, and interspersed with moist alpine meadows that are like terraced floral gardens by July.

Through the pass winds a hiking trail, and there is a stone chalet several miles to the west. Over the years the goats have not only become well accustomed to people, but have made a positive association between them and salt. In the past, salt licks were put out to attract the goats for viewing. That practice has been officially stopped, but people still gave the goats salt, and by now the beasts have developed the not-so-charming habit of licking where people or their horses leave urine, a salty substance in its own right.

To the goats, the entire area for miles around the pass is a salt-lick situation, which means the billies drop their usual role of deferring to nannies. Aside from this it afforded an ideal opportunity for me to live side by side with free-roaming mountain goat bands. At times when no one else entered the pass for days I felt as if I had left my own society and adopted a new one. The problem was that although the goats accepted me as long as I moved slowly and avoided intruding on anybody's personal space, they still treated me as a very dominant animal, which is just what we humans take for granted. They were always watching to see where I would go next so they could get out of the way. When we all bedded down together there would invariably be a wider empty spot around me than around any other individual in the group.

Gore fixed that.

I had an extra interest in him all along, for in addition to being by far the biggest goat, deferred to by all, he had his own extra interest in me. I was lying on my back in a meadow one afternoon when I was awakened by a sound that turned out to be Gore snipping grass a foot away from me. I lay still and looked at him, and our eyes met. I looked away first, not wanting to threaten him. With his head down grazing, his horns were too close if he wanted to respond. Then he stepped right over me and continued grazing, pausing once to look back at me. His tail was tucked down the entire time, betraying not a milligram of fear.

What was it about this huge billy? He, and he alone, trotted back and forth across the pass keeping an eye on the whereabouts of all the other goats. He also kept the closest track of hikers, meeting them as they came up one side and then watching from a promontory as they passed down the other, acting like the true master of the mountaintop. My initial thought was that he was merely making sure he wasn't missing out on any new sources of salt.

Yet there was something more to the way he grew uneasy when he lost sight of the nanny-led bands. Then I recognized that he was acting rather like a billy does during the rut: roaming about the rocks, usually keeping above the female-subadult bands, and checking for the approach of possible rivals. As if to confirm my theory, he began to threaten me when I was in the company of nannies.

The first threat was subtle enough. He merely stood in my path, refusing to give way. I had to go around him to proceed. The next was a mild present-threat I hardly noticed. The third was a present-threat he made sure I noticed. Gore put me a bit on edge at this point, but I was still more interested in watching his behavior than worrying about it. A day later he nailed me.

I was walking alongside a nanny, taking notes. Gore appeared beside me just within my personal space. His tail was tucked down and he was slightly tensed. He watched me intently but made no further move, so I ignored his stare-threat and turned to see what the nanny was doing. The next thing I knew, I was being lifted up with a horn in my knee and spilled onto my back. It was not a vicious thrust. By Gore's standards it was probably more like a warning prod. But it had gone right through my soft hide, and only the leg bone close to the surface at the knee had kept it from penetrating more deeply. If he had struck somewhere else....

Thereafter I had a new place in goat society and new insight into its workings. I was genuinely afraid of Gore now, and both of us knew it. Like other herd members smaller than he, I was careful to give him a wide right-of-way when our paths crossed, respecting his private sphere of influence with the sincerity of a lower-ranking animal. If he drew close purposefully I crouched slightly, then stepped aside. This seemed to satisfy him. But he continued to threaten me occasionally, and I found myself becoming keenly alert to his whereabouts and moods—again as a subordinate must to a dominant goat.

Seeing me defer to Gore as I moved over the rocks and meadows, a few other big billies apparently learned that I was nothing to have to sidle away from and so began to behave more aggressively in my presence, giving me threats of their own when we came together. As my status kept slipping from dominant stranger to familiar subordinate I could do more than record the social encounters taking place around me: I could empathize in a realistic way with the goats involved in them.

I spent three or four muggy, buggy hours lying down among the goats during one long afternoon bedding period. All of us were twitching and fanning mosquitoes and blackflies away from our faces, me with my hands, they with their ears. I was using the time to count chewing rates, noting how often the goats brought up a bolus—the ball of food we call a cud—from the rumen, how many chomps per minute they made in grinding the bolus up, and how long it took the goat from the start of each bolus until it was finished and swallowed it. Pretty trivial stuff in a way, yet I had noticed in the Swans [mountains southwest of Glacier] that the speed of chewing varies from one age class to the next, becoming slower with age. Kids average about two chews per second; yearlings, 1 2/3 chews per second; two-year-olds, 1 1/2; and adults about 1 1/2. Here was a possible way to estimate the age of a goat, for there are many kinds of poor light conditions under which a distant observer with a telescope can see a goat chewing but cannot be sure of its horn length against a dark rock background. Perhaps more importantly, here too was a possible way of estimating stress in the white climbers. When the beasts are disturbed, as they were in the Swans by the sounds of roadbuilding and logging, they slow down their chewing rate and often interrupt the sequences by pausing to listen intently.

So I was jotting down more chomping data to see where it might lead, and every notebook page had seven or eight squashed mosquitoes among the lines. As early evening approached we were all more than a little full of pent-up energy. An adult female was among the first to rise in our band. She started to move off feeding, but none followed, and she returned toward the group. At that point the leader of the band—a nanny with a kid—rose, stretched, shook herself, nibbled some plants, urinated, and then started out in earnest, and all the subadult followers rose to join her.

The climbers began snipping their usual midsummer fare—the most recently blossomed flowerheads from a bouquet of species. Almost at once three fights broke out. They were playful fights, though—mock battles. Michael Fox, a well-known investigator of canine behavior, has shown that wolves, like dogs, will crouch with their heads low and give a shake or shimmy before play-fighting. It is both an invitation to play and an announcement that the attack behavior that follows is a sham, meant to be taken in the spirit of having a good time. Fox calls this signaling of intentions to establish the context of a behavior pattern metacommunication. The goat's way of saying, "Look, this really isn't serious," is to make quick prancing movements accompanied by a lot of head-bobbing and horn-shaking.

High-spirited and sassy, our band was soon in an uproar, with some of the members beginning to rear up, toss their horns, and go on to make whirling leaps. This is the behavior I have referred to several times before by the self-descriptive name of war-dancing. A war-dancing goat looks like a rodeo bull just let out of the chute, bucking, twisting, hooking, and slashing the air with its horns. Sometimes goats leap straight up as they war-dance. More often they spin as they jump, and I've seen goats make nearly two complete revolutions in mid-air before landing.

War-dancing shows up in play, and also during or just after status battles that are less than dead serious, and it is most common in summer when the climbers are well fed and full of pizzazz. I've seen single goats all alone on a mountain slope do it, though it is more of a group behavior. In fact it is tremendously contagious. One war-dancing band member will spark every other within sight into the dance. They do their best dancing on fellfield or meadow slopes steep enough that they can get airborne heading downhill, especially when that slope is covered with old, hard snow. Once in a while just coming upon a tilted snowbank in the midst of a feeding area is enough to send a band boogieing away downhill. Chamois have a version of war-dancing, and they are also given to glissading down snowbanks, their style being to extend their forelegs and leap into a belly slide.

One big billy now pranced my way and gave a horn-toss close to me. I wasn't as nervous about this particular fellow as I was about Gore, not at all; but then I wasn't really dominant to this billy either. In any case, I decided to give a small hop and head-toss myself. It felt kind of good. The billy sidled toward me in a present-threat and then leapt up and spun around one side of me. I didn't quite know what to do next. I wasn't in a mood for yielding, but I didn't want to tempt those horns. Just then a yearling headed down a nearby snowbank, bucking and spinning like a dervish. One by one the rest of the herd took off after him, including the billy and myself, and our troupe continued dancing its way downhill for almost 200 feet in a spray of crystals.

A spiraling kid lost its balance and landed on its chin. A nanny spun out onto her side. I kept leaping higher and higher, making one turn, then two turns while I was airborne. It was a magnificent release of tension, I found out, and just plain fun. Now when I ski down a snowfield on my bootsoles I always throw in a stretch of war-dancing, and from time to time I've been tempted to try a little war-dancing in awkward social situations down at lower altitudes.

NOTE

1. A ring forms at the base of a mountain goat's horn upon the commencement of

renewed horn growth after each winter of the goat's life except the first. In other words, a two-year-old will have a single ring; a five-year-old, four rings; an eight-year-old, seven rings, and so on.

Gore was perhaps an extreme example of the individual variation that makes relative horn size a poor indicator of age. Winter conditions, as they affect nutrition, also cause variations in horn growth. For example, after several light winters in a row in coastal Alaska, Christian Smith began to notice four-year-old goats with horns as long as those of nine-year-olds that had undergone very heavy winters as juveniles.

31

FROM *FATE IS A MOUNTAIN*

Mark W. Parratt
2009

Mark Parratt first came to Glacier with his family in 1946. For the next eighteen summers, his father, Lloyd, served as a ranger naturalist at both Lake McDonald and St. Mary Lake. While spending every summer in Glacier, Mark and his brothers, Monty and Smitty, were constant companions in exploring the park's wonders. The youngest, Smitty, was seriously mauled by a grizzly bear on the Otokomi Lake trail in 1960, when he was ten years old. He recovered from his injuries and went on to a distinguished career with the National Park Service. The middle brother, Monty, worked five summers on blister-rust control crews (blister rust is a fungus that attacks five-needled pines) and was a beloved high school teacher and coach in Marysville, Washington, until 2001, when he was tragically killed in an auto accident near the park. Mark, the eldest, spent six summers working as a fireguard on the east side of the park; he subsequently became a professor of environmental biology at Fullerton College in California, from which he is now retired. These two stories are taken from his Glacier memoir, *Fate Is a Mountain*.

THE ST. MARY LAKE MONSTER—JULY 1954

A venerable Canadian fisherman told us many stories of catching huge lake trout or mackinaw in the frigid waters of St. Mary Lake. Old Man Dahl fished these haunts scores of times from the 1930's to the 1950's. Using a large wooden boat to troll the 200-foot depths, the ruddy-faced Norwegian became quite skilled at catching twenty-five-pound trout. Never verified, however, were his colorful and imaginative tales of landing monster trout weighing fifty pounds or more. On occasion, Dahl docked his boat at our summer residence, the old Sun Camp Ranger Station. Mother [Grace Parratt] always obliged by serving him cookies and coffee.

My brother Monty and I were entranced by the craggy fisherman's stories. No matter how tall the tales, we accepted them as gospel and always begged for more.

Needless to say, the fantasies of two young brothers were greatly fueled by his accounts. One morning in early August, to our delight, Dahl took us fishing in his boat. It was a remarkable day on the lake. He shared his special fishing rigs and showed us many of his favorite trolling spots. At day's end, we gleefully raced into the cabin to display our catch, a pair of fifteen-pound lake trout. Pumped up with excitement, we lay in our bunks and talked late into the night.

Old Man Dahl didn't return to the lake the following summer. Sadly, one night in the midst of the long, bleak Alberta winter, the old fisherman passed away in his sleep. Monty and I felt a dull void in our lives without him. We vowed, then and there, to fish the lake until one of us caught the big one. The catch would be dedicated to the fishing legend and our mentor, Old Man Dahl.

In early June of 1954, the Glacier Park Boat Company launched the new passenger cruiser *Red Eagle* on St. Mary Lake. Located at Rising Sun, the company added several fifteen-foot wooden boats as well. The small craft could be rented as rowboats or fitted with small outboard motors. I was hired that summer to sell tickets for the daily cruises and to handle the small-boat rentals.

Thankfully, the boat dock at Rising Sun is partially protected from the lake's legendary high winds. Even so, with good reason, there were many days during the summer when gale-force conditions compelled us to suspend our rental operations altogether. The lake had a long and storied history of capsizing small craft, sending fishermen to watery graves.

In sharp contrast, there were the rare instances when the lake remained calm and mirror-like for the entire day. One such occasion occurred July 18, 1954 and was destined to hold the most exciting fishing adventure of my young life. Business was slow, so owner Art Burch gave me the use of a rental outboard during my lunch hour. I was eager to try some new heavy-duty fishing gear, a gift from my parents on the occasion of my thirteenth birthday.

The small Johnson outboard purred along as I maneuvered the boat into an area of the lake known as the Narrows. This geographic feature is the result of a large limestone outcrop that juts into the waters near Rising Sun. A corresponding ridge on the opposite shore reaches out to create the narrowing.

Once in position, I cut the motor and hastily rigged my deep-sea rod and reel. The shiny new reel was spooled with 600 feet of well-used fifty-pound-test leaded line. A steel wire leader was attached to a large red and white Dardevle lure. I snapped a two-pound leaded weight onto an extension line and fired up the motor. As the boat entered the Narrows, I released the drag on the reel and tossed the rigging overboard. I watched the lure tumble down through the clear water for some fifty feet, then disappear into the darkness.

A short time later, I felt a bounce as the leaded weight struck bottom. Rapidly reeling in about five feet of line, I kept the weight from snagging the lake floor and then set the drag on the reel. Using fifty-foot increment marks on the line, I guessed the trolling depth at 200 feet. Old Man Dahl favored the Narrows as a prime fishing spot, realizing the large lake trout spent the majority of the summer months in these deeper, cooler waters. As the motor slowly droned on, my thoughts drifted to the crafty old fisherman, and I felt sure he was out there somewhere smiling down upon me.

With one hand steering the boat, I held the fishing rod in the other, locking it between my knees. The warm air hovering on the lake, combined with the odor of the smoky two-stroke engine, lulled my senses into a dream-like state. What a beautiful day to be out on the water.

Suddenly, my rod sprang downward, the tip slamming against the side of the boat. I tightened my grasp and jerked upward on the rod, a flush of excitement coursing through my body. Was it a strike? I felt only the normal drag resistance of the leaded line and the rigging. The euphoria of the moment faded as I reeled in a few more feet of line and whipped the pole upward a few times. No response. I guessed that the rigging had temporarily snagged on a rock.

Once more, I released enough line to feel the bounce of the weight on the lake floor. Again, I tightened the tension on the line. I realized it would soon be time to call it quits and head back to work at the dock. It would take time to reel in the 500 feet of trolling line which now angled into the depths behind the boat.

As I reached toward the knob on my reel, my rod suddenly bent double, slamming hard against the railing. Instinctively, I pulled sharply upward to set the hook. Immediately, a powerful throbbing shook the pole. I felt certain I'd hooked a big mackinaw. Youthful adrenaline surged through my body. As the fish struggled beneath me, the tip of the rod continued to splash the water's surface. Quickly cutting the motor, I swung the propeller out of the water. Using all my strength, I was barely able to keep the rod high enough to clear the edge of the craft.

Slowly, a series of clicking sounds told me the big fish had begun to pull line from my reel. I continued to tighten the drag as the sounds slowed and then stopped. Guessing there were fewer than twenty-five feet of line remaining on the reel, I tightened the drag to a full stop. The aged line would simply have to hold. I could only hang on and hope. The rod bent double as the powerful creature continued to struggle. I winced with every tug, expecting the line to snap at any moment.

The day grew warmer as the summer sun bore down upon the still waters. As I caught a quick glance at the nearby shoreline, I realized the boat was moving. The mackinaw was towing my craft slowly up the lake. Grabbing my canteen with one hand, I gulped down the last of my water. Perspiration poured off my face as the intense afternoon sun beat down upon me. It was hot. Really hot.

Suddenly, the fish changed direction and began to pull the line under the boat. I feared the splintered wood on the weathered keel would surely abrade the line, eventually causing it to snap. Quickly, I backed off the drag on the reel. Guiding the rod carefully around the bow of the boat, I gained a better position for the contest. Now, the great fish began towing the boat slowly down the lake in the opposite direction. Taut line moved through the glassy surface, parting small rafts of floating pine pollen.

With a glance at my watch, I guessed that I'd been hooked up with the fish for a good forty-five minutes. Would the monster ever tire? I was dehydrated and exhausted. The muscles in my back convulsed and my arms became limp with the tension.

A sense of urgency began to overtake me. I desperately wanted to pull this fish off the bottom and bring it in. With repeated attempts, I reeled in ten to fifteen feet of line, only to quickly lose it again to the powerful thrashing of the trout.

My mind wandered. Then, abruptly, my thoughts returned to the boat dock. Reality struck. I was scheduled to sell tickets for the afternoon boat cruise. I was already late. Beyond the Narrows, I spied a faint line of passengers boarding the *Red Eagle*. I promptly decided I was not going to lose this fish. This was a battle I simply had to finish. I could feel my face burning from the intense sunlight reflecting off the still water. Shortly, I heard the rumble of its engines as *Red Eagle* approached.

A familiar voice called out to me from the flying bridge of the cruiser. Louie Cousineau, the boat's captain, hailed me. With the launch idling some 200 feet off my stem, he shouted, "The boss says that you'd better bring this one in. You're on company time now and this will be darned nice for our business." Art Burch had been following my progress with binoculars for several minutes from his vantage point on the dock. He suspected that I'd tied into a good-sized fish. Passengers on the tour cruise lined up along the railings to cheer me on.

The *Red Eagle* slowly moved away and, at last, became a tiny speck in the distance. The encouragement was the very tonic I needed.

With renewed resolve, I pulled the rod upward and rapidly reeled in a few feet of line. By continually repeating the process, I managed to turn the fish toward the boat, coaxing it from the lake bottom. The once powerful tugs were less frequent now. I sensed the great fish was beginning to tire. With smooth cranks on the reel, I could see the line markers moving slowly upward from the depths. Giving a strong kick, the powerful fish once again passed under the boat. No longer a stranger to its tactics, I stuck the rod in the water and guided the taut line following it. I continued to counter as the fish made three more such runs. I was now progressing at a steady pace. It seemed as if the trout and I were matching wits in a game of survival. There had to be less than fifty feet of line in the water. I could feel my heart pulsing strongly in my chest.

Harboring visions of being jerked out of the boat by a mighty mackinaw, I braced my legs against the hull. Peering over the edge, my eyes followed the shards of sunlight as they danced in the blue depths. Suddenly, several brilliant flashes pierced the water as the gigantic fish spun wildly to the surface. Water depth tends to magnify the size of a fish…and, to my boyish eyes, this monster appeared to be as long as the boat. My excitement grew with each passing moment. Slowly bringing the big fish alongside, I began to tremble uncontrollably. I was absolutely stunned by the immensity of this lake trout. He was mine and, amazingly, I was the victor in what is generally the toughest part of the battle.

With one hand cradling the rod, I slowly slid the gaff hook into the water. As the large hook moved near its massive head, the mackinaw thrashed its tail and made a final run, which took it several feet from the boat. Once more, I slowly brought the great fish alongside. Slipping the gaff hook into the water, I aimed at the trout's large gill slit. I connected. Spending my last shred of strength, I dragged the monster into the boat. Jumping atop the struggling fish, I waited for the thrashing to subside.

Too exhausted to rise, I gazed at the sky as I lay beside the quivering behemoth. Occasionally, I'd turn my head to examine the prize…as well as to make certain I wasn't dreaming. The battle with the big fellow had taken just over two hours. All-consuming was the ultimate thrill of landing one of the big ones. Keen memories of Old Man Dahl overtook me. I knew he was proud. Truly, this was his kind of fish.

With arms still weak and trembling, I lowered the propeller housing into the water. I pulled on the engine recoil rope several times. The little motor finally sputtered to life, and I turned the boat toward the distant shoreline. The glow I felt far surpassed the bright sunshine spilling around me.

As I neared the dock, Art Burch stepped forward to congratulate me. A short time later, he hefted the huge fish out of the boat, laying it gently in the back of his pickup. I eagerly climbed in beside him and we drove the half mile to the Rising Sun General Store, site of the only reliable scale in the area.

The massive lake trout weighed in at 42 pounds, eight ounces and measured 49 inches in length. With an immense head, its greatest girth totaled a whopping 27 inches. Later, we were to learn that the lake trout was the largest fish ever caught in Glacier National Park. That record remains to this day.

Word of the big fish spread through the St. Mary Valley like Montana mosquitoes. It wasn't long before the news reached my father, ranger-naturalist Lloyd Parratt, who arrived with camera in hand a short time later. Filled with pride, Dad took several pictures to preserve the moment for posterity. As the fish lay on large blocks of ice near the meat locker, curious onlookers and fishermen filed past with looks of admiration. Absorbing the accolades, I sat in a nearby chair and gazed at my catch. One local fisherman tapped me on the shoulder and said, "You are one lucky guy." Motioning toward the massive trout, he said, "I've been fishing this lake since the early 1950's and I've never seen anything even half this size. Congratulations, young man."

I thought, "Well, luck was certainly part of it...but the know-how gained at the knee of Old Man Dahl was what really enabled it to happen." Even as a youngster, I sensed that this would be the fishing achievement of my lifetime.

We dressed out the fish and carefully examined the contents of its stomach. Here, we discovered five fish in various states of digestion. The largest, a two-pound cutthroat trout, illustrated the predatory nature of the lake trout. The other fish included three good-sized mountain whitefish and a smaller rainbow trout.

As luck would have it, the next evening was the date of the annual east-side potluck dinner. All the Park Service employees at St. Mary were invited. My monster trout was filleted and cooked up in a large outdoor barbecue pit. The rich, reddish-orange meat had a flavor similar to choice wild salmon. The entire fish vanished as over fifty diners devoured the tender flakes. There could be no doubt. The tasty fillets were a resounding hit.

The big fish later gained honorable mention in the 1954 *Field and Stream* magazine's trophy list for lake trout. The big one remains among the larger lake trout ever caught in the State of Montana, possibly a state record but never submitted. The current state-record lake trout was caught in Flathead Lake and was 42.5 inches in length and 42.69 pounds. It was virtually identical in girth and weight to mine, so we'll consider the St. Mary Lake monster as the unofficial record.

During the many summers that followed, Monty and I continued to fish St. Mary Lake. Occasional mackinaws in the fifteen- to twenty-pound range were our largest catches.

We feel certain they are down there…the really big ones…lurking in those dark, cold depths. Why not give it a try? Perhaps Old Man Dahl will smile upon you one day for the catch of a lifetime.

PIKE EYES—LAKE SHERBURNE, JULY 1962

Monty knew, with certainty, that there were large great northern pike in Lake Sherburne in the Many Glacier Valley. Earlier that summer, he'd met up with a pair of Canadian fishermen who spoke of fishing the lake regularly over the years with considerable success. They told tales of great northern pike, or northerns, so large that landing them from shore was virtually impossible. With no access point or ramp from which to launch a boat, fishing from shore was an angler's only option.

Always up for a challenge, Monty ventured to the shores of the lake one morning in late July. As he set out down the trail, my brother had no idea of the terror which lay beneath the murky waters of the lake that day. This would be one fishing adventure he would long remember.

By anyone's estimation, he was an outstanding fisherman. Monty possessed a special finesse, a know-how that made fishing truly an art form. He was known throughout the park as the young man who could catch fish practically anywhere, anytime.

As the sun warmed the morning air, with his fishing gear strapped to his backpack, Monty made his way around the northern end of Lake Sherburne on a portion of the Cracker Lake trail. Eventually, he left the pathway and hiked across the grassy meadows of Sherburne's south shore to a series of shallow fingers or lagoons. The beach there was covered with water-worn rocks mingled with open spots of soft clay silt. From the edge of Boulder Ridge's forested flanks, the shoreline dropped steeply down to the sandy coves.

This was prime grizzly bear country. There had been several sightings of a good-sized male grizzly roaming the lake's edge during the past few weeks.

Monty had duly noted several of the bear's tracks on the trail earlier that morning. Now he saw those same telltale imprints pressed deeply into the silt, mingling with those of his own boots. Wary, he continually glanced at the dense forest behind him and scanned the beaches on both sides of the lake. Not a living creature was in sight. Still, with grizzlies randomly patrolling the shoreline, a certain air of uneasiness persisted. He shuddered inwardly as he thought about the horrific grizzly bear incident two summers earlier that nearly took the life of his younger brother, Smitty.

A week earlier, Monty had purchased a pair of six-inch, red Dardevle lures. The Canadian fishermen felt that big lures sometimes caught big fish. That made perfect sense to Monty as he snapped one of the large spoons onto his steel leader. His spinning reel was spooled with fifteen-pound-test line, enough, he felt, to play almost any large pike.

Making a quick visual check for bears once again, he cautiously approached a nearby lagoon and felt a heady anticipation rise in his chest. He began making long casts into the main body of the lake, reeling the big spoon slowly through the shallow waters. The lure made a whistling sound each time it was flung across the surface of the lake. Water plants were thick at the bottom of the silted backwaters, a perfect hiding place for resting pike. Within minutes, Monty caught and released two small northerns. Patiently moving along the edge of the lagoon, he continued his spin-casting.

Suddenly, a strong tug announced the presence of a larger pike. A quick upward jerk of the pole's tip set the hook. Before long he realized he'd caught the attention of a good-sized fish, a real fighter. After wrestling the taut line for some ten minutes, the fish finally tired of the struggle and sidled up toward the beach. Wearing a leather glove on his right hand, Monty carefully pulled the long reptilian-looking creature out of the water. Grabbing the back of the pike's large head with his gloved hand, he surveyed the remarkable predator. Suddenly, with a powerful twist, the large jaws clamped down on his glove. Fortunately, the needle-sharp teeth just grazed the edge of the leather covering his thumb. Monty quickly struck the fish on the head with a piece of driftwood, ending the struggle. This one was a keeper. The large northern measured 31 inches in length and weighed in at ten pounds.

After resting a bit, Monty dressed out his catch, wrapped it in a special piece of canvas and stuffed it into his rucksack. Bear-wary, he realized the scent of fresh fish wafting through the air could surely attract any grizzly that happened to be nearby. He was careful to throw the entrails and head of the fish far out into the lake and made certain to clean the fishy odor from his hands. Content with his success, he sensed it was time to head back.

Shouldering his pack, he began his trek, skirting the forest that grew just above the water. As he glanced at the remaining lagoons near the end of the lake, a peculiar sight caught his eye. In a deep finger, he spotted a half-dozen large objects hovering just below the surface of the water. He dropped down the steep incline and carefully approached the lagoon. He caught his breath as he noted movement in the water. Closer examination revealed he had come upon a school of very large northern pike. He slowly crept closer and gasped at what he saw. Two of the fish had to be at least four feet in length, possibly even longer.

Monty found his excitement difficult to contain. These fish were unlike anything he'd seen before in Glacier's waters. Using a low embankment nearby as cover, he quickly prepared his spinning outfit. Nervously, he whipped the top of his rod and flung the Dardevle far into the slender finger of water. As the lure splashed near the resting giants, he held his breath. There was no response.

Reeling in, he again tossed his line toward the opening of the inlet. By occasionally jerking the tip of his rod, he made the spoon move erratically. At once, the largest of the basking northerns rose and hit the spinning lure hard. As the rod bent double, the mammoth fish twisted and turned in an attempt to throw off the treble hook that had snared him. Monty briefly spied the white underbelly of the northern rolling just beneath the murky waters. He felt his breath catch in his throat, stunned by the immensity of the creature.

After several more rolls, the giant turned and left the shallow, sheltered waters of the lagoon, heading out toward the main body of the lake. With the drag on his reel set as tightly as possible, Monty hung on, his throbbing pole still bent double. The great pike slowly, deliberately continued to swim toward the middle of the lake. Now sweating profusely, Monty had already given up any hope of turning the great fish around. Against the rapid, clicking sounds of the drag, he watched as 250 yards of monofilament line rapidly disappeared into the depths. Now he could see the spool's chrome center. What had at first seemed like a generous supply of fishing line suddenly didn't seem like much at all.

And then, with only a few feet of line left on the reel, the fish abruptly turned and began to head slowly back toward the lagoon. Quickly reeling to keep the line taut, Monty kept pace with the incoming monster. Wet line began to accumulate on the spool as the pike continued its peculiar course straight toward him.

Thoughts ricocheted through his mind: "Never had a fish act like this before. Maybe, just maybe, I can land this thing."

As the big pike approached, Monty took a wide stance on the steep bank in preparation for what might happen next. Digging the heels of his logger's boots into the rocky silt, he kept a steady eye on the water.

Amazingly, now only ten feet away, the northern continued swimming directly toward him. As its size and length became apparent, Monty began to tremble. Standing there alone on the shore of the great lake, he realized he'd more than met his match. Taking a quick estimate, he told himself the fish had to be close to four feet in length, a good quarter of it taken up by its massive head.

Suddenly, two bulging eyes were fixed on Monty. When the huge fish broke the water, a red spoon could be seen dangling from the corner of its mouth. As my brother held tightly to the rod, his boots suddenly lost traction on the steep bank. He found himself abruptly propelled downward on his back. Reaching the edge of the water with a splash, Monty struggled to regain his stance. An unnerving panic gripped him as he tried to distance himself from the pike's steady glare.

Then, without warning, the huge fish lunged from the water, its great mouth agape. The jagged teeth rimming its powerful jaws grabbed Monty's right boot at the ankle. The pressure was amazing. A harsh jolt of terror seared through him as he struggled to free himself.

Momentarily recalling tactics he'd used in his days of high-school wrestling, Monty dropped his rod and braced himself against the bank. The body of the northern, its wide mouth temporarily imprisoning his leg, made a quick barrel roll. In disbelief, Monty felt himself being flipped onto his stomach. Time seemed to stand still.

With one final lunge, the giant released its grip. His mind racing, Monty quickly grabbed his rod by its midsection and hung on. Giving a parting lash with its tail, the northern turned and once again headed for open water. Hands shaking, Monty shifted his grip, grasping the handle as tightly as he could. As the rapid click of the drag continued, the line tilted steeply downward as the predator dove.

Still shaken, Monty watched the line quickly disappearing from the reel until it abruptly came to the end of the spool. The rod bent double as he struggled to maintain his grip. Then, with a loud ping, the broken line slackened on the water's surface. The fish was gone. Glancing briefly at the bare reel, he quickly scrambled up the rise to higher ground. An examination of his boot revealed three broken razor-sharp teeth embedded in the black leather. He stood there trembling, intensely aware of the pounding of his heart.

Suddenly, he felt an eagerness to distance himself from the troubling event. Hefting his pack, he quickly headed down the beach and then made his way toward the trail. Slowed by his sore ankle, he continued onward as fast as his legs would allow.

Upon reaching the dirt track, Monty stopped to check out the source of his pain. As he began to untie his boot, he detected a slight movement behind him. Quickly turning, he squinted against the glare of the sun. There, along the shoreline, his eyes caught the form of a grizzly. The beast pawed the very spot where Pike Eyes had attacked only moments earlier. He quickly retied his boot, wishing only to get well beyond the bruin's field of vision. Ignoring his throbbing ankle, he once again set off down the trail. Quickening his pace, Monty glanced over his shoulder now and then. The bear quickly became a tiny dot roaming the distant beach.

Weary and worn by his experience, Monty finally walked into the parking lot at Many Glacier Hotel close to an hour later. After dropping his gear in the trunk of his car, he pulled off his boots. His right ankle was red and swollen. To his relief, the skin didn't appear to be broken. The high-top leather boots had saved him from more serious injury. Using his fishing pliers, Monty carefully pulled the jagged fragments out of his boot. Each broad, triangular tooth was a good half-inch wide. Once again, the thought of the northern's gnashing jaws caused him to shudder.

Nearby, a park ranger was posting a hand-written notice at the trailhead to Cracker Lake. It read, "Warning: Grizzly Bear Activity on This Trail." Monty approached the ranger and, after reading the sign, relayed his recent sighting of the big bear. The ranger thanked him for the update and then asked, "So, how was the fishing?"

Monty shrugged his shoulders and replied, "It was good, but I don't know that I'd try it again this summer." True to his word, he did not return to Lake Sherburne that season or for several to follow. Three years later, he chose to fish the lake, bringing along several colleagues with whom he worked on the blister-rust crew. They all caught northerns that day and, fortunately, saw no sign of bear. As a companion passed comment over lunch about what a peaceful fishing spot they'd chosen, Monty smiled that memorable smile and then began to relate the tale of Pike Eyes.

PART VII

MODERN TIMES

In the twenty-first century, Glacier continues to face some of the same problems that confront other national parks, as well as some specific to Glacier. White pine blister rust, the spruce bark beetle, and other invasive species have decimated many of the park's forests, and exotic plants continue to make inroads along roadsides and campgrounds. Diseases have reduced the park's bighorn herds, yet grizzly bear populations continue to rise, which creates potential problems for rangers and visitors. The little pika, a kind of tiny rabbit, is declining, the victim, probably, of global warming. The park's glaciers are shrinking and many have already disappeared. It is doubtful that any will be left by 2030. Forest fires increase in size and ferocity, fueled by warmth, aridity, and winds.

The greatest change, however, is human. In 2016, Glacier set a new record for most visitors—over 2.9 million, an increase of 23 percent in a single year. That number of people, almost all of them crammed into a four-month period, puts tremendous pressure on park resources, its wildlife, and its finances. Traffic control and law enforcement become ever more pressing problems, distracting personnel from managing the park's wildlife and natural resources. The network of hotels, motels, cafes, general stores, chalets, and other facilities—most built one hundred years ago—suffer continual maintenance problems. Campgrounds are jammed, parking lots full, hotels overbooked, and traffic on Going-to-the-Sun Road creeps along during the summer months. The solutions are elusive, complex, perhaps impossible.

Contemporary writers have found Glacier an ideal place to focus their attention on these issues. From global warming to national parks maintenance to preservation of wildlife corridors, Glacier occupies a central position in the western North American ecosystems. As Glacier goes, so will the rest of the North American West.

Robert Wrigley (b. 1951) is a poet of this region. Educated at the University of Montana, he now teaches at the University of Idaho. The following poem, "Ursa Major," written at Trapper Peak in Montana's Bitterroot Range in September 1975, describes the confluence of earth and the heavens. It could apply equally well to Glacier's Trapper Peak, near the center of the park.

On your back in juniper, a skeletal bear
grows above, a dipper full of dream
some mauled Indian spotted
centuries ago. Astronomers draw lines,
circle the dots with full-tailed bearish
shells as crude and empty as cookiecutters.
Here, you watch the starry bones grow
a body. In this place of pure dark,
constellations and nebulae too dim
in the city beam a silver-tipped coat,
and now and then some
distant sun flashes like a fang.

32

FIRE LOOKOUT
Numa Ridge

Edward Abbey
1977

Edward Abbey (1927–1989) was known as a fierce environmentalist, a principled anarchist, a suspected monkeywrencher (one who commits sabotage in the cause of the environment), a classic curmudgeon, and an all-around rabble-rouser. His many books—novels, collections of essays, and the classic *Desert Solitaire: A Season in the Wilderness*, which describes a year as a seasonal ranger in Arches National Park, Utah—made him one of the best-known writers of the American West. Although most of his adult life was spent in the Southwest—primarily New Mexico, Arizona, and Utah—he spent a number of summers working as a fire lookout, including one stint (1975) in Glacier National Park, where he and his then wife Renée lived and worked at Numa Lookout in the North Fork region of the park. This account, written in the form of a journal, describes their summer; it was later published in Abbey's collection of essays, *The Journey Home: Some Words in Defense of the American West*.

JULY 12

We've been here ten days before I overcome initial inertia sufficient to begin this record. And keeping a record is one of the things the Park Service is paying us to do up here. The other, of course, is to keep our eyeballs peeled, alert for smoke. We are being paid a generous wage (about $3.25 an hour) to stay awake for at least eight hours a day. Some people might think that sounds like a pretty easy job. And they're right, it is an easy job, for some people. But not for all. When I mentioned to one young fellow down at park headquarters, a couple of weeks ago, that I was spending the summer on this fire lookout he shuddered with horror. "I'd go nuts in a place like that," he said, thinking of solitary confinement. I didn't tell him I was cheating, taking my wife along. But that can be risky too; many a good marriage has been shattered on the rock of isolation.

Renée and I walked up here on July 2, packs on our backs, two hours ahead of the packer with his string of mules. The mules carried the heavier gear, such as our bedrolls, enough food and water for the first two weeks, seven volumes of Marcel Proust, and Robert Burton's *Anatomy of Melancholy*. Light summer reading. Renée had never worked a fire lookout before, but I had, and I knew that if I was ever going to get through the classics of world lit it could only be on a mountain top, far above the trashy plains of *Rolling Stone*, *Playboy*, the *New York Times*, and *Mizz* magazine.

The trail is about six miles long from Bowman Lake and climbs 3,000 feet. We made good time, much better time than we wished because we were hustled along, all the way, by hordes of bloodthirsty mosquitoes. We had prepared ourselves, of course, with a heavy treatment of government-issue insect repellent on our faces, necks, arms, but that did not prevent the mosquitoes from whining in our ears and hovering close to eye, nostril, and mouth.

We also had the grizzly on our mind. Fresh bear scat on the trail, unpleasant crashing noises back in the dark of the woods and brush, reminded us that we were intruding, uninvited, into the territory of *Ursus horribilis*, known locally as G-bear or simply (always in caps) as GRIZ. It was in Glacier, of course, only a few years ago, that two young women had been killed on the same night by grizzlies. We clattered our tin cups now and then, as advised, to warn the bears we were coming. I was naturally eager to see a GRIZ in the wild, something I'd never done, but not while climbing up a mountain with a pack on my back, tired, sweaty, and bedeviled by bugs. Such an encounter, in such condition, could only mean a good-natured surrender on my part; I wasn't *about* to climb a tree.

Bear stories. My friend Doug Peacock was soaking one time in a hot spring in Yellowstone's back country. Surprised by a grizzly sow and her two cubs, he scrambled naked as a newt up the nearest pine; the bear kept him there, freezing in the breeze, for two hours. Another: Riley McClelland, former park naturalist at Glacier, and a friend were treed by a GRIZ. Remembering that he had an opened sardine can in his pack, Riley watched with sinking heart as the bear sniffed at it. Disdaining the sardine lure, however, the bear tore up the other man's pack to get at a pair of old tennis shoes.

Sacrifice, that may be the key to coexistence with the GRIZ. If we surprise one on the trail, I'll offer up first my sweat-soaked hat. If that won't do, then cheese and salami out of the pack. And if that's not enough, well, then nothing else to do, I guess, but push my wife his way. *Droit du seigneur à la montagne*, etc.

We reach the lookout without fulfilling any fantasies. The lookout is a

two-room, two-story wood frame cabin at timberline, 7,000 feet above sea
level. On the north, east, and southeast stand great peaks—Reuter, Kintla,
Numa, Chapman, Rainbow, Vulture. Northwest we can see a bit of the Canadian Rockies. West and southwest lie the North Fork of the Flathead River, a
vast expanse of Flathead National Forest, and on the horizon the Whitefish
Range. Nice view: 360 degrees of snow-capped scenic splendor, lakes, forest,
river, fearsome peaks, and sheltering sky.

We remove the wooden shutters from the lookout windows, shovel snow
from the stairway, unlock the doors. The pack string arrives. The packer and I
unload the mules, the packer departs, Renée and I unpack our goods and move
in. Except for a golden-mantled ground squirrel watching us from the rocks,
a few Clark's nutcrackers in the subalpine firs, we seem to be absolutely alone.

JULY 14 (BASTILLE DAY!)

The Great Revolution was a failure, they say. All revolutions have been failures,
they say. To which I reply: All the more reason to make another one. Knock-
ing off "work" at five o'clock (the transition from work to nonwork being here
discernible by a subtle reshading in the colors of the rock on Rainbow Peak),
my wife and I honor this day by uncorking a bottle of genuine Beaujolais.
With Renée's home-baked crusty French bread and some real longhorn cheese
from the country store down at the hamlet of Polebridge, it makes a fitting
celebration.

A golden eagle soars by *below us*, pursued by—a sparrow hawk [kestrel]?
My wife the bird-watcher is uncertain; but it must have been. Looking unhur-
ried but pursuing a straight course, the eagle disappears into the vast glacial
cirque above Okokala [Akokala] Lake, followed steadily, slightly above, by the
smaller bird. More Clark's nutcrackers. Chipping sparrows. Mountain chickadees. Oregon juncoes. Clouds of mosquitoes whining at the windows, greedy
for blood. A doe, a fawn, a yearling buck with velvet horns jostling one another
at our salt deposits on the rocks outside. The doe is dominant; the young buck
retreats. Women's Lib has reached out even here, for God's sake, all the way
from Washington Square to Numa Ridge. Depressing thought. Striving to
uphold the natural superiority of the male, I have beaten my wife—at chess—
five games straight. Now she refuses to play with me. You can't win.

What *do* people do on a lookout tower when, as now, the season is wet and
there are no fires? Aside from the obvious, and reading Proust and *The Anatomy of Melancholy*, we spend hours just gazing at the world through binoculars.

For example, I enjoy climbing the local mountains, scaling the most hideous bare rock pitches step by step, hand by hand, without aids, without rope or partners, clinging to fragments of loose shale, a clump of bear grass, the edge of an overhanging snow cornice, above a nightmarish abyss, picking a route toward even higher and more precarious perches—through these U.S. Navy 7x50 lenses. The effortless, angelic, and supine approach to danger.

It's not all dreaming. There are some daily chores. Ever since arrival I've been packing snow to the lookout from a big drift a hundred yards below, carrying it up in buckets, dumping it into steel garbage cans, letting it melt in the sun. Now we've got 120 gallons of snow water in addition to the drinking water brought up by muleback. Then there's firewood. Although we have a propane stove for cooking, the only heat in the lookout comes from an old cast-iron cookstove. And with the kind of rainy, windy weather we've been having, heat is a necessity. Even in July. So a couple of times a week I go down the trail with ax and saw, fell one of the many dead trees in the area—fir, whitebark pine—buck the log into eighteen-inch lengths, tote it up the hill armload by armload.

Three times a day we take weather observations—wind speed and direction, temperature, relative humidity—or my wife does, since she is the scientist in this family. We wash windows, occasionally. We patch and repair things. We listen to the Park Service radio and the Forest Service radio, ready to relay messages if necessary. I entertain the deer and the squirrels with my flute. Renée bakes things, studies the maps, memorizes the terrain. But mostly we sit quietly out on the catwalk, reading about aristocratic life in *fin-de-siècle* Paris and looking at northwestern Montana in the summer of '75.

This is a remote place indeed, far from the center of the world, far away from all that's going on. Or is it? Who says so? Wherever two human beings are alive, together, and happy, there is the center of the world. You out there, brother, sister, you too live in the center of the world, no matter where or what you think you are.

JULY 16

Heavy cloud buildup in northwest. Lightning likely, fire danger rising, humidity dropping. The haze lies heavy over yonder Whitefish Range, obscuring the farther peaks. Looks like smog, but is only water vapor, dust, the smoke from many campfires along the North Fork. They tell us.

One longs for a nice little forest fire. We need some excitement around this joint. Nothing healthier for the forests than a good brisk fire now and then to clear out the undergrowth, give the moose and bear some living room. Besides we need the overtime pay. If that idiot Smokey the Bear (the noted ursine bore) had *his* way all us fire fighters would starve to death.

We see a Townsend's solitaire, abundant here. Hermit thrush. Swallowtail butterflies. Little spiders hanging on threads from the attic trapdoor. A six-legged spider (war veteran) on the outside of the windowpane chewing on a mosquito. Good show! mate. One snowshoe hare loping into the brush.

Gordon the Garbage Man, one of the park's seasonal employees, comes up the mountain for a visit, leaves us two big Dolly Vardens fresh from the lake. Fried by my frau, filleted and anointed with lemon, they make a delicately delicious supper. If I weren't so corrupt and lazy, I'd take hook and line myself, drop down to Lake Okokala 1,200 feet below, and catch a similar supper every evening. According to the old logbooks here, at least some of the previous lookouts used to do that.

JULY 20

Bear claw scratches on the wooden walls of the ground-floor storage room. Last thing before retiring each night I set the bear barrier in place on the stairway leading to our quarters. The bear barrier is a wooden panel with many nails driven through it, the points all sticking out. Supposed to discourage *Ursus stairiensis* from climbing up to our catwalk balcony. In a previous lookout's log we had read this entry:

> Woke up this morning to see a big black bear staring at me thru window, about six inches from my face. Chased him off with a Pulaski.

The Pulaski is a fire-fighting tool, a combination ax and pickax. I keep one handy too, right under the bed where I can reach it easy. I'd keep it under the pillow if my old lady would let me.

Thinking about GRIZ. Almost every day, on the park or forest radio, we hear some ranger report a bear sighting, sometimes of grizzly. Campers molested, packs destroyed by hungry and questing bears. Somebody was recently attacked and mauled by a GRIZ north of the line, in Waterton Lakes. Bear jams on the park highway, though not so common here as they used to be in Yellowstone, before so many of Yellowstone's bears mysteriously disappeared, do occur in Glacier from time to time.

No doubt about it, the presence of bear, especially grizzly bear, adds a spicy titillation to a stroll in the woods. My bear-loving friend Peacock goes so far as to define wilderness as a place and only a place where one enjoys the opportunity of being attacked by a dangerous wild animal. Any place that lacks GRIZ, or lions or tigers, or a rhino or two, is not, in his opinion, worthy of the name "wilderness." A good definition, worthy of serious consideration. A wild place without dangers is an absurdity, although I realize that danger creates administrative problems for park and forest managers. But we must not allow our national parks and national forests to be degraded to the status of mere public playgrounds. Open to all, yes of course. But—*enter at your own risk.*

Enter Glacier National Park and you enter the homeland of the grizzly bear. We are uninvited guests here, intruders, the bear our reluctant host. If he chooses, now and then, to chase somebody up a tree, or all the way to the hospital, that is the bear's prerogative. Those who prefer, quite reasonably, not to take such chances should stick to Disneyland in all its many forms and guises.

JULY 22

Bowman Lake 3,000 feet below looks more like clear Pennzoil than water. A milky turquoise green color, strange to my eyes. The North Fork even more so. The cause is not manmade pollution of any sort, but what is called "glacier milk," a solution of powdered rock washed down from under the bellies of the glaciers hanging all around us under the high peaks.

Toy boats glide up and down the lake, trailing languorous wakes that spread across the oil-smooth water in slow-subsiding ripples. Anglers at work. The fishing is poor this summer, they say; weather too wet, too much insect life in the air and floating down the streams.

Too wet? You can say that again. This is the foggiest, boggiest, buggiest country I have ever seen in my life. Everywhere I look, below timberline, the land is clothed in solid unbroken greenery. Damp, humid green all over the place—gives the country an unhealthy look. I guess I really am a desert rat. The sound of all these verdant leafy things breathing and sweating and photosynthesizing around me all the time makes me nervous. Trees, I believe (in the ardor of my prejudice), like men, should be well spaced off from one another, not more than one to a square mile. Space and scarcity give us dignity. And liberty. And thereby beauty.

JULY 23

Down the mountain I go, returning same day with mail, wine, cheese, other essentials. I sing, as I march along, songs I hope will warn the GRIZ of my approach. But what kind of music does the GRIZ like? Suppose he *hates* old cowboy songs? Or Puccini?

All the way up the mountain, under a dark and grumbling sky, a personal cloud of hungry mosquitoes envelops my head. I am relieved and glad when the first lightning strikes begin to bounce off the crags above. Am less glad when I reach the open ridge at timberline with jagged high-voltage bolts crashing all around. No place to hide now; I keep going for the relative safety of the lookout cabin and reach it just as the storm bursts out in all its awful grandeur.

We cower inside in the dark, Renée and I, trying to stay away from all metal objects, as instructed. But, of course, the lookout is crowded with metallic objects—iron stoves, fire finder, steel cots, water cans, buckets, ax, dishpan. We can feel the next charge building up; we stand on the negative terminal of a high-powered electrical system, the positive pole directly overhead. Our skin prickles, our hair stands up. We hear a fizzing noise above us, on the roof of the cabin where the lightning rod sticks up. A crackling sound, like a burning fuse. I know what's coming now, and an instant later it comes, a flash that fills the room with blue-white light, accompanied simultaneously by a jarring crash, as if the entire cabin had been dropped from the sky upon our rocky ridge. No harm done. The building is thoroughly grounded, top and sides, and Thor's hammer blow passes on safely into the heart of the mountain. Lightning strikes many times in the same place. As every lookout learns.

That evening we spot a couple of small flare-ups across the river in the national forest. But both are soon drowned out by rain and never go anywhere.

JULY 27

The bird list grows slowly. Add barn swallow, cliff swallow, water pipit, raven, blue grouse, white-tailed ptarmigan, rufous hummingbird, brown creeper, gray jay, evening grosbeak, red-shafted flicker, loon. *Loon!*—heard from the lake far below—that wild, lorn, romantic cry, one of the most thrilling sounds in all North America. Sound of the ancient wilderness, lakes, forest, moonlight, birchbark canoes.

We have also seen two cow moose, one with calf, romping through the fields below the lookout, and a badger, several black bear (but no GRIZ yet), elk droppings, mountain goat tracks, least chipmunks, ground squirrels, pikas, hoary marmots, many deer. And there's a big wood rat living downstairs among the water cans, firewood, tools, and boxes. Met him the other day.

JULY 30

I read the old lookout logs. First of all Numa Ridge lookouts was Scotty Beaton, who worked here twenty-two summers, beginning in 1928. Unlike all succeeding lookouts, whose logbook entries tend (like mine) to rant and ramble, Scotty kept his notations terse, laconic, to the point. Viz.:

Aug. 2, 1945: hot & dry done my usual chores

July 28, 1946: Very warm—Hugh Buchanan the ranger came up with a Paper to have me Pledge I wouldn't overthrow the government that never entered my mind in the fifty five years I been in this country

July 5, 1948: Moved up today the bears had moved into the lower part of the Lookout & took a few bites out of the upper story. The lower part a hell of a mess.

July 22, 1949: Done usual chores

Sept. 11, 1950: Found mud in bottom of water barrel put there by youngster from McFarland's dude ranch. Same kid who broke crosshairs on firefinder, tramped down nails in bear board and set my binoculars on the hot stove.

We've had a ranger-visitor too—Art Sedlack, the man who shot the snowmobile.

It happened one night in December 1974. Sedlack, on duty at Walton Ranger Station in Glacier, caught a snowmobiler buzzing around in an area where snowmobiles are not supposed to be. This sort of thing had been going on for a long time, and the operator of this particular snowmobile was a repeat offender. Suddenly inspired, Sedlack drew his trusty .38 Ranger Special and shot the snowmobile right through the head. "One snowmobile, immobilized," he reported by radio. Sensation! For a while Sedlack's rear end was in a sling as the owner of the slain snowmobile and other local motorized recreationists demanded blood, a head for a head. Sedlack might have lost his job but for an outpouring of public support, phone calls and letters from all over western Montana. Reconsidering, the park administration suspended him for one week without pay, then sent him to the service's police-training school in

Washington, D.C. Now he is back in Glacier, an unrepentant and even better ranger.

Art talks about the bear problem in the national parks. Really a human problem. Too many humans crowding the roads and trails, conflict inevitable. Solution: Reduce population. Which population? Ah yes, indeed, that is the question.

A bear, when caught in mischief, is tranquilized and tagged on the ear. Caught again, it is tagged on the other ear. A bear with both ears tagged is in trouble. It may be transported to a locality remote from human activity, but this is not a solution. There are no vacant areas in nature. The newcomer bear is not welcome among established inhabitants, is harried, fought, driven out by native bears, becomes a loner, an outlaw, a rogue—doomed. If caught in trouble a third time he or she will likely be "taken away" for good. That is, shot dead.

AUGUST 2

Fog and rain. Foul is fair and fair is foul. Cut more wood, keeping bin full. When I go down the hill to the john in the morning I find the mosquitoes huddled inside, waiting for me as usual. As usual I light up a Roi-Tan, a good cheap workingman's cigar, and the moquitoes flee, choking and swearing. I sit there and contemplate, through the smoke, the dim shapes of fir tree and mule deer through the mists. On clear mornings, sunshine on my lap, I can look right down on the pearly, oily, iridescent surface of Bowman Lake in all its incredible rich blueness. I think, if I think at all, about simplicity, convenience, the advantages of what I call Positive Poverty.

There is of course no flush toilet on a fire lookout. But the pit toilet is a perfectly adequate, comfortable and even pleasant substitute for the elaborate bathrooms of the modern home. A little lime or wood ashes keep down the odors, discourage flies. In cold weather one kerosene or Coleman lamp keeps the outhouse warm enough. What more does one need? And no freezing pipes, no water pump, no septic tank to worry about, no awful plumber's bills. And the basic good sense of it: Instead of flushing our bodily wastes into the public water supply, we plant them back in the good earth where they belong. Where our bodies must go as well, in due course, if we are to keep the good earth productive.

Nor is there running water up here. Or electricity. I carry the water by the bucketful up from the barrels in the cellar. We heat the water on the wood stove, wash and scald-rinse the dishes in a pair of dishpans, bathe (when we feel like it) in a small galvanized tub set on the floor or out on the catwalk when the sun is shining. Before the big drifts melted, Renée and I sometimes scrubbed ourselves with handfuls of snow, standing naked on the dazzling snowbanks, in the heat of the sun.

AUGUST 3

Done usual lookout chores.

AUGUST 4

Done usual lookout chores. To wit: woke, ate, answered radio check, looked, chopped wood, carried water, read Burton. ("Of all causes of this affliction," he writes, meaning romantic love, "the most remote are the stars"), looked, re-leveled fire finder, washed dishes, played chess then flute, watched sun go down, went to bed.

In the evening after sundown an owl flies round and round the lookout, swooping silent as a moth through the fog and gloom, checking out our chipmunks. Barred owl? Short-eared owl? Hard to tell in this darkness. A spooky bird of ill import.

AUGUST 5

My wife looks prettier every day. By God, a man begins to get ideas in a place like this.

AUGUST 7

High winds all day, clear sky, scudding clouds. The surface of the lake below, stirred by the wind, looks like brushed aluminum, has the color of my knife blade. The peaks round about stand forth in startling, blazing, preternatural brilliance. A cold, immaculate clarity. Shall we climb Rainbow Peak one of these days? Ever see Goat Haunt? Belly River? Mount Despair? Loneman? Gunsight Pass? Rising Wolf Mountain? Spirit Lake? Two Medicine Mountain? Almost a Dog Mountain? Vulture Peak?

AUGUST 11

Storms. Fog and drizzle, brief blaze of sun—a rainbow floats in the fog below.

Lightning again, flashing through the mist; the thunder rumbles in at a thousand feet per second. Pink lightning. Heaven and earth link nerves in illuminated ecstasy—or is it pain? Once, in another place, I saw lightning score a direct hit on a juniper tree. The tree exploded in a burst of flame.

Now comes another direct hit on our lookout. First the buzzing sound, the eerie *hiss* and *fizz* directly overhead. That sinister touch, God's fingertip upon our roof. Light, deadly, an almost dainty touch, you might say. Followed by the flash of light and the *crack!* of a great whip. The building vibrates.

When the hard winds blow the cabin creaks and groans, tugging at the cables that keep it anchored to the rock. On our east side the ridge drops off at fifty degrees down a treeless slope to the bottom of the cirque 600 feet below.

In the evening things settle down a bit. We go for a walk down the trail, down through the drifting fog. The huckleberries are ripening now, but it looks like a poor crop. The bears will be roaming and irritable. Mushrooms bulge through the damp duff under the pines—fat, brown, speckled domes of fungoid flesh. Delicacies for the deer.

AUGUST 18

Somebody falls into McDonald Falls again. "Bring the wagon," radios ranger. The hurry-up wagon. Happens every year. As at North Rim, Grand Canyon, where somebody disappears every summer.

Whole family mauled by a grizzly on Grinnel[l] Glacier trail. Father, mother, two children. Apparently the children had been walking far ahead of their parents, got between a sow and her cub. Children attacked. Their screams bring father running to the scene, who attempts to fight off the GRIZ with his bare hands. Reinforced by mother, the bear knocks them both about, then wanders off. Entire family hospitalized with serious injuries. Rangers close trail to further hiking for time being.

Might be hard to explain to those people why the grizzly bear is a vital part of the Glacier wilderness. But it is. The parks are for people? Certainly. And for bears also? Absolutely. How do we resolve the inevitable conflict? Are we going to ration the wilderness experience? Probably; that process has already begun at Glacier National Park, where back-country camping is restricted to certain sites, requiring written permits and advance reservations. A sad and ominous but unavoidable expedient.

One calamity after another. One mishap after another. A ranger's work is never done. And more and more, in every national park, that work consists largely of police work. The urbanization of our national parks. All through the summer bumper-to-bumper auto traffic crawls up and down the

Going-to-the-Sun Highway. I've said it before and I'll say it again, we've got to close the parks to private cars if we want to keep them as parks. The parks are for people, not machines. Let the machines find their own parks. Most of America has been surrendered to them already, anyway. New Jersey, for example. Southern California.

AUGUST 23

Rain, wind, rain, and fog. When the storm clears I see fresh snow on Kintla, Rainbow, and Reuter peaks, down to the 8,000-foot line. Temperature was 34° F this morning at 0630. Everything wet and slimy. Expect to see snails and other Mollusca crawling up the windowpanes. Horny octopi....

AUGUST 24

Awoke this morning, after a long cold night, to find two inches of snow on the catwalk railing, on the pines, on everything in sight. Wet, fat snow, clinging to every twig and needle.

Renée returns, but only briefly. Has to leave at once for Vancouver. Her grandfather's dying. I am alone for the final week on this cold, dismal, rain- and snow-soaked mountain. I get so lonesome I wash the dishes for diversion. Loneliness. Mount Despair. Wintertime in August.

AUGUST 26

Termination date has now been advanced to August 28.

I go for long walks in the evening, hoping for one clear sight of GRIZ. The silence of the woods. No birds speak except one woodpecker, far below, hammering on a snag. But 1,000 feet below, under the snowline, the weather is late summer. Tufts of moss, like scalp locks, dangle from the branches of the lodgepole pine, the larch, the spruce. This is the forest primeval. Elaborate spiderwebs hang face-high across the trail, each with a tiny golden spider waiting at the center. Damp smells of fern and pine bark, the distant drumming of the woodpecker. Sounds like Red Norvo at the vibraphone. Bluebells still in bloom down here, wild roses covered with dew. Running water across the stones of the trail. I pause on the way back up to drink a handful; the sweet, cold, piney flavor reminds me of boyhood, the Allegheny Mountains back in old Pennsylvania. Lost at twilight in the green depths of the Big Woods.

Back to the cold darkness of the lookout cabin. I build a fire in the stove, sit with my feet on the open oven door and play the flute. The deer outside lift their heads to listen for a moment, then resume their feeding. Down in Arizona I used to rouse the coyotes at dawn, playing certain high notes on this silver-plated instrument. I'd play our tune and wait and after a few moments their wild cries came floating back to me across the desert, mimicking my song.

AUGUST 27

Last full day on the mountain. Sun shining for a change. Many deer hang about, fighting over my various urine-supplied salt deposits. Obvious pecking order among them: One old battle-scarred six-point buck is clearly dominant; the others keep their distance from him but jostle one another roughly.

Always looking and listening, these deer. Even the fawns have that wary look. Danger everywhere. Nor do they look well-fed, even now in late summer. Gaunt and ganted, lean and bony deer, how will they ever get through the coming winter? A tough life. Always hard times for deer. The struggle for existence. All their energy goes into survival—and reproduction. The only point of it all—to go on. On and on and on. What else is there? Sometimes I am appalled by the brutality, the horror of this planetary spawning and scheming and striving and dying. One no longer searches for any ulterior significance in all this; as in the finest music, the meaning is in the music itself, not in anything beyond it. All we have, it seems to me, is the beauty of art and nature and life, and the love which that beauty inspires.

Smell of cooking rubber. I withdraw my booted feet from the oven.

AUGUST 28

Raining again. Storm predicted. The packer with his mules is coming up the mountain this morning. I clean the lookout, put everything away, bolt the shutters back on the windows, pack our baggage, sign off on the radios. "This is Numa Ridge Fire Lookout going ten-seven [out of service] for about ten months. Have a good winter, everybody."

The packer arrives. Followed by the wind. We load the mules in a driving rain and start down the mountain.

33

GLACIER NATIONAL PARK, MONTANA

Terry Tempest Williams
2016

Terry Tempest Williams is a renowned writer of essays and books pertaining to the natural world as well as being an activist for environmental causes. Her lyricism and passion infuse her prose and poetry with a deeply felt commitment to the preservation and restoration of wilderness. Notable among her works is *Refuge: An Unnatural History of Family and Place* (1991), which juxtaposes the devastating effects of a rising Great Salt Lake during the wet years of the mid-1980s and the murderous effects of atomic bomb testing on her own family members during the 1950s. Raised in Utah, Williams has written on women's place in nature, Native American relationships to the land, and the spiritual values of wilderness. She is the recipient of major awards from the Sierra Club and the National Parks Conservation Association. This essay on surviving a forest fire in Glacier National Park is from her 2016 book, *The Hour of Land: A Personal Topography of America's National Parks*, which describes journeys to twelve different national parks ranging from the Effigy Mounds in Iowa and Alcatraz Island in San Francisco Bay to Wyoming's Grand Teton and Montana's Glacier.

For my family, Glacier National Park is a landscape of fire, not ice.

The summer of 2003 is known as "the pinnacle year of fire," in the history of Glacier National Park breaking all records: twenty-six fires were burning in the park, consuming more than 145,000 acres in three months. It was also the summer the Tempests decided to take a family vacation to celebrate our father's seventieth birthday.

On July 23, 2003, we had reservations for twelve at the Granite Park Chalet for one night, and the Sperry Chalet for another, with campsites reserved in between. My father wanted to duplicate the backcountry trip we made in 1982 (the same trip where I met Doug Peacock on the trail), hiking sixty-six miles in six days from the Sperry Chalet to the Granite Park Chalet, over Swiftcurrent Pass, culminating at Many Glacier. This time we were hiking the route in reverse, beginning with the Highline Trail.

More than any other park I know, Glacier embodies the majesty of alpine landscapes, surrounded by rock castles and slow-moving rivers of ice with secret lakes the color of turquoise. The hike into Granite Park Chalet, beginning at Logan Pass, is a glory of wildflowers: red paintbrush, sticky geranium, larkspur, and the flowering stalks of bear's grass appearing as white globes lighting up the meadows. Our family spaced themselves evenly along the narrow trail beneath the Garden Wall, with the strongest hikers in front led by my brother Steve and his wife, Ann, followed by their family, Callie and Andrew (newly married), Sara, and Diane. My father and his companion, Jan, walked with them; my brother Dan and his wife, Thalo, followed behind. And [my husband] Brooke, perhaps the strongest among us, stayed in the rear with me, gathering bones.

There is something soul-satisfying about carrying what you need on your back: water; food; a cook stove; a sleeping bag, pad, and tent; rain gear; a down vest or parka; hat; gloves; a change of clothes; camp shoes; sunglasses; sunscreen; bug dope; a first aid kit; a good book and headlamp to read by; a journal; pens; binoculars; camera. And then, with a topo map in hand, you chart your course and walk.

Some of the miles you may talk to your hiking partner, some of the miles you remain quiet, observant to the world embracing you. And there are other miles when your mind not only wanders through a labyrinth of thoughts but climbs the steep hills of obsession, be it love or loss or laments. "Walking it off" is not just a phrase but a form of reverie in the religion of self-reliance, where every mile is registered in the strength of calf muscles.

Eight miles later, Granite Park Chalet greeted us with an opaque view of Heavens Peak. Visibility is obscured due to the smoke. The Robert fire was raging in a far-off drainage that we could see with our binoculars; and the Trapper fire, with plumes of smoke visible to our naked eyes, had begun earlier in the week. But we had been assured by rangers at Lake McDonald, who carefully checked our itinerary, that the current fires would pose no threat to us.

The Granite Park Chalet is full of alpine charm, a largely stone building that sits at the base of Swiftcurrent Pass with the Grinnell Glacier Overlook just a short, steep hike above. The chalet was built by the Great Northern Railroad between 1914 and 1915 to attract more American tourists with a hut-to-hut trail system like those found in Europe. Of the nine alpine chalets that were built in that era, two remain.

Each of us settled into our designated cabins, furnished with a set of bunk beds that we completed with our sleeping bags. Half the party stayed at the chalet, while the other half hiked up Ahern Pass for a wider view.

My brother Dan and I sat at the picnic table on the chalet's porch and talked about Jim Harrison's *Legends of the Fall*, set in Montana.

"Do you think fathers and sons are fated to destroy each other?" Dan asked.

"I can't answer that—" I said. "But I remember hearing a psychologist talk at a conference on boys. He said, 'If you want to see a man cry, ask him about his father.'"

Our conversation changed to our mother.

"Do you think we'd all be different if Mother had lived?" Dan asked.

"No question."

"How?"

And that conversation carried us into the late afternoon.

We all cooked dinner together inside the chalet, having been warned by a large handwritten sign not to touch the shrimp in the freezer. Rumor had it the shrimp had been flown in as a special surprise for First Lady Laura Bush, who, with some of her girlfriends, was arriving at the Granite Park Chalet toward the end of the week.

We watched the sun burn through the smoke and stare at us like the red eye of a demon. And then a blue haze settled on the valley.

That night, I dreamed a spiral of bats flew out of the forest followed by flames. I woke up anxious.

The next morning, we all noticed the smoke had thickened. As we ate breakfast on the porch of the chalet, fire was on everyone's mind. Chris Burke, a Park Service employee, appeared anxious as well, his worry heightened by the discovery that the water pump at the chalet was broken. He hiked out to meet a maintenance worker on the trail to get a new part as a safety measure.

About midday on July 24, the flames from the Robert fire appeared to be coming closer. Dad walked down to the edge of the chasm, a sizable rock-faced cliff that separated us from the forest, to calculate the distance from the fires to the Granite Park Chalet.

"It's a fair distance," he said. "But if the winds change, we could be in trouble."

Just then, a helicopter hovered above us and landed on flat ground. To our surprise, a captain from the smoke jumpers, stationed out of Los Angeles, stepped out of the chopper looking like Cool Hand Luke. He had been instructed to stay with us in case the fires escalated. He found a canvas director's chair, carried it to the top of the knoll, sat down, and crossed his legs as he gazed toward the burning horizon, offering us a relaxed image, the epitome of calm.

The other guests at the chalet began to gather, also alarmed by the smoke and the fires that seemed to be advancing. Chris was back with the new part needed for the water pump and installed it, and quickly, with the help of Brooke and Steve, began wetting down the roof of the chalet.

Suddenly a spiral of bats flew out of the forest just like I had seen in my dream. They rose in a black column of wings against the gray sky and just as quickly disappeared. My heart began to race. I looked at my watch: 4:30 p.m. The smoke was increasing. The fire was escalating, with spot fires gaining momentum ahead of the blaze, igniting all around us. The captain stood up from his chair. Several deer emerged from the trees and ran behind the chalet. Chris was on his cell phone, talking to the fire lookout. What we didn't hear from the woman on the other end of his conversation was this: "We can't calm the beast of Trapper fire…it looks like it's making a run for the Granite Park Chalet!"

Chris and the fire captain called us together.

"We seem to be at the center of a perfect storm," the fire captain said. "The Robert fire, the Trapper fire, and a new fire unnamed seem to have merged into one crown fire they're calling the 'Mountain Man Complex.' It's all blown up in the last four hours—and it appears to be heading our direction."

"We must prepare ourselves," Chris added. "Keeping the chalet wet will help, and we need to get rid of whatever could burn on the porch. I could use some help."

Brooke, Steve, and Andrew worked with Chris, throwing the picnic tables and chairs off the porch down the hillside so there would be nothing burnable next to the stone walls of the historic chalet.

The propane tank nearby was a concern. The winds were picking up dramatically; it was increasingly hard to hear. Chris and the captain passed out particle masks. We stood on the porch bathed in an eerie orange glow, watching in disbelief as firs and pines exploded into flames with pieces of charred bark raining down on us. We could feel the waves of heat as the flames roared from all directions.

Thalo and Dan ran down to their cabin and returned with their backpacks strapped on.

"We're leaving," Dan said. "Does anyone want to come with us?"

"I'm gettin' the hell out of here, before we burn up!" Thalo said, her blue eyes bloodshot and frantic. "I saw what happened to the people who listened to the authorities inside the World Trade Center on September eleventh and thought they'd be rescued."

"You're better off staying here with the rest of us," Chris said. "Don't panic—I don't think you'll make it up to Grinnell, the fire's moving too fast."

Thalo was already gone.

"I'm going with Thalo," Dan said. And we watched them disappear into the smoke—the Grinnell Glacier Overlook, still a steep mile and a half away.

"Do something, John," the captain said to my father.

"He's a grown man, he's going to do what he's going to do," Dad said. "I can't stop him."

"The next person who leaves is under arrest," the fire captain said. "Everyone needs to put on their hiking boots and make sure you have your personal ID with you. Go—now—hurry! I want to see everyone inside the chalet as fast as you can get there."

Flocks of birds were flying helter-skelter into the chaos of the crosswinds. More deer were running out of the woods ahead of the burn. Heat singed my eyelashes. Our eyes were red and our faces were flushed. Everyone wore masks. I had two extra and put one on each breast for comic relief. Sara and Diane laughed.

Dad, Jan, and I rushed down to our cabin to get our necessary gear, fear accelerating with the advancing fire. Chris had run down to the campground and brought other hikers back to the chalet for safety. He mentioned that two former Bureau of Land Management employees from Alaska who had registered at the chalet earlier in the day had disappeared.

Walking briskly back to the chalet with the heat chasing us, I kept looking up the mountain to see whether I could see Dan and Thalo, but it was consumed in black smoke. The spot fires increased as flames jumped over trees like banshees; the wind howled like a speeding train. I turned to see the blaze, now an inferno, racing up the mountain toward us.

Ann was inside the chalet with the girls. Callie and Andrew were standing on the side porch, watching the flames behind us. Brooke and Steve were still working with Chris, getting rid of more flammables, including trying to move the propane tank farther away from the building, and then, with longer white canvas hoses screwed together, they continued spraying down the roof and porch of the chalet until the very last minute.

"Everybody inside, now!" the fire captain yelled.

A couple had been playing Scrabble. They quickly put away their game. Two women held each other's hands, crying. A young man, crouched in the corner, seeming a bit dazed or drugged, continued playing his guitar, quietly singing, "Come on, baby, light my fire," until Chris put his hand on his shoulder to get him to stop. I stared out the windows. All I could think of was my brother and his wife in the middle of the firestorm.

Chris made a quick count and turned to the captain. "Two others besides the two that left are unaccounted for. Everyone else is here."

Thirty-five of us stood in the center of the chalet, most of us coughing.

"Okay, everybody, listen up: I want the children sitting in the center. Everyone else sits in a circle around them. The fire is going to reach us in minutes. Stay calm—low to the floor. You're going to hear a loud roar coming closer and closer. It's going to get hot, real hot. The windows will shatter. The oxygen's going to be sucked out of the room—temporarily—and then, hopefully, the fire will quickly move over us, and shoot up Swiftcurrent Pass and we'll all be just fine. The Park Service knows we're here. Any questions?"

No one said a word, we just sat on the floor, children in the center, holding each other, waiting,…some with their eyes closed, praying.

We would later learn that we had been taken for dead by the Park Service. Miraculously, we survived—as did Dan and Thalo, who watched the fire come within two hundred feet of the historic Granite Park Chalet, split around us, and rejoin its force as it roared up Swiftcurrent Pass. The windows didn't blow out, nor did the oxygen get sucked out of the room. The fire missed us. We were alive.

In Christopher Burke's words: "We could see that the crown fire that had been coming our way had arced around and above us, burning through Swiftcurrent Pass with two-to-three-hundred-foot flame lengths and seventy-mile-per-hour winds.…At sunset the flames surrounding us lit up the chalet with an orange-pink glow and spot fires continued to burn above and around."

The two former employees of the BLM who had disappeared reemerged from the latrines before dark, where they had positioned themselves next to the pit toilets, ready to jump in the dark, nasty holes if necessary.

Our family stayed up all night and, from the porch of the Granite Park Chalet, we watched the fires burn. The intensity of our focus must have been tied to a delusional belief that if we just kept our eyes on the flames, we could keep them at bay. This kind of magical thinking soothed us, even though we all knew it was only the luck of the winds changing direction that had allowed the flames to split and burn around us instead of through us—leaving behind a circle of bodies, a circle of ash.

Early the next morning, we "escaped" the continuing fires by hiking out the way we had hiked in—single file on the Highline Trail. Only this time, we were led by Christopher Burke, with the fire captain bringing up the rear. Three grizzlies walked out with us, slightly below the Garden Wall ledge, having also survived the historic Trapper fire of 2003.

On February 5, 2005, Secretary of the Interior Gale Norton presented the sixty-second annual awards for outstanding service and valor to government employees. Chris Burke, having just completed his twentieth season with the National Park Service, was among those honored:

> Christopher J. Burke—In recognition of his willingness to place himself at great personal risk in order to save the lives of 39 others.
>
> At 3:30 p.m. on July 23, 2003, while Mr. Burke was working at the Granite Park Chalet, a historic high mountain chalet in Glacier National Park, he noticed heavy smoke coming toward them from the Flattop Mountain area of the Trapper fire. He radioed the Swiftcurrent Lookout for an update on the fire and was told that the wind had shifted. The lookout had been smoked out and was unable to see the fire activity. Mr. Burke and another co-worker scrambled to get pumps running and suppression sprinklers and nozzles charged and ready. Mr. Burke noticed that the drive belt had broken on the main water supply pump. With some very quick and resourceful modifications, he was able to switch to a different pump to supply water to the chalet fire suppression system. The wind was blowing approximately 70 miles per hour, knocking Mr. Burke and his co-worker to the ground. Mr. Burke ran for tools he needed to make emergency repairs to the pumps and water system. Returning, he was caught by thick hot clouds of smoke and had to feel his way back to the chalet. After hearing radio traffic talking about a running crown fire heading in their direction, he and his co-worker opened up all of their charged lines and began the defense of their lives and the historic chalet. Mr. Burke marshaled assistance of seven volunteers and assigned tasks to defend their position. They were being struck hard by burning bark, embers and ash as they wetted down the front of the

chalet. Most of the chalet occupants huddled in the dark and smoke-filled room of the chalet, some praying and some crying. One of the men declared he was going to escape by hiking ahead of the fire over Swift-current Pass. Mr. Burke quickly recognized that he had to establish firm control over the group. Mr. Burke explained that the safest place to stay was in the chalet and that their defense was strong and holding. Over the next several hours, the fire continued to rage around and past the chalet, finally dying down around 9:00 p.m. Mr. Burke and his co-worker had successfully defended the chalet and the lives of everyone in it. In the morning, Mr. Burke and his co-worker organized the group for the hike out to Logan Pass to safety. Before leaving, however, they received a standing ovation and personal thanks for their heroic efforts from each of the grateful survivors. For his heroic actions, courage, and professionalism, Christopher J. Burke is awarded the Valor Award of the Department of the Interior.

Glacier National Park is a landscape of change. Today if you hike into the Granite Park Chalet on the Highline Trail, you will see evidence of the Trapper fire in the standing forest of black-burnt trees now in a state of regeneration, marked by the magenta flares of fireweed. Hike up to the Grinnell Glacier and you will see more change from a different kind of heat.

In 1850, 150 glaciers were recorded within the boundaries of Glacier National Park. In 2015, only 25 active glaciers remain. After decades of research, scientists have concluded that the glaciers for which the park was named could be gone within fifteen years as a consequence of the burn of global warming.

Climate change is not an abstraction here, but real change in real time: the rapid retreat of glaciers. Rock once covered now lies bare. To touch warm granite beds once blanketed by glaciers is both a hard fact and a perversion. No longer do you see the chiseled high peaks defined by fields of snow. In the twenty years our family had been visiting Glacier National Park, from our first visit in 1982 to the fires of 2003, the absence of ice was disorienting and unnerving. A vital characteristic of the terrain is being erased by global warming. The geographic relief of the mountains was rendered monochromatic and bland. The "Crown of the Continent" is slipping. I wonder what the mountain goats are thinking, these "beasts the color of winter." In this part of the world, predicting the future is a foolish proposition.

No one knows this better than the Blackfeet Nation. They are the true witnesses of change. The Blackfeet Reservation borders Canada to the north and Glacier National Park to the west, what the elders call "the backbone of Mother Earth." The Blackfeet have been living in this landscape for generations, spanning hundreds of years and thousands more before that. With the knowledge of their ancestors still present through ceremonies and stories shared, contemporary Blackfeet are able to reach back through time and reclaim traditional wisdom, just as they are in the process of reclaiming the land that was once theirs.

When Glacier National Park was established in 1910, the Blackfeet were displaced and physically removed from their home ground where the men hunted bison on horseback and women gathered berries and roots for their families. It wasn't just their food that was derived from the land, but all their medicine, as well. Not only were they removed from their sources of subsistence, but they lost access to much of the land where their spiritual life took place. They were not only ripped from the land where they lived, but torn from their spiritual traditions, inhibiting songs, dreams, prayers, and ceremonies, especially those ceremonies and vision quests practiced within sight of Chief Mountain, a geologic formation central and sacred to the tribe. By the laws of another nation, foreign and disconnected from their own, the Blackfeet were not only displaced but deceived by the U.S. government, disregarded and dismissed as a sovereign nation with rights.

The first superintendent of Glacier National Park, William Richard Logan, was no friend to the tribes even though he was an Indian agent to the Assiniboine and Gros Ventre at the Fort Belknap Reservation. He wanted Blackfeet land for the minerals believed to be in the mountains and for the future economic value of tourism.

In 1895, the U.S. government initiated a deal with the Blackfeet Nation to trade the western mountains on their reservation rumored to be filled with gold in exchange for cash and the continued nonmineral rights to hunt and fish on their land as they had always done.

White Calf, one of the Blackfeet leaders, said, "I would like to have the right to hunt game and fish in the mountains. We will sell you the mountain lands from Birch Creek to the boundary, reserving the timber and grazing land."

Pressured to sign the agreement, the Blackfeet asked for $3 million. They were paid half that by the federal government. George Bird Grinnell was one of the government negotiators and an early advocate for Glacier National Park.

He gave his word to the Blackfeet that they could retain their hunting and fishing rights as long as these lands remained public. But upon the opening of Glacier National Park in 1910, their native rights were revoked on the technicality that these were no longer public lands but park lands. It made no sense other than Indian removal. The Blackfeet were denied (with some Indians even being arrested) the previous access they had been promised.

Where is the value in these actions taken by the U.S. federal government?

Much of the enduring valor of the Blackfeet Nation is drawn from fire. Between the glaciers that continue to hang in the high peaks above their homes and the slow rivers of ice that have carved the landscape around them, it is fire that helps to maintain their traditions and strength. Whether it is smoking the sacred pipe in ceremony or participating in sweat lodges with steaming stones and smoldering sage to purify the body and spirit, fire is a truth teller among the Blackfeet people. Even the Sun Dance, once practiced secretly for fear of government reprisal, imprisonment, or death, is now practiced openly in the name of prayer, sacrifice, and renewal, honoring the Sun that lights up the world, a force that both gives life and destroys it.

It is said that the Blackfeet get their name from their characteristic moccasins darkened by the ashes of fire.

Fire is akin to many tribes.

There is a long history of Indians as fire preventers and firefighters within the United States. In 1933, with the creation of the Civilian Conservation Corps under President Franklin D. Roosevelt, more than eighty-eight thousand Native Americans were employed in the Indian CCC Division to build fire lookout towers, fire cabins, and hundreds of miles of trails within remote forested terrain that provided access to firefighters should the trees ignite.

In 1948, the famed Mescalero Red Hats organized themselves to become the first Native American fire crew to fight fires in the Southwest. Most of them were World War II veterans. They were also the ones who rescued an orphaned bear cub after a large burn in New Mexico that later fostered the legend of Smokey the Bear, dressed in a ranger suit and advocating for fire safety in our national forests.

During that same period, David H. DeJong of the Native American Research and Training Center writes, "The Hopi Indians organized a trained firefighting crew; two years later, the Zuni Indians did the same. In 1954, the Red Hats and the Zuni Thunderbirds received meritorious service citations for firefighting from the U.S. Department of Agriculture. During 1953–55, Native American crews were formed in Montana from the Crow, Northern Cheyenne, Black-feet, Flathead, Rocky Boys, and Forts Belknap, Peck and Hall reservations. In the mid-1950s, the Bureau of Land Management (BLM) also organized crews from among Alaska Natives."

According to the Bureau of Indian Affairs National Interagency Fire Center, close to 25 percent of all firefighters working today on wildfires on our public lands in the United States are Indians. In Montana, many are Blackfeet. The distinguished "Chief Mountain Hot Shots" are comprised of highly skilled Blackfeet crews who are dropped into dangerous fire zones to tame the flames. They are known as the "Fire Warriors."

I can't help but wonder how many Fire Warriors were fighting the "Mountain Man Complex" we witnessed in the summer of 2003.

Fire has been a traditional tool of warfare among the Blackfeet Nation for centuries, creating fire walls against enemies as well as using fire as a tool of restoration to rejuvenate land through intentional burns and fire management essential to the regenerative health of the prairies. It makes sense the work of the "Fire Warriors" would be heightened in the twenty-first century as global warming is causing bigger and hotter fires due to the ravages of the pine bark beetle in western forests. Freezing temperatures during long, cold winters killed the beetles. Now, no longer. Now, due to higher temperatures in both summer and winter, pine bark beetles go through multiple breeding cycles that kill more trees.

The same climate changes that are creating more wildfires in the American West are creating the retreat of glaciers. Fire and ice are harbingers of change and both are found in the dynamic landscape of Glacier National Park.

A political fire is also burning in Glacier National Park. After more than a century of promises made and treaties broken by the federal government, the Blackfeet are challenging the status quo. They are demanding reinstatement of their reserved treaty rights to hunt, fish, and gather medicinal plants inside the national park boundaries. They are also asking for the voluntary closure of cultural sites essential to their spiritual practices. And their final ask is for joint management of Glacier National Park itself.

Here is one prediction that can be made. Soon, the Blackfeet will stand shoulder to shoulder in shared governance of these parklands with the National Park Service. After more than a century of being forced to retreat, the Blackfeet Nation is advancing like fire. The Blackfeet identity is rising from the ashes of national park history. Two-thirds of the Blackfeet live in Canada.

Like the ecosystem of Waterton-Glacier, they have been divided by an international border. Today, their sky-blue flag flies high at the Lake McDonald Visitor's Center—flanked by the American flag on one side and the Canadian flag on the other—inside America's tenth national park. Three sovereign nations merge in an International Peace Park where Glacier National Park and the Waterton Lakes National Park create a contiguous boundary of faith.

It was at this intersection of nations that we celebrated John Tempest's birthday in Canada on July 26, 2003, across the border in Waterton Lakes National Park, a country away from the fires of northern Montana, but still within sight of melting glaciers.

In 1990, the writers Bill Kittredge and Annick Smith edited a thousand-page anthology of Montana literature including Native storytelling, the journals of trappers, poems, short stories, and essays from close to 150 writers, offering a mosaic of some of the finest writing past and present that had ever been written in the American West. The collection was called *The Last Best Place* and it became a regional phenomenon that both jump-started a western literary renaissance and captured a hard truth in one poignant phrase—the disappearing landscapes within the Rocky Mountains.

Darnell Davis, a Blackfeet elder, said recently, "The last best place is our first place."

34

FROM *THE MELTING WORLD*

A Journey across America's Vanishing Glaciers

Christopher White
2013

Between 2008 and 2012, Christopher White (b. 1956) made frequent visits to Glacier National Park to determine the fate of the park's glaciers and their relevance to climate change. In his travels, Smith focused on the work of U.S. Geological Survey employee Dan Fagre, whose research aims to determine how and why the park's glaciers are shrinking. Fagre's most recent projection, as reported in White's book *The Melting World*, is that Glacier National Park's glaciers will be completely gone by 2050, if not sooner. The question of providing adequate water for urban areas and Indian reservations and agriculture; the impact of higher temperatures on rare and endangered animals and plants; the effect of global warming on forests and wetlands; and the long-term implications of wildfires, avalanches, and other natural phenomena are all part of Smith's book. Smith has previously written three books about the Chesapeake Bay ecosystem and many articles about the natural world. In these excerpts from *The Melting World*, White explains his research goals and the dimming future for the glaciers of Glacier Park, with an in-depth report on research at Grinnell Glacier in the Swiftcurrent Valley.

I have traveled from my home along the foothills of the New Mexican Rockies to Montana to write a profile on Dan Fagre, the leading glacier expert in the country. For years, I have written about water—topics from sailing to canoeing to diving—but now I return to my first passion: mountaineering. Peaks and glaciers have always meant solitude and freedom to me. More recently the melting of the ice fields has been troubling: What will the loss of all that alpine water mean? Most of what I've heard about climate change is remote either in time or distance—impacts that are a century removed or that are as far away as the poles. The search for local and immediate manifestations of warming has brought me to Glacier National Park, to learn what I can about our future.

I feel like one of those lookouts on the *Titanic*, tracking the path of fractured and melting ice.

The distress calls will come soon enough. Fagre picks up a ball of snow from the crest of the crevasse and lifts it to his mouth. It crumbles in his hand like sand. He blows the last snowflakes into the August wind, and a fraction of them boomerang, stinging his face. The snow in the cirque, he says, given enough time, will turn to ice, and the ice to meltwater, the fresh water joining the sea. Formerly this was a slow geological process. But the planet is warming at an unprecedented rate. Already, the burning of fossil fuels has elevated the average temperature of the planet by more than 1.5 degrees F (nearly 1 degree C); the heat keeps climbing. Montana snow from the 1960s, converted into ice, is tumbling into the lake. And melting.

Grinnell Glacier is just one of many to suffer. Worldwide, mountain glaciers are on a fast track to oblivion. They are expected to vanish faster than polar ice, both north and south. Grinnell and the other ice-age remnants of Glacier National Park, Montana, may be the first to extinguish at altitude—they are among the most exposed glaciers in North America (and, relatively, the smallest) and thus most susceptible. In 1850, nearly 150 of these glaciers populated the Rocky Mountains of northwest Montana, what would become the Park in 1910. By 1966, there were thirty-seven glaciers or fewer. In 2008, as I tromp around Grinnell, there are twenty-seven. Fagre knows them all.

Dan Fagre (pronounced FAY-gree) is a research ecologist turned glacier scientist. He has been monitoring the Rockies' northern glaciers for nearly twenty years—checking their pulse. He also takes the temperature of the glaciers' snowpack. He measures their dimensions and densities. He gauges their mass. Fagre is a diagnostician. He is the official monitor of the health and lifespan of glaciers in Montana. In 2003, he predicted that, in the face of climate disruption, the largest icefield in the Park (Blackfoot Glacier) would vanish by 2030—nearly thirty years hence. The day he explores Grinnell with me, five years into his forecast, he is reading the glaciers again to see if his timeline is correct. He may have to recalculate.

Within our immediate view are three glaciers—Grinnell, Salamander, and Gem—all of which were connected before a big meltdown split them into a triptych at the dawn of the American industrial age—the advent of factories coughing carbon smoke. Salamander and Gem are poised above the headwall at the back of the cirque like crusted snow on a rooftop. The two overhanging glaciers seem teetering for a crash—each an ice avalanche frozen in time.

Stepping back from the gaping crevasse at his feet, Fagre points to these two small glaciers overhead and talks of reading the ice.

"We use sophisticated technology to measure the ice," he says to me, "but we can pretty much tell the health of a glacier by eyeballing it." He points upward, to the left. "Take Gem—that round jewel glistening above the headwall—it's impossible to reach on foot. But from a distance we can tell it's still moving, creeping downhill, because you can see crevasses at its base, just before it slips over the cliff. So we know it's a viable glacier, not just a snowfield."

A living glacier is always on the move, kicking and carving its way downhill.

Fagre traces the outline of Gem and then lowers his eyes to Grinnell, sketching its features with his finger. "Gem is shrinking," he continues, "but the real loser is Grinnell, the mother glacier for this valley. Look at the lateral moraine, that pile of rock and rubble plowed aside by the glacier. The ice is at least 200 yards (183 meters) short of it now—that's how much the ice sheet has contracted in 160 years." Fagre turns his back to me to scan the side moraine. I notice some fir saplings growing in new soil, where ice once roamed, another sign that the glacier began receding a while ago.

While pondering the timing of the glaciers' demise, Fagre often asks why the ice is disappearing and why trees are growing in their paths.

"Trees are migrating to higher altitudes," he says, turning and stooping to pick up a cellophane wrapper from the trail. "It's warmer up here now. Would you ever have imagined a lowland fir invading the domain of a glacier? In mountain ranges all over the world, plants and wildlife are forced higher and higher by global warming. Alpine summits are a cul-de-sac; species are running out of room."

Like a geyser between eruptions, Fagre's passion bubbles over on the hour, like clockwork. I sympathize with his concern. The alpine landscape looks different from my memories of it, hiking here in 1976, when nearly forty glaciers reigned. I remember ice shrouding the mountains like a white powdered wig; now the hairline is receding. I ask him about the widening distance to the moraine, whether that is his best forensic clue.

The ecologist scans the rubble and the ravine; it borders the glacier like a skirt. "A broad moraine like this may be old news," he says, "so our best visual gauge of what's happening today is the snow line." This rough line of contour traverses the glacier, showing when there is enough snow to compensate for what has melted. It works like this: In late summer, the visible snow line looks like a meandering hemline with white snow above, which is accumulating, and exposed gray ice below, which is melting. If the snow line is at least two-thirds down the glacier, the ice mass is considered healthy—it is growing or holding its own. Today, the demarcation is clearly up toward the headwall, only one-third down the slope. The rest is wasting away. The official field results: The glacier may be flatlining. In the months ahead I would learn Fagre had a barrage of tests and tools at the ready to profile a glacier. He keeps a diagnostic chart on each, their vital signs carefully listed.

Dan Fagre is a maverick at the U.S. Geological Survey, his employer at the West Glacier Field Station, where he directs the Program for Climate Change in Mountain Ecosystems and a crew of five. He abhors deskwork. Two young men and two women are with him today, presently climbing the last track to join their leader on the ice....

Adjusting to his niche, Fagre has become a jack-of-all-trades in Montana's mountains. As coordinator of glacier monitoring efforts in Glacier National Park, his activities range from computer modeling to GPS (Global Positioning System) measurements, usually atop crampons or cross-country skis. He is a legend to his crew, most of whom are half his age—he is fifty-six—and they hike and climb at a fast pace, often with Fagre in the lead. He is stocky and fit—built like a mountaineer and rugged looking. His boyish haircut makes him seem younger than his years. But, unusual for a scientist, he doesn't mask his youthful passion. "The loss of a glacier hits me hard," he says. "I like snow and ice. I'd rather be living in the Pleistocene."

The mission of Fagre's alpine program is to study the ecological and geological effects of the global warming trend as it manifests locally in the mountains of northwest Montana. The Park is a crucible, a proving ground for the rest of the alpine world. Global environmental problems often appear here first—the world is watching. Besides recording global melting, local monitoring includes reading avalanches, forest fires, stream temperatures (and volumes), and tree line changes, as conditions become more temperate at higher elevations. Not only trees and wildlife are moving uphill. Even coldwater fish are forced upstream as once-cool habitats begin to warm up. Of course, they can't swim much higher—the frigid stretches of streams peter out. They end up in fragmented pockets of cool water. Ecologically, they've been painted into a corner.

Fagre locks eyes with me and clicks a ski pole against his boot like a spoon rapping a wineglass. He and I stand at the base of the glacier, each with a foot on the ice, the other anchored on rock. He has something to say. "We're not doing ice radar or stream transects today; our objective is strictly to get GPS positions for the glacier—to measure the acreage—by boat and land." That's why he has brought along two rubber rafts. Fagre gently taps the yellow inflatable on his uncomfortable-looking pack. The surfeit of straps on the frame looks like something from the Spanish Inquisition. Just then, one of his crew wanders next to us. Chris Miller carries the second raft and other gear. Fagre continues, "Even a major glacier like this is so small, relative to the resolution of satellite imagery, that satellite remote sensing is not accurate, so we employ aerial photography—and ground-truth anything we get from the air."

Miller says, "That's how I've worn the tread off my boots this summer—ground-truthing for the government. Hauling the gear. Checking every corner of the glacier. I'm a government mule. Luckily it's for a good cause." His boots are caked with snow. A healthy snowpack, after years of winter drought, means it is uncertain if the glacier will recede or grow this year, so Fagre and Miller are even more curious than usual. They plan on mapping the glacier's dimensions from GPS coordinates just to make sure they confirm or disprove the trend. The current hypothesis: extinction for the glacier within twenty-two years or less.

35

NORTH FORK

River (Where I Went in Search of Wildness)

Christine Byl

2013

In the mid-1990s, Christine Byl (rhymes with "smile") graduated from college and headed west, ending up with a seasonal job as a "traildog"—a trail maintenance laborer—in Glacier National Park. "I was not born to labor," she writes, "nor led to it by heritage or expectation." With virtually no construction or maintenance experience, she learned the tools and methods of repairing and maintaining trails. She persevered for six seasons, working mostly on all-women crews. She and her husband Gabe, also an experienced traildog, then moved to Alaska, where they led trail crews in national forests and Denali National Park. Eventually they founded their own trail design and construction company, Interior Trails, working in public lands across Alaska.

Byl has published both fiction and nonfiction; she is currently working on a novel set in western Montana. Her trails memoir, *Dirt Work*, is a thoughtful look at what it means to do hard physical labor, learn a new culture, and succeed as a woman in a world of work formerly restricted to men. It also remains probably the best description of trail work and trail workers ever written. This excerpt is from the first chapter of *Dirt Work: An Education in the Woods*, in which Byl describes the North Fork area, named after the river in the northwestern part of the park.

The North Fork of the Flathead is a greenish river, swift in some places and slow in others, forming the western boundary of Glacier National Park. It flows south out of Canada's Kootenai Mountains into northwest Montana, running the international border as if a blinking yellow light, and then farther south through airy meadows and scorched forest, the craggy silhouette of the Northern Rockies' Livingston Range often just in view. The North Fork converges with the Middle Fork of the Flathead about forty miles south of the Canadian border, just upstream of the Blankenship Bridge. West Glacier sits a mile away, the town that houses the park's headquarters.

The North Fork originates in hundreds of feeder creeks that tear down the slopes of the Rockies, creeks flowing from the Forest Service land to the west (Fish, Hay, Camas) and the Park to the east (Kintla, Bowman, Kishenehn, Quartz, Logging, Akokala, Dutch). Topography knows no park boundaries, and on whichever land they began, the creeks end in the North Fork. It's a formidable river and a friendly one at the same time, so cold and clear in some spots you're swimming in tinted air; in others fast and muddy, kicking up silt and stones, jamming logs in narrow canyons until they resemble structures joisted from the force of water.

The North Fork is also the district in Glacier National Park whose trails and bridges and travelers must contend with one or another of the river's tributaries. It's an area of a couple hundred thousand acres—one-hundred-plus miles of trail; a few tire-puncturing roads; scattered cabins and fire lookouts—a wide sweep bordered by the river to the west, the Continental Divide to the east. The North Fork district is dominated and defined by the North Fork River, so when someone says, "I was up the North Fork today," you can only guess whether they mean the region or the river by proximity to a truck or canoe.

Besides the river and its creeks, the North Fork is home to twentysome lakes, a couple of wolf packs, shaggy grizzlies, osprey, fireweed, marmots, old-growth larch groves, snowy passes, and the occasional *Calypso bulbosa*, the fairy slipper orchid. The fairy slipper is purplish-pink and lilylike, a weighty blossom on a bowed stem that looks like a tiny, fancy shoe. *Calypso* is Greek for "concealed," and true to name, the lily grows low to the ground, often obscured by larger undergrowth or fallen needles; a special orchid, it's not exactly rare, but a sighting feels precious. Like many inhabitants of the North Fork, it's often looked for, and easy to miss. It seems that only in the absence of seeking do senses clear enough to see: lily, wolf, falling star.

Who belongs more than the critters? In the North Fork, as in all of the Northern Rockies, there are animals everywhere. Wolf, mountain goat, bighorn sheep, black bear and grizzly, coyote, moose—the superstars. And smaller creatures, too: snowshoe hare half-turned white, marten on a tree branch, dippers nesting beneath a bridge, pika lifting the lid of my Tupperware lunch box, star-nosed mole burrowing in the duff. Animals stay far clear of the chainsaw's roar, but when we lived and worked ten days in the same place, we'd see the fawn sleeping in the stamped-down bear grass, hear the swoop of an owl's wings over the tent in the night.

There are humans out there, too, us working, and hikers, kids with their parents and their pockets full of stones, college students on a long-planned backpack trip, newlyweds from a big city with brand-new gear. They're eager to chat, full of questions, often thankful for our work. But when people grow quiet, or crowds scatter, animals appear. One early morning at the job site, a wolverine ran off a switchback in front of us and we watched it scramble up three tiers of waterfall pouring over sloped rock. Hiking out of [an eight-day] hitch, fast, heading for the truck six miles downhill, we saw a quick snake cross the trail and my crewmate jumped, pack and all, into my arms.

When animals appear, clichés sidle up close. Watch out. Soon there will be "electricity" between a bear and me, "dignity" in a lone wolf's eyes. Trite as it is, such telescoping from the experience of an animal to a philosophizing about it is not such a base instinct. I want to make sense of creatures, at once exotic and kin, and as I try to interpret their presence against the backdrop of my own existence, it's a very short leap to the owl as talisman, elk a stately messenger from a wilder world. I am more eager to see what an animal means to me than what it means to itself.

Why do we do this? (Don't you do it too?) I have some hunches, about power and connection and disappointment, about the margins of ego, and the urge to idolize. Short heroes of our own kind, it's no wonder we build pedestals for bears. But if I push past the initial urge to codify, or else to *ooh* and *aah*, if I force myself to watch without judgment, philosophy soon falls away, the meaning of the animal quashed by the actual animal, moving, through the same world as me. Wait. The same world? Well, that's frightening, isn't it? Me and a grizzly bear, in the same exact world?

Which brings us to danger. Part of what fascinates me about wild animals is the element of threat, not because they are bloodthirsty or even necessarily predators, but because their actions are not about me. My wolf-faced dogs share the social contract of domesticity—I trust they will not hurt me, and they look to me for food, exercise, companionship. With animals I do not feed or sleep beside, there is not trust. I am curious about them, I can guess how they will behave based on other experiences, or what I've read, but I do not know, despite my field guides, what their priorities are, what they aim to do, and when. A grizzly could maul me if I stepped between it and a carcass. A moose might charge if I skied past its calf in the alders. A fisher could bite my leg if I sat too long in the outhouse it has made its winter home.

The specter of danger mingled with curiosity results in an otherness that both beckons and warns. This potent blend leaves me off-balance, invigorated, and by necessity, returns me to watching. To feel as safe as possible in situations I cannot predict among company I don't control, I have to trust my senses and read signs. A congress of ravens circled and hollering might indicate a fresh kill nearby. A calf prompts a look for its mother. On a brushy creek, I scan for fresh bear prints in sand. Evolutionary lessons ring true: keep eyes open, nose pointed into the wind. Notice everything.

There's a funny thing about connection, though. I say it's the animals I'm drawn toward, but these sightings usually bring me closer to humans, whether the crew mate in my arms or the hiker we tell later on the trail, *Watch close for you'll never guess what we how cool was that.* The bond over animals is one of the strongest I have with particular friends; stories about the fox that stood for minutes on a creek bed watching fish, and how the Sandhill cranes seem early this year. We ask questions: This feather frozen in ice, do you know what kind? We point and wonder: How'd that get there, a Dall sheep skull on a gravel bar, half-filled with sand?

The Polish poet Czeslaw Milosz wrote, "We're separated from nature as if by a glass wall....We are akin to it and yet we are alienated by our consciousness—our curse and our blessing." But, Milosz, we *are* nature. Don't you see? Still, he's on to something, the egocentric positioning that lets us fool ourselves. Sharing space with wild creatures stirs me (blessing), and as soon as I've said "stirs me," I cringe (curse). Sheepish or not, proximity to wild things makes me feel feral—incautious and frisky and willing to gamble on what I cannot prove. And proximity to wild things makes me feel tame—glad I don't have to hunt for every meal, eager to hunker next to a fire on a cold night. Wherever I am, banging against the glass.

Randy is a ranger in the North Fork. He lives at the station just inside the boundary, on the Park Service compound near the river, complete with brown buildings and green-and-gray uniforms. The town site of Polebridge is two miles south on the road, made up of an old mercantile, a saloon, a few cabins for travelers, and a bunch of rusty trucks and roaming dogs and horses. People who live in Polebridge can be a little odd, and people who work for the Park Service are also often odd, so people who work for the Park Service in Polebridge are, on the whole, wonderfully odd.

Randy's from Jersey (or Queens?), but he's been working seasonally in the North Fork for so long he qualifies as a Polebridge local. He hikes trails, checks cabins, monitors permits, mans the station, tinkers with vehicles. He's isolated and chatty, a wicked combination, and when the right truck passes through, he'll lean on the driver's rearview mirror. Randy likes to talk shit, to tease and bluff. "I just heard on the radio that Charley's looking for you," he'll say. "He sounded pissed!" When the leader reaches for his radio to call the foreman, Randy slaps the side of the truck and cackles. It's hard not to fall for Randy's jokes. It's almost an agreement: when you talk to Randy, you are buying tickets to a certain kind of show, and you can't ask for different once it's started. If you aren't in the mood to talk, or be ribbed, keep driving, lift two fingers from the steering wheel in the standard rural-road greeting.

You might be sorry you didn't stop. Randy's helpful, and he knows the district. Maybe he needed to tell you that the road is flooded at Kintla Creek, or there are six trees down in the Bowman campground. In that case, when you come back through, Randy will let you hear it, laughing: *You shoulda asked!* And suddenly, you're the joker, not him.

The North Fork in July explodes with flowers: arrowleaf balsamroot, fireweed, trillium, arnica, columbine, lupine, gentian, Indian paintbrush, clematis, larkspur. Spoken, they bloom again.

Polebridge, Montana: town site established in 1911 by a loner from back east who built a homestead cabin on the edge of nowhere, and in the yard planted the first known beech tree west of the Continental Divide. Now, the cabin is a saloon, the only watering hole in the North Fork's only human enclave, where long wooden picnic tables rest in the shade of the beech. The Northern Lights Saloon is more than twenty miles from the nearest town, and in rock-tossing distance of wilderness, you can get most drinks, except a slushy margarita—no blender. But local beer on tap, a shot of Jack, an elk burger? Put it on the tab.

After four o'clock, dusty trucks line the dirt strip out front. The vista from the porch spans a twenty-five-year-old burn, dead trees in front of the mountains beyond, and the foreground props include two ancient gas pumps whose numbers scroll by like a slot machine, a rusty fire engine, two dogs, and a horse foraging the sand pits behind the Mercantile. A hand-lettered sign nailed to a utility pole reads, "SLOW DOWN, People Breathing." Even years after the 1988 fire, char tints the air, mingled with the smell of burnt sugar, from the Mercantile Bakery's daily special. A cardboard sign nailed to the saloon's porch warns, "Unleashed Dogs Will Be Eaten." Under the sign sleeps Sasha, a three-legged

Karelian bear dog. She is black, with a dirty-white fur apron. She lies unleashed with her head on outstretched paws, ready to enforce the local rules.

The North Fork is the only place in the Lower 48 I've seen a wolf. Driving south down the road, back to West Glacier, long past dark on an October night. We'd had a few beers, a big dinner at the saloon, and I leaned my head back against the seat in the drowse between wake and sleep, listening to soft pedal-steel on the radio, washboard ruts vibrating my thighs. The truck lurched as Gabe tapped his foot on the brake and stuck his arm out in front of me, an instinctive gesture. "Look," he whispered, "wolf." I opened my eyes. Gabe turned the wheel slightly, casting headlights toward the shoulder. Twenty feet ahead, it stood just off the road in profile, as still as if zapped in midstride.

If you've ever seen a coyote and wondered, *Could that be a wolf?* it wasn't. I've seen a coyote and wondered the same thing. Seeing a wolf, I did not wonder. Even if I hadn't known anything about how large wolves are, how long their snouts, their legs, I think I would have known. The world seemed to close in around the edges of my perception until *it was only me and the wolf, our eyes locked, some ancient knowledge passing*—stop. Did I think this? Please. That wolf cared nothing for ancient knowledge, and in any case, I had little of it to give. To the wolf, I was neither augur nor soul mate, only an obstacle in the terrain, an odd creature that inched close. Its eyes were distinct, its gaze forward. We sat that way for a minute, probably less. The wolf walked slow, out of the beam of our lights and along the length of the passenger side of the truck, five, eight feet away. Gabe switched off the lights. My window was rolled down a third. It was too dark to see well but I could hear it outside the window. The night's noise went on around us, I'm sure, the squeak of a far-off rusted fence gate, a wind chime clattering in the eaves of an abandoned barn, but I remember those moments as if the world were muted, as if the wolf and I were the only things passing before a set stage. No Gabe. No truck. When it reached the tailgate, the wolf cut across the road and trotted down into the ditch line and up again, vanished into the woods between the river and us. Gabe and I sat in the truck in the dark. No talk. No touch. For a minute, just dark.

Of all the animals I've seen over the years, all the brief glimpses and long stares, I remember the wolf more clearly than many. Not so much the motions of it, not where the wolf walked and how long it took and what I thought when it disappeared. But I remember its eyes reflecting light, how the shoulder muscles undulated beneath the thick beginnings of its winter coat. I remember that it didn't run. It never seemed wary, or curious. Not canny, smart, devious, or fierce. We crossed its path and it regarded us briefly before making its way toward pups in a den, a deer kill buried in a hole, or miles more hungry walking under the slim moon. That night, whether because of culture or nature, my wishful tilt toward wildness or an evolutionary hunch, I felt the borders of physicality and transcendence shift until one allowed the other in, and when the wolf slipped into the woods, I wanted to follow it. I wanted to dip my face to the river to drink, tear flesh with my teeth, flatten myself a bed of needles with a circling pace before sleeping. Never mind the blood on my face. Never mind the cold.

When it's clear in the North Fork and you're having a beer at a picnic table outside the saloon, you can see east across the river valley to the mountains, twenty miles away. Long Knife, Kintla, Rainbow, Bowman, Vulture, Nahsukin. Beyond those, more, and beyond those, still more, over the divide to the east side of the park, the rain shadow where red talus slopes run into prairie's edge. Gunsight, Bearhat, Two Medicine, Sentinel, Apikuni, Rain Shadow, Bad Marriage. Animal names, Native names, white men's names—mountain names. Rainbow Peak's name nods to three snowy couloirs on the south face that mimic, in monochrome, the spooned arcs of refracted sun. *Kintla* is the Kootenai word for sack: the drainage that leads up to that peak is like a loose bag, wide at the bottom, drawn tight at the top where the creek rockets down off the cliffs through a tapered gap. The summit ridge of Gunsight looks like the notch on the muzzle of a shotgun, from such height the world a target below.

Most peaks have other names, too, names that aren't on the map, the ones chosen by those who have slept and played and traveled and worked in them. *Cabin mountain; the peak where the snow stays year round. Thirsty Pass. The blond bear's mountain, the ridge I climbed in a hailstorm, the one where you left a shovel lying in the thimbleberries, the summit where two old friends died.* Names are our most condensed narrative, the one-, two-, three-word stories we tell ourselves about places we know, or wish to.

The mountains in the North Fork, as in all of the park, were formed by the creative force of tectonic upheaval and glacial revisions. Near a large body of water, an open meadow, or above tree line where the view is unobstructed, geology's alchemy is evident. Eras ago, through compression and uplift and carving, dirt and rock, water and ice turned into mountains. And since then, over centuries, the process reverses. A hard rain, hot summer sun, the freeze and thaw of the darkest days. A forest fire, the warming Arctic's winds. Mountains revert again to dirt and rock, water and ice.

From the high peaks, or the passes below them, you can see glaciers hanging shiny gray in the sun, scant remnants of the ones that shaped this land. Some of them are named, too: Agassiz, Weasel Collar, Harris, Thunderbird, Two Ocean. They look impressive, but not vast; small, really, in the context of the world's great ice fields. It's hard to believe these little patches of ice could have once dominated the faces that tower above them. Earth's constant scientific lesson: size is never the whole story. A new reality has emerged in the years since I first discovered Glacier. If I have children, and if they do, those kids won't see a glacier in the park. Like the grizzly bear on California's state flag, the story in Glacier's name will be a nod to something gone, the fact of language no longer matched to the truth of place. How startling, that a world I knew so well could vanish. And that despite my loving it, *in* my loving it, I helped it disappear.

What is *wild*? To Henry David Thoreau, it's "the thrill of savage delight" at a woodchuck in his path, and the urge to sink his teeth in; it's "the preservation of the world." Gary Snyder says the wild is the process and essence of nature, an ordering of impermanence. Annie Dillard gives a lyric: a cat's bloody paws on a pillowcase, things whole and things broken. To Edward Abbey, wild is the one true place, and there are many of them. Wallace Stegner says wilderness is "the geography of hope."

In margins, bedrooms, maps, and minds, wild hovers, lingers, skulks.

Morel mushrooms are hard to cultivate. Once domesticated, certain wild plants—huckleberries, too—do not thrive absent the indigenous chemistry of the places where they grow on their own. Musky and sweet, morel caps look like tiny cone-shaped brains, rutted with grooves and wrinkles. They grow all over the Northwest, dotting especially the understory of a forest recently burned. The first growing season after a fire, the woods burst with both the mushrooms and the camo-clad foragers who crawl on the ground after them. Morels are the North Fork's midsummer currency, bringing in fifteen bucks a pound in the height of the season, and pickers come from all over to fill buckets, pockets, trucks. Picking mushrooms is illegal within the boundaries of the national park except for immediate consumption, so commercial traffic clusters on the dirt road leading north to Polebridge, with limitless access to national forest land on both sides. Mushroom buyers' camps sprout up in response to the supply, huge tents in fields off the dirt road, and the atmosphere is all backwoods Wall Street, people throwing elbows and eyeing the competition, trying to unload their crop before the word comes from buyers' headquarters in Portland that the price has dropped. By late summer the frenzy dies down as pickers migrate to the next seasonal hot spot; locals are left with morels overlooked, the ones hoarded, dried, or stashed in a brown bag under the basement stairs to keep them cool. In late October, when even Indian summer's long gone and the fall rains have begun, morel gravy on mashed potatoes tastes nothing like the distant commerce, only like a chewy mouthful of summer dirt sweetened by fire.

In the North Fork, the bugs can be bad, one of the worst places in the park, everyone agrees. By midsummer in a year of normal precipitation, mosquitoes run the place, trailing warm-blooded critters like the cloud of grub that follows Pigpen. They swarm anything that stands still—elk, mules, bears, people—burrowing in ears and nostrils, inserted into any crevice. Which is worse, the raw itch of a bite on sweaty skin, or the whine of a single bug circling the cabin at 2 a.m. when everyone is asleep but you? (Both are worse.)

Forest fires shape the North Fork, as commanding a force as glaciers in eras past. Decades of misguided suppression tactics and climate change's heavy hand have resulted in tinderbox groves throughout the West, and the North Fork's dog-hair lodgepole and spruce forests are easy fodder for conflagration. Late-summer heat, a dry year, a lightning strike, and the skies grow apocalyptic with ash and plume, a dirty glow visible from miles away. Some fires burn out fast and others are nipped in the bud, spotted by the fire lookout, extinguished by initial-attack teams or the glamorous smoke-jumpers who leap from the sky like superheroes. But every few years, Glacier sees a big one, often in the North Fork.

Trail crews are backup Type II firefighters; when the need for people power trumps expertise, we get called in. Sometimes we do day work, washing hoses and cleaning saws, or, if lucky, fly in a helo to a remote cabin for structure protection. Other times, the stint is longer, a detail in fire camp, a little boomtown with canvas tents and trailers, IT systems for payroll, and two catered meals a day, more meat than even a cowboy can stomach. No steaks if you're spiked at a backcountry site or unexpectedly out overnight—then it's MREs [military

"Meals Ready to Eat"] with microscopic bottles of Tabasco sauce and space-age meatloaf salty enough to sap out of you whatever moisture hasn't already gone by way of smoke or sweat. Our yellow shirts and green pants, made of fire-resistant Nomex, chafe the skin, and by the end of a two-week tour, they smell like a laboratory that went up in flames.

The world of fire evokes ambivalence in me. Fighting fire can be fun, a welcome late-season break from the monotony of trailwork, a chance to envision ourselves heroes. There's adrenaline and camaraderie, doing good work and bacon every morning, and, of course, overtime pay plus occasional hazard premiums. (Fire seasonals in the West like to sniff smoky air and say, "Smells like money!") But there's also the militarized mentality, the "hurry up and wait," macho smoke-jocks strutting like hopped-up Marines, and the almost-too-hot-to-bear weather that nurtures fire, underwear soaked with sweat. Eventually the sneaky pleasure at getting paid premium wages to play Hacky Sack while "standing by" gives way to demoralizing sluggishness. Weeks of inefficiency and the rumbling machinations of bureaucracy grind all but the staunchest work ethic to a pulp.

Nationwide fire policy has improved dramatically in the past thirty years, with an increasing emphasis on fire ecology and the role it plays in forest health. Some of my best friends work in fire, mapping fuels, plotting burn patterns, and prescribing where to manage a burn and when to let the flames do their work. On the ground, though, a crisis-response outlook still eclipses the long view, and the tone of fire camp lingo is all battle and charge. Epic blazes predicated on prior mismanagement don't do much to help the ordinary citizen see the benefits of fire (for example, certain plants need fire to propagate the way other plants need water), and the media fuel the problem with their drama-hungry emphasis on *homes lost! acres devastated!* In mainstream rhetoric, there's little critique of a continuing trend—multimillion-dollar home construction in fire's version of a flood plain, which increases the human-fire interface and the likelihood of displacement. No one, it seems, can look a guy who's lost his house in the eye and ask him, *Why the hell'd you build it there?* So fire remains nature's whipping boy; a century of bad press is hard to undo in a decade or two, and for many, fire will always be the enemy to be vanquished, not a necessary part of ecosystem health. Smoky the Bear can't be part of the problem, right?

In spite of the media and politics fanning the flames, the smoke eventually goes out. Enough crews on the ground, a rainy spell that raises relative humidity and dampens fuels, or the inevitable September frost puts an end to the burning season. After fire camps pull up stakes and the fat paycheck's been spent on a new truck or a plane ticket or last year's bills, the ash begins to work its way into the soil. Charred stumps smoke and underground roots cradle fire's warmth. Lodgepole pines incorporate the chemistry of ignition into their reproductive ritual, some cones opening to spread seeds only under extreme temperatures. By the following summer, morels will peek out of the ground. Fireweed leads the flower brigade, and in two years, a burn is laced with green plants that draw ungulates to forage.

The talking heads call the blackened landscape of a very hot fire a "holocaust," a "ruin," and people watching TV say, *What a shame.* Which it is, and it isn't. On one hand, this landscape has burned and bloomed for centuries without spokespersons or contingency plans, and really, what lies ruined? Our fragile illusion of control, mostly, which needs a good drubbing. On the other hand, forests are different than they were even ten years ago. Climate change has had documented effects on tree mortality, temperatures, increased lightning strikes, snowpack depth, and snowmelt timing, all of which create imbalance. Fires burn longer and hotter and more frequently than ever. Because of us. There is the shame.

Forest fires strike a chord in part because they force us to confront a fierce Mother Nature, with everything at stake that matters: work, shelter, money, ruin, ego, remorse, power. And also, somewhere in there, love. Love for forests, and for the creatures that live in them, and love for trees, especially the green-needled Christmas-y kind, strung with glittering symbols we don't even realize we've asked them to bear.

Larch trees grow all over western Montana, from Yellowstone to the Canadian border, bristling the west side of the divide like a five o'clock shadow. They are dense in the North Fork, growing small on the mountains in twisted subalpine form, or in forested valleys, clumped in old-growth groves. The western larch, cousin to the eastern tamarack, is a deciduous conifer, a tree in the pine family that sheds its needles every year and grows new ones the following. In summer, to the unknowing eye, it looks like any evergreen, its brushy branches and elliptical cones blending in amid the Engelmann spruce and Douglas-fir. But closer inspection reveals the larch's distinctive needles clustered on twigs, a vibrant, almost neon-green compared with the duller needles of other trees. Larch feels most singular in autumn, when it shucks its evergreen guise and the needles turn yellow-orange over the course of September and October. A hillside of larch in late fall is a spectacle, trees lighting hills in wavy colored swaths like the aurora borealis gone to ground.

The larch is a well-loved tree in the North Fork. Aside from its autumnal beauty and the brilliant green it lends the summer canopy, it thrives in cold climates, burns hotter in the woodstove than many conifers, makes decent timber for building, and better survives the frequent fires that clear out junk pine and brush from the understory. Also, larch has personality. Its slender branches ringing a one-hundred-foot trunk look, I swear, joyful, silhouetted against sky. The needles bristle, standing at attention like they've been shocked and the tree's aura is at once stately and gleeful, bringing to mind an old man with a joke or a dizzy child balancing.

Up Kintla Lake, the snowstorm dumped a foot and a half in twelve hours. It was May, and assigned to an alpine crew for the rest of summer, this would likely be my only hitch in the North Fork for the year. The foreman sent me and Gabe and our housemate, Kent, an old friend from Missoula days, the one who'd gotten us into this world in the first place. *I work trails,* he'd said when Gabe first met him in the apartment they'd shared on Front Street. *Park Service, up in Glacier. You guys would love it.* In six years, we'd never been on a hitch just the three of us before. Old friends, chainsaws, the North Fork, beer and brats coming in on the mules. Nothing to add.

The first day we'd hiked in seven miles to the cabin at the head of Kintla Lake, clearing light deadfall, maybe two trees per mile, hardly enough work for three. The next day we planned to hike to Upper Kintla Lake, clearing as far as we could get. It was usually a long day, but with such sparse downfall, it looked doable. We woke at dawn and peeked out the cabin window to things changed: blowsy snowflakes, a winter sky over spring ground.

Gabe went to the outhouse first and came back urgent: *Come look, quick!* The new snow was thick and unmarred, a sea of white on which bear tracks stood out like flares: prints as big as pie pans emerging from the woods, past the cabin, disappearing at the shore of the lake. Where did it go? For a swim? We investigated, followed the tracks backward from the beach into the woods. Under the cabin window near the bunks, the four-paw gait pattern shifted to two where the bear must have risen up on its back legs, paws to the pane above Kent's bunk, and peered in while we slept, nose pressed against cool glass. *Them again. Winter's over. The cabin creatures are here.*

Inside, we ate a quick breakfast. Steeped hot drinks, packed our backpacks, topped off the saw and filed the chain, fitted the scabbard around the edge of the felling axe. Bears, snow, whatever. Trail crews work no matter what, something we're proud of.

An hour into morning, a quarter mile from the cabin, we realized the futility of it. The snow was heavy and wet, burying fallen trees so that sinking the saw in where the tree should have been was like slicing through the frosting on a cake, the bar invisible beneath snow. Through safety goggles and thick snow, we could hardly see. As Kent bucked one tree, two fell around us. The late snow, accumulating on branches with roots in thawing ground, was too heavy for the trees to bear and they dropped hard, the way tired kids who've been up too long finally collapse.

In a wet, dark forest with saws running and trees falling, the three of us called it a day. This was nearly unprecedented—in five seasons, I had had perhaps half a day where inclement weather was stiff enough to warrant truancy (then, it was lightning at a high alpine work site, our hair fuzzed out, metal tools tossed aside in the brush.) This day off wasn't hard to justify. Visibility was shit, sawing sketchy. At this rate, we'd have to clear the trail again anyway; and there was no other task to do instead, the drains all covered in snow, the tool cache organized, the cabin clean from last season's closing-up hitch. Reasons aside, why turn down a free day in such a strange and quiet world? We stashed our tools and hard hats, opening senses to the unexpected snow. We hiked a while together before Kent, with wet feet and a sore Achilles, headed back to the cabin, promising hot drinks for us when we returned. After two miles, I turned around, my mind on the book I'd left beneath my sleeping bag that morning, and the hot chocolate Kent would have waiting. Gabe said he wanted to get to the clearing ahead, and he'd catch up. We parted, disappearing into opposite ends of the whiteout.

On the hike back, my noisy mind shut up. Walking in the woods alone, in the snow, in May, was lovely and weird—snow on green ferns, inches of melting white beneath my boots, the sway of quiet through branches. I forgot, as I often do, to call out, to yell, *"Hey bear!"* as is prudent when hiking alone. I forgot myself. Halfway back to the cabin, I saw a bear. Off the trail to my left, lumbering through the trees, snapping branches beneath its feet, a huge male grizzly moved, also alone, parting the snow in the air before it. Unaware of me. Had this one peeked through our cabin window? A stripe of white mapped its spine, flanks falling away like slopes off a high ridge, corniced along the top. I stopped, blood rackety in my veins. I watched the bear move in steady snow with an ambling poise, rolling to one side and the other like a graceful fat man in no particular hurry. Thirty yards away? I saw my hand stretched out in the air, separate from me, palm out, inviting in, warding off. Noticed, it fell to my side.

I didn't want to surprise the bear. It was too late to yell out without alarming it, and I didn't want to jar the stillness. I wanted to watch the bear, keep it in sight for the rest of the day in the snow. But really. I couldn't hike along parallel, risk surprising it suddenly. It would charge me if startled. It was so close.

I kept walking. So did the bear. A minute later it turned toward me, swung its square head, and paused. It wasn't a stop, exactly, just a longer moment between strides. Had it noticed me, or known I was there all along? The bear loped into the woods, disappearing from my view as if it had been erased. I saw its rump peppered with white, then nothing. Snow kept falling. "Hey bear," I sang out when I started walking again. *Hey bear, hey, I saw you, brown bear in a white world, so big how can you be so graceful, so close to me, so far away?*

The next day, the snow had mostly melted and left trees down everywhere. We hiked to our stashed gear and cleared as far as we could, two on saws, one hauling brush, busting ass to absolve ourselves of the previous day's secret. We barely made it to the foot of Upper Kintla Lake, slowed by heavy steps in the last inches of muddy snow and tangled piles of trees to cut, one after another with barely any hiking between. We followed more bear tracks in the trail, half brown, half white, one set bigger than my hand, a second set much smaller. They preceded our path all day, sometimes veering off trail for a few yards, then joining us again, until, crossing a snow-covered meadow, we lost them for good. The tracks were fresh, from that morning, still crisp around the edges. Two bears together, probably a mother and a subadult cub. Not the curious lake bear, nor the lone male of the day before, his paws like snowshoes. We never saw the mother and cub that day, but they were there, watching for us as we watched for them.

36

WATERTON-GLACIER

Keystone of the Yellowstone to Yukon Corridor

Harvey Locke
2015

Harvey Locke (b. 1959) is a leading expert on national parks, wilderness, and large-landscape conservation. He has worked extensively on preserving the Waterton-Glacier area since 1989 and was involved in the effort to gain UNESCO (United Nations Educational, Scientific, and Cultural Organization) World Heritage status for Waterton-Glacier International Peace Park. He is a co-author of "The Waterton-Glacier International Peace Park: The First of Its Kind" in *Transboundary Conservation: A New Vision for Protected Areas* (2005) and "The Flathead River Basin" in *Water Without Borders? Canada, the United States, and Shared Waters* (2013). He is also the co-founder of and strategic advisor to the Yellowstone to Yukon Conservation Initiative and editor and lead author of the book *Yellowstone to Yukon: The Journey of Wildlife and Art* (2012). A resident of the town of Banff in the Canadian Rockies, Locke wrote this essay especially for this volume.

The Rocky Mountains of Canada and the United States extend in an almost unbroken arc from below Yellowstone National Park in Wyoming up to Canada's Yukon Territory. Straddling the border in the heart of this vast mountain corridor lie the two national parks that make up Waterton-Glacier International Peace Park. Though Yellowstone and Banff National Parks are more famous and Nahanni National Park Reserve in the Northwest Territories of Canada is much larger and wilder, no parks in the Rockies are more importantly situated for large landscape than Waterton and Glacier. They are the keystones that hold the whole Yellowstone to Yukon corridor together.

All around the world, national parks are the best land designation we have for ensuring that nature thrives, especially for large inconvenient species like lions, elephants, tigers, mountain gorillas, rhinoceroses, grizzly bears, and wolves. In our human-dominated world, national parks provide a secure place for species to live, breed, and raise their young. In the past, Yellowstone played a critical role in the survival of elk and bison at the beginning of the twentieth century. And without Glacier and Yellowstone National Parks, grizzly bears would have gone extinct in the lower forty-eight states by 1970. National parks are indispensable sanctuaries for nature.

Yet in the 1980s, we became aware that national parks are not by themselves adequate to protect these sensitive species. Parks started to lose these animals when they became islands of habitat isolated within a larger landscape of incompatible land uses. This "island effect" is well illustrated in the case of grizzly bears in the lower forty-eight states over the last 150 years. In the early nineteenth century, these bruins were widespread in the West from northern Mexico through the Rocky Mountain region of the continental United States to Alaska. By the 1920s the grizzly had been pushed back into islands of habitat in isolated mountain ranges. Some of these habitat islands were very large; the central Idaho wilderness, for example, was close to eight million acres. Yet one by one these habitat islands lost their grizzlies, whether to overhunting, disease, or fire, because once the bears left these habitat islands they, or their potential replacements, could not get back. One by one their populations disappeared or "winked out," from Mexico's Sierra Madre, from New Mexico's Gila Wilderness, from California's Sierra Nevada (notwithstanding the national parks there), from the Colorado Rockies, and even from the vast wilderness area of central Idaho.

The only "islands" where they survived were Glacier and Yellowstone National Parks. But Yellowstone's bears were already showing signs of inbreeding due to their genetic isolation from other populations, so by 1970 the only fully robust population of bears in the contiguous United States was in Glacier National Park. This was because the bears were not marooned on an "island" but rather lived at the tip of a long peninsula of habitat that ran from Alaska and the Yukon south through Banff National Park in Alberta and across the U.S.-Canadian border to Glacier.

It wasn't just bears that made Waterton-Glacier stand out in the Yellowstone to Yukon habitat corridor. Around the same time that we learned about the "island effect," field scientists began affixing radio collars to animals to monitor their movements in the wild. The collars sent signals to satellites that allowed the researchers to follow the animals' travels over the broader landscape. Then new DNA sampling techniques enabled researchers to understand which populations were connected and which had become isolated.

In the early 1990s, researcher Diane Boyd studied the return of wolves to the western United States. They had previously been killed off across the American West as vermin, even in national parks. But they came back because of landscape connectivity. They had come down that peninsula of life from Banff to recolonize the Flathead Valley of Glacier National Park after a half-century of absence. But this time they were protected by the park because predators were now understood to be important to overall ecosystem health, with additional protection afforded by the profoundly important U.S. Endangered Species Act of 1972.

It was already well known that the wolves had migrated in from Canada and that they were capable of traveling long distances with their easy loping gait. But Boyd's research revealed something startling. One wolf radio-collared in Glacier traveled hundreds of miles north before being shot near Mile Zero of the Alaska Highway in northern British Columbia. Another traveled south as far as Yellowstone. Even more surprising was finding wolves with radio collars that Boyd did not recognize. They came from a similar study going on near Banff National Park led by Dr. Paul Paquet, who was at the same time finding wolves wearing Boyd's collars. The implications, when supplemented by DNA findings, were clear. The wolves in the Flathead Valley of Glacier National Park were not a new colony that had migrated into a vacant habitat island but rather were part of one continuous population that ranged from Waterton-Glacier to Banff and beyond.

Thus these wide-ranging animals taught us that our national parks were providing vital security in a portion of their range but that parks, no matter how well managed, are not sufficient in isolation to maintain viable populations. Other studies around the world have reached similar conclusions. It was obvious that something additional had to be done if these rare species were to prosper. A new branch of science called conservation biology developed to define the theory and methods to tackle this challenge.

The simple idea that emerged is to protect parks and wilderness areas as secure habitat and to connect them to each other with corridors that allow animals to move among the core areas in search of food and mates. Other land uses that do not compromise the function of the corridors can be compatible with them.

In the Yellowstone to Yukon region, the essential building blocks for such a network were already in place: the Greater Yellowstone Ecosystem centered around Yellowstone National Park and the designated wilderness areas in surrounding national forests; Waterton-Glacier International Peace Park and Biosphere Reserve together with the adjacent Bob Marshall Wilderness Complex in the Flathead National Forest of Montana (sometimes called the Crown of the Continent Ecosystem); and Banff, Jasper, Kootenay, and Yoho National Parks of the central Canadian Rockies coupled with adjoining provincial parks and wilderness areas in Alberta and British Columbia. These established parks together formed the southern nucleus. Beyond them to the north some of the world's greatest wilderness conservation opportunities were available in the vast areas that stretch across the northern Rockies of British Columbia (now sometimes called the Muskwa-Kechika), the Nahanni area of the Northwest Territories, and the wild Peel watershed, which ends at the Arctic Circle in the Yukon. So in 1993 a community of conservationists and scientists from both Canada and the United States came together to create the Yellowstone to Yukon Conservation Initiative.

We analyzed the whole system for its wildlife values and located the most vulnerable links in the chain of the northern Rocky Mountains. There was an obvious need to repair the broken triangular link between Yellowstone National Park, central Idaho, and Glacier. We also recognized quickly the central importance of not breaking the most vulnerable and most critical link of all—the one stretching north from Waterton-Glacier to Banff National Park, that peninsula of life that runs up to the Canadian Rockies starting in the Flathead Valley. However, just north of the border, along Highway 3 in southern Canada, housing developments and open-pit mines had a high potential to sever this vital connection for wildlife. If these human developments were not carefully managed as part of a broader landscape that also protected wildlife connectivity, Waterton-Glacier could be cut off from its connection to the north and become an island of extinction.

Such an event would be catastrophic for nature. Waterton-Glacier is the ecological crossroads of the entire Yellowstone to Yukon system for many species besides bears and wolves. The unique position of Waterton-Glacier in the landscape enables it to support extraordinary biodiversity. The High Rockies, by which I mean those summits that rise high enough above timberline to harbor glaciers and true alpine plants, are at their narrowest here. To the west are heavily forested waves of mountains too low to strip off all the precipitation from the moist Pacific air that frequently blows in from the West Coast. When those moist currents hit the Continental Divide in Waterton-Glacier, it rains heavily in the spring and snows heavily in winter, creating pockets of interior cedar-hemlock rainforest on the west slope. Much less rain makes it over the high rock walls to fall on the east slope, where the mountains meet the plains.

Although such rain shadows are common in the world's mountainous areas, the one at Waterton-Glacier is unusually productive. Arctic blasts of cold air roll down the Great Plains from Canada, creating long cold winters that keep evaporation and transpiration rates low. The cold air masses battle with pulses of warm, wet air flowing up the Great Plains from the Gulf of Mexico. The combination keeps the east slope moist enough along the eastern edge of Waterton-Glacier to support lodgepole pine forests and Douglas-fir savannas with glades of grass and aspen. In parts of Waterton, the Great Plains stretch their dry fingers right into the mountain valleys.

These wildly varying conditions caused by tangles of mountains and collisions of weather from the north, south, east, and west make Waterton-Glacier the great ecotone, or transitional area, of the Yellowstone to Yukon corridor. Plant species from the U.S. Rockies reach their northern limit and Pacific species reach their eastern limit here. Prairie species meet their western limit and Arctic boreal plants their southern. The result is an astonishing diversity of over one thousand native plants, 25 percent more than are found in Banff. Waterton is the richest area for vascular (stemmed) plants in all of Canada.

Great diversity of landscape, climate, and plant life combined with abundant fresh water creates ideal conditions for sixty mammals, including three native species of cats (lynx, cougar, and bobcat), four species of dogs (wolf, coyote, red fox, and swift fox), six native ungulates (Shiraz moose, elk, white-tail and mule deer, bighorn sheep, mountain goat), two kinds of bears (grizzly and black), and at least eight native weasels (wolverine, fisher, river otter, badger, pine marten, mink, short-tailed weasel, long-tailed weasel). A herd of bison is kept in a fenced area of Waterton grasslands. Some of us dream of the native bison being allowed to run free again to interact with the landscape.

This area is importantly the mother lode for grizzly bears. The Waterton-Glacier International Peace Park's adjacent neighbor, the as yet unprotected Flathead River Valley in Canada, is home to the densest population of grizzly bears in the interior of North America. The iconic grizzly is immensely powerful, but it is also extremely vulnerable. The Yellowstone to Yukon Conservation Initiative relies on its presence to measure the health of the landscape and to guide our conservation actions. Grizzly bears are a good indicator because they are wide-ranging habitat generalists that do not survive well around large numbers of people. They have a very low reproductive rate and take a long time to become independent adults. Thus, they are an umbrella species, which means that if we can meet their needs and keep them in the landscape, we will also be meeting the needs of about 80 percent of all the other species that belong there. And Waterton-Glacier provides a source population of grizzly bears that radiates out to a much broader area.

The North Fork of the Flathead Valley on both sides of the border is the hub. This low-elevation valley is drained by a pure, wild river that rises in southeastern British Columbia and flows south, forming the western boundary of Glacier. On the Canadian side, the Flathead Valley is completely uninhabited by people and the river is unrestrained. Its rich riparian floodplains support an astonishing diversity and abundance of birds. A 2013 bioblitz by knowledgeable birders found 115 species in a week. True to the ecological diversity of the region, they found all four species of chickadees: standing in one spot, they heard boreal, mountain, black-capped, and chestnut-backed chickadees all singing at once. Even more remarkable was that they found no nonnative species of birds. Similarly, snail researchers found no exotic snails. Spider researchers found no exotic spiders. That such a stronghold of native species could exist along the Canada-U.S. border is astonishing.

Rare native bull trout (once called Dolly Varden) and native cutthroat trout move up and down the North Fork of the Flathead to breed and feed among robust and highly diverse populations of mayflies, stoneflies, and caddis flies (some species identified here were new to science). The Flathead River system along the western edge of Glacier has also been used as a global benchmark for water-quality studies, and research done in the Flathead River system has transformed our understanding of the way that gravel-bed rivers work in mountain systems all over the world.

Yet the Canadian headwaters are not protected, and until recently, the Flathead Valley in British Columbia was zoned for open-pit coal mining. The fact that Waterton-Glacier was recognized as a UNESCO World Heritage Site played a major role in preventing a proposed mine from proceeding. It is no exaggeration to say that the whole world got involved. Indeed, the decision to ban mining on both sides of the border was announced at a joint press conference held by the premier of British Columbia and the governor of Montana on the eve of the Winter Olympics in Vancouver, British Columbia, in 2010. Legislation to make good on the mining ban followed from the province of B.C. and the U.S. Congress. But it did not protect the missing piece of Waterton-Glacier, that vitally important forested area between the western boundary of Waterton and the Flathead River. Logging, off-road vehicle use, hunting, and quarrying for rock still continue.

That missing piece of Waterton-Glacier is obvious to anyone who looks at a map. Both parks extend from the plains on the east up to the Continental Divide. Then Glacier continues west, down to the North Fork of the Flathead River, but Waterton does not. Its western boundary is the Continental Divide, so the western slope of the mountains is excluded from protection, one of the great conservation anomalies of the entire Yellowstone to Yukon region. A coalition of conservation groups from both Canada and the United States, working together under the name Flathead Wild, are striving to fill in the missing piece by publicizing the opportunity to add it to Waterton Lakes National Park and to create a wildlife management area that would connect the entire region to Banff National Park.

Connectivity is essential to keep healthy populations of wide-ranging mammals in the landscape, but in an era of rapid climate change, connectivity becomes critical for plants and smaller animals, too. We know that after the last ice age ended, plants and animals slowly made their way toward the north as the climate warmed. They also migrated upslope to cooler areas. At latitudes like the 49th parallel—the border line between the United States and Canada—plants and animals can also seek moister and cooler environments by moving "around aspect" to the northern slopes of the mountains. Intact river systems also provide naturally cooler habitats within landscapes.

In the twenty-first century, providing for this northerly movement up, around, and across the landscape will be critical as the climate warms. Transitional areas like Waterton-Glacier take on even greater significance in these times. The leading edge of plant distributions may well turn out to be the center of their range in a warmer world. Connectivity helps keep the earth resilient and gives us hope that life may be able to adapt to climate change. Perhaps most important of all is to keep north-south river systems like the Flathead intact with all their natural processes functioning, because they are the ecological backbone of the entire landscape.

Beyond the astonishing ecological values of Waterton-Glacier International Peace Park, there is also something unique about these particular mountains when compared to the many landscapes I have visited in the Rockies, Himalayas, Alps, and Andes. The mountains of Waterton-Glacier are neither the highest nor the most dramatic, and the two parks are not particularly large nor as culturally iconic as Yellowstone, Yosemite, or Banff, yet they get hold of you and make you want to return over and over again. For years I have tried to put my finger on what it is that gives them such power. On a backpacking trip in the remote Belly River area of Glacier, it came to me.

We camped out at the head of Glenns Lake beneath Pyramid Peak. From there we hiked up over a headwall to Stoney Indian Pass, one of the most remote areas of Glacier Park. It is a magnificent area. Being a photographer, I took my time coming down to wait for the evening light while my wife and companions went ahead to set up camp. With the sun's last rays illuminating the high flanks of the mountains around me, I began to realize that the landscape of Waterton-Glacier has an intimacy that is unique. The parks' rock walls are as colorful as they come—massive bands of red and purple and tan rock standing bare, sometimes painted with brilliant yellow and orange lichens. The cliffs erode to form stacks of ledges that in summer are draped in green and speckled with snow-white mountain goats. Grasslands dotted with bushes full of purple serviceberries yield to forest glades lined with huckleberry bushes and lit with the torchlight parades of the giant white blooms of waist-high beargrass. Dark forests of towering spruce are interspersed with avalanche slopes that are a riot of luxuriant shoulder-high plants. High meadows in season are masses of knee-high color from hundreds of wildflowers crowded together. Alpine summits feature rock gardens of hardy blooms of tiny yellow poppies and purple moss campion that hug the ground to stay out of the wind. And networks of artfully constructed trails weave their way over easy grades in both parks, so all this diversity can be sampled in a single day or over many. John Muir had it right when he said it is some of the best care-killing scenery on the continent.

The mountains, valleys, and plains of Waterton-Glacier are an ecological crossroads of critical value to the Yellowstone to Yukon region and to the world, but they are more than that: their exquisite, intimate, and unique beauty has made them of inestimable value to the human heart.

37

IN GLACIER

Sonata in Earth Minor

B. J. Buckley
2014

B. J. Buckley is a Montana poet who has taught poetry and writing in public schools for over forty years. Her most recent poetry collection is *Corvidae* (2014). Section I of the following poem was first published in *About Place Journal*, May 2015.

IN GLACIER: SONATA IN EARTH MINOR

I. *Largo sostenuto*: Vespers

In earliest evening the day lets out its breath,
riffling the aspen leaves, long exhalations
through the green throats of the grass,
and the slant light draws a darkness out of the pines,
out of my body.
When my shadow crosses the shadows of pine
we become,
like brief lovers,
one—
flow together, deep currents of the water of light.

If my darkness speaks to the darkness of trees, have I
spoken?
If we are all shadows,
am I the pine?

II. *Gigue*: September Rain

The first rain of autumn
never happened and
the one that's falling now
knows it's an interloper,
an impostor,
faux precipitation, its drops
too tinsel-y, tawdry with
all summer's dust
poofing up around their edges
as they hit the ground, *plop*!
and roll, acrobats
in a second-rate circus who
keep tripping over their own wet feet and
slide off the roof ending up
with something sprained, at least,
and probably broken, and
there they lie trying to
get all our sympathy
by shining on the late asters
like rhinestones,
like stars!

III. *Andante*: Horses Standing in the River

Their manes dripping, in the mist, before the sun
floats into the sky from behind the mountains.
To the river, their legs are sudden trees
sprung up out of nothing,
to the water their hooves
are smooth and heavy stones,
to the current their tongues, their velvet noses,
are transitory as fallen willow leaves.
Little fish take shelter
in blue belly-shadow, mistake them
for clouds,

who snort, occasionally,
startling silver out like lightning.
One horse lies down on a sandy bar
and rolls, another trots up
a shallow side-channel.
Flies land, and the horses flick their tails,
quiver deliciously inside their skins,
which are colored like the hours:
black, white, red, yellow.
When they lower their long heads again to drink,
their necks are bridges of light.

IV. *Allemande*: Winter

Foot   notes.   Elusive
music of tracks across or
through
the snow, melodies that sing out
weasel   deer   lynx   sparrow
the blue lines cast by aspens
a staff
marking the register: deep bass
of drifts, tremolo of flight,
each tone
concave, a bowl for scent
and silence to rest in,
little cup of hunger:
bow made from owl wing,
the mouse, its broken strings.

V. *Allegro ma non troppo*: This Life

I watched her, she-fox
emerging from her den, a bright fire
out of darkness and the green
of the underbrush more green because
the vixen was washing

her sooty feet, delicate as a cat,
smoothing her white apron.
How sounds beyond my hearing
made her ears dance,
how all the perfumes of the world
gathered to tease the wet blackness of her nose,
tail like a great cottony spike
of a flower, like its own animal
curled around her body,
and I knew that beneath the fur
she was smaller than a rabbit,
how without her skin she would look most like
a naked, sharp-nosed child.
A few flakes of snow
whirled up from the powdery drifts
mounding the stones of the riverbank,
and she rose on her hind legs
to pirouette with them, to lick them out of the air!
Then, in the cold, sharp raven's-cry—
and she yawned,
and yipped,
and was
gone.

ACKNOWLEDGMENTS

In addition to the many great writers who have contributed encouragement and suggestions, as well as their work, to this collection, I want to acknowledge these long-time Glacier Park stalwarts: George Bristol, Curt Buchholtz, Don Burgess, Daryl and Kate Gadbow, Mike Gerard, John Gray, Bill Hutchison, Dave Krake, Doug Medley, Jan Metzmaker, Bruce Murphy, Mike Ober, Mark Parratt, Jack Potter, Bill Schneider, and Bill Yenne. Thanks to you all.

Thanks are also due to the Westminster College Giovale Library, the University of Utah Marriott Library, the Indiana University Herman B. Wells Library, the Indiana State University Fairbanks Library, and the Vigo County (Indiana) Public Library (Brigitte Gardner). Also to the Charles M. Russell Museum in Great Falls, Montana (Brenda Kornick and Emily Wilson), the Glacier National Park Archives (Deirdre Shaw), the Glacier National Park Library (Sheree West and Anya Helsel), and the Montana Historical Society (Molly Holz and Lory Morrow).

I owe special thanks to Jane and Tom Petrie of Denver, Colorado, for funding the reproduction of the Charles M. Russell letters, and to the Petrie Collection for loaning images of three of the letters. Artist Kathryn Stat of Salt Lake City, Utah, kindly allowed us to reprint her painting, "Running Eagle Falls," as the frontispiece. Janis and Wiley T. Buchanan of Washington, D.C., also loaned a Russell letter. I received additional help from Pamela Bomphart Davis, Kristy Buchanan, B. J. Buckley, Christine Byl, Doug Chadwick, John Fraley, Jack Gladstone, Pat Hagan, Harvey Locke, Willie Matthews, Kendra Newhall, Glen Olson, Doug Peacock, Ann Regan, Mimi Ross, Russ Schneider, Marcella Walter, Christopher White, and Terry Tempest Williams. I've benefited greatly from the advice and assistance of Brian W. Dippie, Elizabeth Dear, Amy Fairchild and Lance Newman of Westminster College, and work-study student Diandra Ryan-Mas. My greatest debt is to my wife, Nan McEntire, whose patience and support for a never-ending project never wavered; she's also an ace editor who loves Glacier as much as I do.

TIMELINE OF MAJOR EVENTS
IN PARK HISTORY

20,000–10,000 BCE	Glaciers formed during the ice age move through the mountains, sculpting the peaks, shaping the distinctive U-shaped valleys, and leaving behind moraines, lakes, and other features.
10,000–5,000 BCE	Native Americans travel through and eventually settle in the Glacier-Waterton area, using the mountains' resources of game, timber, vegetation, and fruits and berries.
1730s	The Niitsitapi (Blackfeet) acquire horses for the first time and begin using them for bison hunting.
1790s	Fur-trading companies sponsor exploratory expeditions, seeking abundant beaver populations. Peter Fidler publishes a map that locates Kings Mountain (now called Chief Mountain) near the Canadian border. David Thompson also explores both sides of the Rockies.
1806	Meriwether Lewis and three other men journey from the Missouri River to ascertain the course of the Marias River and its possible future influence on the U.S.-Canada boundary line. They camp about twenty miles from the park boundary, within sight of the Front Range of the Rockies. A party of eight Niitsitapi warriors attempt to steal the party's guns, and one, possibly two, of the Natives are killed in the ensuing fight.
1883	James Willard Schultz makes his first journey to the Glacier region from the east, explores the St. Mary Lakes, and begins publishing articles about the region in George Bird Grinnell's magazine, *Forest and Stream*.
1885	An intrigued Grinnell arranges to meet Schultz and they explore the St. Mary region.
1887	Schultz, Grinnell, and others explore the Many Glacier Valley, including the glacier eventually named for Grinnell.
1891	Grinnell, William H. Seward III, Henry Stimson, and several guides explore the upper St. Mary Valley, including the Gunsight Pass region. The Great Northern Railway builds track along the Middle Fork of the Flathead River and a few homesteaders begin constructing cabins at the foot of Lake McDonald.
1893	The Great Northern Railway completes its transcontinental line to Seattle and passengers begin arriving at Glacier.

1895	Under pressure from prospectors, miners, and others, the Niitsi-tapi agree to sell their mountain lands to the United States for $1.5 million. That land eventually constitutes the eastern half of Glacier National Park. A 54-square-mile area around Waterton Lakes is protected as a Dominion Forest Park. It is eventually expanded and now totals 186 miles.
1895–1906	Dr. Lyman Sperry of Oberlin College makes a number of journeys to the park with college students, exploring Lake McDonald, the Avalanche Basin, and the northern part of Glacier. He also lays out and pays for the construction of the trail to Sperry Glacier, later named for him.
1897	The first bridge over the Middle Fork of the Flathead River is constructed at Belton (West Glacier), enabling tourists to reach Lake McDonald.
1899–1902	A short-lived mining boom begins, fueled by rumors of rich mineral strikes on the east side of the mountains. It soon fizzles.
1901	George Bird Grinnell publishes his essay "Crown of the Continent" in *Century* magazine and begins his campaign in Washington, D.C., to make Glacier a national park.
1910	On May 11, President William Howard Taft signs the bill designating Glacier a national park. Almost immediately, Louis W. Hill, president of the Great Northern Railway, orders the construction of chalets, hotels, "tepee camps," roads, and trails throughout the park. The first chalet, Belton, opens near the Belton (now West Glacier) depot.
1911	Waterton Lakes Dominion Park is officially designated, and John George "Kootenai" Brown, who first saw the region in 1865, is appointed superintendent.
1913	Glacier Park Hotel opens for business near the Midvale (now East Glacier Park) depot.
1914	The Great Northern Railway begins an advertising campaign based on the slogan "See America First," with the mountain goat as its symbol. Lake McDonald Hotel, constructed by John Lewis, opens near the head of the lake.
1915	Many Glacier Hotel opens for business on July 4. Howard Eaton leads his first horseback party through the park; guests include Mary Roberts Rinehart and Charles M. Russell.
1916	The National Park Service is created by Congress and training of rangers begins.
1923–1924	Norman Clyde of the Sierra Club climbs over sixty of the park's peaks, many of them first ascents, and guides club members to some of the summits.

1927	Prince of Wales Hotel opens in Waterton Lakes National Park in Canada.
1930	U.S. Highway 2 between West Glacier and East Glacier is completed, allowing vehicles to travel from one side of the park to the other along its southern border.
1932	With the urging of Rotary Clubs in both the United States and Canada, Waterton-Glacier International Peace Park is dedicated as a monument to lasting peace between the two nations.
1933	After years of construction, the Going-to-the-Sun Road is dedicated in a ceremony at Logan Pass. The road enables vehicles to cross the middle of the park and contributes to a surge in auto traffic.
1933–1941	Civilian Conservation Corps camps are constructed in the park, and crewmen begin work on campgrounds, ranger stations, trails, and other facilities.
1949	Dr. George C. Ruhle publishes his *Guide to Glacier National Park*, the first of several editions. It soon becomes an indispensable guide for visitors.
1960	J. Gordon Edwards publishes *A Climber's Guide to Glacier National Park*, the first published description of many climbing routes. Expanded editions follow.
1964	Huge spring floods wash out roads, trails, campgrounds, and buildings; it takes the park several years to repair the damage.
1967	Two backcountry campers are killed by grizzlies in unrelated incidents on the same August night; the park responds with changes in bear management policies. These were the first bear-caused fatalities in the park's history.
1985	The first wolves seen in the park in many years arrive from Canada, and their population expands.
1995	Waterton-Glacier International Peace Park is named a UNESCO World Heritage Site.
2003	A series of massive forest fires burn nearly 15 percent of the park; many facilities are threatened. This year becomes probably the worst fire season in the park's history.
2006	Severe winter and spring flooding again damages roads, trails, and other facilities.
2010	Glacier celebrates its centennial as a national park.
2016	The National Park Service centennial spurs record crowds in national parks across the country, including Glacier.

FURTHER READING

In addition to the works excerpted in this collection and those mentioned in the introductions to each piece, the following publications are recommended. Some are no longer in print but can be found through online booksellers.

Buchholtz, C. W. *Man in Glacier*. West Glacier: Glacier Natural History Association, 1976. First complete history of the park area through the 1970s.

Christopherson, Edmund. *Adventure among the Glaciers: The Story of America's Most Exciting Scenery!* Missoula: Earthquake Press, 1966. Brief chapters and lots of photographs, but written in an engaging style that well represents what the park was like in the mid-1960s.

Dear, Elizabeth A., and David Stanley. "Charlie Russell and Glacier Park." *Montana the Magazine of Western History*, 63,2 (Summer 213), 42-57.

Diettert, Gerald A. *Grinnell's Glacier: George Bird Grinnell and Glacier National Park*. Missoula: Mountain Press, 1992. Comprehensive study of Grinnell's work to publicize and advocate for Glacier National Park, as well as his negotiations with the Pikuni (Blackfeet) people to acquire the mountainous part of their reservation for the park.

Djuff, Ray, and Chris Morrison. *Glacier from the Inside Out: Best Stories from "The Inside Trail."* Minneapolis: Glacier Park Foundation, 2012. A collection of personal narratives from an occasional journal; the focus here is on the personal experiences of concession employees—the seasonal workers who staff the hotels, cafes, general stores, and other facilities in the park.

Edwards, J. Gordon. *A Climber's Guide to Glacier National Park*. Missoula: Mountain Press, 1984; second edition 1990. Edwards pioneered many of the routes up Glacier's peaks, including some of considerable technical difficulty (though Norman Clyde gets credit for many first ascents back in the 1920s). The book is a cut above most climbing guides; Edwards was well versed in the park's human and natural history, and his engaging writing style makes the book a pleasure to read even for nonclimbers.

Ewers, John C. *The Blackfeet: Raiders on the Northern Plains*. Norman: University of Oklahoma Press, 1958. Despite its age, this book is a solid study of Blackfeet history and culture, though some of Ewers's conclusions have been vigorously questioned by the Blackfeet people.

Glacier Centennial Program Committee. *A View Inside Glacier National Park: 100 Years, 100 Stories*. West Glacier: Glacier Association, 2010. Assembled by a committee to celebrate the centennial of Glacier National Park, this volume consists of one hundred brief narratives of personal experiences in the park. Most of the writers are former park employees.

Grant, Madison. *Early History of Glacier National Park, Montana.* Washington D.C.: Department of the Interior, 1919. One of the first histories of Glacier based in part on the memories of old-timers.

Guthrie, C. W. *Glacier National Park: The First 100 Years.* Helena: Farcountry Press, 2008. Guthrie has written several popular books about Glacier; this one is a decade-by-decade glance at Glacier's history. The historic photographs are fascinating.

Hanna, Warren L. *James Willard Schultz.* Norman: University of Oklahoma Press, 1986. Well-researched biography of a man who married into the Blackfeet tribe and lived among them for most of his adult life, publishing dozens of books on their way of life.

Hanna, Warren L. *Montana's Many-Splendored Glacierland: All You've Ever Wanted to Know about Glacier Park.* Seattle: Superior Publishing, 1976. Originally written in 1925 by a newly married young couple who had met while working at the Many Glacier Hotel, the manuscript was updated later and not published until 1976. It covers the most important aspects of the park, from geology to human history to bears. Hanna's clear writing style and thorough research make the book still relevant.

Hanna, Warren L. *Stars over Montana: A Centennial Celebration of the Men Who Shaped Glacier National Park.* West Glacier: Glacier Natural History Association, 1988. Published just after Hanna's death at age eighty-nine, the chapters cover early explorers, writers, and artists, including Charles M. Russell, Hart Merriam Schultz, and Winold Reiss.

Holterman, Jack. *Place Names of Glacier National Park.* West Glacier: Glacier Natural History Association, three editions from 1996 to 2006. Holterman was a local teacher with a fascination for history; the third edition traces the origin of 663 geographic names.

Holtz, M. E., and Katherine I. Bemis. *Glacier National Park: Its Trails and Treasures.* New York: George Doran, 1917. Written for potential tourists, this is an early description of the park's facilities for travelers as they were being developed. This is, by the way, one of a number of books written by women during the first two decades after the park's designation.

Jenkins, McKay. *White Death: In the Path of an Avalanche.* London: Fourth Estate, 2000. Jenkins, a journalist, compiled this report on the deaths of five young men in an avalanche on Glacier's Mount Cleveland, the park's highest peak, in December 1969. It is a careful study of the commitment and expertise of Park Service professionals in searching for and eventually recovering the bodies.

Linderman, Frank. *Kootenai Why Stories.* New York: Scribner's, 1926. A friend of Charlie Russell, Linderman lived in the Glacier area for many years, and he eventually built a home on Flathead Lake, west of the park. He collected most of these origin narratives (the "why" of the title) from residents of the reservation south of the lake.

MacDonald, Graham A. *Where the Mountains Meet the Prairies: A History of Waterton Country.* Calgary: University of Calgary Press, 2000. Engaging history that covers Kootenai Brown, Death-on-the-Trail Reynolds, and other local characters. Glacier in the United States and Waterton Lakes in Canada are, by international agreement, collectively known as Waterton-Glacier International Peace Park, a designation formalized in 1932.

Ober, Michael J. *Glacier Album: Historic Photographs of Glacier National Park*. Helena: Riverbend Publishing, 2010. This centennial project collects a fascinating variety of photographs from archives around the state and nation, arranged chronologically and thematically. Ober is a librarian, historian, and seasonal ranger who knows the park inside and out; his captions are truly informative.

Reeves, Brian, and Sandra Peacock. *"Our Mountains Are Our Pillows": An Ethnographic Overview of Glacier National Park*. West Glacier: Glacier National Park, 2001. A complete survey of the Native American presence in the Glacier Park area, based on extensive research and archaeological fieldwork.

Robinson, Donald H. *Through the Years in Glacier National Park*. West Glacier: Glacier Natural History Association, 1960. An "administrative history," as the title page says, this study focuses on the legislation, organization, and development of the park.

Ruhle, George C. *Guide to Glacier National Park*. Minneapolis: Forney, 1949 and several subsequent editions. Ruhle was a long-time naturalist at Glacier, and his guide remains a landmark for its depth and clarity.

Russell, Austin. *C. M. R.: Charles M. Russell, Cowboy Artist*. New York: Twayne Publishers, 1957. The great "cowboy artist" of the West, Charlie Russell and his wife, Nancy, had a cabin on Lake McDonald, where they spent every summer from 1906 to 1926. Charlie's nephew, Austin, was a frequent visitor, and this long-out-of-print book remains the best description of the quirky life the Russells and their friends led at the cabin they called "Bull Head Lodge."

Schneider, Bill. *Where the Grizzly Walks*. Missoula: Mountain Press Publishing, 1977. Schneider has had an extensive career in publishing, editing, and writing, including the publication of many guidebooks to national parks and wilderness areas. This, his first book, was based on his experiences working on trails in Glacier.

Schullery, Paul. *Glacier and Waterton: Land of Hanging Valleys*. San Francisco: HarperCollins, 1996. One of the most renowned writers on national parks in the American West, Schullery is primarily identified with Yellowstone, but he has a special affection for Glacier as well. This coffee-table book has lots of wonderful color photos, but its highlight is Schullery's evocative text and the experiences he records.

Schullery, Paul. *This High, Wild Country: A Celebration of Waterton-Glacier International Peace Park*. Albuquerque: University of New Mexico Press, 2010. Another centennial volume celebrating Glacier's one hundredth birthday, this one is spiced with Schullery's personal experiences and wonderful watercolor art by Marsha Karle. Perhaps the best contemporary book on Glacier.

Thompson, Margaret. *High Trails of Glacier National Park*. Caldwell, Idaho: Caxton Printers, 1936. An entertaining excursion through the park, circa 1930s. Thompson was apparently the wife of Otto Thompson, chief engineer for the chalets and hotels in the park, so she must have had lots of opportunities to explore the park.

Thompson, Sally. *People before the Park: The Kootenai and Blackfeet before Glacier National Park*. Helena: Montana Historical Society Press, 2015. A survey of Native American presence and activity in the Glacier area, noteworthy because the major chapters are the product of work by tribal elders and authorities. In this text, Native Americans tell their own stories.

Waldt, Ralph. *Crown of the Continent: The Last Great Wilderness of the Rocky Mountains*. Helena: Riverbend Publishing, 2004. Like Schullery's *Glacier and Waterton*, this is a large-format volume with many color photographs. Waldt was for many years resident naturalist at a Nature Conservancy preserve just southeast of Glacier. Though his subtitle is debatable, his experiences with rare animals in the Crown of the Continent ecosystem are well worth reading.

Yenne, Bill. *Glacier National Park*. Images of America Series. Charleston, SC: Arcadia Publishing, 2006. A compact description of the park with many black-and-white photos, this book was written by someone raised in the park from childhood (see entry below). Bill Yenne is deeply knowledgeable about the park and is a widely published author.

Yenne, Bill. *Going-to-the-Sun Road*. Images of America Series. Charleston, SC: Arcadia Publishing, 2013. Describes the construction in the 1930s of the spectacular highway that connects the east west sides of the park. Contains many photos, most by the author.

Yenne, W. J. *Switchback*. Kalispell: WY Books, 1983. Yenne (father of Bill, above) was a longtime packer, wrangler, and trail-crew supervisor in Glacier; many said he had ridden more miles of trails in Glacier than anyone else. The book is especially interesting to those curious about the maintenance of the park and the dedicated nonrangers who do much of the work.

SOURCES AND PERMISSIONS

Native People: lyrics for "Legends of Glacier" courtesy Jack Gladstone.

Walter McClintock, "My Introduction to the Blackfeet," from *The Old North Trail: Or, Life, Legends and Religion of the Blackfeet Indians* (London: Macmillan, 1910), 6–27.

Percy Bullchild, "My-stu-bun, Crowfeather Arrow's Revenge," from *The Sun Came Down: The History of the World as My Blackfeet Elders Told It* (San Francisco: Harper and Row, 1985; reprint, Lincoln: University of Nebraska Press, 2005). Copyright 1985 by Percy Bullchild. Reprinted by permission of HarperCollins Publishers.

George Comes at Night, "The Last Great Battle of Eagle Head," from *Roaming Days: Warrior Stone*, ed. Jane Bailey (Browning: Blackfeet Heritage Program, 1978), 31–37.

James Willard Schultz, "The Jealous Women," from *Blackfeet Tales of Glacier National Park* (Boston and New York: Houghton Mifflin, 1916), 226–32.

Peter Beaverhead, "Mountain Sheep Boy," from Leslie B. Davis, ed., *Remnant Forms of Folk Narrative among the Upper Pend d'Oreille Indians* (University of Montana Anthropology and Sociology Papers No. 31, ca. 1961), 28–30. Reprinted with permission of Pamela Bomphart.

Explorers: Maynard Dixon, "Camp in the Rockies," from *Rim Rock and Sage* (Los Angeles: California Historical Society, 1977), 67. Reprinted with permission of the California Historical Society.

Raphael Pumpelly, from *My Reminiscences* (New York: Henry Holt, 1918), 631–45.

Charles Spencer Francis, from *Sport among the Rockies: The Record of a Fishing and Hunting Trip in North-Western Montana* (privately printed, 1889), excerpts from Tenth and Eleventh Letters.

George Bird Grinnell, "The Crown of the Continent," *Century Magazine* 62 (September 1901), 660–72.

John Muir, from *Our National Parks* (Boston: Houghton Mifflin, 1902), 17–19.

Helen Fitzgerald Sanders, "Lake Angus McDonald and the Man for Whom It Was Named," from *Trails through Western Woods* (New York and Seattle: Alice Harriman, 1910), 89–94, 22–37, 245–68.

Albert L. Sperry, from *Avalanche* (Boston: Christopher, 1938), 53–56, 72–79, 142–43, 146–47.

Visitors: Vachel Lindsay, "The Bird Called 'Curiosity,'" from *Going-to-the-Sun* (New York: Appleton, 1923), 14. Reprinted with permission of Nicholas Lindsay.

Carrie Adele Strahorn, from *Fifteen Thousand Miles by Stage: A Woman's Unique*

Experience During Thirty Years of Path Finding and Pioneering from the Missouri to the Pacific and from Alaska to Mexico (New York: Putnam's, 1911), 605–17.

Mary Roberts Rinehart, from *Through Glacier Park: Seeing America First with Howard Eaton* (Boston and New York: Houghton Mifflin, 1916), 14–16, 18–36, 38–39, 41–43, 45–56, 58–61, 85.

Mary Roberts Rinehart, from *Tenting Tonight: A Chronicle of Sport and Adventure in Glacier Park and the Cascade Mountains* (Boston and New York: Houghton Mifflin, 1918), 12–16, 17–21, 63–78, 80–86, 88–89.

Agnes C. Laut, "Two Medicine or White Magic Lakes," from *Enchanted Trails of Glacier Park* (New York: Robert M. McBride, 1926), 34–41, 42–44.

Dorothy M. Johnson, "Carefree Youth and Dudes in Glacier National Park," from *When You and I Were Young, Whitefish* (Helena: Montana Historical Society Press, 1982), 142–60. Copyright 1982 by Dorothy Johnson. Reprinted with permission of McIntosh & Otis, Inc.

Characters: Jim Whilt, "The Outside Trail," from *Mountain Echoes* (Kalispell: O'Neil Printers, 1951), 66–67.

Dave Walter, "Louis Hill's Dream: Glacier National Park in 1915," from *Encounters* 8, no. 4 (July/August 1985), publication of the Science Museum of Minnesota, St. Paul, 24–27. Reprinted courtesy of Marcella Sherfy Walter.

Jerry DeSanto, "The Legendary Joe Cosley," from *Montana The Magazine of Western History* 30, no. 1 (January 1980), 12–27. Reprinted courtesy of Montana Historical Society.

Irvin S. Cobb, from *Exit Laughing* (Indianapolis, Bobbs Merrill, 1941), 407–10.

Charles M. Russell, Letters from Bull Head Lodge. See notes below.

John Fraley, "Bootleg Lady of Glacier Park," from *Wild River Pioneers: Adventures in the Middle Fork of the Flathead, Great Bear Wilderness and Glacier National Park* (Whitefish: Big Mountain Publishing, 2008), 134–55. Reprinted courtesy of John Fraley.

Jim Whilt, from *Giggles from Glacier Guides* (Kalispell: O'Neil Printers, 1935), 10, 11, 12–13, 14, 16–17.

Adventurers: G. N. Paige, "Winter Patrol in Glacier Park," from *Glacier Nature Notes* (January 1930).

Stephen Graham, "Climbing Red Eagle," from *Tramping with a Poet in the Rockies* (New York: Appleton, 1922), 82–94.

Norman Clyde, "Wanderings Afoot," from *Nature Notes from Glacier Park* (November 1929), 54–56.

H. T. Gisborne, "A Forest Fire Explosion," from *Western Prose and Poetry*, ed. Rufus A. Coleman (New York: Harper, 1932), 423–28.

Andy Russell, "Some Early Recollections of My Own" and "Along Wilderness Trails." Excerpts from Andy Russell, *Grizzly Country* 137–43, 182–91. Copyright 1967 by Andy Russell. Used with permission of Alfred A. Knopf, an imprint of the Knopf Doubleday Publishing Group, a division of Penguin Random House, LLC. All rights reserved.

Animals: Maxine Kumin, "In the Park," from *Selected Poems 1960–1990* by Maxine Kumin. Copyright 1997 by Maxine Kumin. Used with permission of W. W. Norton & Company, Inc.

Don Burgess, "Grizzly Encounters," from *Montana Magazine* (May/June 1980). Courtesy of Don Burgess.

Doug Peacock, "The Black Grizzly," from *Grizzly Years* (New York: Henry Holt, 1990), 214, 220–24, 227, 230. Reprinted courtesy of Doug Peacock and Henry Holt, Inc.

Pat Hagan, "Predator Puma," from *Seasonal Disorder* (Boulder: Johnson Books, 2006), 93–100. Reprinted courtesy of Pat Hagan and Big Earth Publishing.

Douglas H. Chadwick, from *A Beast the Color of Winter: The Mountain Goat Observed* (San Francisco: Sierra Club, 1983), 146–51. Reprinted courtesy of Doug Chadwick.

Mark Parratt, "The St. Mary Lake Monster" and "Pike Eyes," from *Fate Is a Mountain* (Whitefish: Sun Point Press, 2009), 63–71, 147–54. Reprinted courtesy of Mark Parratt and Sun Point Press.

Modern Times: Robert Wrigley, "Ursa Major," from *The Sinking of Clay City* (Port Townsend: Copper Canyon Press, 1979), 23. Reprinted courtesy Robert Wrigley.

Edward Abbey, "Fire Lookout: Numa Ridge," from *The Journey Home* (New York: Dutton, 1977), 30–57. Reprinted with permission of Don Congdon Associates, Inc. Copyright 1977 by Edward Abbey.

Terry Tempest Williams, "Glacier National Park, Montana," from *The Hour of Land: A Personal Topography of America's National Parks* (New York: Farrar, Straus and Giroux, 2016), 331–47. Copyright 2016 by Terry Tempest Williams. Reprinted with permission of Farrar, Straus and Giroux, LLC.

Christopher White, from *The Melting World: A Journey across America's Vanishing Glaciers* (New York: St. Martin's Press, 2013), 6–12. Reprinted courtesy of Christopher White and with permission of Macmillan Publishing.

Christine Byl, "North Fork: River (Where I Went in Search of Wildness)," from *Dirt Work* (Boston: Beacon Press, 2013), 6–34. Copyright 2013 by Christine Byl. Reprinted with permission of Beacon Press, Boston.

Harvey Locke, "Waterton-Glacier: Keystone of the Yellowstone to Yukon Corridor" (2015). Courtesy of Harvey Locke.

B. J. Buckley, "In Glacier: Sonata in Earth Minor," from *About Place Journal* (May 2015). Reprinted with permission of B. J. Buckley.

CHARLES M. RUSSELL ILLUSTRATED LETTERS

Plate 1. "Bulls Head Lodge," image courtesy of Buffalo Bill Center of the West, Cody, Wyoming.

Plate 2. "Greetings from us all," watercolor on birchbark, sent to Albert and Margaret Trigg and their daughter Josephine, July 23, 1906. Image courtesy of C. M. Russell Museum, Great Falls, Montana. Gift of the Josephine Trigg Estate.

Plate 3. "Best wishes to Mr. and Mrs. Calvert, Kootnaei Lodge" (1906), watercolor on birchbark. Image courtesy of Petrie Collection.

Plate 4. "Says the halk with a stare" (August 1905), watercolor on birchbark. Image courtesy of C. M. Russell Museum, Great Falls, Montana. Gift of William J. Roberts.

Plate 5. "In remembrance of August Ninth, 1905, Lake McDonald, from your friends at Kootnaei Lodge," 1906, watercolor on birchbark. Image courtesy of C. M. Russell Museum, Great Falls, Montana. Gift of Jeffrey M. Roberts.

Plates 6–9. To Edgar I. Holland, September 4, 1908, watercolor and ink on paper. Private collection. Image courtesy of Gerald Peters Gallery, Santa Fe, New Mexico.

Plates 10–11. "Friend Bill [William H. Rance] ("Boose for Boose Fighters"), watercolor on paper, August 12, 1912. Image courtesy of Montana Historical Society, Helena, Montana.

Plate 12. "Friend Bob" [Robert J. Benn] (1908). Image courtesy of Petrie Collection.

Plate 13. "I have just returned from the glasier Bill" [to William H. Rance], September 4, 1908. Image courtesy of Montana Historical Society, Helena, Montana.

Plate 14. "Mr and Mrs John Lewis, Aug 11 1918," watercolor and ink on paper. Image courtesy of C. M. Russell Museum, Great Falls, Montana. Museum purchase.

Plate 15. "Dudes." Image courtesy of Rockwell Museum, Corning, New York.

Plates 16–17. "Carl Borg / Friend Borg, Aug 29 1925," watercolor on paper. Courtesy of Mr. and Mrs. Wiley T. Buchanan, Washington, D.C.

Plates 18–19. "Miss Isabel Brown, July 30 1926." Private collection. Image courtesy of Rockwell Museum, Corning, New York.

Plates 20–21. "Dr. Philip Cole, September 26 1926," watercolor on paper. Image courtesy of Gilcrease Museum, Tulsa, Oklahoma.

Plate 22. "Friend Bob, Dec 25 1910," watercolor on paper. Image courtesy of Petrie Collection.

SOURCES AND PERMISSIONS FOR BLACK-AND-WHITE PHOTOGRAPHS

1 and 2 are courtesy of National Archives, Edward S. Curtis Collection.

4, 8, 9, 11, and 13 are from the archives of the Montana Historical Society Research Center, Montana Historical Society, Helena, Montana.

3, 5, 6, 7, and 10 are from the archives of Glacier National Park, West Glacier, Montana.

12 is courtesy of National Archives, Ansel Adams Collection.